On Three Pillars

On Three Pillars

ק"ק חזוק אמונה

THE HISTORY OF CHIZUK AMUNO CONGREGATION
1871-1996

by

Jan Bernhardt Schein

Chizuk Amuno Congregation, Baltimore, Maryland
September, 2000

On Three Pillars
The History of Chizuk Amuno Congregation
1871-1996

Published by
Chizuk Amuno Congregation
8100 Stevenson Road
Baltimore, Maryland 21208
www.chizukamuno.org

Library of Congress Control Number (LCCN): 00 133342
International Standard Book Number (ISBN): 0-9673940-1-5

Printed and bound in the United States of America
by
Signature Book Printing, Inc.
Gaithersburg, Maryland

עַל שְׁלשָׁה דְבָרִים הָעוֹלָם עוֹמֵד
תּוֹרָה, עֲבוֹדָה, גְמִילוּת חֲסָדִים
—פִּרְקֵי אָבוֹת א:ב

The world rests on three pillars;
Torah,
Avodah (worship),
and Gemilut Hasadim (acts of loving kindness)
—Pirke Avot 1:2

.

The synagogue is not a 'house of prayer' merely. We have not fulfilled our mission as God's chosen people in depositing the Ark in the shrine and allowing it to be read during service. We are also bound to teach its contents to our children and to preserve the traditions of the synagogue as transmitted unto us... We have always endeavored to carry out the rabbinical injunction to combine a thorough acquaintence of our sacred books with the requirements of secular education, loyalty to the traditions of our fathers with a full recognition of the wants of the present. Our fathers have been conservative Israelites, they were happy in the practices of their religious customs and observances; they witnessed the fruits of their religious training in the morality of the household and dutifulness of sons and daughters, and with the help of God, we expect to remain thus.

Rev. Dr. Henry W. Schneeberger
Dedication of McCulloh Street Synagogue
December 20, 1895

This synagogue, Chizuk Amuno Congregation, a place of assembly, a place of prayer, a place for study. That institution responsible for preserving the Jewish people because it is the repository of Torah, not given to the fashion of the moment, the fad of the hour, the philosophy of the day. The synagogue, this synagogue, affirms that we are created in the image of God, that God who revealed Himself to the people of Israel and taught us his Torah—which is now our Torah—that we must live and teach. And Chizuk Amuno is doing precisely that. Just think of it. We are what we pretend to be—a place for the study of Torah.

Rabbi Joel H. Zaiman
Laying of the Educational Wing
Cornerstone Ceremony
May 3, 1987

Contents

Introductory Message

It was Abraham Joshua Heschel who wrote: "It is incumbent upon us to remember those events that occurred to our ancestors, events through which the spirit of God established residence in the history of our people. The days of the past and the present are inextricably tied together." *On Three Pillars* gives testimony to Rabbi Heschel's observation.

Chizuk Amuno has celebrated its 125th Anniversary. It is only proper that as part of this celebration, we understand and acknowledge those before us upon whose significant achievements we continue to build. In each generation, men and women dedicated themselves to furthering the mission of this synagogue. A careful reading of our history indicates that the achievements of each generation have been remarkably consistent.

Against a backdrop of evolving American Judaism, continuous affirmation of Torah has enabled this congregation to persist in its mission. Chizuk Amuno remembers. It is our sacred duty. Yet, we will continue contributing to the intellectual, spiritual and social lives of our membership and of this community not simply because we remember. Our ability to be a vital force depends on what we believe and affirm.

Were it not for the persistence of Dr. Jerry Buxbaum and his band of donors, and were it not for the tenacity of Jan Schein, our author, this history would never have seen the light of day. We are deeply indebted to them.

I think you will enjoy reading our history. I know that you will enjoy it even more if you read yourself into our history. You are related to what is written in these pages. You have a role to play. The coming decades are up to us.

Rabbi Joel H. Zaiman
September, 2000

Preface

The more things change, the more they seem to stay the same. This old adage occurred to me, time and time again, as I read Jan Schein's journey into our congregation's past. Back in 1996, amidst the celebration of Chizuk Amuno's 125th Anniversary, it was hard to conceive of what shape our history might take on paper, not to mention how much work and perseverance it would require on the part of the history's author and editorial committee.

The following pages have been painstakingly researched, documented, and written with dedication and love. This volume serves as a lasting testament to the men and women who helped to build and sustain our vibrant Jewish community and as a promise to future generations. With the publication of *On Three Pillars*, we close the final chapter on our 125th Anniversary celebration and look ahead to the next 125 years. Enjoy.

Dr. Jerry Buxbaum,
125th Anniversary Celebration Chair
September, 2000

Sponsors

A grateful congregation acknowledges the following sponsors whose generosity sustained the programming for the entire 125th Anniversary celebration, including the publication of *On Three Pillars: The History of Chizuk Amuno Congregation.*

Gail & Jack Baylin
Linda G. Blumenthal
Marcia & Jerry Buxbaum
Shoshana S. Cardin & Family
Deborah & Louis Cohen
Nancy R. Cohen
Suzanne F. Cohen
Annette & Joseph Cooper
Deborah & James Effron
Harriet & Lowell Glazer
Florene & Ronald Goldner
Sharon & Phillip Goldstein
Toba & William Grant
Lois H. Halpert
Ina & Calvin Hamburger
Debby & Jesse Hellman
Lee M. & Nelson H. Hendler
Sandra & Fred Hittman
Bluma & Leonard Jed
Harriet & Alan Kanter

Suzanne & Gerald M. Katz
Isobel & Sydney S. Kemper
Ronnie Kleiman
Zanvyl Krieger
Harriett & Mende Lerner
Rhona & Martin A. Levin
Mimi Blitzer & David Mallott
Bernard Manekin & Family
Bonnie & Pacy Oletsky
Marilyn & Jack Pechter
Pamela & Jeffrey Platt
Sue & Howard Platt
Marlene & Irvin Pollack
Ilene & Alvin Powers
Kathy & Sanford M. Shapiro
Carole & Hanan Sibel
Janet R. Tolbert
Kathy & Stevan Weinberg
Sharon & Jay Yospe
Ann & Rabbi Joel H. Zaiman

125th Anniversary Year Committee Chairs

Celebration General Chair	Jerry Buxbaum
"Foundations"	Debby Hellman David Roffman
"Historical Journeys"	Linda Diamond Edward Sandler
"A Celebration through Music"	Toba Grant Calvin Hamburger
Interfaith Series	Tammie Plant Sanford M. Shapiro
125th Year Study Program	Barbara Berg Ellen Friedman Debby Hellman Jeffrey Platt
Appreciation Dinner	Sandy Baklor Pacy Oletsky Carole Sibel
In Concert with Vladimir FeltsmanWeekend Shabbat Dinner	Janet R. Tolbert Alan N. Kanter Michelle & Howard Rosenbloom
Concert Event	Linda G. Blumenthal John Blumenthal
School Program	Ellen & Neil Meltzer

Editorial Note

Differences in the spelling of certain words and Hebrew trans- literations throughout this volume are a result of direct references to the primary source materials. Such differences add to the uniqueness of our history and should not be seen as inconsistencies or errors in the author's writing and/or research. Also, please note that words, sentences, and paragraphs found in this volume that are denoted with italics represent direct quotations from original source materials.

FOREWORD

Rabbi Israel M. Goldman announced his intended retirement in a letter to the president of the Board of Trustees dated January 7, 1975. He wrote: *"The first item on my personal calendar upon retirement is to complete a book on the history of the Chizuk Amuno Congregation – a book on which I began to work about twenty years ago. This will be a gift of gratitude from me to the Congregation I love."*

That goal was never realized. Handwritten notes, yellowing newspaper clippings, hundreds of pages of correspondence, poorly recorded audiotapes, and boxes of archival materials from the rabbi's research remained at the synagogue – clues to the story he had hoped to tell. Perhaps we are fortunate that another twenty-five years passed before the publication of Chizuk Amuno's history. Rabbi Goldman's own tenure can now be placed in proper context.

The factual information presented has been gleaned from original source material held in the archives of the Congregation, and from microfilm and archival holdings of Baltimore Hebrew University, the Jewish Museum of Maryland, and the Rare Book Room of the Jewish Theological Seminary. Hundreds of documents were critically examined. Undoubtedly, many more items exist that could reveal additional information of interest, but the essential history of the Congregation is here in sufficient detail to provide a comprehensive picture of the Chizuk Amuno community.

By researching primary sources, rather than conducting personal interviews, I was able to analyze historical events as they were reported at the time. Profiles of individuals and groups emerged from the available records. The words of the clergy and laity, recorded contemporaneously in archival documents, speak for themselves, without being distorted by sentimental remembrances or selective memories. Wherever possible, I have cited original sources for statements of fact. This dependence on documentary proof presumably has kept errors to a minimum.

Viewed too closely, moments that are still fresh in our minds cannot be examined with the same critical eye as those from which we have distanced ourselves. The first hundred years of Chizuk Amuno's story have been placed against a backdrop of world events, sociological changes, and demographic adaptations. We can only imagine what consequences the most recent twenty-five years will have on the future of the Congregation. The historians who write the next volume of Chizuk Amuno's history will be able to offer much more perspective to frame these years.

This project would not have come about were it not for the support and assistance of many. My sincere appreciation and gratitude to:

- The Committee, chaired by Dr. Jerry Buxbaum, who had the guts to agree that a CPA could write a synagogue history
- Larry Shuman, who persuaded the Committee to take my offer seriously, and coordinated production logistics
- Stanley I. Minch, whose meticulous thirty year files captured details which would otherwise have been lost to memory
- The librarians and archivists at the Jewish Museum of Maryland and Jewish Theological Seminary for graciously guiding me through their collections
- Anna Goldman, who shared not only her father's personal papers, but also the stories of her family which enabled me to gain insight into a man I never had the pleasure of meeting
- The late Alexandra Lee Levin, whose fascination with the Friedenwald family and respect for Rabbi Goldman's projects provided published and unpublished scholarly material illuminating much of the early history of the Congregation
- Norman Brotman, whose request for help in locating the graves of his Hartogensis ancestors led me to explore the Congregation's first Minute Book
- Judy Meltzer, who reunited my split infinitives, kept watch over my tendency to slip emotional adverbs into an objective

presentation of facts, and granted me borrowing privileges in her personal library of references

- Susan Vick, Debby Hellman, and Doris Tanhoff, who tolerated not only a mountain of boxes containing archival materials stacked in their office suite, but also humored me when my enthusiastic shouts of *"look at this!"* interrupted their work
- Barbara Leibowitz, who served as my guide to the records of the Congregation's Arlington Cemetery and yahrzeit files, and didn't even blink when I requested a six-foot ladder to photograph gravestones
- Ellen Kahan Zager, whose graphic expertise and computer design savvy proved invaluable
- Dr. Paul D. Schneider, who offered Hebrew translation, rabbinic interpretation, his collection of scholarly texts, and words of encouragement
- Rabbi Joel H. Zaiman, who, without saying a word, set the standard by which I approached this project. His availability, and patience for my fervent style of research, is much appreciated.
- My parents, Jay and Doris Bernhardt, whose love of Judaism and involvement in synagogue life was inherited from their own parents
- My daughters, Hallie, Johanna and Chelsea, who, after awhile, stopped asking, *"Why is Mommy writing a book?"* and began monitoring my progress by asking, *"Are you up to Rabbi Zaiman yet?"*
- My husband, Jay, whose calming, gentle nature and loving support were repeatedly tested as I vented my frustrations, stacked more binders and microfilm copies on the dining room table, and pleaded for him to *"just read this section one more time."* We will never be *"married too long."*

Many facets of the Chizuk Amuno community have remained remarkably consistent over 125 years. Members are still counted among the leaders of Baltimore's communal organizations and Jewish agencies worldwide. Support of the Jewish Theological Seminary and United Synagogue of America has remained steadfast. Dynamic professionals and dedicated lay leaders have brought standards of excellence to their positions. Thousands of devoted volunteers have spent countless hours providing support for Congregational activities. The generosity of members still assures that the financial demands of maintaining quality programming and facilities will be met. Learning and living Jewishly have always been of paramount importance.

It would have been impossible to name each and every person whose energies and spirit contributed to the perpetuation, evolution, and growth of the Congregation. The fear that I might have unintentionally slighted someone by neglecting to mention him or her by name, motivated my decision to limit acknowledging individual efforts.

The story of Chizuk Amuno Congregation is dedicated to each and every one of these people. It is a great honor to complete a project so long in the making.

Jan Bernhardt Schein
April 2, 2000

INTRODUCTION

Baltimore City's Jewish population increased from an estimated 150 in 1825, to nearly 12,000 in 1855. Much of this growth was attributable to a wave of German immigration as Bavarian Jews, denied civil liberties, immigrated to Holland, England, and America. Baltimore was a popular port of arrival. Shipping lines, delivering tobacco from Maryland farms to the port of Bremen, Germany, increased profitability by selling discounted tickets of passage on the empty ships returning to Baltimore.

Upon arrival, the Jewish immigrants of the mid-nineteenth century settled within walking distance of where they had disembarked. The streets of East Baltimore – Lombard, High, Exeter, Aisquith, and Central – became a hub of Jewish activity and prayer. In 1830, Baltimore's first organized congregation was established. Baltimore Hebrew Congregation received the first corporate charter issued to a Jewish entity in Maryland. Being the sole synagogue in Baltimore, the congregation was known as the "Stadt Shul" – the City Synagogue. Eight years later, Fells Point Hebrew Friendship Congregation was established. In 1848, the group constructed a synagogue commonly known as the "Eden Street Shul." Although the congregation had ceased operations by 1902, a surviving corporate entity maintains ownership of the Hebrew Friendship Cemetery on East Baltimore Street.

Baltimore's third congregation, Har Sinai Verein, was established in 1842. Protesting the orthodoxy of the other two synagogues, Har Sinai followed the influence of the Hamburg, Germany Reform Temple, thus relinquishing most of the rituals associated with Judaism. Other members of Baltimore Hebrew Congregation, unhappy with both the traditional orientation of Rabbi Henry Hochheimer and the reforms at Har Sinai, formed a fourth congregation in 1853, Oheb Shalom (Lover of Peace). In 1859, Rabbi Benjamin Szold arrived in Baltimore to lead Oheb Shalom on its moderate path of Historical

Judaism. Rabbi Szold eventually developed a close personal and professional relationship with the leadership of Chizuk Amuno.

Traditional German Jews worshipping at Baltimore Hebrew Congregation were constantly on the alert for even the slightest hint of reforms being introduced at their synagogue. Member Jonas Friedenwald, destined to become the leading force of Chizuk Amuno, filed a court suit in 1857, to block the pending contract renewal of Rabbi Hochheimer. The rabbi had advocated introducing a confirmation service for girls, and the use of Dr. Isaac M. Wise's <u>Minhag America</u> prayer book – views which Friedenwald felt were suspect. Although this action was settled out of court, Friedenwald had made his point and the rabbi's contract was only extended for a few months.

In 1860, Friedenwald again challenged efforts for reform. The Board of Baltimore Hebrew Congregation approved a motion to exclude *piyutim* (liturgical poems) from the prayer service, but Jonas Friedenwald demanded that the minutes record his negative vote. Only a slight minority of the Baltimore Hebrew Congregation membership shared Friedenwald's level of strict religious observance. Hired in 1868, Rev. Abraham Hofmann took decisive steps to lead Baltimore Hebrew Congregation toward Reform Judaism. On January 2, 1870, a motion was proposed to organize *"...a choir composed of male and female voices."* The resolution was defeated at that meeting, but was passed when reintroduced six months later.

Joined by eighteen other Baltimore Hebrew Congregation members, Jonas Friedenwald filed a class action suit in federal court charging the officers with violating the congregation's constitution on several counts. It was very unusual for a religious matter to be adjudicated in a secular court. On August 18, 1870, the <u>Baltimore American and Commercial Advertiser</u> reported news of Napoleon's naval blockage in the North Sea on page one, but carried the story of the local religious conflict on page four:

A SCHISM AMONG THE HEBREWS
CUSTOMS OF THE FATHERS SET ASIDE
THE TRADITIONS OF AGES MADE OF NO ACCOUNT

AN UNORTHODOX CHAZAU AND A MIXED CHOIR
NEW AND STRANGE DOCTRINES PREACHED
FEMALES TAKE PART IN SONGS OF ZION
AID OF COURT OF EQUITY INVOKED
AN INJUNCTION PRAYED FOR

A Schism in a Hebrew Congregation
*APPLICATION FOR AN INJUNCTION AGAINST
PROGRESSIONISTS*

*In the Circuit Court for Baltimore City, Judge Pinkney,
there was filed by Wm F. Frick, Esq., counsel for com-
plainants, Jonas Friedenwald, Louis Goodman, Isaac
Arnold, Herman Halle, Bernard Stern, Simon
Greensfelder, Hertz Blonheim, Simon Halle, Abraham
Rothschild, Abraham Rosenfeld, Abraham Neuberger,
Nathan Greenebaum, Hertz Oppenheimer, L. Heilner,
Moses Friedenwald, Lazarus Engel, Philip Herzberg,
H.L. Heussler and S. Harman, on their own behalf, and
other members of the Baltimore Hebrew Congre-
gation...a bill for an injunction.*

The complaint focused on three points –

1) the hazzan had been elected to a five year term instead of the
   one year stipulated in the constitution,
2) *"according to the custom of the Orthodox German Jews from
   time immemorial, it has not been allowed that females should
   take part in the rites and ceremonies...by singing in a choir
   with males"* and adoption of such a choir is in direct violation of the constitution and,
3) the hazzan had *"preached doctrines which are not in accordance with Orthodox German Jews"* and *"introduced unau-
   thorized changes in the ancient form of worship..."*

Although a hearing date of September 13 had been set for the
court of Judge William S. Pinkney, agreement was reached between
the parties and the case was *"allowed to sleep on the docket of the
court"* indefinitely. Many of the dissidents resigned from Baltimore

Hebrew Congregation in final protest, anxious to continue the rituals of Orthodoxy. Led by Jonas Friedenwald, they would form the nucleus of the emerging Chizuk Amuno Congregation.

FORMATION   (1871–1876)

The traditionalists resigned from Baltimore Hebrew Congregation in December 1870 and January 1871, and formulated plans to establish a new congregation. Jonas Friedenwald rented Exeter Hall, owned by ex-Governor Bradford, at 2 North Exeter Street, and began outfitting the two-story building for use as a synagogue.

The first floor was designed as a Bet Hamidrash, a House of Study. The second floor would serve as the Bet Tfilah, House of Worship. In anticipation of opening, the building was cleaned, whitewashed, and painted. Workmen installed an Ark, laid carpets, hung a clock, placed two dozen spittoons, and positioned six cane officer chairs on the bimah. Friedenwald advanced a total of $570.84 to cover all of the expenses. An ad placed in the local English and German-language newspapers invited interested men to attend a meeting on April 2, 1871, to form a new Orthodox congregation.

On Saturday, April 1, 1871, Shabbat Hagadol, Inaugural Services were conducted. The group had already chosen to call themselves, **Hebrew Chizuk Amuno Congregation**, "Strengthening of the Faith," a direct barb at the emerging reforms at their prior congregation.

The original Minute Book recorded the events of the following day, and the months and years to come. Artistically handwritten by Henry S. (H.S.) Hartogensis, these entries provide insight into the earliest decisions of the founders. The following entry is transcribed directly from page one of the leather-bound Minute Book, with spellings appearing as they were written:

Baltimore April 2ⁿᵈ 1871

A special meeting was held this day at 10 A.M. at the call of Jonas Friedenwald Esgr. in the בית המדרש *Beth Hamedrasch Exeter Hall. By an unanimous vote Mr.*

Judah Rosewald was elected Chairman and Mr. S. Altmyer as the Secretary pro.tem.

The meeting having regularly been opened, the Chairman Mr. Rosewald stated that the object for the call of said meeting was, for the purpose of establishing a Hebrew Congregation, where our Prayers daily will be offered in accordance with the Orthodox Rituals, the very same manner of worship, as it was inherited to us by our Forefathers.

Mr. Jonas Friedenwald moved that if there are any of the Gentlemen present, who feel disposed of becoming a member of this now newly organized Congregation, he requested to apply to the chairman in order to have their names recorded as members by the Secretary p.t. which was adopted.

The hereby following named Gentlemen made application and were duly accepted as members viz

Isaac Arnold
Simon Altmyer
Jacob Behrens
Samuel Bergman
Raphael Berliner
Jonas Friedenwald
Joseph Friedenwald
Isaac Friedenwald
Moses Friedenwald
Asher Heilner
H.S. Hartogensis

Tobias Harts
Philip Herzberg
Morris Levy
Samuel Nuberger
Herts Oppenheimer
Nathan Oppenheimer
Judah Rosewald
Moses Rosenthal
Benjamin Stern
Benjamin Simon
Samuel Sondeimer

and Morris Weil

These twenty-three names would forever be recorded as the founding members of Chizuk Amuno. Many of their names are still announced in the sanctuary on the anniversaries of their yahrzeits.

Many of the twenty-three original members of Chizuk Amuno had roots in Bavaria and carried with them strong memories of the rising anti-Semitism of the early 1800's. They emigrated to escape repression and arrived in America with little more than their personal belongings and deep convictions of maintaining the Orthodoxy of their fathers. Highly motivated to create a better life for their families, many of the founders entered commercial trades and profited from Civil War industrialization.

There was a common thread that linked the founders together. Most of them found time to serve as lay leaders for the major communal associations in Baltimore. This trend would continue over the next century as succeeding generations emulated the example set by the founders of the Congregation. These men and women led lives characterized by Jewish culture emanating in Jewish observance, in Jewish piety, in Jewish service, and in Jewish leadership.

Jonas Friedenwald

The individual most responsible for the founding of Chizuk Amuno was unquestionably Jonas Friedenwald. Not only was he the primary motivator in establishing the new congregation, Friedenwald was also its staunchest supporter and greatest benefactor.

The son of Chayim Friedenwald, Jonas was born in Altenbuseck in Hesse Darmstadt, Bavaria, on November 9, 1801. At the age of twenty, he married Merle Bar Stern, the widow of a "kinsman" and eight years his senior. The couple lived on their small farm near the village of Altenbuseck, along with Jonas's father and Merle's young son, Bernard Stern. After spending the early hours of the day working in the fields, Jonas earned extra money as a trader. His industrious nature enabled the family to accumulate enough money to emigrate from Bavaria, hoping to achieve freedom and opportunities in America.

By 1831, the family had grown to include daughter Betsy (born 1825), and sons Joseph (born 1827), and Isaac (born 1831). Along with Merle's son Bernard and Jonas's father Chayim, the family sold everything to finance passage from Bremen, Germany to Baltimore. To prepare for the trip, Jonas purchased kosher meat from a butcher in Bremen and had it smoked and packed for the voyage.

Unfortunately, the captain of the *Louise* insisted that the Friedenwalds place their food under his supervision. Deeply concerned that passing the kosher meat through non-Jewish hands could render it traif, Jonas traded the meat for herring and potatoes – all that the family ate during the voyage. The ship was battered by constant storms, making the Atlantic crossing uncommonly harsh. Passengers taunted the Jewish family and blamed them for the rough seas. The travelers feared the strange sounds coming from the captain's cabin where he had agreed to let the Friedenwald family gather for their daily prayers.

On Thursday, January 19, 1832, after four months at sea, the *Louise* reached the mouth of the Chesapeake Bay and traveled slowly to the ice-blocked Patapsco River. Jonas, fearing the ship would arrive in Baltimore after Shabbat had begun, left the ship, and walked on the frozen river to the port of Baltimore where he managed to find shelter. By the time his family arrived at port the next day, Jonas had arranged to rent two small rooms on the upper story of a house owned by a fellow Jew.

Jonas Friedenwald earned his first wages in America mending broken umbrellas, a skill he learned before leaving Bavaria. Within four months, he had earned enough money making and selling umbrellas to move his family to Bond Street near Shakespeare Street. In 1834, Jonas started another trade – hardware. Family legend has it that Jonas would buy old nails and have his sons hammer the nails straight. He then resold the nails at a price under that of his competitor, Mr. Enoch Pratt. By 1840, the Friedenwald family moved to Bond and Thames Streets where Jonas opened a small grocery store managed by his wife and daughter Betsy.

The growing American economy brought success to Jonas Friedenwald, and in 1850, at the age of forty-eight, he announced his retirement. By his own calculations, Friedenwald had amassed $90,000 in savings, which he deemed enough for his wants. A four-story brick house was built for the family at 111 E. Baltimore Street (now 1111), near Aisquith Street.

Jonas Friedenwald was very devout, strictly following Judaism's teachings, traditions and ancient rituals. Upon arrival in Baltimore in 1832, he joined the Orthodox Baltimore Hebrew Congregation and remained an active member until resigning to establish Chizuk Amuno. After retiring, Jonas Friedenwald filled his days with daily prayer, community service, and philanthropic activities. One of Friedenwald's personal projects was his "Matzah Fund." Every year he purchased close to 3,000 pounds of flour and distributed it to the poor for Passover. A provision to continue this practice after his death was included in his will.

Among his many charitable interests was the Hebrew Free Burial Society. Jonas owned several burial plots in the Oheb Shalom Cemetery on O'Donnell Street. When the community determined that a free burial site was needed for unfortunate Jews who died destitute, Friedenwald traded his plots in a prime location in the Oheb Shalom Cemetery for four acres of ground in the rear of the cemetery. Those acres were then donated in 1869 to the Hebrew Free Burial Society, and Jonas purchased new lots for his family at the Baltimore Hebrew Cemetery on Belair Road.

Jonas Friedenwald's piety, generous spirit and devotion to his community were legendary. His children, grandchildren and great-grandchildren inherited Jonas's passion for Judaism and carried on his legacy for many decades.

Bernard Stern

Bernard (recorded as "Benjamin" in the Minute Book) Stern was the son of Merle Bar and Moses Stern. From age one, he was raised as the stepson of Jonas Friedenwald. Unfortunately, he died an untimely death on October 26, 1873, at age fifty-three.

Joseph Friedenwald

Joseph, the oldest son of Jonas and Merle Friedenwald, was born in 1827, and traveled to America as a youngster with his parents. Joseph Friedenwald joined his sister's husband, Moses Wiesenfeld, in the wholesale clothing business. The firm of Moses Wiesenfeld and Company manufactured uniforms during the Civil War and became one of the leading wholesale clothiers in America. However, Joseph Friedenwald's most lucrative business venture was the establishment of Crown Cork & Seal Co. where he held the position of President.

Many communal organizations benefited from Joseph Friedenwald's philanthropy. He served as the first president of the ten-room Hebrew Hospital and Asylum (later to become Sinai Hospital) for sixteen years, and was the first President of the Hebrew Orphans Asylum. The Purim Association, organized in 1868 through the action of Joseph Friedenwald, gave an annual masked ball with proceeds going to the Hebrew Hospital and orphan home. Friedenwald was the first Jew to serve as a member of the Board of Baltimore's almshouse – Bay View Asylum – a position he held for twenty-one years.

Isaac Friedenwald

The third child of Jonas Friedenwald was only two months old when his family sailed to America. During the Civil War, Isaac Friedenwald served with the Confederate Army, much to the dismay of some in his family. Isaac, known in the family as "Ike", established Isaac Friedenwald Press, a printing and engraving business, and was the official printer for Johns Hopkins University. The business later became Lord Baltimore Press.

Moses Friedenwald

Moses was the first American-born child of Jonas and Merle Friedenwald. After working at a clothing business in St. Louis for a few years, Moses returned to Baltimore and joined his brother-in-law's business. At age thirty-seven, he was the youngest of the Friedenwald siblings to have the distinction of being a founding member of Chizuk Amuno.

Judah Rosewald

Very little is known about the early life of Judah Rosewald – the Congregation's first president. Born in 1806, he was the son of Issachar. Rosewald served terms as secretary and treasurer at the Baltimore Hebrew Congregation prior to the formation of Chizuk Amuno. Traditionally trained in Talmud and Jewish worship, Rosewald served as Baal Shaharit on the High Holy Days and delivered many discourses to the Congregation during Chizuk Amuno's earliest years. The Baltimore City Directory, published in 1872, revealed that Judah Rosewald earned his living as a bookkeeper and lived at 25 East Fayette Street. Also listed at that address was Jacob H. Rosewald, a music teacher. The name "Prof. J.H. Rosewald" is noted in several Chizuk Amuno programs as providing the musical accompaniment for special programs.

Personal insight into Judah Rosewald's character was offered in a statement made on January 16, 1956, by Dr. Edgar Friedenwald, grandson of founder Jonas Friedenwald:

> *While the German Jews of that generation were a fairly uneducated group; they were industrious and good business men, but had little appreciation of learning and culture. Judah Rosewald was a high exception in his generation. He was a highly cultured gentleman, well educated, and had a keen appreciation of music. He read a great deal, mostly in German. He was a quiet, modest man. He and grandfather Jonas were great friends and very observant Jews.*

On February 14, 1852, Rosewald's daughter Rosa married Jonas Friedenwald's oldest son, Joseph. They had fourteen children, of whom twelve survived to adulthood.

Philip Herzberg

Born in the town of Klingenberg au Main, Bavaria, Germany, Philip Herzberg came to Baltimore as an eighteen-year-old in 1840, and established a successful manufacturing wholesale and retail clothing business. Herzberg is credited with being an organizing member of the Eden Street Congregation in 1843, and served as its Treasurer for many years. In 1849, Herzberg's name appeared on a Baltimore Hebrew Congregation membership list where he remained a member until resigning to establish Chizuk Amuno in 1871.

Herzberg was actively involved with many communal organizations in Baltimore. He was a founding member of the United Hebrew Assistance Society (which amended its name to the Hebrew Benevolent Society of Baltimore ten years later) and served as its president for twelve years. Herzberg also served in leadership positions with the Hebrew Hospital and Asylum Association, the Hebrew Orphans Asylum, the Hebrew Educational Society, the Hebrew Free Burial Society and other non-sectarian institutions.

Henry S. Hartogensis

One of the most colorful personalities among the founding members of Chizuk Amuno, H.S. Hartogensis, served the Congregation as secretary for nineteen years. A descendant of the distinguished Rabbi Arye Loeb of Breslau, Hartogensis was born on Rosh Hodesh Cheshvan (October 27, 1829) in the town of 's Hertogenbosch, Holland. His father, Samuel, was ordained as a rabbi, but elected to enter the Dutch banking industry and was well known as a philanthropist and scholar. The Queen of the Netherlands knighted Hartogensis's brother, Abram, for his communal efforts.

In 1848, the impending French Revolution prompted Hartogensis to leave Holland and travel by sailboat to New York. During the four-week tempestuous journey, most of the passengers died of cholera. Upon arrival in America, Hartogensis began in the stationery business and is acknowledged as the man who introduced Baltimore to the form of check payable "to the order of" instead of "to the bearer." In 1870, the Baltimore City Directory listed Hartogensis as a storeowner, peddling *"clothing, guns, revolvers and musical instruments."*

Hartogensis achieved prominence for his service to the Baltimore Jewish community. He served as a director and officer of the Society for the Education of Poor and Orphaned Hebrew Children (later known as the Hebrew Education Society) for forty years, and devoted a quarter of a century as a manager of the Hebrew Free Burial Society. Although he never received formal training, Hartogensis was considered a *"Chazan"* and often offered his services to the synagogue. A 1910 profile of Hartogensis published in The Jews of Baltimore noted that:

> *...because of his sacrifice of time for communal work, he has never amassed any wealth. This unselfish devotion to the interests of others without a thought of himself, following closely rabbinical tradition and observances and his unbounded faith in God, he considers as the keynote of his beneficent activity, although it has not brought him success in life in the common acceptation of the term.*

The essay continues:

> *...a genial companion and an entertaining talker, his familiarity with Talmudic and Jewish lore rendering his anecdotes especially interesting. Moreover, his time, his efforts and his purse, as well as his counsel, have always been at the disposal of the many who came to see him; wherefore he was most serviceable in helping young men in starting their careers.*

Asher (Lehman) Heilner

Lehman Heilner was also born in Bavaria in the year 1803. He and his wife, Caroline, immigrated to New York where Heilner served as the first cantor of Congregation Rodeph Sholom from 1842 until 1852. The family grew to include five daughters and four sons. It is unclear exactly when Heilner came to Baltimore, but he served as cantor of Baltimore Hebrew Congregation from 1856 to 1859.

Other Founding Members and Key Personalities

Personal information on the remaining fourteen founding members is limited. Early Baltimore City Directories reveal the following facts:

Name	Address	Occupation
Simon Altmeyer	45 Watson Street	
Isaac Arnold	36 Holland Street	
Jacob Behrens	93 N. Gay Street	watchmkr.
Samuel Bergman	320 Eastern Avenue	butcher
Raphael Berliner	———	
Tobias Hartz	77 E. Lombard Street	
Morris Levy	19 N. Frederick Street	tobacconist
Samuel Neuberger	19 N. Frederick Street	boarding
Hertz Oppenheimer	361 E. Baltimore Street	
Nathan Oppenheimer	176 E. Lombard Street	gents furn.
Moses Rosenthal	43 Harrison Street	clothing
Benjamin Simon	204 S. Bethel Street	butcher
Samuel Sondheimer	191 E. Lombard Street	tailor
Marcus Weil	222 S. Broadway	liquor

Michael Simon Levy

Michael Simon (M.S.) Levy does not technically qualify as a founding member of Chizuk Amuno because his official membership did not appear in the records of the Congregation until February 4, 1872. Nonetheless, his influence regarding the founding of Chizuk Amuno warrants his inclusion here.

Born in the Province of Posen, Germany in 1836, M.S. Levy moved to Manchester, England as a young man to join his older brother in the cap business. It was there Levy married his wife, Betsy Jacobs, and his first four children, William, Esther, Jacob and Rose were born. After some initial success, Levy's business venture faded and he decided to immigrate to New York, ultimately settling in Baltimore in April 1866. With very little money to spare, Levy began selling a product he knew well – cloth caps and hats – experimenting with the manufacturing of men's straw hats. He eventually prospered and earned the title of "King of the Straw Hat Industry."

Levy affiliated with the Baltimore Hebrew Congregation upon his arrival in Baltimore, later joining with the group of Orthodox men who seceded to form Chizuk Amuno. A leading philanthropist of the Jewish community, Levy was deeply religious, and scrupulously observed Jewish law and custom. In a memorial volume published after his death, it is noted:

> *Mr. Levy carried out the rabbinical dictum that whenever Jews meet together religious topics should be the subject of at least a little discussion. He was fond of such discussions and found keen pleasure in arguing on religious questions. He often tried to convince less conservative Jews of the value and importance of the customs and ceremonials which were to him so rich in meaning.*
>
> *Their home was pervaded by a Jewish atmosphere, for both Mr. and Mrs. Levy were strongly attached to their faith and their conduct at home and abroad was guided and fashioned by the law and the spirit of Judaism. The*

Sabbath was welcomed each week as a bride, the har-
binger of rest and bliss. The holidays and festivals were
celebrated with love and with understanding of their
meaning and significance.

Many of Levy's children and grandchildren continued to support Chizuk Amuno and were instrumental in the development of
the Baltimore Jewish community.

Betsy Friedenwald Wiesenfeld

Married at the age of nineteen, Betsy Friedenwald Wiesenfeld
was devoted to her parents, brothers, and her own nine children.
Although she had limited formal education (not unusual for women
of that time), Betsy was known for her strong management skills.
Her husband, Moses Wiesenfeld, and her father, Jonas Friedenwald,
encouraged Betsy to become involved in communal activities.

Betsy Wiesenfeld was deeply committed to the Hebrew Ladies Sewing Society (founded in 1856) and was elected president of
that group in 1862.   She served for the next twenty-nine years.
Meeting every Monday afternoon, Society members sewed clothing
to donate to the underprivileged, and sponsored annual banquets and
balls to raise money for a variety of Jewish causes.   Privately, Mrs.
Wiesenfeld used her evening hours sewing shrouds for the Chevra
(Jewish Burial Society).

It can be assumed that Moses Wiesenfeld would have become
a founding member of Chizuk Amuno if not for his untimely death
in February 1871. Instead, it was Jonas Friedenwald's daughter who
stood by her father's side in support of the new congregation. Betsy
Friedenwald Wiesenfeld's generous contributions of both time and
money greatly enabled the establishment of Chizuk Amuno.

In keeping with formal rules of order, the next order of business at the inaugural meeting was to elect officers. The minutes of
April 2, 1871 continue:

Mr. Moses Friedenwald moved that in order to organize we proceed immediately to nominate and elect our officers for the coming Six Months ending on the first of October 1871 which was adopted.
The following nominated Gentlemen were then duly elected for the coming term of Six months.
Mr. Judah Rosewald for President
Mr. Jonas Friedenwald for Vice President
Mr. Tobias Harts for Treasurer
Mr. H.S. Hartogensis for Secretary

Mr. Hartogensis stated that he accept said office to serve without salary the coming six months. Mr. Benjamin Simon was next elected for Shammes at a salary of twenty dollars for the coming six months ending October 1ˢᵗ 1871 for him to attend faithfully to the cleaning and lighting of the Synagogue also.

Mr. Jonas Friedenwald stated that Mr. Heilner had to attend to some business which prevented him from being present at the meeting, that Mr. Heilner offered his services as Gazan for one year without any salary gratiously.

Simon Altmyer and Hertz Oppenheimer were then elected as Electors to serve for six months. Following this announcement, Philip Herzberg moved that the Secretary should be allowed to keep the Minute Books and financial records in any language convenient for him. Hartogensis, perhaps realizing that the future of the Congregation would lie with English-speaking Jews, decided to keep all records in the language of their adopted country.

Lastly, Moses Friedenwald proposed the formation of a five-member Constitution Committee to draft proper documents. Rosewald, Jonas Friedenwald, Altmyer, Herzberg and Hartogensis were appointed to serve on the committee. They were instructed to insert a notice in two daily newspapers after completion of a draft Constitution and By-Laws *"...inviting those Israelites who wishes to become members of this Congregation to be present at said meeting."*

Hartogensis concluded his report of the meeting with the words he would use to sign every entry in the Minute Book:

> *Nothing further claiming attention*
> *The meeting closed By order of the President*
> *Respectfully yours*
> *H.S. Hartogensis*
> *Secretary*

One would have expected Jonas Friedenwald to have been elected the first president of the Congregation. Although there is no written explanation as to why he was not elected, it is reasonable to assume that it was due to the illness of his wife, Merle, who died a few months later on July 9, 1871. Family records note that Jonas was grief-stricken by Merle's death and at the urging of his sons, spent close to two years traveling in Europe to recover.

The Constitution Committee met shortly after charged, reconvening only three weeks later, on Sunday, April 23, 1871, at the first Regular Meeting of the Congregation. Secretary Hartogensis read the proposed Constitution and By-Laws, paragraph by paragraph. The assembled group discussed each section and voted on each paragraph separately.

Seventeen of the twenty-three Founding Members listed above were present to sign the Constitution of *"Hebrew Chizack Amuno Congregation of Baltimore City."* The following men joined them:

Emanuel Cohen
Joseph Benedict
Nathan Kaufman
Julius Ely
Charles Levy
A. Rosenberg
A. Sinzheimer
Joseph Levy
Abraham Neuberger
Joseph Newman

S. Bachrach
David T. Sakolski
L. Elsasser
Solomon Goodman

Excerpts from the 1871 Constitution clearly reveal their intent in establishing Chizuk Amuno:

- *All prayers shall be read in the original Hebrew language and according to the custom of the Orthodox German Israelites. Minhag Ashkenaz.*
- *No alterations whatsoever shall be made in our daily Prayer, Pejutim Jotserous Ceremonies or Customs as long as one member of this Congregation opposes it.*
- *No member shall hold any office of this Congregation who publicly violates the Shabbat or Hollidays*
- *No Israelite can be elected as a member of this Congregation who has married contrary to our Mosaic Laws. If a member marries out of the faith, he shall be expelled.*

As an emphatic response to the process that brought reforms to Baltimore Hebrew Congregation, the final paragraph of the constitution is entitled "Alterations of the Constitution:"

This Constitution shall never be altered, amended, or any addition added to it, unless said alteration, amendment, or addition be submitted in writing signed by five members of the Congregation and before the regular meeting of the congregation. If at the next stated meeting the proposition is approved of by the concurrent vote of two-thirds of the members present it shall then be considered a part of this constitution thereby annulling and repealing all such parts as conflicts therewith excepting **however the mode of Worship which cannot be altered, amended, or any addition whatsoever added to it.**

Members voted to adopt the proposed Constitution as amended and turned their attention to more routine matters. Jonas Friedenwald had rented the Exeter Street space and furnished it with his own funds. H.S. Hartogensis moved to ask Friedenwald to disclose the terms of the lease and the total expense of *"furniture and fitting up of the Synagogue."* Friedenwald divulged that the yearly rental cost was $500, but that the Bet Hamidrash Association would pay $72 per year for use of the first floor space. However, he avoided a direct answer to the question of furnishings. The group voted to assume responsibility for the costs of their new facilities and to reimburse Jonas Friedenwald for his expenses. The last order of business during that "First Regular Meeting" was the announcement of membership dues, and an installment payment option. *"The Board of Managers reported that they have regulated the contribution of members at the rate of eight dollars per year or two dollars per quarter till after the coming 1ˢᵗ orOctober said contribution to commence from the 1ˢᵗ of April."*

Following the full Congregation meeting on April 23, 1871, the Board of Managers met privately. They discussed and approved the membership applications of five men – Joseph Adler, B. Gomprecht, Joseph Newman, Mendel Herzberg and S. Baumgarten. Announcement was made that the next monthly Board meeting would be held to *"divide by lot"* the seats assigned to members.

The precursor of the contemporary Seating Committee met on May 14, 1871. In full sight of the members, Herzberg, Altmyer and N. Oppenheimer simultaneously drew slips of paper from three containers – the member's name, the number of the *"Gents Seat"* and the number of the *"Ladies Seat."* Thirty-four sets of seats were assigned. Before the High Holy Days, the Seating Committee established a price of $2.00 per additional seat which could be rented for unmarried children of members who were under the age of thirteen. The remaining open seats were made available to non-members, termed *"strangers."* These seats came at a premium – sold to the highest bidder, with a minimum bid of $3.00.

Historically, the honor of receiving aliyot was auctioned off to the highest bidder or sold outright for a fixed price, termed an "offering." At the Monthly Board Meeting held on May 7, 1871, the managers set the following fees:

Aliyot or Mi-sheberah on each Shabbat during the year
— 25 cents

Aliyot or Mi-sheberah on Yom Tov or Festival Day
— 50 cents

One additional fee was set on May 14, 1871. To comply with state law, impending marriages needed to be announced publicly on three occasions before the marriage could be performed. Four dollars and fifty cents, payable in advance, was charged to *"...any one wishing to be proclaimed for marriages in the synagogue."* The funds received were to be allocated as follows:

To the *"Gazan"* for performing the marriage — $2.50
To the *"Shammes"* — $1.00
To the Secretary for recording the names in the registry of marriages — $1.00

A formal petition for incorporation was drafted in May 1871, signed by the four officers and two electors. These men appeared before the justices of the Supreme Bench of Baltimore City and presented the four-page document. The opening paragraph slightly amended the official name of the Congregation by inserting the word "Baltimore."

Whereas certain parties, all citizens of the state of Maryland, did on the second day of April 1871 unite and organize themselves into a Jewish or Hebrew congregation and did unanimously adopt Articles of Religion as their form of doctrine and declared themselves to be the Hebrew congregation of the City of Baltimore under the name and style of the Baltimore Hebrew Chizuk Amuno Congregation of Baltimore City, and that the government of said congregation should be independent of all other ecclesiastic bodies.

The group distinguished their mission to "strengthen the faith" by inserting the phrase "Chizuk Amuno" after the name of their predecessor congregation. Approval of the incorporation was dated May 24, 1871.

Clearly concerned about maintaining proper decorum at meetings and avoiding possible conflict-of-interests accusations, the Standing Rules of Order were written. The twenty rules included:

- *Any member who shall deliver his opinion or speak in any debate, shall arise in his place and respectfully address the Chair. He shall confine himself to the question under discussion and avoid personalities. If two or more members rise to speak at the same time, the Presiding Officer shall decide who shall speak first.*
- *No member shall speak longer than 10 minutes each time or more than twice on the same question without leave, nor shall any member, while speaking, name another except respectfully by his proper name.*
- *No member shall vote on any question in the event of which he is immediately or personally interested.*
- *No member shall be appointed on a Committee of which he is immediately personally or even partially concerned.*
- *No member shall speak to another; disturb or interrupt another while he is speaking in debate or otherwise disturb the business of the Congregation while the minutes or other papers are being read. Members shall always confine themselves to the question under debate.*
- *Any member refusing to obey the Presiding Officer using improper or indecorous language during the meeting the Presiding Officer shall have the right to impose a fine upon him from 25 cents to one dollar.*

Responsible fiscal management was always a priority for the Congregation. At the end of the first fiscal quarter, June 30, 1871, the report of the Committee on Books was recorded in the Minute Book. Serving as the precursor of a modern day Finance Committee, these men reviewed the financial data of Secretary Hartogensis, verifying all receipts and disbursements. Each reviewer signed his name under the statement, *"Your Committee on examining the books of Your Treasurer and Secretary hereby respectfully report that we have examined their books and found them correct."* Treasurer Tobias Harts repeated the same verification procedures and attested to the accuracy of the report.

As the first summer came to a close, a new committee was established – the Committee on Fuel and Heating the Synagogue. Concerned about controlling costs, the committee was instructed to contract for two tons of coal, and investigate the *"best and cheapest manner"* to heat the synagogue through the winter. The Congregation's president, vice-president, and secretary served on this first House Committee.

In preparation for the first High Holy Days season an extra Board meeting was convened on August 27, 1871. The Board set prices of:

Aliyot and Mi-sheberah – each 50 cents

Opening and Closing the Ark – each $1.00

Maftir Yonah – $2.00

Haftorah – $1.00

Judah Rosewald chanted Shaharit on the first day of Rosh Hashanah and H.S. Hartogensis davened Shaharit on the second day and on Yom Kippur. Cantor Heilner led Musaf services on both days of Rosh Hashanah, as well as Kol Nidre, Musaf and Neillah services on Yom Kippur. During the Festival of Sukkot, the honors of Hattan Torah and Hattan Bereshit were auctioned to the highest bidders.

Membership was about forty when the first "Yearly Congregational Meeting" was held on October 15, 1871. The officers were each re-elected. Cantor Heilner was elected to serve another year without salary, but was offered a $25 gift in appreciation of his services. He declined to accept the money. Benjamin Simon agreed to serve as Shammes for the coming year at a salary of forty dollars.

Secretary H.S. Hartogensis took the opportunity to offer his own perspective on the first six months of the new Congregation in the minutes of October 15, 1871:

> *Allow me, Gentlemen, to congratulate you. With the help of God our enterprise has succeeded. We have shown the world that the old roots of our holy religion notwithstanding which a great many want and are seeking to destroy have not died away yet but started again. Thy beginning has been small because the latter end will grow up greatly. Let however Shalom, Peace, be our motto rule and action so that with our name Chizuk Amuno may be added, Abundant peace have they who love thy Law and none shall obstruct them.*

Hartogensis conveyed similar thoughts on the occasion of the Congregation's first anniversary. Proud that the bank balance was $346.43 and that the Congregation was stable, Hartogensis concluded his minutes of April 7, 1872:

> *A year has passed in Shalom-Thank God. It being this day our Anniversary let us give thanks to our God that we have succeeded in our undertaking and let us pray to Him that in future we may prosper and exist, so that every Israelite may say of our House of Prayer and of us: Blessed are they that keeps His testimonials and that seek Him with their whole heart and blessed is the man that heareth me and visits daily my gates...*

Members of Chizuk Amuno involved themselves not only in the business of maintaining their new Congregation, but also involved their congregation in the greater Jewish community. Determined to maintain observance of the Laws of Kashrut, the members discussed organizing a Ritual Slaughtering Board. Joseph Friedenwald introduced the following resolution, at the January 7, 1872 meeting:

> *Resolved by the Baltimore Hebrew Ghizack Amuno Congregation that in order to devise some suitable plans to*

form a regular Shechitah Board in the city of Baltimore,
all the Orthodox Congregations of this city are solicited
for each of them to appoint a Committee of two and to
instruct their Committee to meet in conjunction our com-
mittee for said pirpose on any date and day they may set.

The first meeting of this group was held in Chizuk Amuno's Bet Midrash room on February 11, 1872. The Congregation had approved a contribution not to exceed fifty dollars to support the work of these ritual slaughterers. Unfortunately, the Shechitah Board was not long-standing. In December 1872, the minutes record that the organization had dissolved, refunding $3.75 to Chizuk Amuno.

Another joint effort of the Orthodox community was the continued maintenance of the Mikvah (ritual bath), located on Lloyd Street and no longer used by Baltimore Hebrew Congregation. In February 1873, Shevet Achim Congregation on Eutaw Street informed Chizuk Amuno that they had rented the Mikvah and asked for financial assistance to cover proper management. The Board voted to donate $6.25 per quarter. Two years later, the Mikvah needed repairs. Chizuk Amuno President Rosewald met with officers of several other Orthodox synagogues and agreed to split the cost of repairs. Chizuk Amuno's share amounted to twelve dollars.

Of the many examples of individual acts of Gemilut Hasadim, one incident deserved special recognition in the minutes of Chizuk Amuno. A traveling peddler, Abraham Abrahams of Charleston, South Carolina, died suddenly while in Baltimore. H.S. Hartogensis performed last rites for the deceased and escorted the body to burial. During the monthly Board meeting held on March 3, 1872 an announcement was made that the Abrahams family had contributed a small Sefer Torah and its silver ornaments to the Congregation in gratitude for the kindness shown by Mr. Hartogensis. The Secretary was instructed to send the family a letter of appreciation and *"...tender to the bereaved family in their trying affliction our heartfelt sympathy and assure them of our firm belief that God will be the Protector of the disconsolate widow and father to the fatherless."*

Members continued to donate additional gifts. During a European trip in 1872, Jonas Friedenwald purchased many ritual objects for possible use at Chizuk Amuno. He donated a Sefer Torah, Purim Megillah scroll, shofar, silver yad (Torah pointer), Kiddush cup and a spice box. During the next sixteen years, he donated three more Sifrei Torah, a Purim Megillah, a crystal gas chandelier and a silver-plated bowl and pitcher to be used for the Ducheanen (ritual washing of the hands prior to the Kohanim blessing the congregation). The bowl was inscribed, *"To the Chizuk Amuno Congregation from Jonas Friedenwald."*

Members also recognized the greater Jewish community worldwide. At the Board meeting held on June 7, 1874, Mr. Isadore May moved to send a contribution of $20 to the *"Sufferers"* of Eretz Israel. This would signal the beginning of Chizuk Amuno's strenuous support of Zionism. Responding to requests from Jewish relief organizations in Amsterdam and Jerusalem, members unanimously voted to send $10 or $20 dollars every few months to help their brethren in the Holy Land.

The founding members took very seriously the Jewish obligation for life-long learning. A library of sacred texts was assembled and organized in the first floor meeting room. On February 1, 1874, the Bet Hamidrash Association, which had been an integral segment of Chizuk Amuno since its inception, wrote its formal Constitution with seven articles. The first article reveals that meetings and study sessions were to be held "...*at the Vestry Room of the Ghizack Amuno Synagogue at Exeter Hall No. 2.*" Article seven details the operations of the Association:

> *The room of the Association shall be open to the public daily from 2 o'clock P.M. till Sundown and any member or visitor shall have free access to the books of the library but no books from the library shall be allowed to be taken away or home, unless by a member of the Association and not without having first asked the privilege thereof of the Presiding Officer present, and of which a*

*memorandum shall be kept by the Secretary but no mem-
ber has a right to retain any book for a longer period
than two weeks. Any book kept longer than two weeks
shall subject the holder thereof to a fine of 25 cents per
week, for each and every week for each book so retained.*

Signing the "Beth Hamedrasch" Constitution were three officers of Chizuk Amuno — Judah Rosewald, Tobias Hartz, and H.S.
Hartogensis. H.P. Cohen served as treasurer of the group. Serious
adult learning would continue to be a priority for the Congregation.

Within months after Chizuk Amuno was established, the Board
began discussing the need to relocate. Membership had been growing slowly, but steadily, and a permanent synagogue was called for.
On November 5, 1871, a Search Committee was appointed to find a
"more suitable place for worship." Possible site locations for the
Congregation were limited to those within walking distance of members' homes. Although some lived as far west as Charles Street, the
great majority of Chizuk Amuno members still lived in East Baltimore.

It would take almost a year for the committee to identify two
possible properties. At the Congregation meeting held on
October 6, 1872, the Search Committee reported *"...that a building
on S. Eden St. near Gough St. was for sale, also the Har Sinai Temple
on North High St could be had...".* The High Street Temple had
been built in 1849 by the Har Sinai Congregation after a group of
reformers seceded from Baltimore Hebrew Congregation. The
Chizuk Amuno Search Committee inspected the High Street building and reported back to the Congregation on February 2, 1873, *"(we)
have thoroughly examined Har Sinai Temple and find said property
not fit and entirely of no use whatsoever for a synagogue for our
congregation."* Several times during the following year, the President of Har Sinai offered their building for sale at progressively de-
creasing prices. Chizuk Amuno members always voted to reject a
possible move to the High Street Temple.

At a special Congregation meeting held on April 20, 1873, the Search Committee, led by Jonas Friedenwald's son Joseph, reported that a lot on Front Street was available for purchase at a price of $8,000. Interest in purchasing the Front Street property was strong and the Board authorized the younger Friedenwald *"...to purchase said lot in the name of the Congregation."*

A motion was passed at the very same meeting asking for pledges ("subscriptions") towards a new building. As an incentive to encourage contributions, members were told that all paid subscriptions would be applied to reduce the cost of their permanent seat in the new building. Amounts were to be paid in cash immediately or one half in 30 days and one half in 60 days. Secretary Hartogensis was ordered to keep a separate "book of account" in order to maintain careful documentation of the Building Fund. A three member committee was appointed to solicit subscriptions and immediately $950 was pledged by twenty-five of the members present. A special committee of two was appointed to canvas personal friends for additional subscriptions. The first Chizuk Amuno Capital Campaign had been launched.

Unfortunately, the Search Committee announced to the Board on February 1, 1874 that the owners of the Front Street property now declined to sell the site. H.S. Hartogensis was instructed to return all amounts and notes collected towards subscriptions. Notification was sent to the landlord of the Exeter Street building that Chizuk Amuno would renew their lease and the owner agreed to a rental charge of $40 per month.

The search began again, and new committee members were appointed. Sol Goodman, H. Nussbaum, N. Kaufman, Judah Rosewald, S. Altmyer and Jonas Friedenwald continued pursuing leads on possible locations to build a synagogue. At a special meeting called on August 29, 1875, the committee reported that the public school building at Front and Fayette Streets might be available for sale by the city. Some members had heard the unfounded rumor that the Baltimore Hebrew Synagogue building on Lloyd and Watson

Streets would be put on the market. It was the third possible site described that evening that would eventually become the new home of Chizuk Amuno:

> *They were offered also lots 48 feet front by 90 feet deep on Lloyd St. near Lombard St for which the owner wants $3500, $2500 for one lot and $1000 for the adjoining lot in fee. On motion of N. Kaufman committee was empowered to purchase in the name of the Cong. the last named lots...Said motion passed unanimously.*

Once again, a subscription list was opened and $372 was pledged on the spot:

A. Altmyer	*$25*	*Hertz Oppenheimer*	*$50*
Philip Hertzberg	*$25*	*Judah Rosewald*	*$25*
S. Katz	*$25*	*Joseph Bennedick*	*$25*
H.S. Hartogensis	*$20*	*Jacob Behrens*	*$20*
N. Kaufman	*$20*	*H. Nussbaum*	*$20*
Joseph Newman	*$15*	*S. Baumgarten*	*$15*
Asher Rosenberg	*$10*	*A. Bachrach*	*$10*
Joseph Weil	*$10*	*L. Heilner*	*$10*
H. Bucksbaum	*$10*	*N. Oppenheimer*	*$ 5*
Benj. Simon	*$ 5*	*A. Nuburger*	*$ 5*
A. Sindsheimer	*$ 2*		

On October 3, 1875, the Search Committee reported that they had purchased the Lloyd Street lot for $2500 from Christopher Hirsch and paid $50 for a small house on the same lot. Architect and marble cutter Henry Berge drew preliminary plans for a synagogue building and furnished them to the group at no cost. The first Chizuk Amuno Building Committee, established to coordinate the construction, was comprised of:

> *Sol Goodman, Chairman*
> *H. Nusbaum, V.P./Treasurer*

H.S. Hartogensis, Secretary
N. Kaufman
Philip Herzberg
S. Altmeyer
Judah Rosewald
Jonas Friedenwald
Tobias Hartz

Henry Berge was officially approved as the building's architect for a fee of $100. After two small buildings on the lot were destroyed, the committee discovered that the site was ten feet short in width to make the building square. Jonas Friedenwald came to the rescue and purchased the adjoining lot, No. 2 Lloyd Street, for $2000. Graciously, Mr. Friedenwald immediately presented the property deed to the Congregation.

Construction began. The Building Committee decided to *"...build ourselves and to contract separately for each branch of work to the lowest bidder. Wm. Devere was engaged Superintendent, salary $4.00 per day for each and every day work is done."* Progress reports were made to the membership, disclosing the names of firms providing materials:

Chas. B. Getz – bricks
Richard Mooney – flagstones at 62½ cents per running foot
John A. Allen – lime at 33 cents per bushel, cement at
$1.60 per barrel
Patrick McNatty – sand at 40 cents per 1000 and plastering
sand at 40 cents per load
E.W. Scott Co. – bricklayers
M. Gault Son – granite work

Several times during the construction period, the Board passed formal motions acknowledging certain *"liberal donations."* Jonas Friedenwald contributed $1000 in cash towards the construction costs. His daughter, widow Betsy Wiesenfeld, *"...presented to the Congregation some granite sills, joice and bricks which will be used when needed."* A notation in the Minute Book of December 5, 1875 reveals that Mr. Isaac Hecht of San Francisco donated $50 towards the erection of the new synagogue. On February 27, 1876, Jonas Friedenwald stated for the minutes that through the influence of his son, Isaac Friedenwald, and his relative, Goody Rosenfeld, Halle Stieglitz of 21 White Street, NY had contributed twenty yards of white velvet for a perachos.

Not every gift, however, was accepted by the Building Committee. On May 7, 1876, the Baltimore Hebrew Congregation offered the "Almemar Bench" formerly used at their "Mother Congregation." Philip Herzberg proposed a motion on June 4, 1876, that Secretary Hartogensis thank Baltimore Hebrew Congregation of Lloyd Street for their kind offer and state that *"...whereas we cannot well use them* [the Almemar Benches] *we have to decline accepting them."* During that June 4, 1876 meeting, the Board also discussed the plan to vacate Exeter Hall, where they had worshipped for five years. The Secretary was instructed to notify the landlord that the Congregation intended to move out by July 17, but would appreciate the flexibility of remaining a few weeks longer.

One last task was accomplished before the move to Lloyd Street. A Special Congregational Meeting was held on Sunday, July 13, 1876, to hear the report of the Committee for the Revision of the By-Laws and Constitution. Many revisions were accepted as read however, some were considerably debated. The most emphatic wording was contained in Article 2, Section 2 entitled *"Mode of Worship"*:

> *No change or alteration in or addition to our daily Prayers, Pijoetims, Jothserous, Ceremonies or customs whatsoever shall be made unless with the assent of every member belonging to this congregation, and should any member offer a motion or resolution to make any change or alteration in or addition to the daily Prayers, Pejoetim, Jothserous, Ceremonies or Customs, he shall ipso facto forfeit his membership.*

From Article IV, Section 8 - *No member shall hold any office of this congregation who publicly violates the Sabbath or Hollidays.*

From Article IV, Section 10 – *No Rabbi or Lecturer can be elected in the congregation unless he receives a three fourth vote of the Congregation.*

Matters of seat distribution and fees were addressed in Articles XIII and XIV. With the additional space the new sanctuary would provide, three classes of seats were defined in each of the Mens and Ladies sections based on row location:

> *There shall be three classes of Seats among the Gents, also among the Ladies Seats in the gallery. The prices for the two Seats namely, one Gentlemans and one Ladys Seat shall be as follows: 1st Class $80 Eighty dollars, 2nd Class $60 Sixty dollars and 3rd Class $40 Forty dollars. Seats to be sold with a premium to the highest bidder.*

Members were granted the "privilege" of paying for their seats over a period of two years in quarterly installments.

The Board of Managers had intended to set dues for the coming year at $12, but opposition was raised by wealthy Joseph Friedenwald. His motion to maintain the current $10 contribution was approved. Immediately following this resolution, Jonas Friedenwald and Philip Herzberg each offered a one-thousand-dollar, interest-free loan to the Congregation for a year.

Seat assignment procedures had been determined. Construction of the synagogue was in its final stage. Now the membership acknowledged their need for spiritual leadership from an ordained rabbi. First, however, they needed someone to be the keynote speaker at the official dedication of their new synagogue building scheduled for August 18, 1876.

As construction on the new synagogue was nearing completion, Philip Herzberg introduced the name of Dr. Henry W. Schneeberger as a possible guest speaker for the dedication services.

Henry W. (Pinchas Halevi) Schneeberger has the distinction of being the first American-born, university-trained, ordained rabbi in the United States. The Chizuk Amuno archives contain numerous items documenting Schneeberger's family background, his education, and his tenure as rabbi. In 1967, a forty-page article, written by Rabbi Israel M. Goldman, appeared in the <u>American Jewish Historical Quarterly</u> profiling Schneeberger's many accomplishments. The article provides insight into why the traditional members of Chizuk Amuno originally selected Schneeberger, and why his tenure lasted nearly forty years.

Rev. Dr. Schneeberger was the son of Sigmund Schneeberger, a journeyman weaver, and Regina Kohn, both from the Kingdom of Bavaria. The young couple executed a traditional Jewish Engagement Contract on November 8, 1845, containing the following provisions:

> *The groom promises to bring along his property and to outfit himself properly. The bride's mother promises her daughter a dowry of 500 florins which the bride herself has earned, as well as to outfit her properly for Sabbath and the Festival days and to furnish bed linens...It has been agreed upon that the young couple shall settle in North America and there, with God's help, as soon as possible, get married according to aforesaid ritual.*

Six months later, on the 18th of Iyar 5606, their ketubah confirms that the couple was married in the Province of Hanover, Germany.

Two years after his parents immigrated to America, Henry W. Schneeberger was born on August 29, 1848. He attended New York public schools, then Columbia College, earning his Bachelor of Arts degree in 1866, at the age of eighteen. The following year, he received his Master of Arts degree. A program of Jewish studies in Mishna and Talmud, taught by private tutors, supplemented Schneeberger's secular studies. Apparently, the young man was stirred by these teachings, and in 1867 he left New York to study with the great Jewish scholars of Europe.

Schneeberger's first Talmud teacher in Germany was Dr. Marcus Lehmann, the Rabbi of Mayence, and a proponent of traditional German Jewry. After studying together for almost two years, Dr. Lehmann advised Schneeberger to continue his studies at the Hungarian rabbinical school of Dr. Israel Hildesheimer, the Rabbi of Eisenstadt. In 1869, Hildesheimer – considered to be the leader of the modern Jewish Orthodox movement in Western Europe – was invited to join the Jewish community in Berlin. Schneeberger was one of only a handful of students who traveled with the rabbi from Hungary. Within four years, a rabbinical school, known as the Hildesheimer Seminary, was established in Berlin.

Concurrent with his rabbinical studies, Schneeberger was preparing to earn his Doctor of Philosophy degree from the University of Jena. His thesis, "The Life and Works of Rabbi Jehuda Ha-Nasi," was published in Berlin, but printed in English.

The theological approach of Dr. Hildesheimer appealed to Schneeberger and greatly influenced the ideology of the young student. On February 22, 1871, Dr. Hildesheimer hand wrote two copies of Henry Schneeberger's rabbinic ordination papers – one in Hebrew and one in German. Carrying the titles of both "Reverend" and "Doctor," Schneeberger returned to New York in late winter 1871, only weeks before the founding of Chizuk Amuno was to occur in Baltimore. Dr. Lehmann wrote the newly ordained rabbi a letter of praise, in Hebrew, commenting on the current condition of American Jewry:

> *This excellent young man, Pinchas Halevi Schneeberger, came to me from the City of New York in North America in order to study our Sacred Torah, the Talmud and the Codes of Jewish Law. He came fully prepared and eager to receive in purity and to learn with concentration. Praised be God that the Almighty strengthened him in his endeavors and he has succeeded. Since he came a great distance having crossed the great Atlantic Ocean in a boat – and since 'God's word is not beyond the sea'*

[Deuteronomy 30:13] he has received the reward which is promised for a long journey undertaken in a sacred cause. To him has been vouchsafed reverence for God which is his enduring treasure and firmness on the path of righteousness which leads him upward to the House of God. May God continue to bless him with merit so that he shall further pursue with diligence the study of the Torah so as to empower him to stand in the breach to do battle for our Faith in the land of his birth.

Interested in immediately assuming a pulpit position, Schneeberger offered his services as guest lecturer at several synagogues in New York City. After each appearance, the officers of the congregation would publicly thank the rabbi for his address by publishing a resolution in the local Jewish newspaper. Finally, after delivering a sermon on Shavuot 1873, Congregation Poel Zedek of New York hired Schneeberger to serve both as rabbi and principal of the congregational school.

It is unclear exactly how Baltimorean Philip Herzberg knew of Rev. Dr. Schneeberger of New York City. Nevertheless, it was at Herzberg's recommendation that the rabbi was invited to deliver the dedication address for Chizuk Amuno's first building on Lloyd Street.

The Building Committee disclosed that the total cost of the new synagogue, including the purchase of the property, construction, and furnishings, was $19,810. Among the listed expenses were:

74 spittoons	$18
4 officer chairs	$80
Benches	$855
Cushions	$398.75
Stained glass	$155
Wall frescoes	$300
Carving for Ark	$75.75

On Saturday, August 19, 1876, the <u>Baltimore American &
Commercial Advertiser</u> published a detailed description of
Baltimore's newest Orthodox synagogue, built just down the street
from the home of Baltimore Hebrew Congregation:

*The synagogue building makes an imposing appearance,
being built of brick, trimmed with Indiana stone and granite. After entering the front door, there is a vestibule
thirteen feet wide with a wide stairway on either side.
The first, on ground floor, contains the Beth Hamidrash
and several classrooms and meeting rooms for the Board
of Directors and the members of the congregation. The
second floor is the synagogue proper and has a seating
capacity for 425 persons. The gallery for the females
runs the entire length of the synagogue and at the lower
end are two rows of seats for the accommodation of a
male choir. The walls and ceiling are frescoed in a plain
but very tasty manner, and a circular window of stained
glass is situated on either side of the Ark, which is of
wood, painted white and ornamented with gold and beautiful carved work. The Ark is surmounted by marble Tab-
lets of an ashy color and the Ten Commandments are
inscribed on them in letters of gold.*

At 2:00 p.m. on Friday, August 18, 1876, the members of
Chizuk Amuno gathered at Exeter Hall for the final Minha service in
their temporary home. Rev. Dr. H.W. Schneeberger delivered the
closing sermon in German. Five Torah scrolls were lifted out of the
Ark and placed in the arms of Judah Rosewald, Jonas Friedenwald,
Hertz Oppenheimer, Asher Rosenberg, and a "youth," for transfer to
the new shul.

As those assembled exited Exeter Hall behind the Sifrei Torah, they formed a processional headed by Professor Linhardt's Reed
Band. The group walked along Exeter and Watson Streets, turning
onto Lloyd Street and stopping in front of the new façade. At the
closed entrance to the synagogue stood a men's choir under the direction of Professor J.H. Rosewald singing, "It is pleasant to give

thanks unto the Lord" in Hebrew. Newspaper coverage of the dedication provides a first-hand account of what happened next:

> *The Rev. Mr. Schneeberger exclaimed, 'open unto us the gates of righteousness, that we may enter through them and offer homage to the Lord.' Mr. Heilner, the Reader of the congregation, responded from within: 'This is the gate of the Lord; the righteous shall enter therein; enter yee His gates with thanksgiving, His courts with praise.'*

The doors of the synagogue swung open allowing entrance to the procession, choir, and musicians. As the Congregation and invited guests were seated, the group chanted "Mah Tovu." This was followed by the recitation of the Shema. Circling around the altar seven times carrying the Torah scrolls, the honored men joined in the responsive reading of a Psalm of David. The scrolls were placed in the Ark, which was covered by velvet curtains. President Judah Rosewald recited an opening prayer in German, followed by the singing of Adon Olam. The program booklet issued for the ceremony noted that donation tickets were distributed during the singing. Dr. Schneeberger delivered a sermon in English focusing on the first verse of the 122nd Psalm, "I was rejoiced when they said unto me, unto the house of the Lord, let us go."

Schneeberger discussed the significance of the synagogue as a House of Prayer and House of Instruction, warning those present not to follow the false teachings which were leading so many away from the truths of traditional Judaism. Challenging them to battle for the maintenance of what is holy, Rev. Dr. Schneeberger attributed the success of the young congregation to their "upholding a sacred cause." This thinly veiled reference to the separation from Baltimore Hebrew Congregation served as an inspiring message. Donation tickets were collected immediately following Schneeberger's remarks, before Shabbat began.

Guests at the Consecration of the Synagogue included the Mayor of Baltimore, the City Comptroller, the Sheriff, a Federal Tax Court Judge, and several members of other congregations. Published reports of the service noted that Schneeberger held the audience "spell-bound" and spoke "in flawless rhetoric." These accolades were accompanied by similar praise for the elegance of the building itself. The following day, Dr. Schneeberger delivered the Sabbath sermon in German with equal ease.

Filled with joy over the success of the dedication ceremonies, the Board gathered on Sunday, August 20, 1876, for a special meeting. They voted to send Schneeberger $75 in consideration for his services, and passed the following resolution:

Whereas we have listened with much gratification to the very able and eloquent discourses delivered by the Rev. Dr. H.W. Schneeberger of New York in our New Synagogue at the dedication of Friday evening Elool 5636 Aug. 18, 1876,also of Sabbath morning פ' ראה ערב ר"ח אלול *Aug. 19 therefore be it,*

Resolved, That we acknowledge ourselves deeply indebted to the learned Doctor, for his kindness in accepting our invitation to deliver a Sermon

Resolved, That the lectures of the Rev. Dr. Schneeberger were calculated to elevate the mind, and purify the religious ideas and to strengthen the belief in our faith

Resolved, That a copy of these resolutions be presented to the Reverend Doctor also that a copy be sent to the Jewish Messenger for publication

Resolved, That a copy of these Resolutions be spread upon the minutes of the Congregation.

Chizuk Amuno had survived as a congregation for five years, built a magnificent synagogue in which to center their prayers and learning, and set a path for strengthening their devotion to Judaism. Quite an accomplishment considering the membership in 1876 – forty-six families without the benefit of an ordained rabbi.

A committee was appointed to approach Schneeberger with an offer to become the first rabbi of Chizuk Amuno. Within days the young rabbi accepted. The one-year contract was to begin October 1, 1876, and set a yearly salary of $1,200. As an endorsement of this decision, Jonas Friedenwald personally pledged a donation of $400 per year to be specifically used towards the rabbi's salary. Other Friedenwald family members also pledged lesser amounts for this restricted purpose.

Rev. Dr. Schneeberger delivered his farewell sermon to the Poel Zedek Congregation in New York. He assured his congregants that he was leaving them only because he viewed Baltimore as a larger field where he could spread the knowledge of positive, genuine Judaism. The American Israelite, a publication of the Reform movement, published criticism of Schneeberger's sermon in their September 22, 1876 issue:

> Good Dr. Schneeberger, I have heard you speak, and your honest, sincere, fervid manner could not help impressing me; what a pity that these qualities – not too common now-a-days – should be wasted in the service of orthodoxy, which to be sure "is not yet dead," but which is wasting away gradually, and when it is dead, every one will wonder that it lived so long!

An unlabelled New York newspaper clipping in the Chizuk Amuno Archives echoes a similar feeling:

> We are pleased to learn that Rev. Dr. Schneeberger, a native of this city, has received a call as preacher and minister of a Baltimore congregation. He is a young man of talent and considerable learning, and above all devoted to his calling. We differ with him in our views of the requirements of modern Judaism, but we know him to be honest and sincere and feel confident that he will do good work in his congregation.

During the last quarter of the nineteenth century, separate branches of Judaism slowly emerged, although labels of "Orthodox," "Conservative," "Historical Conservative," and "Reform" were not clearly defined. As Abraham Karp commented in his 1965 article, "The Origins of Conservative Judaism," the supporters of Historical Judaism would interchangeably describe themselves as "orthodox" and "conservative", but would adamantly avoid use of the word "reform."

Henry Schneeberger considered himself a member of that group. He was clearly a perfect fit for the members of Chizuk Amuno. His family roots were in the Bavarian region of Europe, his ideology was orthodox, his training was traditional, and his birthplace was America. Schneeberger would reconcile the founding principles of Chizuk Amuno with the developing needs of an evolving American Jewish community.

THE SCHNEEBERGER ERA 1876-1912

A tall, erect, well-dressed, 19ᵗʰ Century American gentle-man. A beautiful speaking voice. Impeccable diction. Excellent command of the English language. A well-trimmed gray beard. Dignified in thought, manner and bearing; from appearances and from his speech he could have been taken for a banker, a doctor, a member of the Cabinet, a philanthropist, or a business man.

I never heard him addressed or referred to as <u>Rabbi</u> Schneeberger; it was always <u>Dr.</u> Schneeberger, although people would naturally refer to him as "the Rabbi."...I never heard anyone, even the heads of the congregation, call Dr. Schneeberger by his first name; it just was not done in those days.

I never saw Dr. Schneeberger wear a yarmelke. Of course, his head was always covered in synagogue or when he prayed. If he did not wear his high silk hat, he would wear his silk cap...

Moses W. Rosenfeld, 1967
Great-grandson of Jonas Friedenwald

The Board clearly defined their expectations of Dr. Schneeberger in the minutes recorded on August 30, 1876. He was to *"...lecture in English and German in the synagogue alternately; to open a school in the schoolroom of the synagogue, there to instruct daily at such time and hours as will be designated."* There was no indication at the time that impending world events would ultimately cast Schneeberger in an intensified role of communal worker, Zionist, and fundraiser. During his forty years at Chizuk

Amuno, Schneeberger, along with the lay people he inspired, would become leaders in local, national, and international Jewish communities.

Dr. Schneeberger's early popularity was attributable to his mastery in delivering a sermon. At ease speaking both German and English, he attracted the interest of other Orthodox congregations in Baltimore and nearby states. Within months of the rabbi's arrival, Chizuk Amuno was offered $150 by the Howard Street Shearith Israel Congregation for the privilege of having Dr. Schneeberger occasionally lecture in their synagogue. Congregations in Pennsylvania, Virginia, Washington, D.C., and around the city invited Schneeberger to speak at their dedication services and other special events. Resolutions of praise were published in newspapers and recorded in the Minute Book.

Keenly interested in events affecting Jews around the world, Schneeberger clipped articles from Jewish periodicals published in London, Palestine, New York, Philadelphia and Cincinnati, saving them as sources for future sermons. Over a hundred of Rev. Schneeberger's sermon drafts and outlines are in the archives of Chizuk Amuno. Donated by his son in 1951, these original writings provide insight into the eloquence of the rabbi's dissertations. From a lecture given in 1876:

> *Happy, thrice happy should we be that we are scions of that nation that in antiquity received the law, suffered persecutions in the Middle Ages, and at present has triumphed gloriously. Be grateful to the supreme Being for having enlightened the minds of the founders of this glorious republic with that heavenly boon, equality to all creeds. Let us be grateful to God that He has placed us with a nation that knows of no persecution for conscience's sake, but that receives all its children with paternal love and freedom.*

And from 1902:

Proverbial wisdom declares time as precious as money. The fact is we measure the value of time by the rates of interest it brings in any business investment or industrial employment. Yet this is a very false and low standard. The value of money is – aside from all vibrations and oscillations of the market – only relative: that of time is absolute. The one can always be replaced, the other never. The one is a gift of circumstances, the other of God's grace. We must learn how to prize time and each single part of it as the key to immortality's treasures.

Not everyone, however, appreciated the rabbi's sermons. A Special Board Meeting was called on February 11, 1878 to discuss a complaint from a member of the Congregation. Secretary Hartogensis was instructed to write a *"very polite letter"* to Rev. Schneeberger informing him of the following resolution:

Resolved, whereas objections having been taken for some remarks made in Dr. Schneeberger's last sermon as well as in some previous one, that Dr. Schneeberger be respectfully requested to abstain in future from any remarks likely to be construed personal in his sermons.

Immediately after arriving in Baltimore, Schneeberger met with the Board to discuss the fundamental structure of a new religious school. Classes were to be conducted seven days a week, twelve months a year. Tuition, payable in advance, was set at one dollar per month for Chizuk Amuno members and $1.25 for children of non-members. All books would be paid for by *"the scholar's parents."* Estimates of expected enrollment convinced the Board that they needed to hire an assistant teacher and Mr. E. Eiseman was hired for the position at a salary of $12.50 per month. Joseph Friedenwald, M.S. Levy, and David Halle were appointed to serve as the first School Commissioners – the forerunner of the modern-day School Board.

From its inception, the Chizuk Amuno religious school admitted both boys and girls however, the groups were separated for translation instruction. As boys were learning to translate the Bible, girls were given prayers to translate. Not all parents agreed with the regimen of sending their daughters to school seven days a week. Mr. Simon Halle petitioned the Board to discount the standard tuition fee and allow his two daughters to attend classes Saturday and Sunday only for a fee of one dollar per month. The Board refused. There is no mention of whether the girls studied elsewhere or enrolled in the complete program. Several children were enrolled in the religious school by the Society for Educating the Poor. The charitable organization requested that tuition for these children be reduced to the member rate of one dollar per month, but the discount was denied. A similar request from the Hebrew Orphans Asylum was also denied. Commissioners argued in private session that these charities conducted fund-raising efforts to subsidize their mission, and Chizuk Amuno should not relieve them of that charge.

It was not, however, the school's salaries or fees that caused controversy among the leadership, but rather the issue of including a course in German language. The Board voiced no objection when Dr. Schneeberger decided that instruction in Judaic studies be given in Hebrew or English, but they requested that the curriculum also include teaching the German language twice weekly. It is important to note that at the time, German was still the language spoken among the older members of the Congregation and used, along with Hebrew, in worship. The parents of first-generation American children were convinced that Jewish heritage and culture could best be transmitted in the language that their families had spoken for generations. Schneeberger vehemently disagreed with this position and requested that a decision on the matter be postponed until the following spring.

The issue of German language was again discussed at a meeting held on March 11, 1877. Schneeberger, still adamant in his opposition, stated:

> *...that he will not under any circumstances sacrifice the Hebrew language for the German or any other language, and particularly not at this time, but will instruct the German language when the children are more or better*

advanced in the Hebrew language or when he considers
the proper time has arrived.

Apparently his argument was convincing. The minutes of that meeting continue:

The Board resolved unanimously that the instruction of
the German language be postponed till we receive a com-
munication of Dr. Schneeberger that the time has arrived
and he considers it expedient to commence.

It took a full year until Schneeberger notified the Board that German language instruction could begin at the school. However, interest in continuing to teach German waned, and the course was dropped as a requirement for the 1885 school year. In 1888, Schneeberger appeared before the Board and *"...stated that in order to give the children a better Hebrew education, he would advise to do away with the instruction of the German language."* The Board accepted his advice, and the course was discontinued.

Enrollment in the religious school during the first few years averaged seventy students and provided approximately $1,000 of revenue annually. Space for classroom seating was constantly at a premium in the Lloyd Street building. After only one year, the room was furnished with nine additional six-foot benches and divided by a wooden partition and sash windows. Jonas Friedenwald contracted for the work and personally settled the bills amounting to $98.

Lay leaders exercised considerable control in shaping the initial Chizuk Amuno religious school. The Commissioners drafted formal rules governing school discipline and specific curriculum guidelines to assure that the priorities of the Congregation were adhered to. The following rules for the youngest class of students were recorded in the minutes of October 21, 1877:

School Discipline

1. *All cases of lateness are to be marked in the roll book of the*
   class.
2. *Repeated cases of tardiness are to be reported to the princi-*

pal of the school and cases of unexcused absence likewise are to be investigated.

3. *Severe corporal punishment is not tolerated. Children misbehaving are to be marked in the roll book, repeated insubordination to be reported to parents.*
4. *No pupil is allowed to leave the room unless it is absolutely necessary and in that case no more than one at a time.*

Course of Instruction

1. *The course of instruction for the second class shall begin from the rudiments of the Hebrew language.*
2. *Children studying the alphabet and spelling are to receive daily instruction.*
3. *The teacher will be requested to practice the morning prayers and such [boruchot] as a child may require orally.*
4. *Hebrew reading shall be combined with practical illustrations of the Hebrew grammar.*
5. *With the advanced class of boys the translation of the Bible will be had 3 times weekly and while the boys translate the girls shall have a prayer translation assigned them.*
6. *When sufficiently advanced the entire class shall have a slate exercise once a week at least practicing declension of simple nouns etc.*
7. *A short time shall be devoted at every lesson and at least ½ hour of Saturdays and Sundays for biblical History combined with religion and the study of the Jewish months shall be taught.*
8. *A review of studies shall be held twice a month.*
9. *The English language is to be used in the translation and in conversation with the pupils.*

One instance of rule enforcement is specifically noted in the minutes. The son of Mr. Oppenheimer apparently misbehaved and was ordered to leave classes until bringing an excuse from his parents. The humble parents appealed to the Board for return of their $1.25 tuition for the month, but the refund was denied.

The first year of the congregational school concluded with an examination of the students on the second Sunday in May, 1877. Not only were parents invited to attend, but an advertisement placed in the Jewish Chronicle also invited the public to witness the testing. Jonas Friedenwald and his daughter, Betsy Wiesenfeld, personally funded the post-examination party to *"entertain or regale"* the children. The tradition of distributing candy sweets at the end of a school year continues to this day.

Although laymen serving as School Commissioners drafted the religious school program, Dr. Schneeberger had very definite ideas on early childhood education. The following extract is part of an undated newspaper clipping found in a collection of Dr. Schneeberger's personal papers. It was most likely published between 1877 and 1890, though the argument may still be deemed valid 100 years later:

HOURS SPENT IN SCHOOL

The question of regulating the hours for a pupil's confinement in school should, I think, be submitted to the medical profession in conjunction with the school board. Every physician will tell us that too close and constant confinement to study is detrimental to the physical improvement of a child...

For this reason I would suggest that the primary schools should not discriminate nor submit to the votes of parents, for many parents, alas, look very frequently upon the school and its teachers as so many nurseries and nurses obliged to take care of the little ones. Three to four hours steady confinement for the children of the primary schools should amply suffice. The balance of the day can then be given up to play and wholesome recreation....

It should not be forgotten that advanced pupils frequently attend religious schools or are taxed with lessons in music or other studies after the public school sessions.

Rev. Schneeberger believed in using positive praise to motivate the students. One hundred cards of merit were ordered in 1877, at a cost of $1.80, to be distributed to deserving pupils. Ice cream parties ($5.00 for ice cream, $9.56 for lemonade and candies) were sponsored by the Congregation and organized by the Committee on Entertaining Children, perhaps the forerunner of the PTA.

In subsequent years, more elaborate celebrations were held to entertain the students. Excursions away from the streets of East Baltimore offered the youngsters an opportunity to interact outside of the classroom. Great care was given to planning the school's first picnic held in July, 1878 at Darley Park, near North Avenue and Harford Road. Park owners agreed to provide the site and furnish music at no charge. All Chizuk Amuno members, schoolchildren, and their parents were invited to attend for free. As a means to raise additional funds for the school, three hundred admission tickets were printed *"...to be sold to strangers through our school children at 20 cents each."* The following year, a gala event was held at Rusk's Garden. Rosewald engaged a four-piece band to play from one until ten o'clock (at a cost of $12), and Herzberg arranged for the Baltimore transit authorities to have two of their Red Line cars waiting at the corner of Lloyd and East Baltimore Streets to transport the children to the picnic.

Although treated to frequent trips and parties, the students soon grew weary of daily instruction. A petition, signed by a majority of the scholars, was presented to the Board in March, 1878, requesting that classes not be held on Saturdays, but rather an extra hour of instruction should be scheduled on Sundays. The Board amended this proposal and ruled to eliminate Saturday classes during the months of June, July and August. A year later, at the request of Rev. Schneeberger, a full month of summer vacation was allowed. The eleven-month school year remained in place until 1888.

With the hiring of Rev. Dr. Schneeberger and the formation of a new school, the Congregation turned its attention to replacing Cantor Heilner with someone who could serve both as cantor and teacher. Cantor Lehman Heilner served Chizuk Amuno from its inception in

1871, but Board minutes of August 27, 1876 document him as *"aged and infirm"* – he was then seventy-three years old. At the yearly meeting held on October 1, 1876, managers recommended that congregants not re-elect Heilner, but the suggestion was ignored. By a vote of sixteen to nine, Heilner was re-elected at an annual salary of $300.   It would be his final year of service. In August, 1877, an ad appeared in the New York weekly Jewish Messenger for a *"...strict Orthodox Gazan who is also capable to be an assistant teacher and competent of translating the Hebrew into the English language. None others need apply and no expenses paid."*

Just before the High Holy Days, Chizuk Amuno hired Mr. M.L. Lilienthal as *"gazan"* and teacher at a salary of $800 per annum. Within two months, conflicts surfaced between Lilienthal and Schneeberger. Lilienthal resented the supervision of the school principal. He informed the Board that *"...under no consideration whatsoever would he serve as assistant teacher under the guidance of a Principal of School, let alone under the management of the Board of Managers and School Commissioners."* Lilienthal refused to sign his contract and refused to teach students, but did offer to serve as cantor and reader for the reduced salary of $600. The offer was unacceptable, and Lilienthal was asked to resign. At a special congregational meeting convened on December 9, 1877, President Rosewald explained the difficulties with the cantor and asked the congregants to support the action taken by the School Commissioners to sever the relationship with Lilienthal. The motion passed with only one dissenting vote. Accepting a settlement of $140, Rev. Lilienthal signed his resignation on January 6, 1878, putting the unfortunate episode to rest.

Still troubled by their experience with Lilienthal, the Board slightly amended the description of the cantor's position to include the requirement that the cantor serve not only as reader and assistant teacher, but also as Baal Koreh. Mr. Herman Glass, barely twenty-six years old, officiated at Shabbat services in January 1878, and applied for the position. He was offered the job as described, but for reasons unknown, at a salary of $600 per annum as opposed to the

$800 provided to Lilienthal. Cantor Glass accepted and was destined to devote more than four decades in the service of Chizuk Amuno.

The original contract with Rev. Glass reveals the demanding responsibilities assigned to the cantor:

- *To attend to the reading and officiate as Gazan and Baal Korah in accordance with the Orthodox Rituals and Minhag Ashkenaz at all times when services or divine worship are held in the Synagogue unless excused for causes by the President or acting presiding officer of the Cong.*

- *To attend to the funeral, in case of the death of one of the members of the Congregation or one of his family and also to be present during the Shivah days of mourning at the house at such time and hour when divine worship is held provided however that said attendance does not interfere with the divine worship held in the Synagogue or regular school hours.*

- *To assist daily, Fridays excepted, the Principal of the school by instructing the Second or lower classes in the Hebrew language at such time and hours as will be designated by the Principal of the School and to be subjected to such rules and regulations as laid down by the Board of Managers and School commissioners of the Congregation.*

Herman Glass was born on January 24, 1852, in the town of Sorau, Upper Silesia, Germany. Following his education in the public schools of the area, Glass trained for the cantorate under the renowned Cantor Deutsch of Breslau. He began his professional career as teacher and cantor to congregations in Leweren, Westphalia and Solingen, Rheinland. Known for his cheerful disposition and pious devotion, Glass is considered the first true cantor of the Congregation. The following eulogy, written by Dr. Harry Friedenwald in 1925, serves as insight into Cantor Glass's vocal ability:

As Chazan, his singing had the element of beauty and sympathy of a mother's lullaby and his chanting the clearness and the dignity befitting the "Messenger of the Con-

gregation." He looked upon his profession as the per-
formance of a sacred duty and his entire life, private and
public, was in perfect conformity. Mild in expression,
he was inflexible in doing what he regarded as right.
Deeply religious, he always showed a broad tolerance
to those of other views. He was the pious Zaddik, whose
life was rich, not in earthly goods, but in the respect and
the honor in which the community held him.

Dr. Schneeberger and Cantor Glass worked well together, both on the pulpit and in the classroom. The only reported conflict occurred in 1886, when Cantor Glass felt that there was inequity in the size of the classes taught by the two men. Rev. Schneeberger taught twenty-two advanced students in the "first class," while Cantor Glass was responsible for forty-six students, some of whom he thought could pass an examination to promote them to the other group. After hearing Rev. Glass's position, the Board graciously decided not to enter into the dispute, but rather suggested that the professionals settle the matter amicably between themselves.

Schneeberger strongly supported the cantor's proposal to form a choir of male schoolchildren. A motion to create such a choir was introduced by Jonas Friedenwald on March 3, 1878 – but it was rejected. After President Rosewald gave Glass permission to have a boys' choir sing at Friday night service in April, the matter was again brought before the Board. This time the motion passed with the provision that the group would not incur any expense to the Congregation.

Membership in the Congregation hovered around forty during the first decade and there was a strong sense of community among the Chizuk Amuno worshippers. Recognition of a member's illness or death deserved comment by Secretary Hartogensis in the Minute Book. Board members attended each funeral, usually travelling in a rented carriage:

Special Board Meeting　　　*Baltimore July 10, 1878*

*At the call of the President, the Board of Managers as-
sembled at the vestry rooms of the Synagogue this
Wednesday afternoon at 5 o'clock P.M. The President
stated the object of this meeting was whereas after long
suffering it pleased our just and true God and judge
דין ושופט צדק ואמת to take unto him the Soul of our worthy member Simon Altmayer on Tuesday morning July 9
יום ח' דתמוז at the advanced age of 72 years we the Board
of Managers are hereby enjoined to pay the last tribute
of respect to our deceased member by attending to his
חלוויח which takes place this day July 10 ט' תמוז תרח"פ
at 5 o'clock P.M. The meeting closed and Board attended
to the funeral.*

Administrative responsibility for the management of the Congregation rested with the laymen serving as the Board of Managers.
They handled all financial matters, resolved personnel issues and
determined ritual practices. Officers of the Congregation served
without salary except for the position of Secretary which, beginning
in 1873, paid $100 a year. Election of officers took place on
October 1 each year, as did appointments to the Book Committee
(financial oversight) and School Commissioners. Members gathered to vote on the slate of officers, who were usually unopposed.
Votes were tallied and results announced by two *"tellers"* appointed
by the President.

Financial shortfalls plagued the young congregation. Rather
than increase dues and risk losing members, the Board depended on
careful spending habits and the contributions of its wealthier constituents and strangers. The Bet Hamidrash Association of Chizuk
Amuno continued to pay $100 each year for the privilege of meeting
in the vestry. Several other communal groups contracted to use space
at the synagogue for their meetings, usually at a fee of $1.50 an
evening. Members were allowed to hold weddings in the building at
no fee, but seatholders and strangers were charged $10 to cover the

expense of extra gaslights. Frequent contributions of necessary items helped to defray expenses. Simon Halle offered to donate all candles needed for Shabbat and Hanukkah. Other members contributed Sifrei Torah, ritual items, and their time to help with building repairs. Each year, Jonas Friedenwald was granted permission to decorate the synagogue with flowers for Shavuot.

Collection of past due amounts was usually the responsibility of the Secretary. When a member was behind on remitting his $10 dues, paying for his seats, or fulfilling a pledge for an aliyah privilege, the Secretary was ordered to contact the person by mail and, with increasingly stern dunning tactics, demand payment. Extended default on amounts due would result in the member forfeiting any installments already paid and possible legal action in civil court. Only after all efforts had failed, the declaration was officially recorded in the Minute Book to strike the person's name from the rolls of the Congregation. Even though strict collection policies were enforced, the Board agreed to grant the president the power to sell High Holy Day seats for a reduced price, or give them away for free if he felt that someone could not afford a seat.

Occasionally non-members would make sizeable contributions to Chizuk Amuno. In September, 1876 Jonas Friedenwald announced receipt of a $100 contribution from Col. Mendes J. Cohen, a prominent member of one of Baltimore's first Jewish families. One year later, Col. Cohen applied to become a dues-paying honorary member of Chizuk Amuno and requested that at his death, the Congregation would see to it that he was buried in accordance with *"Hebrew Orthodox Ritual."* The request was granted, and in May, 1879 Secretary Hartogensis recorded the attendance of the Board at Cohen's funeral.

Non-interest bearing cash loans from Jonas Friedenwald and Philip Herzberg, along with loans from the Permanent Land Company, financed cash shortages. The short-term bank notes were rolled over each time they came due with only the accrued interest paid. Slowly, as cash became available, the obligations were reduced. As of January 1, 1879, the Congregation showed accounts receivable of

$814.96 and notes payable of $4,000 – of which $1,150 was due to Jonas Friedenwald.

Even with cautious management, Chizuk Amuno did not have sufficient funds to meet the salary expectations of its rabbi. Schneeberger, hired in 1876 at the annual salary of $1,200, was earning significantly less than the $4,500 paid to his colleague and friend Rabbi Benjamin Szold at Oheb Shalom. However, it was the one-year contract term that bothered Schneeberger the most. In January, 1879, he made a passionate plea in a letter to the Board that was summarized by the Secretary:

> *Dr. states in said letter that 9 months ago and even previous to his third election he requested his friends to change the law and elect him for a portion of years. He doesn't see why the minister elect should have not the confidence of his congregation to be elected for a longer period than one year and where mutual confidence exists then labor is Sweet and Success is doubly sure. He further stated that he is very sorry indeed to state that if his congregation will not trust him for no longer period than one year and should this be the will and decision of the members of Chizack Amuno Congregation he must most reluctantly resign his position as lecturer and teacher and stay only till Feb. 1 to enable you to elect in the meanwhile one whom you see fit to serve you.*

Mr. J. Eichengreen immediately proposed to extend Rev. Schneeberger's term to October 1, 1882. Acceptance of the motion was unanimous.

On April 1, 1882, the Board met to discuss possible methods of increasing the rabbi's wages. Philip Herzberg proposed that dues be raised to $15, but the motion failed. As an alternative, a committee of three, N. Kaufman, M.S. Levy, and H. Nusbaum, was appointed to solicit subscriptions to generate additional funds. Eleven members present at the meeting pledged an aggregate of $80 per year for three years toward this cause. When Rev. Schneeberger married Sarah

Nussbaum of New York City in April 1882, the Board collected $87 for a wedding gift of *"parlor furniture"* and voted to give the rabbi a $200 raise effective October, 1882. Although grateful for the proposed increase and the wedding gift, Schneeberger nevertheless requested a $300 increase and a contract term of five years. The request was denied. Every renewal period, the issue of salary caused friction between the rabbi and the Board. As the rabbi's family grew to include six children, his pleas for more money took on greater importance. Ultimately, Schneeberger's maximum salary would only reach $1,800 before being reduced to $1,000 a year when he was elected Rabbi Emeritus in 1912.

Shortly after Dr. Schneeberger came to Chizuk Amuno in 1876, he became involved with organized efforts to collect funds for the support of Jews in Palestine. He was appointed chairman of the Executive Committee representing Baltimore Orthodox congregations Chizuk Amuno, Shearith Israel, Bikur Cholim, and B'nai Israel. Greatly appreciative of the committee's support of Jerusalem, Sir Moses Montefiore sent the community a priceless gift – a Sefer Torah which he himself had finished writing. Montefiore requested that the Sefer Torah be kept and used in each congregation for one year beginning with Shabbat Bereshit and ending with Simchat Torah. Chizuk Amuno paid for one-half of the expenses related to clearing the Torah through U.S. Customs. The relationship with Sir Moses Montefiore would lay the groundwork for the Friedenwald family's interest in Zionist causes.

In January, 1879, President Judah Rosewald submitted his letter of resignation to the Board. A committee of Philip Herzberg, H. Nusbaum and M.S. Levy met with Rosewald to convince him to reconsider his decision. Their argument prevailed and the Congregation's first president did complete his term of office, but Rosewald declined when nominated for president at the October, 1879 election. Founder Jonas Friedenwald was nominated and began serving his term as president – a position that he held for thirteen years.

When Jonas Friedenwald's tenure as President of Chizuk Amuno began, membership had dropped to thirty-six as several of the older members died. The decline in membership caused a reduction in dues, seat rental, and offering income, resulting in severe financial shortfalls. President Friedenwald often covered cash needs personally, and by September, 1881, the Congregation's indebtedness to him had grown to $2,500. Rather than forgive the debt, Friedenwald converted the balance into five $500 non-interest bearing, demand notes. Annually, beginning in 1888, each of these notes was presented to Chizuk Amuno as a gift to the Congregation in celebration of Friedenwald's birthday. The loans from Jonas Friedenwald reduced the need for further borrowing from the Permanent Land Co. , whose obligation amounted to $1,100 by November, 1883. In order to liquidate the bank debt, accruing interest at the rate of 6%, Friedenwald donated an additional $600 and Hertz Oppenheimer the balance of $500.

Seven years later, Hertz Oppenheimer became the first member to establish an endowment fund for the benefit of Chizuk Amuno as a legacy upon his death. On October 22, 1890, the Congregation was informed of the generous bequest contained in Oppenheimer's will:

> *I give to the Chizuk Amuno Congregation on Lloyd St.*
> *Baltimore City, the sum of One Thousand dollars to be*
> *by it safely invested and to be known and designated as*
> *the Hertz Oppenheimer Fund, the annual interest only*
> *to be used. Further it is my wish that the several societ-*
> *ies herein before mentioned, as beneficiaries after my*
> *death, from time to time look after my grave and see that*
> *it is kept in good order and condition.*

The proceeds of the endowment were invested on December 1, 1890, in a 4% North Carolina bond.

Jonas Friedenwald's primary focus was not the financial condition of Chizuk Amuno, but rather it was balancing the Congregation's adherence to traditional German Orthodox ritual and decorum with the lifestyles of its American members. Rev. Schneeberger continued the centuries old Jewish tradition of including a prayer in the service on behalf of the ruler of the land. Although Chizuk Amuno's entire service was recited in Hebrew, the words *"the President of the United States of America"* in the Prayer for the Government were recited in English. Several Schneeberger sermons related the themes of American holidays, such as Thanksgiving and Independence Day, to the tenets of Judaism. National events affecting the country were publicly acknowledged at the synagogue. When President Garfield was the victim of an assassin's bullet, a special meeting of the Board was called on July 3, 1881:

> *Whereas with painful sorrow we have received the dreadful news that an attempt on the life of the President of this U.S. has been made on yesterday Saturday July 2, 1881, 5641 whereby the life of our Chief Magistrate has been endangered,*

> *Resolved that a prayer meeting for the recovery of the President of the U.S. be held in our Synagogue this afternoon at 4 o'clock P.M. also for the Secy to insert in two daily papers that on tomorrow July 4 at 3 ½ o'clock P.M. public service will be held in our Synagogue and supplications made to the Eternal for the speedy recovery of the President of the U.S. Hon. James A. Garfield.*

These interactions with American culture exhibited to both the secular community and the reformers that traditional religious practice was compatible with being an American citizen.

Resolved to keep proper decorum at worship services, the Board passed two new rules of conduct on November 2, 1884. It was to be announced that *"...in future no one will be allowed to leave the Synagogue from the time the sefer Torah is taken out of the Ark until it is deposited back again, neither to take off the tallit until the entire service is completed."* Excessive chatter during services and loitering in front of the synagogue were not tolerated. By April 1890, Chizuk Amuno had initiated congregational singing, but only at the appropriate time.

Although finances were tight, the religious school was thriving. In May, 1881, the students participated in a public Hebrew Reading Match – much to the satisfaction of the Board and School Commissioners Joseph Friedenwald, M.S. Levy and H. Goldsmith. After the school exams of May 1882, Rev. Schneeberger presented books to the best scholars. As a token of their appreciation, the Board presented Schneeberger and Rev. Glass with engraved silver goblets.

The education of adults was also important to Rabbi Schneeberger. In conjunction with his participation in the Beth Hamidrash Association, the rabbi instituted an advanced class in rabbinical literature. To attract younger men to study, Dr. Schneeberger organized the Chizuk Amuno Young Men's Association in 1885. Classes in Jewish History, Bible and Hebrew language were held Saturday and Sunday afternoons and guest lecturers spoke once a month. A young friend of the Friedenwald family, Cyrus Adler, was a Fellow at the Johns Hopkins University and frequent speaker at these lectures. By their second year, the Young Men's Association included over eighty members receiving instruction in Jewish rituals, ceremonies, and leading the synagogue service. As the average age of their membership sharply increased, the Congregation recognized the need to attract and retain the younger generation. Programming directed towards young men was intended to assure that strong, committed lay leadership of Chizuk Amuno was being developed.

Another segment of the congregational community, however, had not yet received attention. Until the mid-1880's, there is very little mention of the role women played in the life of the Congregation. Occasionally, there was a note in the Minute Books about a widow requesting transfer of her husband's membership to their son or a comment that courtesy seats were assigned to Mrs. Schneeberger and Mrs. Glass for the High Holy Days. The women of Chizuk Amuno were involved in many Jewish communal organizations but no formal women's group existed inside the congregation until April 21, 1886. That evening, thirteen women met in the schoolroom of the synagogue, under the leadership of Mrs. Rosa Wiesenfeld Rosenfeld, to formal organize *"The Ladies Chizuk Emoonah Auxiliary Association of Baltimore City."*

Rosa Wiesenfeld Rosenfeld, most often referred to as Mrs. Goody Rosenfeld or simply "Rosie", was the daughter of Betsy Friedenwald Wiesenfeld and the granddaughter of Jonas Friedenwald. Emulating the dedication of her family to communal causes, Mrs. Rosenfeld served as the secretary of the Hebrew Ladies Sewing Society, director of Women's Hospital, chairperson of the Committee on Religion of the Council of Jewish Women and founder of the Jewish Newsboys Association. After graduating from Notre Dame in Baltimore, Rosie married Col. Goody Rosenfeld in 1877.

The preamble of the group's constitution stated that they had *"...associated ourselves for the purpose of advancing the welfare of the Chizuk Emoonah Congregation."* Only wives and daughters of members and seatholders were eligible for membership in the Auxiliary. Quarterly dues, payable in advance, were assessed at fifty cents for wives and twenty-five cents for daughters. Honorary membership was extended to male members and seatholders for a five-dollar contribution. Meetings were to be held on the first Tuesdays of May, August, November and February.

Almost immediately, the Ladies Auxiliary began supporting the needs of the Congregation. A *"vote of thanks"* was extended to the Auxiliary on July 1, 1886 for *"...their kindness and great interest they have taken by providing articles needed for the use of the congregation."* A few months later, the women of the Auxiliary volunteered to assist with the routine maintenance of the synagogue – one of the congregation's most troublesome problems. In the ten years since Chizuk Amuno had occupied the Lloyd Street building, six men had been employed as sexton. For a variety of reasons, each was accused of neglecting his duties, which included cleaning the building, kindling the gaslights, and maintaining the coal furnace. On November 7, 1886, the Minute Book recorded the following resolution:

> *Whereas it has been reported to the Board of Managers that the Ladies Auxiliary Society of this Cong. resolved to appoint some Ladies of their Society to act as a committee to superintend and to see to it that the building is kept in a clean condition. Be it resolved that the Board accepts with thanks the kind offer of said Ladies Society.*

The Ladies Auxiliary involved themselves in many facets of Chizuk Amuno life. Among their activities in 1887 were:

- Regaling the school children with small gifts after their Purim shpiel
- Sponsoring a Lag B'Omer festival with the proceeds donated for the benefit of the congregation
- Decorating the synagogue for Shavuot

When Jonas Friedenwald stated that a new oilcloth was needed for use in the vestibule, the Ladies Auxiliary Society volunteered to *"purchase one of the very best material and pay one-half of the expenses toward it."* The cloth was purchased for $50. The Society called attention to needed improvements even when they did not have sufficient money to help in the purchase. In 1888, Mrs. Herman Glass presented a letter to the Board commenting that the stairs needed new carpeting, *"...but the Society has not the funds to procure said carpet."* Partnering with the Congregation to fund essential items would continue to be a major role of the Auxiliary.

Meeting the needs of their own members came as a secondary focus of the Ladies Auxiliary. In July, 1886 the women contemplated building a mikvah and presented the idea to the Board. While the men approved of the idea, they emphatically stated that the Congregation would not be responsible for any debt incurred by such a building. The Auxiliary did not let the issue rest and on October 3, 1886, the wife of the rabbi again conveyed their wishes:

A letter was presented from Mrs. Schneeberger, Secy of the Ladies Auxiliary Society asking this congregation to aid the holy cause they adopted to build a mikvah by subscribing a sum of money towards erecting said building. On motion Pres. appointed a committee of two to solicit subscriptions from our members to further this holy cause.

The campaign for subscriptions was not successful and the matter was again raised in April 1889. Two women from the Auxiliary appeared before the Board urging them to find funds for the construction of a mikvah. President Jonas Friedenwald responded with a challenge grant. *"President stated that whenever Congregation will raise $2,000 cash funds for this purpose he will donate towards it the sum of $1,000."* A mikvah was never built.

The last fifteen years of the nineteenth century marked a period when the attention of Chizuk Amuno members was directed away from their own needs and toward the needs of fellow Jews nearby and far away. The dramatic migration of Jews from the Russian Empire would impact the entire Baltimore Jewish community and greatly influence the direction that Chizuk Amuno would take as the new century began. To fully understand the changes occurring in the Baltimore Jewish community between 1880 and 1920, and the unique role that Chizuk Amuno Congregation and its members played during that period, it is essential to understand the background of the Eastern European immigrants who would comprise the next generation of Baltimore Jewry.

By the late 1860's, the rate of German immigration had slowed and a handful of Jews were beginning to arrive from areas within the Russian Empire. Regional conflicts during the seventeenth and eighteenth centuries had carved and re-carved the geographic boundaries of Eastern Europe into three major empires – Prussian (German), Austrian and Russian. The Polish-Lithuanian Commonwealth, home of Jews for hundreds of years, was dismembered by its neighbors in three stages. With the final partition in 1795, the independent nation of Poland completely disappeared, not to reappear until 1918. The Russian Empire, largest of the three powers, encompassed a vast geographic territory gathered into one national state. The area included what are now the countries of Poland, Lithuania, Latvia, Belarus, Ukraine, Slovakia, Russia, and portions of Hungary and Romania. This amalgamation of land formed an empire whose inhabitants displayed tremendous ethnic diversity. Families often found that the shifting borders of Eastern Europe had resulted in their moving from one province to another, or even one country to another, without ever having left home.

The absence of a strong national identity was replaced by a strong cultural identity. Although the Jews in scholarly cities of Kovno Guberniya (province) in the north differed in Yiddish dialect and kugel recipes from their fellow Jews in the southern Kherson Guberniya, the underlying unity of Judaism linked the groups together as a civilization of Ashkenazic Jews. This civilization shared three traits – pattern of habitation, adherence to halakha and formation of kehilla/chevra organizations. These traits formed a web – uniting religion, economics, culture, politics, society and daily life for the Ashkenazic Jews as they lived in their own universe, coping under the governance of Czarist Russia. Jews in Eastern Europe adapted to dictated changes by relying on their fundamental beliefs and depending on the communal infrastructure which they had developed.

The marketplace economy centered around the weekly market day when Jewish traders, artisans and crafters gathered to sell their finished goods and services for the agricultural products brought by the Polish peasants. Professor Michael Stanislawski of Columbia University analyzed the registration lists of the Russian Empire and noted that most Jews were registered as "urban-dwellers" reflecting their lower middle-class status. He inferred that the introduction of a cross-continental railroad system and the development of industri-alized cities disrupted the market economy of the countryside, in-ducing a steady stream of Jews to migrate towards urban centers in search of employment.

In an attempt to "Russify" Poles and Ukrainians, the Russian government forced alien culture, customs, and laws on the people, thus creating a chaotic environment. Ashkenazic Jews, however, maintained their daily life according to halakha (Jewish law), turn-ing to the local rabbi for responsa (rabbinical answers to posed ques-tions). Detailed rules governing kashrut, business practices, holiday celebrations, rituals of life cycle events, and other more mundane topics were applied to Jews throughout the vast region. The com-mon underpinning – Torah – maintained a sense of continuity to their disrupted lives.

Most important to our understanding of the mesh between the Russian immigrants and the existing Baltimore Jewish community is the Ashkenazic trait of forming kehillot. Acting as self-governing bodies of each community, the kehillot collected taxes from resi-dents and were responsible for the administration of the town. The kehilla paid the rabbi, ran the mikvah, handled burials, established study houses and also served as the intermediary between govern-ment officials and the people. Linked to the kehillot were chevrot, voluntary charitable associations. Small groups of men would gather together to daven, study Talmud, and then discuss solutions to com-munal problems. Jews were afforded wide latitude in self-gover-nance and established not only kehillot, but also guilds, councils, and boards. The continually changing Russian political environment served to strengthen the Jewish community's experience in design-ing communal infrastructures to deal with their own problems.

The lack of a strong nationalistic presence served to strengthen the religious identity of the Jews in the region. Most did not con-sider themselves Russian Jews or Polish Jews, but rather Jews who lived in the Russian Empire. Stereotypical myths describe the Rus-sian immigrants of the 1880's as the world's poorest, least educated, and most oppressed Jews leaving a primitive and moribund country.

However, the most compelling reason to leave Eastern Europe was economic. The sons and daughters of small town merchants and artisans did not possess the skills to find employment in an increasingly industrialized society. There was sweeping anti-Semitism and local hatred of Jews, especially after the assassination of Czar Alexander II in March, 1881, but the majority of the immigrants arriving in America 1880-1903 were from towns where there had been no pogroms.

Common lore and Hollywood movies lead us to assume that the masses of immigrants all arrived through the gates of Ellis Island, but the ports of Boston, Philadelphia, and Baltimore were also the first American stops of thousands of arriving Russians, Poles, and Litvaks. In the early twentieth century, ships owned by the North German Lloyd Line docked at Locust Point in Baltimore every few days carrying hundreds of steerage passengers, with their nationality documented simply as "Hebrew." Approximately 10,000 Jews lived in the city of Baltimore in 1880. During the period 1881-1890, another 24,000 Jews arrived at the port of Baltimore, most of them deciding to settle in the city. Immigrants arriving at other East Coast ports also found their way to Baltimore, a city known for its sizable Jewish community.

As these early Russian immigrants arrived in Baltimore, they naturally gravitated toward other "landsmen" (fellow Jews from the same town or region) who spoke the same dialect, cooked the same recipes, and davened in the same manner. Just as the earlier German immigrants were not comfortable worshipping with the Baltimore Portuguese Jews in the 1830's, so the Russian immigrants were not comfortable with the German Jews who appeared to them as well-dressed aristocrats. Striving to continue their religious practices, the first congregation of Eastern European Jews in Baltimore, organized in 1865, was the Bikur Cholim Congregation (the "Prushnitz Shul"). B'nai Israel Congregation (the "Russiche Shul") followed in 1873, then the Anshe Chesed Bialystok congregation in 1875.

The nineteenth century Baltimore Jew of German descent is

often cast as belonging to one homogeneous group defined as successful men, promoting German secular culture, reform religious practices, and acculturation into the mainstream American economy. The often-repeated folktale is based on stereotypical profiles, and as dramatic as the generally accepted rendition may be, it is the antithesis of the Chizuk Amuno experience. An examination of the actions of individual congregation members and the rabbi of Chizuk Amuno illustrates how they differentiated themselves from the German model promoted by some historians. In his book documenting the development of the Baltimore Jewish community, Uncommon Threads, Philip Kahn, Jr. (himself the descendent of a Reform German Jewish family) acknowledges that there existed a *"small group of highly cultured and well-to-do Baltimore German Jews [who] responded more receptively"* to the arrival of the Russian immigrants. The *"small group"* Kahn refers to was the laity of the Chizuk Amuno Congregation.

Whereas some established German Jewish immigrants considered the Russian Jewish immigrants to be completely foreign, Chizuk Amuno members recognized that their own migration to America was now being repeated by another group. Inherent in the two groups was the strength of their religious convictions, the Hebrew language, and a realization that their faith played a major role in their identities. The Russian immigrants asserted their Jewish identity and did not hesitate to subscribe to Zionism, Orthodoxy, and other ideologies inconsistent with American culture. Members of Chizuk Amuno were also strong supporters of the Zionist movement, and their adherence to traditional Orthodox rituals was considered by their Reform neighbors to be out of step with modern American culture. This parallelism distinguished the efforts of Chizuk Amuno members in welcoming the new Jews of Baltimore.

The explosion of the immigrant population resulted in ghetto-type conditions in East Baltimore neighborhoods as Jews of all ages arrived unable to speak English and unaccustomed to American habits. In the 1880's, the volume of immigration increased significantly in a short period of time, and many blocks had the flavor of East

European towns. When the Germans had arrived decades earlier, they were forced to learn English quickly out of necessity. The sizable Russian population could still buy food, receive care, and sell services by speaking their native language – Yiddish. More "landsmanshaft shuls" were organized as immigrants from the same European area attempted to recreate a microcosm of the life they had left behind. Most of these congregations met in small rented rooms or storefronts, and followed Ashkenazic Judaism with two daily services and Talmud study groups. Although the religious aspects of these new shuls were important to their constituents, the social support system they offered was of equal importance. The shul was not just where you came to worship; it was where an immigrant could find relief from the struggle of cultural adaptation, and comfort in the company of community. It was this communal characteristic that differentiated the landsmanshaft shuls from the established German Orthodox synagogues, such as Chizuk Amuno. Dr. David Kaufman, in his book <u>Shul with a Pool</u>, summarizes the essence of each type of community:

> *The shul was thus backward-looking and transitional, while the synagogue had settled in for the duration, looking toward a more permanent future. Furthermore, the small shul luxuriated in its inner-directed intimacy, while the larger synagogue reveled in its outer-directed showiness. Paradoxically, the former fulfilled all the functions of a community, while the latter was somewhat curtailed in function as a congregation...Though different in many ways, both types perpetuated the European Jewish past in the new American context. Both would also provide models for the modernized synagogues of the following generation, establishing institutional precedents that ultimately influenced the development of the modern Orthodox synagogue-center.*

Areas from throughout Eastern Europe were represented as these landsmanshaft shuls multiplied downtown. The immigrant shuls exemplified piety and prayer in a much-relaxed format, which to the outside community seemed rowdy and lacking in decorum and dignity. Reform German Jews, who held little respect for the ritual traditions of Judaism, were appalled. They shared little in common with the newcomers – not social standing, language, worship, or dietary restrictions. Conversely, Chizuk Amuno members did share many characteristics with the Russian immigrants – kashrut, daily prayer in Hebrew, involvement in establishing communal organizations, and a strong sense of Jewish identity. They focused on these similarities and took the lead in welcoming the Russian immigrants.

Rev. Schneeberger took an active position in aiding the welfare of the Russian immigrants and in encouraging them to meld into the Baltimore Jewish community. In addition to his responsibilities at Chizuk Amuno, the rabbi taught evening courses for immigrants at a school established by the Hebrew Education Society, named in honor of Sir Moses Montefiore. While attempting to elevate the newcomers to a level of self-sufficiency, Dr. Schneeberger welcomed them to associate with Chizuk Amuno. Several of the rabbi's lectures were reported in Baltimore newspapers, including this one from <u>The Baltimore Sun</u>, October 5, 1890:

> *Rev. Dr. H.W. Schneeberger addressed a large congregation yesterday afternoon at the regular service of the Russian Congregation worshiping on North Exeter Street. He spoke in German, advising them not to be contaminated by associating with Socialists…He strongly advised them not only to be good Jews but to live up to the ideals of good Jews; be exemplary men, respectable in every sense – good, peace-loving, upright, patriotic citizens, who respect public opinion.*

Newspaper articles and biographical sketches provide detail to the activities of Chizuk Amuno members during the flood of immigrant arrivals. One of the most involved was Aaron Friedenwald – the third president of Chizuk Amuno Congregation.

Aaron Friedenwald

The minutes of October 3, 1880 document the acceptance of Dr. Aaron Friedenwald, youngest child of Jonas Friedenwald, as a member of Chizuk Amuno. Aaron, who shared his father's strong religious convictions and dedication to philanthropic causes, was destined to lead the Congregation into the twentieth century, serve on the boards of many Baltimore communal organizations, and become instrumental in the development of the Jewish Theological Seminary.

Born December 20, 1836, Aaron attended a school maintained by the Baltimore Hebrew Congregation. He received his bar mitzvah instruction from Rabbi Henry Hochheimer, who also introduced the studious youngster to Rashi's biblical commentaries, and encouraged his study of Hebrew. At age fourteen, Aaron was forced to leave school and work as a bookkeeper for his brothers at Wiesenfeld & Co. Determined to continue his education, Friedenwald studied at night, learning physics, chemistry, and mathematics from his readings at home. His appreciation of literature and history was refined by participating in debates held by a literary society that met at the corner of Calvert and Centre Streets. These debates also developed the oratory skills that would qualify Friedenwald as a much sought-after lecturer and dinner speaker in later years.

Unlike his brothers, Aaron Friedenwald pleaded to attend college, but it was not until he reached age twenty-one that he informed the family that his days of bookkeeping were over. On March 5, 1858, Aaron entered the University of Maryland Medical School office of Dr. Nathan R. Smith and was accepted as a medical student. Jonas and Merle Friedenwald were among those present when their son, Aaron, received his medical degree on March 3, 1860, only two years after beginning his formal studies. Aaron's medical education continued in Europe where he studied ophthalmology at the University of Berlin, and attended eye clinics in Paris, Prague, Vienna, and London.

Aaron maintained a scrapbook of letters he received from family and friends while in Europe. These letters, along with those he himself had written, were preserved by the family and bound into volumes. One such letter described a visit to his family's ancestral hometown in Altenbuseck, Germany. While davening with his father's cousins, Aaron was appalled at the lack of decorum in their services:

> *Sunday August 20, 1860: Cannot help noticing the mockery which many bestow in the name of prayer. While through their lips escape a gibberage neither intelligible to God nor man by peculiar nod's of the head, shaking of the hands and peculiar intonations of the word (ain)* אין. *They are enabled to direct the household affairs and salute and give signals to passersby. This I observe in Labche and Meyerche, both of these would not feel well if they did not go daily through this exercise. And yet while thus the Lord is so dreadfully sinned against, and his name spoken so oft in vain, we who cannot feel edified through this sort of smuttering are called enemies of Judaism. I do not wish to be understood as blaming the peculiar form of prayer as the curse of this much-to-be-regretted sort of devotion. But I am convinced that this evil is hereditary. The enlightened son has observed it in his ignorant father and, as we all are apt to imitate, they too have accustomed themselves to an evil which they do not like to rid themselves of since it has become a custom. I have no doubt that any prayer taught in our edifying manner would be of sinctised with for better results than this mechanical gibberage called "Imug". I need not be told that many do pray fervently, but I need not to say that this is the exception.*

Returning to Baltimore in 1862, Dr. Aaron Friedenwald soon married Miss Bertha Bamberger and opened his practice. When the house directly across the street from his own became available, Jonas helped his son purchase a home at 126 East Baltimore Street. Aaron's early years in practice were interrupted by the Civil War, when he worked day and night caring for wounded soldiers at a temporary shelter on what is now Central Avenue.

Aaron Friedenwald expressed his concern that Jewish patients had no choice but to receive care in medical facilities that did not consider the religious restrictions of their patients. Opportunities for Jewish medical students were also limited. The concept of a Jewish hospital was explored in 1859, led by the efforts of Friedenwald, who insisted that it was needed so that young Jewish doctors could have a place to be trained like *"their non-Jewish colleagues, for whom abundant hospital experience was available."* In 1868, when the new Hebrew Hospital opened, Dr. Friedenwald was appointed one of its visiting physicians.

Friedenwald's colleagues urged him to move out of his East Baltimore home office to the more prestigious neighborhood "up-town." Although married with a family, Aaron asked his father's consent to move. Jonas disapproved of the decision but was finally convinced by his son Moses that it would be in Aaron's best interest. In July 1868, Dr. Friedenwald moved to 88 North Eutaw Street (later number 310) and his practice flourished. Elected Professor of Diseases of the Eye and Ear at the newly organized College of Physicians and Surgeons in 1873, Friedenwald encouraged his students to consider medicine a noble calling.

Judaism always played an essential role in Aaron Friedenwald's life. Although they lived quite a distance away, the family still attended services at Chizuk Amuno on Lloyd Street. Much time was also spent with the family of Rabbi Benjamin Szold of Oheb Shalom Congregation. Friedenwald served as the family's physician and once remarked that he had five sons to match the five Szold daughters. Although Aaron's oldest son, Harry, was four years younger than Henrietta Szold, the two children became life-long friends.

Aaron Friedenwald's involvement with the plight of persecuted Jews in Eastern Europe was multi-faceted. Shortly after the emigration wave began, Friedenwald was selected to direct the Baltimore operations of the Baron de Hirsch Fund. Established in 1881, the Fund aided in the reception and protection of newly arrived Russian

Jews. He also founded the Baltimore branch of the "American Committee for the Amelioration of the Condition of the Russian Refugees" in 1892, after conditions in the Russian Empire worsened. According to Aaron's son Harry Friedenwald in 1904:

> *During his tenure of the chairmanship of the two committees my father disbursed over fifty-eight thousand dollars, 4391 cases, aggregating 10,534 persons, being relieved. An idea of the importance of this work may be gathered from the fact that the total number of Jewish immigrants landing at Baltimore during this period was 24,095.*

Government officials, worried that the newcomers would become public charges, carefully inspected immigrants and did not hesitate to classify them for deportation. In the 1890's, an immigrant could avoid deportation if a $1,000 bond was pledged to guarantee that the newcomer would not become a public charge. Shortly after Aaron Friedenwald's death, Mr. S. Baroway, agent for the Baron de Hirsch Fund in Baltimore, related the following story, which appeared in the August 29, 1902 issue of the <u>Jewish Comment</u>:

> *Two shiploads of Jewish immigrants arrived from Hamburg and were about to be deported...the offer to pledge the buildings of the Hebrew Hospital and Orphan Asylum was rejected by the Treasury Department. Dr. Friedenwald had a busy time then; he did not rest, he could not sleep. He knew the return of those people to Russia at that time meant starvation to many, baptism to some. He neglected his practice and duties to his family to save the unfortunate immigrants, and he succeeded. He found some influential man...who went to Washington to lay the case before the government, resulting in the release of the immigrants. I remember with what joy he greeted me when I brought him the message from the Canton pier, 'Come and get your people.'*

Outspoken in his support of the immigrants, Rev. Schneeberger became well known in the neighborhoods, attracting many of the Russian Jews to sample services at Chizuk Amuno. In a February 25, 1888 letter to his son studying in Germany, Aaron Friedenwald wrote, *"We went downtown to hear the Megillah read. The Schule was filled to its capacity. Russia of course furnished its contingent."* Remarking on the Passover services held two months later, Friedenwald commented, *"Our Schule was quite crowded on both days since the Russian peddlers come to us in large numbers."* Many members accepted the inclusion of their less sophisticated brethren grudgingly. A letter written by Aaron's wife Bertha Friedenwald reported:

> *Yesterday Dr. Schneeberger gave us a preach. He directed his venom against the Russians because they have so many little Schules, and not always in the best neighborhoods. He thought they ought to go to our Schule and that we should not be unkind to them and if they wanted to come in, we should let them in.*

As Russian immigrants acclimated to American society, many wanted to move away from the "old country" style of the landsmanshaft shul, but still held dear the orthodoxy of their past. The outstretched hand of Chizuk Amuno – coupled with its adherence to Orthodox rituals – drew the interest of the Eastern European Jews.

Most of those in the established German Jewish community belonging to Reform synagogues had moved uptown, away from the East Baltimore neighborhoods, as the Russians arrived. Due to their strict Shabbat observance, many members of Chizuk Amuno still maintained homes in the midst of the immigrant settlements. Communal support organizations previously founded by Baltimore's German Jews, such as the Hebrew Benevolent Society, the Hebrew Hospital and Asylum, and the Hebrew Ladies Sewing Society, rushed to provide services for their fellow Jews, but were overwhelmed. Chizuk Amuno members H.S. Hartogensis, Betsy Wiesenfeld, Max Skutch, Louis Steppacher, Silas Fleischer, Philip Herzberg, Joseph

Friedenwald, and M.S. Levy served pivotal roles in relief organizations. Although their intentions were well meaning, some of the charitable projects were perceived as patronizing and offensive. The Eastern European Jews had great pride and were determined to provide for themselves.

Based on the kehilla philosophy of Eastern European Jewish communities, the immigrant shul was considered multi-functional and central to the lives of its members. As these congregations attempted to care for their members, the Russians created new communal agencies such as Hebrew Friendly Inn and Aged Home (1890), Hebrew Free Loan Society (1898), and Hebrew Immigrant Aid Society (1903). The duplication of services offered by the German-sponsored "uptown" charities and the immigrant-founded "downtown" charities frustrated both groups, but would not be reconciled for many decades.

Of all the relief organizations established in response to the Russian immigration, one of the most successful was the Russian Night School. Henrietta Szold suggested to the I.B.L. Hebrew Literary Society of Baltimore that they sponsor evening classes for recent immigrants. With the administrative assistance of Chizuk Amuno member Benjamin H. Hartogensis (the son of Chizuk Amuno Secretary H.S. Hartogensis) and the financial support of the Friedenwald family, Szold was able to open the school in November, 1889, teaching English to thirty students. By the second season, enrollment had jumped to over 300 students necessitating the addition of more faculty, one of whom was Hartogensis's childhood friend, Louis H. Levin. For two years, Levin taught bookkeeping and assisted Szold with administrative tasks. Although Levin and Hartogensis spent many evenings at the family dinner table of Rabbi Benjamin Szold of Oheb Shalom Congregation, the young men regularly worshipped at Chizuk Amuno. Henrietta Szold described Levin in letters to her younger sister Bertha who was then attending college at Bryn Mawr. Louis H. Levin would eventually marry Bertha Szold, become a leading community social worker, and play an integral role in the formation of The Associated Jewish Charities of Baltimore.

Even as Russian Jews poured into Baltimore, efforts were organized to aid Jews in other areas of the world. On May 12, 1888, a meeting was held at the home of Dr. Aaron Friedenwald to create a Baltimore branch of the Alliance Israelite Universelle. The Alliance, established by Baron Maurice de Hirsch in 1860, was the first international Jewish agency formed for the benefit of distressed Jews anywhere in the world. The Baltimore branch mobilized to raise its share of funds in support of the Alliance's mission:

> ...to educate Jews in benighted lands where education is denied them. It provides schools where governments do not maintain them, and that for girls as well as boys. The principle business is to make the condition of our downtrodden co-religionists in Southeastern Europe, in the Far East and in Africa better and more endurable so that they need not give up their homes and emigrate. It procures for them, where possible, civil and religious liberty, renders them assistance in dire distress, whether caused by persecution or by mobs.

Also in attendance at the organizational meeting were Rev. Schneeberger, Rev. Benjamin Szold, Julius Friedenwald (Aaron's son), Dr. Cyrus Adler, and Benjamin H. Hartogensis. Aaron Friedenwald was elected president of the group, with M.S. Levy and Schneeberger serving on the first Board of Directors.

In 1891, as word of bloody pogroms in the Russian Empire reached America, Rev. Schneeberger and Dr. Aaron Friedenwald were invited to speak at a conference of interfaith clergy. Chaired by Cardinal Gibbons, the meeting was called to protest against the persecution of Russian Jews. The Jewish Messenger of New York quoted Rev. Schneeberger as saying:

> It does not become the Hebrews as interested parties to take the lead in this movement. On this platform Jew and Gentile can meet without any difficulty. We should protest not as individual denominations, but as men, as Americans.

Dr. Friedenwald continued:

Such kind words spoken by my Christian friends have afforded me much satisfaction. I am convinced that eventually justice will prevail. I feel that the Israelites of Baltimore deeply appreciate this movement by their Christian friends. The Czar eventually will be forced to yield.

Each of the Chizuk Amuno rabbis over the next hundred years would maintain strong relationships with clergy of other faiths.

The Founding of the Jewish Theological Seminary

The Reform movement attracted increasing interest during the 1870's and 1880's, leading to the establishment of a Reform seminary in Cincinnati to train American rabbis for pulpit positions. Although the Union of American Hebrew Congregations approached Chizuk Amuno in 1877 with an offer of membership, the Board refused to send dues to the Reform association. In 1885, Reform rabbis met in Pittsburgh to draft principles of Reform Judaism. Rev. Schneeberger delivered a vehement sermon directly responding to the radical agenda. As reported in the <u>American Hebrew</u> issue of November 27, 1885, Schneeberger preached:

In these times, when a morbid desire for constant change and variety in matters of religion is dominant, it is necessary to retain a certain amount of stability. God's Word, as revealed, is as true today as it was when first promulgated. Virtue, truth, morality, will always remain old-fashioned...Who does not deeply deplore the arrogance and despotism of those enemies of Judaism, who had the audacity to denounce "The Lord and His Anointed," and to arrange a platform based on individual convictions only?

As early as 1883, Reverend Sabato Morais of Philadelphia expressed the need for a seminary to be established in America that would combat the trend to abandon traditional rituals and ceremonies. After the Pittsburgh Conference, Morais surveyed other colleagues to gather support for the establishment of a traditional seminary. One of Morais' most ardent admirers was Cyrus Adler, Doctor of Semitics from Johns Hopkins University, whose childhood was spent at Morais's Philadelphia synagogue. On January 10, 1886, Adler wrote to Morais suggesting that Aaron Friedenwald and Dr. Schneeberger be invited to a founding meeting to explore the possibilities of creating a "Conservative College." Adler, destined to serve a long tenure as president of the Jewish Theological Seminary following the death of Solomon Schechter, described his relationship with the Friedenwald family in his 1941 autobiography, I Have Considered the Days:

> *With my strong Jewish background and the Jewish interests that I had, I sought out Jewish homes in Baltimore. First was the house of Dr. Aaron Friedenwald, well known physician and oculist, a good companion and a man of genuine piety... I was permitted to regard their house as my second home, and I was always invited to Saturday dinner. Other people came in and there was much joyous talk. His father, Jonas Friedenwald, a tall, fine looking old man who lived to past ninety, sturdy and inflexible, had met the wave of changing ceremonials in the Synagogue, due to the Reform movement, by establishing a congregation of his own which was called Chizuk Emunah, but commonly known in Baltimore as the Friedenwald Schul. It was several miles from where I lived, but I went to it with great regularity, and then, after the service was over, with Aaron Friedenwald and his sons visited the home of the president and at times those of some of his sons. It was through this connection that I got to know the family of Moses Friedenwald and met there his charming daughter Racie who years later was kind enough to accept me as her husband.*

Apparently, Morais took Adler's suggestion. Rev. Schneeberger and Dr. Aaron Friedenwald were two of only twelve men present in the Trustee Room of the Shearith Israel Synagogue in New York City on January 31, 1886, to found the Jewish Theological Seminary of America (JTS). As the Constitution and by-laws stated, the mission of the Seminary was to keep *"alive true Judaic spirit...where the Bible shall be impatiently taught, and Rabbinical literature faithfully expounded."* A series of parlor meetings and guest sermons by Morais was proposed to garner support for the project and raise the funds necessary to meet the expenses of the new seminary. Just a week after the initial meeting in New York, Morais offered to address the Chizuk Amuno Congregation for one such presentation.

A large crowd was present on Sunday, February 14, 1886, as Rev. Morais spoke from the pulpit of the Chizuk Amuno Congregation. He stressed the need to establish a seminary whose curriculum was based on the original words of the Pentateuch. News of the lecture, published in the February 15, 1886 issue of the <u>Baltimore American</u>, reported that the audience included Dr. Szold and representatives of nearly every other congregation in Baltimore. Response to the lecture was very positive, as Schneeberger reported to Morais in his letter of February 17, 1886: *"Wherever I go, I hear the profound satisfaction and unanimous praise your address has created here. I hope and sincerely pray that the response to your able efforts will be in proportion to the sincerity of your eloquence and the approbation of the public."* The Friedenwald family was firmly convinced of the need for a non-Reform seminary. Jonas Friedenwald pledged his personal financial support, and Aaron Friedenwald volunteered to canvas the city for subscriptions.

A second meeting of the founding group, along with representatives of twenty-two supporting congregations was held in March, 1886 to finalize the formation of the Jewish Theological Seminary Association of America. The archives of Chizuk Amuno preserve a page from materials released after that meeting. The printed page lists the members of the *"Committee on Circular"* including Jonas, Aaron and Joseph Friedenwald, Jacob Hecht, and Philip Herzberg, all of Chizuk Amuno Congregation. The Ministers' Committee included the name *"Rev. Dr. H. W. Schneeberger, Baltimore, Md."* It should be noted that this artifact was not originally saved because of its historical significance to the formation of JTS, but rather because Dr. Schneeberger appreciated the scarcity of paper and used the blank side of the JTS page to draft a sermon. Later that year, Aaron Friedenwald was elected Vice-President of the Board of Trustees – a position he would hold until his death.

The minutes of Chizuk Amuno first mention JTS on May 2, 1886, when the Board accepted the motion of Dr. Schneeberger *"...that all monies contributed and paid over by our members and Seatholders for the Jewish Theological Seminary be handed over to Dr. Schneeberger and be placed in the name and title of the Hebrew Gizuk Amuno Cong. of Baltimore City."* The minutes of February 3, 1892 record that Joseph Blumenthal, president of the JTS Association, had written asking that Chizuk Amuno become a member. Approval of the $25 membership fee is documented without any mention of discussion.

Aaron Friedenwald juggled his successful medical practice, teaching responsibilities, and local communal activities with frequent trips to New York for Seminary business. As might be expected, Bertha Friedenwald was often concerned about the toll this hectic schedule was taking on her husband. The strength of Aaron Friedenwald's devotion to both the Seminary and Chizuk Amuno would permanently cement the relationship between the two entities.

During the late 1880's, Chizuk Amuno again found itself in a bleak financial position. Jonas Friedenwald had continued to retire one of the $500 promissory notes due him every year on his birthday, but sufficient cash was still not available to pay Schneeberger, Glass, and the sexton adequately. Once again, an appeal for contributions was launched at a special meeting of the Congregation on April 28, 1889. Anticipating shortages for a few years, members were asked for commitments, payable in each of the following three years from October 1, 1889 until October 1, 1892. As usual, Jonas Friedenwald took the lead in making the first commitment:

Jonas Friedenwald	*100*	*A. Rosenberg*	*5*
M.S. Levy and family	*50*	*H. Pflaunlacher*	*5*
Joseph Friedenwald	*50*	*H. Nusbaum*	*5*
H. Oppemheimer	*25*	*L. Rosenauer*	*5*
Aaron Adler	*10*	*S. Cotton*	*5*
A. Beckenheimer	*10*	*David Simon*	*5*
J. Joseph	*10*	*Isaiah Weil*	*5*
Mrs. B. Wiesenfeld	*10*	*A. Snattinger*	*5*
G. Rosenfeld	*10*		*$320*
H.S. Hartogensis	*5*		

Jonas Friedenwald appointed Nusbaum, Adler and Beckenheimer to solicit subscriptions from those not present at the meeting. Within the next few days, the Committee obtained commitments for another $80 each year:

Moses Friedenwald	*$ 10*
Dr. A. Friedenwald	*10*
Isaac Friedenwald	*10*
H. Goldsmith	*5*
M. Kellner	*5*
M. Rosenfeld	*10*
M. Skutsch	*10*
Emanl Wolfram	*5*
Joseph Wiesenfeld	*5*
S. Fleischer	*5*
Solomon Stern	*5*

Jonas Friedenwald continued to make gracious contributions to Chizuk Amuno. Although approaching ninety with his eyesight failing, Friedenwald walked twice daily to services at the synagogue. In 1889, he bought carpet for the entire first floor and secured the ground rent for the property on which the synagogue was constructed. Tragically, 1889 also brought the death of Jonas's son Moses, one of the founding members of the Congregation.

For over nineteen years, Henry S. Hartogensis had held the position of Secretary of Chizuk Amuno Congregation, recording the minutes of each meeting and handling all financial transactions. In the spring of 1890, his third-person commentary records a personal note:

> *A letter of resignation of Secy H.S. Hartogensis was presented. Secy stated that after having faithfully served the Cong. from the moment of its existence since April 1, 1871 on account of going on to his native country to visit his family, coming week he is compelled to offer his resignation as Secretary assuring the Board that everything is correct. Should however any mistake be found big or little your Secy will gladly rectify. My books, vouchers accounts also of Treas. have been thoroughly examined up to May 15, 1890 and all monies paid over to the Secy appointed in my place. I will instruct him in anything and everything possible, wishing God's blessing* שלום *in our Congregation.*

On July 1, 1890, Alfred Scholle assumed the role of Secretary, and the flowing penmanship of Hartogensis was replaced by the small, uniform letters of a new officer. Scholle, a 28-year-old German Jew, had arrived in America about 1882, but was not naturalized as an American citizen until April 4, 1902. The accounts were still balanced and the writing was still precise, but the Minute Books no longer spoke in the Victorian flavor that Hartogensis brought to Chizuk Amuno.

In recognition of the tremendous contributions of Jonas Friedenwald, the members of Chizuk Amuno Congregation paid tribute to their president on the occasion of his 90th birthday. The committee, chaired by M.S. Levy, sent invitations to Friedenwald relatives, members of the Congregation, representatives of Baltimore's synagogues and communal organizations, and friends of the Congregation. At 2:30 pm on Sunday November 29, 1891, the crowd that filled the synagogue on Lloyd Street included Mr. William Rayner, Rev. Dr. A. Guttmacher, Rev. Dr. Henry Hochheimer, Dr. Israel Hildesheimer of Berlin, and Rev. Dr. Nathan Bamberger of Wurzburg, Bavaria. As reported in the <u>Baltimore American</u> the next day:

> *The Ladies Auxiliary Society of the congregation hand-*
> *somely decorated the synagogue. Evergreen leaves were*
> *festooned over the Ark, and from it to the galleries, Mr.*
> *Friedenwald's initials, "J.F." hung from the center of*
> *the arch. The congregation presented their president with*
> *a life-sized portrait of himself, and also with handsomely*
> *engrossed resolutions. These, placed on easels, were*
> *just behind the cantor's desk. Potted plants were abun-*
> *dant among the decorations.*

After Rev. Herman Glass led the assembly in Mincha services and a recitation of Psalm 100, "A Psalm of Thanksgiving," Dr. Schneeberger welcomed the guests to a celebration *"not of longev- ity, but virtue and piety."* Dr. Sabato Morais delivered an eloquent keynote address, noting Friedenwald's many charitable gifts and his dedication to the Congregation. Close family friend Dr. Benjamin Szold followed with a brief address of praise in German. Szold cred- ited Friedenwald as being a *"...splendid example of high dignity and nobility of character, proving that it is possible to harmoniously com- bine being a good Jew and a good man."* Jonas Friedenwald, as- sisted by his oldest son, Joseph, responded to the accolades saying: *"I shall appreciate this offering as long as I live, and it will ever be a pleasant memory to me. I hope all of you will have nothing but blessings upon you every day you live."*

A booklet of the proceedings privately printed in May, 1892 included reprints of Schneeberger's, Morais's, and Szold's speeches. The work also included a lengthy biography of Jonas Friedenwald, most likely authored by Jonas's daughter, Betsy Friedenwald Wiesenfeld. In a most erudite manner, the biographer emphasized the importance of Friedenwald's life:

But when the good, the noble and the true representa-
tives of the human race have passed away, unseen, their
memories are reflected in the pillars and walls of our
philanthropic institutions; unheard, their voices admon-
ish us to enlarge their works and to cherish the heir-
looms their beneficence has left us.

An original program from Jonas Friedenwald's 90th birthday celebration now lies in the archives of JTS in New York City. A corsage, possibly that worn by Friedenwald himself, is pressed inside the back cover.

Age did not diminish Jonas Friedenwald's administrative oversight of Board matters, or his influence in family matters. When Aaron Friedenwald's eldest son, Harry, became engaged to Birdie Stein, Jonas insisted that the couple be married at Chizuk Amuno, even though the bride's father was then the president of Baltimore Hebrew Congregation, by then located on Madison Avenue. The Board of Chizuk Amuno quickly adopted a constitutional amendment declaring that all weddings held at the synagogue were to be performed by Rev. Schneeberger and Cantor Glass. As Jonas had decreed, Harry Friedenwald married Birdie Stein June 28, 1892, on Lloyd Street, according to Orthodox ritual.

Congregation membership had reached fifty-three when the annual meeting was held in October 1892. A few weeks earlier, Jonas Friedenwald had privately asked his son Aaron to assume the presidency of Chizuk Amuno for the coming year. Edgar Friedenwald, Aaron's youngest son, repeated the family story for author Alexandra Lee Levin, daughter-in-law of Louis H. Levin:

"Bertha," Aaron said one day to his wife, "Father has
asked me to become president of the Synagogue."
"Aaron, you're not going to do it!" exclaimed Bertha,
who felt he was already over-burdened. "Well," replied
Aaron, "I have never said 'no' to him in fifty –five years,
and I'm not going to start now."

When Jonas Friedenwald was nominated for President, he declined and recommended that Dr. Aaron Friedenwald become the third president of the Congregation. The recommendation was accepted and the second generation of Friedenwald leadership was unanimously elected. Jonas was designated "Honorary President." Although Aaron was offered the president's seat on the bimah, out of respect for his father, he refused to occupy the chair during Jonas' lifetime.

Aaron Friedenwald's tenure as president of Chizuk Amuno lasted ten years and encompassed a relocation of the synagogue, doubling of the membership, and increased involvement with the Zionist movement. A sampling of entries from the Minute Book of 1892-1893 offers a glimpse of congregational life at the time of Aaron's election:

- President stated that the boiler has busted, and that he has ordered a new one, which was approved by the Board.

- Total funds of the Congregation: $761.18

- Motion by Mr. Abe Rosenaur, that all those attending worship in our synagogue shall be requested to remain seated during reading of the Torah, provided Dr. Schneeberger decides that it would not be in opposition to our Shulhan Auruch.

- Motion by Mr. J. Joseph that a vote of thanks be extended to the Ladies Chizuk Amuno Auxiliary Society for the interest they have taken, for the welfare of our Congregation, also for their trouble and kindness in decorating our Synagogue in such a beautiful manner on last שבועות.

Aaron Friedenwald's first act as president was to entertain a motion *"...to open a branch of the Chizuk Amuno School uptown under the supervision of Dr. H.W. Schneeberger & Rev. H. Glass."* The motion carried, and Aaron appointed his son, Harry Friedenwald,

Eli Rosenauer, and M.S. Levy to a newly formed School Committee for Uptown. This Minute Book reference is the first indication that some members of Chizuk Amuno had moved out of the East Baltimore neighborhood. Apparently, fourteen scholars attended classes held at 714 Madison Avenue in October, 1892, but the project was short-lived and the school was discontinued in mid-November.

Although not recorded in the Minute Book of the Congregation, a meeting was convened in April, 1893 to discuss forming a branch of Chizuk Amuno uptown. The local newspaper announced the plan:

FOR AN UPTOWN BRANCH

A meeting was held at Covenant Hall, corner Lexington and Eutaw streets, yesterday afternoon, of members of the Chizuk Emoonah Orthodox Synagogue congregation, on Lloyd street, Rev. Dr. Henry Schneeberger, pastor. The object of the meeting was to take action in regard to forming a branch of the congregation, which is to locate in West Baltimore – probably somewhere in the neighborhood of Eutaw street and Madison avenue. It is understood that Dr. Schneeberger will serve both congregations. He now lectures only alternate weeks at the Lloyd Street Synagogue, and if the west branch congregation is organized, he will lecture alternate weeks at the Lloyd Street Synagogue and to the new branch.

The branch is intended specially to accommodate members of the present congregation living near the new location, and also new members who are expected to join...A leading object of the movement is also to organize a day Hebrew school in the new neighborhood.

In the 1980's, Professor Marsha L. Rozenblit conducted an in-depth study comparing the memberships of Chizuk Amuno and Oheb Shalom congregations. The results of her study, entitled "Choosing a Synagogue: The Social Composition of Two German Congregations in Nineteenth-Century Baltimore," provides analytical evidence

that describes the demographics of the Congregation at the time relocation was being considered:

> *In 1889, two-thirds of all Chizuk Amuno members still
> lived east of Charles Street, with over one-quarter of them
> living in quadrant V, east of Central Avenue, where al-
> ready a large community of Russian Jews had begun to
> settle in the 1880's. Very few lived far from Chizuk Amuno
> itself in the western parts of downtown Baltimore, where
> a large number of Oheb Shalom members resided. Thus
> in 1889 about 43 percent of all Chizuk Amuno members
> lived within a half-mile of the synagogue in east Balti-
> more, and another 27 percent lived between eleven and
> twenty blocks away.*

By comparing the occupations of members, Rozenblit concluded:

> *Preference for east Baltimore did not derive from the
> fact that Chizuk Amuno members were too poor to move
> uptown but rather from the genuineness of their religious
> orthodoxy. As long as Chizuk Amuno was located on
> Lloyd and East Lombard streets, most members contin-
> ued to live in east Baltimore so that they could walk to
> the synagogue on the Sabbath, even though it was no
> longer fashionable to live in that part of town. The
> wealthiest members of the congregation were only slightly
> more likely than others to live over a mile away. In 1889,
> about 30 percent of Chizuk Amuno members lived a mile
> or more away from the synagogue; 40 percent of the five
> manufacturers lived over a mile away, and 28.6 percent
> of the merchants with firms did so. The willingness to
> ride was not related to occupation.*

One of the most prominent members of Chizuk Amuno, M.S.
Levy, had moved from the Lloyd Street area in 1885, and established
a home at 747 West Lexington Street. Levy had been an active participant in the affairs of the Congregation since its inception in 1871,

serving terms as School Commissioner, and member of the Book and Building Committees. On July 1, 1893, the general membership of the Congregation was asked to consider a motion by M.S. Levy to sell the Lloyd Street shul and move uptown. Mr. Jacob Joseph amended the motion, changing it to propose appointing a five-member committee to investigate the legality of the proposed action. The motion carried by a vote of 16 to 3, and Aaron Friedenwald assumed the chairmanship of a committee composed of M.S. Levy, Jacob Joseph, Abe Rosenauer, and Joseph Benedict. Immediately following the vote, former Secretary H.S. Hartogensis proposed another motion – *"not to sell the Schule."* The motion failed.

As the concept of a possible relocation was introduced, the man most responsible for the formation and survival of Chizuk Amuno Congregation, Jonas Friedenwald, died on Shabbat Kee Tavo, 21 Elul 5653 (September 2, 1893). His widowed daughter, Betsy Wiesenfeld, who had compassionately cared for him throughout his later years, passed away barely five months later.

The Baltimore American Sunday edition of September 3, 1893 carried a full column tribute detailing Friedenwald's life and history of communal involvement. The page eight article entitled "Close of a Long Life" included a drawing of the gentleman:

> *Mr. Jonas Friedenwald, one of the oldest, most prominent Hebrews in Baltimore, died at half-past six o'clock yesterday morning, at the residence of his daughter, Mrs. Betsy Wiesenfeld, No. 1111 East Baltimore Street. He was ninety-two years of age, and his death has been expected for some time. He had been failing in health for many months. He was surrounded at the time of his death by the members of his family...*

The article concluded:

> *The funeral will be as plain and simple as was the life of the old gentleman himself. This is in accordance with the Jewish custom, as well as his own personal instructions. There will be no panegyric, and the only outpour-*

*ing of respect of his fellowmen.   The coffin will be of
plain pine boards.   The school children of the congregation will attend the funeral in a body.*

Four years earlier, at a Board meeting on July 7, 1889, Jonas
had informed the leaders of the Congregation of his wishes regarding his death.   He requested that an eternal light be burned in his
memory during the first year of mourning in the Bet Hamidrash Room,
and that the Kaddish prayer be recited for him at every daily service
during the year of mourning, in case none of his children was present
to do so.   The Board granted the President's wishes and provided
him with a copy of their resolution.

Chizuk Amuno held a special memorial service in honor of
Friedenwald on September 17, at the synagogue.   One last resolution
of thanks was presented to the bereaved family:

*Whereas, it has pleased our All-wise Providence to re-
move from our midst our dear and venerable friend, the
devoted supporter and counselor of our Congregation*

Mr. Jonas Friedenwald

*Be it therefore Resolved, that we deeply deplore the loss
of our veteran leader, under whose faithful administrative ability, keen judgement, availability of character and
above all his unbounded generosity our Congregation
has flourished and been enabled to fulfil its great and
responsible mission in Israel.*
*Resolved, that his memory will ever linger in our midst
and that we will constantly cherish his noble attributes
of heart.*

Safeguarded in the archives of the JTS Library is a collection
of Jonas Friedenwald's personal papers, including letters dated as
early as 1832.   One letter drafted in 1876 resembles an ethical will
and details instructions for his funeral and his hopes for family members.   The hand-written letter is in German (with a smattering of
Yiddish), using Hebrew characters.   It reflects both Friedenwald's

adherence to Jewish rituals surrounding death and mourning, and his concern that future generations continue on the path he had set. Loosely translated, Friedenwald's requests included:

- a simple coffin built by good Jews
- a simple monument on his grave inscribed with his name, in Hebrew, and the year of his death
- no music, regaling or other decorations at the funeral
- a learned man cover his grave with the dirt from Land of Israel that Jonas possesses
- the rituals of Shiva and Sheloshim to be strictly followed by his children
- his children should do all that is in their power to keep the shul and the Hebrew school in order, and that his children's children will do the same
- a hope that his children live in peace and unity as long as they live
- his gold watch be given to his son Aaron's oldest son, Harry, as a perpetual remembrance of his grandfather

An article entitled "Legacies to Charity," printed on an unknown date in the Baltimore American, detailed the charitable bequests in the probated Friedenwald will. These included gifts to the Hebrew Benevolent Society, Hebrew Hospital, Hebrew Orphans Asylum, Hebrew Free Burial Society, and the Association for Poor & Orphan Children. The deed to the Lloyd Street property was to be transferred to Chizuk Amuno Congregation. Similarly, other ground rents were transferred to the charitable organizations resting on their property. Perhaps the most thoughtful bequest was the creation of an endowment, funded with $5,000 worth of Consolidated Gas stock, to provide *"Passover Bread every March first for the poor Jews of Baltimore."*

Jonas Friedenwald's devotion to Torah, Avodah, and Gemilut Hasadim molded not only the foundation of Chizuk Amuno Congregation, but also the lives of his children and grandchildren. Many of his descendents continued his legacy of compassion, making remarkable contributions while serving the Baltimore Jewish community and Jewish causes around the world. Two succeeding generations of Friedenwald men would serve as presidents of Chizuk Amuno.

McCulloh Street Shul

Following the High Holy Days of 1893, the committee on selling the shul verified that it would be perfectly legal to dispose of the Lloyd Street property, and reported their results at a congregational meeting on October 8. Although one would expect that this announcement would cause great excitement among the Board, it is not even mentioned in a letter that President Aaron Friedenwald wrote to his wife the next day. Bertha Friedenwald had traveled to the World's Fair in Chicago hoping to relieve her depression over the recent loss of their third son, Dr. Bernard Friedenwald. Between comments about patients and family members, Aaron informed Bertha on events of the meeting:

> We had a Congregational meeting last night…There was a little unpleasantness between Mr. Nusbaum and Mr. Rosenberg about as to who was to say Tehilim, early in the morning. The matter was temporarily settled by Rosenberg offering to pay 5 dollars for the privilege. Mr. Nusbaum who now is the oldest member of the Congregation was very much offended that he had to abdicate, and the Board reconsidered the action taken and that peace should reign ordered that Nusbaum should officiate on Saturday & Rosenberg during the week. Both parties are now satisfied, but I question whether the soul of King David is, and I fear he would not have written his Psalms if he would have known that they would ever have been sung in that way. There must have been a good many Nusbaums and Rosenbergs all living and it was no doubt considered a nice arrangement to have them enjoy themselves very early morning when not many people could hear them.
>
> For a change, perhaps better said, for a little change,

> *the Ztaka box was evidently opened on yesterday after-*
> *noon. I don't think ___ did it this time, for 67 cents were*
> *left remaining. ...If you come across any small, strong,*
> *fireproof, burglar proof Ztaka boxes at the fair make a*
> *note of where that much needed article can be*
> *obtained. ...Uncle Joe was at the meeting of the Congre-*
> *gation last night and delivered a speech about a yard*
> *long on the Jewish Theological Seminary. One uniniti-*
> *ated might have thought that he had just come down from*
> *Mt. Sinai. I must say that he can talk very well. But talk*
> *is cheap.*

A month later, Building Committee member M.S. Levy alerted the Board that a site to build a new synagogue was available on McCulloh Street near Mosher for a price of $9,000. Aaron Friedenwald called a special meeting of the Congregation on the evening of November 12, 1893, for the purpose of discussing the issue of relocation. Reaction was positive and $2,600 was pledged immediately toward purchasing the ground. On April 4, 1894, the Building Committee reported that the asking price for lots 50-105 on McCulloh and Mosher Streets had dropped to $6,666, and that the pledges towards purchase now amounted to $4,600. Those pledges would never be applied to the purchase of the property; M.S. Levy purchased the ground personally on January 2, 1895. In an act of great generosity, Levy announced at the quarterly meeting on January 8, *"...that he got a clear title from the Court for lot of ground on McCulloh and Mosher Str. and that he is ready to deed the same to the Congregation."*

The final decision to relocate the Chizuk Amuno Synagogue from Lloyd Street was settled at that January meeting with a vote on a motion by Bernard Wiesenfeld, grandson of founder Jonas Friedenwald:

> *Resolved that it is the sense of the Chizuk Amuno Con-*
> *gregation of Baltimore City, that it is for the welfare of*
> *this congregation that it remove its present place of wor-*
> *ship to the site of the Northeast corner of Mosher and*

McCulloh Str., recently acquired by deed dated the 2ⁿᵈ of January 1895, by Michael S. Levy…and further that it is the sense of the Congregation that it is for its welfare to sell the Synagogue and the lot of ground on which the same is situated, now owned by it on Lloyd Str., and where it at present worships and to purchase the lot of ground from Michael S. Levy, above described and referred to, and further to apply the proceeds of sale of said lot of ground and Synagogue situated on Lloyd Str. to the erection of a new building, on the above mentioned site…

Twenty-six men out of a total membership of forty-four were present at the meeting. Twenty-one voted in favor of the motion. Four men abstained. The sole dissenter was stalwart member H.S. Hartogensis.

The new Building Committee, chaired by M.S. Levy, took immediate action and just one month later, reported that their Lloyd Street synagogue had been sold to Congregation B'nai Israel of Baltimore City for a price of $12,000, subject to a $73.50 annual ground rent. The large chandelier, which had been a gift of Jonas Friedenwald, was specifically excluded from the sale. Transfer of possession was to take place September 8, 1895. Levy formally gifted the ownership of the McCulloh Street property to Chizuk Amuno on February 26, 1895. In his role as Committee Chair, Levy engaged Joseph Evans Sperry as the architect, and contracted the firm of George A. Blake as the builders. An article, appearing in the national weekly <u>American Israelite</u> on May 2, 1895, provided details about the new synagogue as construction was taking place:

The temple will front fifty feet on McCulloh Street, and have a depth of 104 feet on Mosher Street, running back to an alley. The main entrance will be on McCulloh Street, and will be reached by seven steps leading through a colonnade. There will be three doors at the front, over which will be a massive arch. Two massive pillars will stand between the doors. The roof will be four-sided, and will be surmounted by a cupola. The basement will contain three class-rooms, 18x27 feet each, which will have a separate entrance on Mosher Street, with a corridor leading to the other rooms in the basement, among which there will be a library, coat and toilet-rooms. A stairway from the minor sanctuary will lead to the main floor above. The main auditorium will have a total seating capacity of 750, and it will be accessible from the rear as well as the front. Along the main entrance, will be a choir gallery, 22x12 feet. The entrance to the auditorium will be from a large vestibule, in which will also be stairways leading to the galleries. The pulpit platform, reading desk and shrine will be at the end of the auditorium, opposite McCulloh Street, and their arrangement will follow closely the orthodox traditions. The shrine is made the central feature of this end, occupying the entire breadth of the recess and extending almost to the ceiling. It will be elaborately carved and ornamented. On each side of the shrine will be small rooms, each 10x10 feet – one to be used as a study and the other as a reading-room. The ceiling of the auditorium will be divided into deeply-recessed panels with enriched members. There will be two aisles five feet wide, and three rows of pews. The middle row will be double and fifteen feet in length, and the side rows ten feet long. The building will be heated with steam, and lighted by both gas and electricity. The exterior will be of North Carolina granite and a granite cornice will extend around the entire building.

The Globe Furniture Company built the pews and constructed the gallery screens. Main floor pews, made from red oak lumber, were designed with an area under each seat where prayerbooks could be stored. The $12,000 cost of furnishings was supplemented by many gracious gifts from congregants. In December, 1895, Baltimore's <u>Jewish Comment</u> published announcements that Mrs.

Harry Friedenwald, Mrs. M.S. Levy, Mrs. Jacob Levy, and the Ladies' Auxiliary Society had donated the perpetual light, two handsome candelabra, cushions, carpets, curtain for the shrine, decorations for the reading desk, and two handsome platform chairs.

According to the terms of their agreement with B'nai Israel Congregation, members of Chizuk Amuno removed Sifrei Torah, ritual items, and altar furniture from the Lloyd Street Shul on Sunday, September 8, 1895. Construction on the McCulloh Street sanctuary had not been completed, necessitating the use of the new basement vestry auditorium temporarily for Shabbat and the High Holy Day services. Rev. Schneeberger and his family moved into their new home at 1628 Druid Hill Avenue shortly before the holidays. Joseph Friedenwald moved to his new residence, 1916 Eutaw Place, near other wealthy German Jewish families. The movement of members, after the Congregation had relocated, again demonstrates the level of their religious conviction. Professor Rozenblit comments on this characteristic:

> The fact that Chizuk Amuno's members lived in east Baltimore for religious and not financial reasons is amply demonstrated by their very rapid movement into northwest Baltimore after the congregation move to McCulloh and Mosher streets in 1895. By 1896, only one year later, over a third of the members had already moved to northwest Baltimore, led by the richest members: professionals, manufacturers, and merchants who owned their own firms. In that year, therefore, almost half of Chizuk Amuno's members did live over a mile from the synagogue. The situation was remedied by 1900, however, when...82% lived in upper northwest Baltimore and only 6% lived over a mile away. CA members had always had enough money to buy homes uptown, but had delayed doing so until their synagogue, to which they had to live near for religious reasons, moved uptown.

Not every member moved uptown. As expected, H.S. Hartogensis formally resigned from Chizuk Amuno as of October 1,

1895, along with six others. Membership dropped to thirty – the lowest level in more than twenty years. But the decision to relocate would prove positive as close to one hundred new members would join Chizuk Amuno within the next ten years.

Invitation and Reception Committees planned the formal dedication of the new synagogue for the weekend of December 20, 1895. An eighteen-page commemorative booklet containing the order of the services, printed in both Hebrew and English, was distributed to each guest. The festivities began with Mincha services, held in the downstairs vestry rooms. Eight men, each carrying a Torah, followed Rev. Herman Glass into the vestibule where the cantor sang, *"Open to me the gates of righteousness: I will enter into them, I will give thanks unto the Eternal."* A choir, composed of five local cantors and led by Rev. Alois Kaiser of Oheb Shalom Congregation, sang *"Mah Tovo"* and joined the processional towards the sanctuary. The procession encircled the synagogue three times, then stopped to place the scrolls in the Ark. The president of the Congregation, Dr. Aaron Friedenwald, was given the honor of lighting the Ner Tamid.

Rev. Dr. Henry W. Schneeberger recited a passage from I Kings 8:22-66. He then introduced guest speaker Rev. Dr. H. Pereira Mendes to deliver the dedication sermon. A primary force behind the Jewish Theological Seminary, Rev. Mendes was a Sephardic rabbi serving New York's Shearith Israel Congregation. The full text of Mendes's sermon, printed in the December 20, 1895 issue of Baltimore's <u>Jewish Comment</u>, reflects his adamant support of traditional Judaism. Rev. Schneeberger led the Congregation in Shehecheyanu, then began his remarks. He paid tribute to the memory of Jonas Friedenwald, and offered thanks to the many men and women whose *"noble efforts and wonted generosity"* had contributed to the building of the new synagogue. The rabbi concluded by admonishing the audience to stand firm in their convictions:

> *The synagogue is not a "house of prayer" merely. We have not fulfilled our mission as God's chosen people in depositing the Ark in the shrine and allowing it to be*

*read during service. We are also bound to teach its con-
tents to our children and to preserve the traditions of the
synagogue as transmitted unto us. As members of Chizuk
Emoonah we must never lose sight of the significance of
our name "Strengthening in Faith." Our synagogues
are founded on the principles of historical Judaism. We
have always endeavored to carry out the rabbinical injunction to combine a thorough acquaintance of our sacred books with the requirements of secular education,
loyalty to the traditions of our fathers with a full recognition of the wants of the present. Our fathers have been
conservative Israelites; they were happy in the practice
of their religious customs and observances; they witnessed the fruits of their religious training in the morality of the household and dutifulness of sons and daughters, and with the help of God, we expect to remain thus.*

Photographs of Schneeberger, Mendes, and Glass appeared on
the cover of the December 20 issue of the <u>Jewish Comment</u>. Editors
dedicated the issue to: *"Chizuk Emoonah Congregation with hearty
good wishes for its advancement, growth, and prosperity."*

A special meeting of the Congregation was convened on the
Sunday after the dedication to set the price of yearly dues and fix the
price of seats in the new synagogue. For the first time in twenty-five
years, members voted to raise annual dues from $10 to $20. Rows of
benches were designated as either Class I, II or III and assigned a
related minimum price of $100, $75 or $50. Jacob Joseph was ap-
pointed to act as auctioneer on January 7, 1896, when the highest
bidders were allowed to purchase prime seats. Nineteen seats were
auctioned off that day, generating a premium of $235 over the mini-
mum prices.

The increased costs of maintaining a larger building, coupled
with the drop in membership, caused the Congregation to again suffer cash shortages. Even after applying the proceeds of the Lloyd

Street property sale and Building Fund contributions, contractor Blake & Sons was still owed $24,566. Six members personally guaranteed notes to secure a $20,000 mortgage agreed to by the builder. The debt, structured as a five-year balloon note, demanded interest every six months at the rate of 5 ½%. The same six gentlemen – Aaron Friedenwald, Joseph Friedenwald, M.S. Levy, Goody Rosenfeld, L. Steppacher, and Jacob Joseph, also guaranteed a $4,500, 6% demand note for the balance due by the Congregation. Staff salaries continued to be paid and suppliers were sent partial payment "on account." The bank balance dipped to a dangerous low of $173.81 at July 31, 1896. It was obvious that Chizuk Amuno needed an infusion of cash to remain solvent.

A committee was appointed to confer with the Ladies Auxiliary Society about conducting a "Fair" with proceeds to be used to liquidate the debts of the Congregation. As plans were being made, the Board alerted Rev. Schneeberger to the possibility that there might not be sufficient funds to pay for his services. After twenty years with Chizuk Amuno, the rabbi was earning a salary of $150 per month. As the Congregation had done for their first five years, they were prepared to conduct services themselves if necessary. Schneeberger responded in a letter to the Board dated January 8, 1897:

> *Ever since I have received the sad communication about the critical financial condition of our congregation and of the precarious situation of my position, I have been in a very nervous condition of mind and a deep anxiety for the future is ever before my thoughts. In order to be relieved of this unsettled state of affairs and to give me an idea of what I may expect in the future, I am forced to take this measure of ascertaining your view on this subject of vital importance to me and I trust you will give your close consideration thereto. I have been advised to look around for some other position in order that the congregation expenses may thus be reduced. I now take this opportunity to make renewed application for a position which I had the pleasure to occupy for over 20 years*

and to whose interests and welfare I have devoted the best years of my life to the best of my ability.

Word of Rev. Schneeberger's predicament spread to his colleagues who quickly rose to his aid. As plans for the Fair were formulated, the association of Baltimore rabbis publicly announced their support. The following letter was printed in the December 18, 1896 issue of the Jewish Comment:

To the President and Members of the Chizuk-Emoonah Congregation, City:

Gentlemen – Having learned that your worthy congregation contemplates holding a fair for the promotion of its interests, we, the members of the Rabbinical Association of the City of Baltimore, have resolved to lend our best efforts toward the success of your undertaking, in order to strengthen the position of our worthy and esteemed colleague, Rev. Dr. H. W. Schneeberger, whom we, his colleagues, esteem highly, and who contributed materially toward the elevation of our holy faith in our midst, and whom we know to be highly honored by all.

> *Yours very respectfully,*
> *A. GUTTMACHER*
> *Secretary of the Rabbinical*
> *Association of the City of Baltimore*

The Ladies Auxiliary Society, under the chairmanship of Bertha Friedenwald, assumed responsibility for organizing, promoting, and hosting the Fair. The role of the women's group had evolved from simply providing housekeeping services to the Congregation, to shouldering financial support. The six-day event was to be held at Lehmann's Hall, March 22 to 27, 1897. Notices of meetings, published in the Jewish Comment, provide insight into the fund-raising effort:

December 18, 1896: *The following ladies were elected to preside over the different tables: Fancy tables, of which* *there will be five – Mrs. A. Friedenwald, Mrs. M.S. Levy, Mrs. Jos. Friedenwald, Mrs. Jos. Levi, Mrs. Ph. Hamburger; confectionery – Mrs. A. Harris; lunchroom – Mrs. L. Rosenaur; flower booth – Miss Laura Levy; postoffice and cigars – Miss Marie Oppenheimer; race-horses – Mrs. S. Rosenheim; advertising wheel – Miss Hulda Rohr; fortune-teller – Miss Florence Rosenfeld; Rebecka's well – Miss Hortense Rosenfeld; fair journal – Mrs. Wm. Levy.*

December 25, 1896: *The fair will be open afternoon and evenings. Miss May Rosenfeld was appointed as the head of the Registrar Office. Season tickets for the fair will be twenty-five cents each, single admission tickets ten cents, children same price.*

March 19, 1897: *The Fair will be opened to the public on Monday, March 22, at 8 P.M. It will be open daily from 10 A.M. to 11 P.M. Prof. D. Emerich's orchestra will render a fine musical program on Monday evening. On Saturday evening Professor Fisher's orchestra will furnish the music. Musical entertainments will be given by prominent artists on the other nights of the week. The "Fair Journal" will be distributed gratis to all who attend.*

The final meeting of those in charge of the Geisha Lunch Room was held on Wednesday. It was decided that hot dinners be served from 12 to 2 o'clock P.M. daily during the Fair, at reasonable prices. The room will be made as attractive as possible. The decorations will be Japanese, and the young lady assistants will wear the conventional Geisha costume.

The Fair was a remarkable financial success. Results, recorded in the minutes of May 17, 1897, indicate that the women earned $9,429.46, including $11 from the *"Hat Room."* The entire amount was presented to the Congregation, which used $8,500 of the proceeds to retire a portion of its debt to Blake & Sons. The remainder of the funds paid the accrued interest on the mortgage and other small bills. Support provided by the Ladies Auxiliary Society of Chizuk Amuno most likely saved Rev. Schneeberger's job, and helped stabilize the financial condition of the Congregation.

With Chizuk Amuno's arrival "uptown," there were now four synagogues located within a few blocks of one another – Chizuk Amuno, Baltimore Hebrew, Oheb Shalom and Har Sinai. The great majority of members of these congregations resided on six main streets – Eutaw Place, Madison Avenue, Linden Avenue, McCulloh Street, Bolton Street, and Druid Hill Avenue. Interestingly, Rozenblit found that Chizuk Amuno contained a growing percentage of professionals, mostly doctors and lawyers. In 1889, professionals comprised 7.7% of the Congregation; in 1900 that percentage had increased to 15.1%. The presence of so many professionals at Chizuk Amuno led Rozenblith to conclude that:

> *...religious Orthodoxy was by no means related to low social status or lack of Americanization...Normally, increased professionalization among Jews is associated with decreased religious observance, yet Chizuk Amuno, an Orthodox congregation, proved attractive to Jewish professionals who preferred traditional worship.*

Despite differing religious preferences, the German Jews of Baltimore lived side-by-side, served communal organizations together, often intermarried with one another, and some German Jews maintained dual memberships – paying dues to more than one synagogue.

Zionism

The last decade of the nineteenth century was a turning point not only for Chizuk Amuno, but also for the concept of a Jewish Homeland. The prosecution and conviction of Captain Alfred Dreyfus, in late 1894, captured worldwide attention. The Morning Herald of September 3, 1898 carried the news that Dreyfus had finally been pardoned of treason charges and printed opinions of local rabbis about the French scandal. A sketch of Rev. Schneeberger accompanied his comments about the true culprit of the treason:

> *Esterhazy is a good-for-nothing scamp; an unsightly deformity in military France; a blot on the escutcheon of her honor; a name her lowest street rabble will revile in the future. By intrigue which was more than treachery, and connivance that was more than cowardly, he succeeded in committing one of the most inhuman crimes of the present century; shielded the real perpetrator of the deed by well-laid plans and then, when military justice demanded a victim, he held up Dreyfus and delivered him over to shameful persecution, disgrace and imprisonment.*

Stirred by the stories of thousands of arriving Russian immigrants and by the news that anti-Semitism was surfacing in Western Europe, Aaron Friedenwald joined the Chovevei Zion movement founded in Eastern Europe in the 1880's. He delivered a powerful address – "Lovers of Zion" – to Mickve Israel Association of Philadelphia on December 23, 1894. The following passages are from the text of that address which was reprinted in a privately published volume edited by Harry Friedenwald entitled, Life, Letters, and Addresses of Aaron Friedenwald, M.D.:

> *Everywhere the relation of the Jew to the rest of the world has been and is being busily discussed, and there has arisen what has been called the "Jewish Question." Those who have been forced to contemplate expatriation with all the hardships necessarily attending it felt*

that they would be unwelcome guests wherever they came. It has become more and more evident that the Jew is more or less hated everywhere.

It would be a sad mistake to continue to suffer and to wait for that period when the brotherhood of man will be fully established, and those enmities based upon differences in descent and belief will cease.   The Choveve Zion...is based upon the conviction that the preservation of the dignity of the Jewish people all over the world depends upon the revival of the national idea.

Anxious to see the settlements forming in Palestine for himself, Aaron and Bertha Friedenwald traveled to Europe and the Holy Land in the summer of 1898. As always, Aaron wrote many letters home to his children while traveling, providing details of his activities. Friedenwald was quite taken by the courage and determination of the colonists. The return trip included a stop in London, where the Friedenwalds were guests at the home of Dr. Solomon Schechter, instructor at Cambridge University.

Friedenwald was still in Europe at the time the Federation of American Zionists (FAZ) was formed, combining nearly one hundred small Zionist clubs. Rabbi Stephen Wise, the first secretary of that organization, had heard of Friedenwald's support of the Zionist movement, and invited him to New York to deliver a lecture on the colonies of Palestine to Zionist societies. By 1899, Friedenwald was serving as vice-president of the FAZ, while also actively serving on the boards of JTS, the Jewish Publication Society, the Hebrew Hospital, the Hebrew Orphans Asylum, and – last but not least – holding the position of President of the Chizuk Amuno Congregation.

While on his trip to Palestine in 1898, Friedenwald stopped in Beirut, for what would prove to be a momentous meeting. Samson Benderly, a native of Safed, was in his second year of medical studies. Dr. Friedenwald was quite taken by the young man and invited him to complete his medical training in Baltimore. Benderly accepted Friedenwald's invitation, and upon arrival in September, 1898,

Friedenwald arranged to have Benderly admitted to the College of Physicians and Surgeons. As his medical education continued, Benderly earned a living teaching Hebrew at the Chizuk Amuno religious school and privately tutoring Aaron's son, Harry, and two daughters of Rabbi Szold – Henrietta and Bertha. After completing his medical degree, Benderly surprised his patron by announcing that he would not enter the practice of medicine, but rather the field of Jewish education. As Dr. David Kaufman explains in his essay, "Jewish Education as a Civilization: A History of the Teachers Institute:"

> *Benderly was largely responsible, in fact, for the introduction of a novel method of Hebrew instruction into American Jewish education: a pedagogical technique utilizing spoken Hebrew that he called "Shitah ha-Tiv'it" (the natural method) or "Ivrit bi-Ivrit" (Hebrew in Hebrew). Others simply called it the "Benderly method."*

After moving to McCulloh Street, the Congregation established a Hebrew school, but also continued holding classes on Lloyd Street. Rev. Glass was assigned to teach uptown, while Rev. Schneeberger and various part-time teachers taught downtown. To compensate the rabbi for commuting between locations, the Board voted to pay him $2.00 per month for carfare during the school term. The parallel schools continued for three years until, in October, 1899, Rev. Schneeberger was directed to be the Superintendent and Instructor of the uptown school, with Rev. Glass serving as his assistant. The downtown school continued under the supervision of Dr. Samson Benderly. The success of Benderly's approach to teaching Hebrew language is evident in a letter to the editor published in the June 15, 1900 issue of the Jewish Comment:

> *The children were instructed not merely to read the Hebrew mechanically but were taught to read it intelligently, to know the principles of Hebrew grammar, and to study Biblical History with the aid of the map of Palestine....The examinations of these various disciplines*

*proved to the satisfaction of all that the school is con-
ducted on modern methods, and that the teachers know
what they are about, especially the Principal, Dr. Samson
Benderly, who possesses remarkable skills in imparting
as well as examining.*

In 1903, the Hebrew Education Society purchased a building
at Asquith and Jackson Streets, and appointed Benderly to head the
school. With an enrollment of 300 students, Benderly struggled to
find competent teachers to institute his methods. His interest in turning teachers of Hebrew into true educators led Benderly to assume
the head of New York's Bureau of Jewish Education in 1910, and a
thirty-year association with Dr. Mordecai Kaplan, head of the Teachers Institute of JTS.

November 6, 1898 marked a red-letter day in the history of
Chizuk Amuno, for it was at a meeting on that date that the Board
approved the transfer of a membership from the widow of Simon
Fleischer to her son, Milton. The elder Fleischer joined the Congregation in September, 1886, and had been an active member until his
death in March, 1892. Milton would continue the family's relationship with Chizuk Amuno by assuming leadership roles for over fifty
years. When he was barely two years old, his father took Milton to
the synagogue. An article written by Rabbi Israel M. Goldman re-
counts the story:

*The father was called to the Torah and given the honor
of performing the act of "Gelilah" – of rolling together
the open Torah Scroll. It was at that point that the pious
Simon Fleischer followed an old German-Jewish Minhag,
or custom, which requires that on the occasion of the
first visit of a male child to the Synagogue, the father
donate a wide linen band called a "Wimple" which is
used to wrap around the Scroll and to hold it secure...The
beaming and happy mother, Betty Fleischer, looked down
from the Women's Gallery with tears of joy in her eyes as*

she saw someone bring young Milton – an infant in arms – to the Torah and there help his father place the "Wimpel" around the Scroll. Upon this linen wrapper there was inscribed in colored Hebrew letters the name of the child and that of his father: "Mordecai ben Reb Shamshan." Every time Mr. Milton Fleischer recalled this incident of his early childhood, his eyes twinkled, his lips smiled, and he gave expression to a characteristic witticism by saying, "That was more than 75 years ago and I've been wrapped up in Chizuk Amuno ever since."

Fleischer was nominated to replace Alfred Scholle as Secretary. Scholle had submitted his resignation, stating that business obligations forced his decision. With unanimous consent, Milton Fleischer was elected to be the third Secretary of Chizuk Amuno. The minutes of the Congregation are recorded in his hand through June 1910. As the nineteenth century was coming to a close, Chizuk Amuno was in a period of no-growth, with membership hovering around thirty-five. From the minute book entries of 1899 to 1901:

- *...letter of thanks be tendered Mr. Jos. Friedenwald for his extreme kindness in having presented the Congregation with a handsome Chupah.*

- *Rabbi to announce from the pulpit that morning service during the week will commence at 6:15 A.M. instead of 6:30 A.M.*

- *The attention of the Board was called to the fact that on Shabbos last, our Chazan took the authority upon himself to ask one of our seatholders to officiate during a part of the service. Motion by Jos. Levi ...that the Sec'y write a dictated letter to our Chazan setting forth our most strenuous disapproval of such action.*

Another matter that had stagnated was Rev. Schneeberger's salary. Although his employment had been saved by the funds contributed by the Ladies Auxiliary, the rabbi was still paid only $1,500 a year. His requests for increases were routinely turned down, but on June 11, 1901 the Board resolved to honor their spiritual leader by sponsoring a celebration commemorating the 25th anniversary of Rev. Schneeberger's service to Chizuk Amuno. The <u>Jewish Comment</u> of October 18, 1901 carried the announcement of the celebration and, in a rather curious statement, the editor wrote: *"It is to a great extent owing to him that the services of his congregation, though strictly orthodox, have all the dignity and decorum of our great temples."* Obviously, the remarks allude to the stereotypical belief that the orthodoxy practiced by the Russian immigrants was lacking in dignity. Engraved programs were distributed at the celebration, held on Sunday afternoon, October 20, 1901. President Aaron Friedenwald, Rev. Adolph Guttmacher, Rev. William Rosenau, and attorney Isaac Lobe Strauss, a former student of the rabbi's, delivered speeches of praise. As tokens of their appreciation, the Board presented Schneeberger with a cash contribution referred to as a *"purse."* Among the other gifts the rabbi received were silver tableware, a check for $660, and a leather-covered rocker. The boys of the choir expressed their gratitude by presenting their rabbi with a silver-headed walking stick.

As the average age of Chizuk Amuno members edged higher, the need for new members intensified. Although membership records indicate that the Congregation only had thirty-five "Members," it must be remembered that approximately 100 additional men were considered "Seatholders" – those who rented seats each year for the High Holy Days and who regularly worshipped at the synagogue. Board members prepared lists of friends and acquaintances for possible membership, and voted to have Aaron Friedenwald, Rev. Schneeberger, and Rev. Glass call on these prospects. An announcement was recorded in the minutes of March 13, 1902 that the Eden Street shul was disbanding and a motion was made to contact those worshippers and invite them to attend services at Chizuk Amuno.

Even with these efforts to increase membership, in 1905 the Board approved spending up to six dollars a month to pay men to attend minyan.

Through times of prosperity and times of financial hardship, Chizuk Amuno continued to support the Jewish Theological Seminary in New York. Annual dues were always paid – even if delinquent at times. Besides the leadership positions held by Aaron Friedenwald and Rev. Schneeberger, M.S. Levy and Max Skutch also attended biennial conventions of the organization and reported back to the Congregation on Seminary activities. Unbeknownst to all but a few insiders, a plan to reorganize JTS was formulated in 1900, by Cyrus Adler, Judge Mayer Sulzberger, and Dr. Solomon Solis-Cohen. Their plan – to bring Professor Solomon Schechter to New York as president of a restructured JTS, controlled by laymen and not clergy.

In his essay, "Schechter's Seminary," Professor Mel Scult of the City University of New York explains that the group hoped to secure sufficient financial backing for an endowment, which would enable the institution not to need support from rabbis and congregations. In a 1901 letter to Schechter, Adler stressed the secrecy of the plan and noted that the *"chief conspirators"* felt that Adler himself should be slated to chair the new Board of Trustees. As evidenced in Scult's essay, Adler included *"A. Friedenwald a silent partner"* in his list of conspirators. When the annual meeting of the JTS Association occurred on March 30, 1902, the necessary money had been pledged, Schechter had resigned from Cambridge University, and the newly chartered Jewish Theological Seminary of America proposed merger with the existing JTS Association. With disagreements resolved, the merger was approved. Most trustees of the "old" JTS believed that seven members of their Board would serve as trustees for the "new" JTS, but in fact only three existing trustees were named "Class B Directors" – one of whom was Chizuk Amuno's president, Aaron Friedenwald.

Only five months later, on August 26, 1902, Dr. Aaron Friedenwald died at the age of sixty-five. He had suffered from severe pain months earlier, and had gone to Europe with hopes that the hot springs would alleviate his pain. When it became apparent that surgery was necessary, Friedenwald and his wife hurried back to Baltimore. Within the week, Dr. John Chambers performed surgery for a cancerous growth, but the surgery was not successful, and Friedenwald never regained consciousness. Articles in the <u>Baltimore American</u> and <u>Jewish Comment</u> detailed Friedenwald's accomplishments in their obituaries. As was the custom, the funeral was held at his home which the papers reported *"was crowded with friends and relatives from all parts of the city, representing the whole Jewish community."* Active and honorary pallbearers included officers of Chizuk Amuno, Cyrus Adler, the president of the Hebrew Orphans Asylum, several doctors from the College of Physicians and Surgeons, Dr. William Osler of Johns Hopkins Hospital, and Congressman Frank Wachter. Perhaps the most fitting tribute was paid by the editors of the <u>Jewish Comment</u> in the August 29, 1902 issue:

> *Dr. Friedenwald was indisputably our first Jewish citizen. Whether we view him as a successful physician, jealous for the honor of his profession; as a citizen, taking a keen and high-minded interest in public affairs; as a lover of the oppressed, distributing with conscientious care the Baron de Hirsch funds and gathering money for the Alliance Israelite Universelle; as an intelligent lover of Jewish progress, evidenced by his interest in the Jewish Publication Society and in the Jewish Theological Seminary; as a plain Jew, devoting his time to the affairs of his synagogue – we see him everywhere exhibiting high qualities of mind and heart, a view of life and a conception of duty as noble as they are rare. In these days of Jewish indifference the passing of a man who stood for all that is intelligently Jewish is a loss not easily overestimated.*

A memorial service in honor of Aaron Friedenwald was held at the McCulloh Street synagogue on November 9, 1902. After the Mincha service, led by Rev. Glass, concluding addresses were delivered by Rev. Dr. H.P. Mendes of New York City, Rev. Dr.

Schneeberger, Dr. Cyrus Adler, and Professor Solomon Solis-Cohen of the Jefferson Medical College, Philadelphia. A booklet of the speeches and tributes from Friedenwald's medical colleagues was privately printed and distributed by the family.

At the death of Aaron Friedenwald, M.S. Levy assumed the presidency of Chizuk Amuno. Levy had been intimately involved with the Congregation since its inception, and as one of its major contributors, was highly qualified to assume the leadership position. Outside of synagogue life, Levy had served as the treasurer of the Hebrew Benevolent Society, and director of both the Hebrew Free Loan Association and the Talmud Torah Society. As M.S. Levy was elected president of the Congregation, his wife, Betsy Jacobs Levy, was in the midst of her six-year term as president of the Ladies Auxiliary of Chizuk Amuno.

Aaron Friedenwald's oldest son, Harry, was elected to become the vice-president of Chizuk Amuno. Besides assuming this position, Harry Friedenwald also stepped into the presidency of the Baltimore Alliance Israelite Universelle, was appointed honorary president of the Baltimore Y.M.H.A., a trustee of JTS, and chairman of the Eye and Ear Department at the College of Physicians and Surgeons. Harry Friedenwald's life had echoed that of his respected father. After graduating from City College in 1881, Harry matriculated at Johns Hopkins University, majoring in chemistry. Life-long friend Henrietta Szold and her sisters attended the Hopkins commencement, in June, 1884 to congratulate Harry when he received his degree and a Phi Beta Kappa gold medal. Friedenwald entered the College of Physicians and Surgeons, and graduated first in his class three years later. As had his father, Harry lived in Germany for three years studying surgery and diseases of the eye. While in Munich, Harry received the following letter from the Assistant Secretary of the Smithsonian Institution in Washington, D.C. dated September 11, 1889:

The National Museum is desirous of securing a collec-
tion to illustrate Jewish ceremonial. It is difficult to ob-
tain in this country good examples of objects desired for
this collection. Doctor Cyrus Adler, a member of our
scientific staff, has suggested that you would be willing
to undertake some commissions for us in this direction,
and that your interest in the subject, as well as your con-
nections in Europe, would enable you to be of much as-
sistance to us in this matter. We should like to have, for
example, a Kiddush cup, a spice box used in the cer-
emony of Habdalah, photographs of old or famous Eu-
ropean synagogues etc.

While traveling in Europe, Dr. Harry Friedenwald purchased a spirally curled Italian shofar and several other ritual objects for the museum. After returning home in March, 1890 he entered his father's medical practice. Dr. Friedenwald published many professional articles and served as Associate Professor of Ophthalmology and Otology at the College of Physicians and Surgeons. In the fall of 1893, Harry joined his friend Henrietta Szold in founding what is considered the first American Zionist society – the Chevras Zion.

The 1903 atrocities in Russia prompted Friedenwald to campaign actively for aid to victims and their families. Harry solicited his wealthy uncle, Joseph Friedenwald, for a contribution while the latter was vacationing in Europe. Although Harry's letters to his uncle were never found, Joseph Friedenwald's responses are held in the archives of the Jewish Museum of Maryland:

I beg you will excuse my tardiness in acknowledging your
very interesting letter, painful as it was about the Mas-
sacre of our Brethren in Faith in that Hellish Country
Russia. I deplore to refer to it, but share my sympathies
with those who like yourself, have taken an active part
to relieve the living, or in other words, those who suf-
fered from the murderous atrocities, and you have my
permission to add to the sum collected 50 dollars which
I will gladly repay on my arrival with thanks, if you think

the emergency fund is sufficient for the present which is being sent to Russia, you may place the 50 dollars to the funds of our Congregation.

Inspired by his father's Zionist sentiments, Harry Friedenwald attended the Sixth Zionist Congress in Basel, Switzerland in August, 1903. He wrote to his mother of the dramatic address by Theodore Herzl in which the Zionist leader read the names of those *"prominent in our cause who had died, the entire audience standing – Dr. Herzl's father, Papa, and Dr. Szold were mentioned."* One year later, Harry was unanimously elected president of the Federation of American Zionists. He became one of the leaders of the Zionist movement for the next forty years.

In late 1900, the Board voted to set aside excess cash, whenever possible, in preparation for the maturity of the $16,000 mortgage still held by Blake & Sons. This "Extinguishing Fund" grew slowly, and only amounted to $1,000 by November 1902. Fortunately, the Ladies Auxiliary Society, led by Mrs. Betsy Levy, had maintained an investment account of their own. In October, 1902, the Board minutes indicate that the ladies organization was donating $5,000 worth of railway bonds to the Congregation. The bonds were to be converted to cash, and used to reduce the outstanding mortgage.

Two representatives of the Auxiliary, *"Mrs. E. West and Mrs. J. Levy,"* attended a Board meeting on April 4, 1905, to inform the members that the Ladies Auxiliary had been discussing the matter of beautifying the synagogue. The group was willing to contribute $600 towards the cost of having *"the interior woodwork (excluding benches) repainted, the walls whitened, the chandeliers remodeled and the carpets cleaned."* Repairs, cleaning and new wiring for electricity totaling $1,400 were conducted during the summer – in time for the High Holy Days of 1905.

Chizuk Amuno took a great step toward equality in April, 1906, when President M.S. Levy appointed two women, Mrs. Goody

Rosenfeld and Mrs. Louis Steppacher, to the School Committee. Just one month later, the new School Board asked permission to establish a one-day a week Sunday School. The issue was debated for months, and finally, in December, 1906 the Board approved *"Sunday morning sessions free to all members and seatholders."* The addition of this abbreviated track, with instruction in Biblical History and Ethics, proved very popular at a time when the Congregation was struggling to attract new members. In March, 1909 there were seventy-eight students enrolled in the Sunday School.

At the Annual Congregation Meeting on April 3, 1906, members postponed voting on Rev. Schneeberger's re-election, but a committee was appointed to meet with him to discuss unspecified matters. The conversation with the rabbi is not documented in the minutes, but on March 5, 1907 the Board unanimously approved a motion *"that we recommend to the Cong. that we pension Dr. Schneeberger for the period of 1 year at a salary of $1200 and that we make him 'Rabbi Emeritus.'"* A committee of three was then appointed to solicit candidates to serve as rabbi. Louis Stepplacher traveled to New York, where he was favorably impressed with a service led by JTS graduate Dr. Mordecai Kaplan. Harry Friedenwald contacted his associates at the Seminary for their opinion of Kaplan. Drs. Schechter, Magnes, Friedlaender, and Margolis highly recommended Kaplan, but the rabbi was not interested in leaving New York City. With no other acceptable candidates identified, Chizuk Amuno suspended the search and kept Rev. Schneeberger on staff at his existing salary. Although he continued to lecture from the pulpit and teach an occasional class, Dr. Schneeberger was relieved of his responsibilities of supervising the school. Cantor Herman Glass was promoted to Superintendent of the Hebrew School in 1908, and under his leadership, enrollment significantly increased. By the fall of 1911, Rev. Glass reported 126 students in the Sunday School and sixty-eight students in the Hebrew School – each group divided into five grade levels. Women teachers, hired at a salary of $15 per month, assisted Rev. Glass with instruction. Appreciative Board members periodically voted cash bonuses to Rev. Glass for his enthusiasm and dedication. As the cantor's responsibilities grew, the Board approved paying member Benno W. Hummel seventy-five dollars to serve as *"Assistant Chazan"* during the year.

Another repercussion of Rev. Schneeberger's decreased responsibilities was the establishment of a new Divine Service Committee in 1908, *"whose duty will be to confer with the board and our Rabbi and Chazan, to arrange all matters appertaining to our service."* The first major issue assigned to the committee was the question of changing the mahzor used on the High Holy Days. The existing prayerbooks, individually owned by congregants, still reflected the founding traditions of the Congregation, and were written in Hebrew, with German translation on the facing page. By 1910, many of the worshippers were second, third, or even fourth generation Americans, and no longer spoke or understood the German language. Eastern European seatholders could read the Hebrew, but had no use for the German. At the Annual Congregation Meeting held on January 10, 1910 the Divine Service Committee initiated a proposal to adapt the English translated *"Machsorim"* currently used in England. After full discussion, Dr. Harry Friedenwald introduced a motion to appoint a committee to ascertain from competent authorities whether a change to Rabbi Adler's <u>Service of the Synagogue</u> would constitute a change in ritual, and therefore be prohibited under Chizuk Amuno's constitution. The committee had anticipated this question and presented a letter from Rev. Glass which stated:

> *I will state that the introduction into our service of the English "Machsor" specially on Rosh Hashonah and Yom Kippur would greatly benefit the future of our Congregation as it surely will increase the interest of our rising generation in the orthodox service. I would therefore advocate its introduction if:*
> *1ˢᵗ – you find that there is no law in our constitution against the changing of the "Minhag Ashkenas" to the "Minhag Polen", and 2ⁿᵈ – the price of the new Machsors can be reduced so much as to enable the general public*

who rent seats in our synagogue for the holidays, to purchase them.

Six months later, on June 26, 1910, the motion to adopt a Hebrew/English holiday prayerbook was approved with no opposition noted.

Leadership of the Ladies Auxiliary Society passed to Bertha (Mrs. Aaron) Friedenwald in 1906. As younger women completed their education, they expressed interest in forming their own auxiliary. Late in 1908, Rena Glass (daughter of the cantor), Fannie Schneeberger (daughter of the rabbi), Hilda Wolfram, Regina Weinberg, Pauline Nussbaum, and Mignon Levin organized the *"Junior Auxiliary."* Intended to provide religious, literary, and social programming, the group requested improvements be made to the Vestry Rooms so that meetings and lectures could be held in the basement of the McCulloh Street synagogue. Their request was accompanied by a $600 donation to the Congregation – proceeds of a fair conducted by the young ladies. As the Junior Auxiliary's membership grew, a mild generational struggle ensued. Two officers of the Auxiliary appeared before the Board on December 13, 1910 to present *"facts that they were criticized in and interfered with in their transactions."* The men assured the young ladies that their efforts were greatly appreciated and *"that unity and peace"* would be restored.

The pace of Jewish emigration from the Russian Empire quickened during the first decade of the twentieth century, prompting the formation of more communal support organizations. By 1902, there were more than a dozen Jewish charitable organizations, each soliciting members for funds. A practical solution to end the duplication of appeals and fund-raising events was discussed among the leaders of German-founded "uptown" charities, and in June 1906, the Federated Jewish Charities was formed. The Federated was designed to serve the ten independent agencies under its auspices as an administrative structure responsible for all fund raising. Chizuk Amuno trustee Louis H. Levin served as the first Executive Secretary of the Federated. In accepting the job, Levin gave up his active law practice, but did retain his position as editor of the <u>Baltimore Jewish Comment</u>. When the Jewish Consumptive Hospital was established in 1907, it joined the Federated group and Levin accepted a Board position, serving under the leadership of President Harry Friedenwald. A 1910 essay by Rabbi Adolf Guttmacher, entitled "Charities of Baltimore Jews," stated: *"Prior to the federation, $47,000 was the maximum sum collected for one year; this year it looks as if the $100,000 mark will be reached."*

The leaders of the "downtown" charities originally founded by the Russian community carefully observed the success of the Federated. In December, 1907 seven charities aligned for a similar administrative purpose, and formed the United Hebrew Charities. The family of M.S. Levy, although of German descent, assumed leadership positions in the United. At varying times, M.S. Levy served as a director on the boards of the Baltimore Talmud Torah Society, Hebrew Free Loan Association, Hebrew Friendly Inn and Aged Home, and the Hebrew Children's Sheltering and Protective Association. Levy, along with his children, funded the construction of the Betsy Levy Memorial Building of the Hebrew Children's Sheltering Association, located at Broadway and Fairmount Avenue. M.S. Levy served on the Board of the United Hebrew Charities from the time of its inception until his death. His son, William, assumed the presidency of the "downtown" association in 1909, and developed a close, trusting relationship with the Russian-born leaders of participating agencies. Ironically, Louis H. Levin would latter serve as vice-president of the United, and William Levy would serve as the president of the Federated. Involvement of Chizuk Amuno members in both associations would pave the way for the eventual merger of the Federated Jewish Charities and United Hebrew Charities into The Associated Jewish Charities.

On May 8, 1911, Chizuk Amuno's fourth president, M.S. Levy, died at the age of seventy-five. An obituary printed in the <u>Jewish Comment</u> of May 12, 1911 described the scene at Levy's funeral as attended by *"a throng that gathered early and came from all parts of the city."* Besides the multitude of public tributes, M.S. Levy was immortalized in the minutes of Chizuk Amuno Congregation:

> *...the loss that this congregation has sustained is also the loss of the Jewish community, of which he was so useful a member; of Judaism, of which he was so staunch a supporter, and of the city & state of which he was so valuable a citizen. He was a true, kind & generous father of our congregation, anxious to promote its welfare solicitous for its development as a spiritual force and devoted to its interests and its progress. He was also a devout Jew, to whom the teaching & practices of our faith were as dear as life itself and throughout his life he showed an unwavering attachment to Judaism which left its impress upon all who came in contact with him. He helped to weld the members into a harmonious whole, so that we are not a mere list of members, but, according to the ancient custom of Israel, a holy congregation.*

Included in Levy's generous bequest to Chizuk Amuno was an endowment fund of $10,000, which stipulated that interest was to be used for the support of three scholars who committed to studying Talmud daily. Congregant Dr. David Macht was selected to participate as one of the scholars receiving funds from the M.S. Levy Endowment. He donated his share of the income back to the Beth Hamidrash Association of Chizuk Amuno for the acquisition of more books.

During the summer of 1911, Harry Friedenwald, his wife Birdie, and their children, Julia and Jonas, took a trip to Palestine. As the group toured agricultural colonies, hospitals, and schools, they were greatly moved by the need for medical help in the developing country. Anxious to assist in the development of Palestine, Friedenwald purchased thirty acres of barren land in Hadera. Upon their return to Baltimore, Harry strongly encouraged his friend, Henrietta Szold, to promote a program of health care. Within a year, two nurses were sent to Palestine, sponsored by Szold's chapter of the Daughters of Zion. Dr. Harry continued providing moral and financial support to Zionist relief projects.

Dr. Harry Friedenwald, the third generation of his family to serve the Congregation, assumed leadership of Chizuk Amuno after the death of M.S. Levy, but was not officially elected until January 12, 1912. One of the first issues that the new president had to deal with was the December, 1911 decision to retire Rev. Schneeberger and award him a pension of $1,000 per year. As adamant supporters of JTS, the Board naturally looked toward the Seminary for their next rabbi. Harry Friedenwald reported that Seminary President Dr. Solomon Schechter strongly recommended one of his senior students, Eugene Kohn.

THE KOHN ERA 1912-1918

Our task, therefore, involves a two-fold activity, on the one hand, to learn to understand our Judaism; on the other to study modern conditions with a view to rendering our Judaism effective in modern times.

Rabbi Eugene Kohn
Installation Address 1912

Dr. Solomon Schechter informed President Harry Friedenwald that Eugene Kohn was one of the Seminary's finest scholars and an eloquent orator. Based on that recommendation, Chizuk Amuno invited the young man to officiate during Shavuot. Kohn's performance was impressive. On May 26, 1912, the Board unanimously agreed to recommend to the Congregation that Eugene Kohn become not only their rabbi, but also the chief of the Beth Hamidrash Association. In their offer to Kohn, the Board clearly stated that the Congregation was strictly Orthodox, and that they expected their rabbi to *"abide by the Sholchan Aruch."* The $1,500 annual salary offered included a share of the M.S. Levy Fund granted to Talmudic scholars. The newly ordained rabbi accepted Chizuk Amuno's proposal in his letter of June 3, 1912, stating: *"My most heartfelt prayer at this moment is that I may prove worthy of the confidence thus placed in me, and may lead the congregation successfully in the holy cause that it represents."*

This was the second time that an American-born rabbi was to take the pulpit at Chizuk Amuno, but Eugene Kohn was the first to graduate from the Jewish Theological Seminary. Kohn, born in 1887 in Newark, New Jersey, was educated in public schools and graduated from New York University in 1907. His entrance into JTS followed the path set by his older brother, Rabbi Jacob Kohn (class of

1907), spiritual leader of Ansche Chesed Congregation of New York. Although Rabbi Kohn's contract was to go into effect on October 1, 1912, he was invited to begin one month earlier and officiate for the High Holy Days. Installation services were held at the McCulloh Street synagogue on the weekend of September 6 and 7 with the highly respected Dr. Schechter delivering the keynote address. Rabbi Jacob Kohn and Rabbi Emeritus Henry W. Schneeberger also spoke. Eugene Kohn's remarks, preserved in the Chizuk Amuno archives, reflect his concept of *"a virile and progressive Judaism, true to the Torah and Jewish Tradition."* An editorial printed in the September 6, 1912 <u>Jewish Comment</u> welcomed the new rabbi to Baltimore, and remarked on the challenges he would face:

> *The coming of Rabbi Eugene Kohn to this city is a matter of considerable local importance and interest. He comes to a congregation with a long and honored history, and into a community singularly harmonious so far as the clash of religious opinion is concerned...There is a marked desire on all sides to hear what the conservative has to say, though no great alacrity to put his teachings into practice...The task before an Orthodox rabbi, and therefore, before Rabbi Kohn, is to free his camp from the unwelcome baggage with which it is cluttered, and to show that conservative Judaism can be satisfying to the man and woman of today. This is a serious undertaking and by no means easy, but he comes well prepared and well endowed to grapple with it. His colleagues and the rest of the community will welcome him and watch with interest the career he will carve for himself.*

As had his predecessor, Kohn continued to welcome the new Eastern European immigrants.

Six months after Kohn's arrival, Chizuk Amuno representative William Levy attended the organizational meeting of the United Synagogue of America. Plans for the group had been under discussion since 1909, when a few JTS alumni, including Rabbi Jacob Kohn, formed the Committee on Conservative Union to create a centrist modern-traditional movement. Twenty-two congregations were represented at the February 23, 1913 meeting led by Solomon Schechter, seeking a course between traditional practices and moderate innovations in congregational life. William Levy was elected to the Executive and Finance Committees, and Harry Friedenwald was appointed to the Education Committee. The following year, Rabbi Eugene Kohn was appointed to the "Propaganda Committee" – the group responsible for promoting Historical Judaism. Over the coming decades, Chizuk Amuno members would continue to serve pivotal leadership roles in the United Synagogue of America.

Rabbi Kohn focused the Congregation's attention on two main areas – education and Zionism. The Beth Hamidrash Association of Chizuk Amuno was re-energized and began enhancing their library of Judaic text, purchasing scholarly and religious volumes with fees from their members. The group sponsored a series of lectures addressing the current status of Jewish education, including one in December, 1913 by Dr. Mordecai Kaplan, Professor of Homiletics at JTS, entitled, "Ancient and Modern Jewish Education." Rabbi Kohn wrote the handbook, A Manual For Teaching Biblical History – the first book published by the United Synagogue of America.

With the arrival of thousands of immigrants, many new religious schools were formed in Baltimore, some without qualified teachers. On May 16, 1914, the Board of Jewish Education (BJE) held its first meeting, with Harry Friedenwald elected the first president. He proposed setting standards for Jewish education in Baltimore and hoped to train competent teachers and outfit proper classrooms. The Jewish Comment published Rabbi Kohn's lecture entitled, "The Significance of the Board of Jewish Education" in its June 12, 1914 cover story. Kohn noted that there were over 2,000 Jewish children who were not enrolled in any Jewish school. He stressed the importance of Jewish education for both the children of the wealthy and of the poor:

> *The work of Jewish education is as essential an activity*
> *of a Jewish community that lays any claim to idealism as*

is the work of charity. It was, perhaps, excusable for the first generation or two of Jewish settlers in this country whose lives were necessarily so largely taken up by the struggle for their own maintenance, to limit their altru- istic activities to helping their neighbors in this same struggle, but in our own day we have no longer such an excuse and must assume our larger responsibilities.

The authority of the new organization was limited at first, but the BJE did help monitor the need for schools in response to the changes in Jewish neighborhood demographics. In <u>The Making of an American Jewish Community</u>, author Isaac M. Fein relates a story that Rabbi Kohn once asked the Baltimore School Board to provide him with a list of Jewish students near his synagogue. *"He hoped that by personal contact with their parents he might induce them to send their children to a Hebrew school."* The School Board denied the request.

During the years preceding World War I, Chizuk Amuno was considered the center of Baltimore's Zionist efforts. Harry Friedenwald continued his father's leadership role in the Federation of American Zionists (later renamed Zionist Organization of America), and maintained frequent correspondence with notable Jew- ish leaders around the world, including Chaim Weizmann, Louis Brandeis, and Dr. Judah L. Magnes. Returning to Palestine in the summer of 1914, Friedenwald toured health facilities and performed eye surgery in Jerusalem and in several settlements throughout the colonies of Galilee. Although conditions had improved since his visit in 1911, he recognized the urgent need for medical facilities in the region. Determined to intensify his support of the Zionist dream, Friedenwald departed for America just as the first shots of World War I were fired.

In Baltimore, Zionist organizations often used the vestry rooms of Chizuk Amuno for meetings. On May 8, 1913, Henrietta Szold used the space to organize a local chapter of the Daughters of Zion, later renamed Hadassah. In an effort to bring the Zionist message to people not regularly attending worship services, Rabbi Kohn led small study groups in the homes of congregants. Occasionally his discussions were critiqued in the Jewish press:

> **November 6, 1914** - *He gave a succinct explanation of the "Fundamentals of Zionism," and then answered questions propounded chiefly by the non-Zionists present. Rabbi Kohn's answers and explanations not only met the point, but showed alike originality in his method of approaching topics and depth of thought. In throwing light on Zionism, he incidentally illuminated ethical relations of broadly human interest. In short, in the words of one of his hearers, he made the meeting an "intellectual treat."*

In 1967, Kohn was asked to record his memories of those years. He noted that Henrietta Szold frequently worshipped at Chizuk Amuno when she returned to Baltimore to visit family. Kohn described Szold's brother-in-law, Louis H. Levin, as *"an ardent worshipper at the synagogue and a student of the Talmud and Jewish traditional lore."* The Levin family lived on Chelsea Terrace in the Forest Park area of Baltimore, three miles from the McCulloh Street synagogue. As Shabbat observers, the family walked to Chizuk Amuno for services, often stopping to admire the wildflowers on the way back home.

Louis Levin was a pioneer in the development of social service programming in Baltimore. In October, 1914 his concern over the delinquency of Jewish boys led Levin to establish the Jewish Big Brothers Bureau. In an article published on November 6, 1914 Levin stated, *"it has become manifest that there are many Jewish boys weakened by street associations who would, if surrounded by proper influences, develop into self-respecting men."* The Jewish Comment noted that Rabbi Kohn had actively taken part in the organizational meetings.

As the war in Europe intensified and trade routes closed, Jewish suffering in Palestine worsened. Harry Friedenwald led fundraising efforts among American Zionist groups, but food and medical supplies were more urgently needed. The American Jewish Relief Committee lobbied Secretary of State William Jennings Bryan in 1915 to provide space on a U.S. Navy vessel for an emergency shipment to Jews in Egypt and Palestine. Space for one thousand tons of supplies was allocated aboard the United States Collier *Vulcan*, scheduled to sail from Philadelphia into Turkish waters. A representative of the Jewish community was needed to accompany the relief supplies, and Harry Friedenwald suggested Chizuk Amuno's Louis Levin. The Baltimore Sun reported:

> *The selection of Louis H. Levin to take charge of the distribution of relief for Palestine war sufferers is regarded as one of the greatest honors that can come to a man engaged in Hebrew philanthropic work at this time. It is considered another tribute to the pre-eminence of Baltimore in the field of social work.*

The trip took twenty-five days. With contributed funds, Levin managed to purchase tons of sugar, potatoes, and rice when reaching Alexandria, Egypt, and had them loaded aboard the *Vulcan* for delivery to Palestine. During the dangerous four-month mission Levin managed to distribute food and medical supplies, organize Jewish relief operations in Egypt, form representative relief committees throughout Palestine, and evaluate the conditions of refugees in the colony. In her biography of Levin, Alexandra Lee Levin notes that the Secretary of State had appointed Levin to be a *"Special Agent of the Department of State to assist the American Ambassador of Constantinople,"* thus adding the question of whether Levin's mission also included clandestine activities on behalf of the U.S. government. Levin frequently lectured on his experiences, encouraging continuing support of the Zionist movement. The Jewish Comment, published on September 24, 1915, noted that Levin had delivered an address on "Zionist Work in Palestine" at Chizuk Amuno before an unusually large crowd. His conclusion – *"Palestine is our spiritual fatherland."*

On the national level, several Chizuk Amuno members were involved with the American Jewish Committee, a group organized in 1906 to protect the religious and civil rights of Jews around the world. In 1915, political disputes developed within the Committee as some challenged the aristocratic manner in which the organization was managed and its passivity in making demands on the United States government. The dissenters, under the leadership of Louis D. Brandeis, wanted to convert the Committee into a democratic American Jewish Congress with equal rights for members without regard for their financial position or social standing. Support for a democratic organization was especially strong among Eastern European immigrants and their American-born children. After a unanimous vote taken on May 9, 1916, Chizuk Amuno publicly announced the resolution *"That the Congregation Chizuk Emunah affiliate with the Jewish Congress movement."* Rabbi Kohn, Louis H. Levin, and Herbert Moses (grandson of M.S. Levy) were appointed to represent the Congregation on the local level. Harry Friedenwald, once a major supporter of the American Jewish Committee, submitted his resignation on June 12, 1916, in a letter to Dr. Cyrus Adler, Chairman of the Executive Committee:

> *The issue has become clearer and clearer. A class of Jewry is ranged against the overwhelming masses – the unorganized masses which have so long been silent. ....I wish to remove all doubt as to which side has my sympathy. Those of us that feel their life is part of the throbbing, anxious, suffering Jewish life, belong to that body which is now seeking self-expression in the Congress movement. I find no difficulty in making my choice. I am obliged to resign from the American Jewish Committee.*

On June 10, 1917, the Jewish community voted to select delegates to represent Baltimore at the national level of the American Jewish Congress. As expected, Harry Friedenwald collected the greatest number of votes, but surprisingly, a woman from Chizuk Amuno was elected to the third spot on the delegation. Sadie J. Crockin was the only woman among the ten nominees listed in the Jewish Comment of June 15, 1917. Chizuk Amuno's alliance with the democratic Congress and the Zionist movement drew the respect and admiration of the growing Jewish community of Eastern European arrivals.

The women of Chizuk Amuno continued supporting the Congregation financially, socially, and spiritually. Literary meetings and lecture programs were held several times a year for members of the Ladies Auxiliaries. Bible study classes met monthly and included discussions on current events. In March, 1916 the women began the tradition of sponsoring an annual Purim festival. Held at the Veteran Corps Hall on Madison Avenue, the musical program was under the leadership of *"Toast Mistress"* Bertha Friedenwald. Song lyrics, printed in the programs, were written by Rabbi Kohn and Charles Schneeberger. In the spirit of Purim, the audience joined in singing:

To the tune of "Maryland My Maryland"

Dear Congregation, hail to thee,
Chizuk Emuno,
Nurse of our tender infancy,
Chizuk Emuno.
Thou taught us wisdom from thy scroll,
And tales of heroes great of soul,
And heroines whom all extoll,
Chizuk Emuno.
Now on the festive Purim Day,
Chizuk Emuno,
We pledge to thee our faith always,
Chizuk Emuno.
We will not let thy banner fall,
We'll ever rally to thy call,
And homage pay thee, one and all,
Chizuk Emuno.

The 1917 Purim entertainment, held at the Academy of Music Concert Hall, included dancing and refreshments. Three of the song parodies performed in 1916 were repeated – this time with the name of the congregation noted as *"Chizuk Amunah."*

Extending themselves outside of the synagogue community, women from Chizuk Amuno held leadership positions in communal organizations. In 1912, the Baltimore Association of Jewish Women was organized, and Hortense G. Moses was elected president. By 1915, the organization had over 1,000 women as members from throughout the Jewish community. A cover article, published in the May 7, 1915 issue of the <u>Jewish Comment</u>, described the dilemma that the women faced as their individual charitable efforts were being centralized within the Federated and United Hebrew Charities. As the "profession" of social work evolved, the well-meaning but untrained women perceived that their philanthropic work would no longer be needed. Hortense Moses countered that contention by summarizing the mission of the Association of Jewish Women – fostering solidarity among the women, and creating *"an intense and all-pervading Jewish spirit"* in the Jewish community, including keeping *"our children Jews."* Adding a personal reflection, Mrs. Moses described how the experience of serving as president had affected her own life:

> *Among the many benefits which I have thus enjoyed, I count one above all most precious, and that is the awakening of Jewish consciousness, the quickening of that instinct, be it racial or religious, which has made me realize what it means to be a Jewess; what it means to have the right to be a Jewess; what it means to pass on to our children much that is fine and good...*

Etta Levy, wife of Julius Levy, served as General Chairperson of the Fourth Center Baltimore Chapter of the American Red Cross during the war years. Several other women from Chizuk Amuno served on the chapter's Executive Committee, including Bertha Friedenwald, Julia Friedenwald Strauss, Hortense Moses, and Mrs. Meyer Halle. The membership of over 100 women assisted the

American war effort by sewing, knitting, and making surgical dressings. In 1917, the cost of wool increased, as did the demand for more sweaters, socks, and clothing. A garden party, held at the summer home of Mr. and Mrs. William Levy, raised the additional funds needed for materials.

Dr. Solomon Schechter, the leader of the Conservative Movement, died on November 19, 1915. He not only had a close relationship with many members of Chizuk Amuno, but also served as Rabbi Kohn's mentor while at the Seminary. The Congregation held a special memorial service on January 2, 1916, not merely to honor the scholar's memory, but to serve as an occasion for a discussion on Jewish ideas in Schechter's honor. President Harry Friedenwald remarked:

We Jews are not hero worshipers; neither during the lives of our great men nor after their death are we unmindful of the fact that they are human beings, made of flesh and blood as ourselves and therefore not free from frailty and from fault. We do not canonize those who have lived pure and saintly lives and pray to them for aid and succor. But our appreciation is none the less of those men who have spent their lives in noble self-sacrifice, in study, practice and love of the law and in devotion to the interests and the ideals of Israel.

Dr. Schechter's widow, Mathilde Roth Schechter, continued her husband's vision by organizing the Women's League for Conservative Judaism in 1918. She stressed the need to develop continuing Jewish education for women and designed programs in which women would perpetuate the traditions of Judaism in the home, synagogue, and community. The Chizuk Amuno Ladies Auxiliary was a founding member of the Women's League.

Death Of Rev. Dr. Schneeberger

Following several years of poor health, Rev. Dr. Henry W. Schneeberger, the first rabbi of Chizuk Amuno Congregation, died on Thursday, November 2, 1916. The obituary printed in the Baltimore Sun carried the headline, *"Beloved Rabbi Dead; Grand Old Man Dies After Long Illness."* Rev. Herman Glass led funeral services in the rabbi's home the following day, and Dr. William Rosenau, spiritual leader of the Eutaw Place Temple, delivered the eulogy of his long-time colleague. The November 10, 1916 issue of the Jewish Comment printed an editorial praising Schneeberger:

> *...thirty-five years of steady service to the community, always rendered with dignity, self-respect and due regard for the rights and opinions of others, must have had an abiding influence, making for what is right, and stable and God-fearing. His young people have become leaders in the community; the patient teaching of a lifetime has given many a man and woman the stimulus and support of their Jewishness.*

As a Kohen, Rabbi Eugene Kohn could not be present at Dr. Schneeberger's funeral or burial. The following words of praise from Kohn were published in the weekly Jewish paper:

> *To him in great part belongs the credit that at a time when other congregations felt compelled to compromise with the prevailing ignorance of Hebrew and of Jewish literature, and with the consequent misunderstanding of Jewish law and observance, his own remained, like himself, loyal to the ancient standards.*

Henry Schneeberger was laid to rest in the Hebrew Friendship Cemetery on East Baltimore Street. The Hebrew inscription on his gravestone, worn thin over time, declares that he was the rabbi of Chizuk Amuno Congregation of Baltimore. Sarah Schneeberger donated her husband's extensive personal library to the Beth Hamidrash Association – several volumes of which still line the shelves at the Stevenson Road synagogue.

In February, 1918 the Congregation had reason to celebrate as Rev. Herman Glass marked his fortieth year as Chizuk Amuno's cantor. In addition to speeches made by the president and the rabbi of the Congregation, the cantor's colleagues from Baltimore Hebrew and Oheb Shalom treated the audience to a musical presentation. A tribute by Mrs. Jesse S. Fleischer, published in the February 1, 1918 issue of the Jewish Comment, reflects the affection that the Congregation had for its cantor:

He laid the foundation of Judaism in our homes and often his good advice has been sought. He is beloved by all, old and young, and I, as an old scholar, can speak for one. In pleasures and sorrow he is with us all, ready to serve us at any time. His prayers are issued from the depths of sincerity.

At age sixty-six, Glass would soon be called on to provide spiritual leadership to the Congregation as they once again searched for a rabbi.

Rabbi Eugene Kohn resigned from Chizuk Amuno in October, 1918, and accepted a position in the Educational Department of the Zionist Organization of America in New York. However, in November, 1920 he wrote to JTS President Cyrus Adler expressing dissatisfaction with his job and interest in returning to the active rabbinate. After serving congregations in New Jersey, Wisconsin and Pennsylvania, Kohn eventually worked for the Jewish Reconstructionist Foundation as managing editor of the foundation's journal. Although his tenure at Chizuk Amuno lasted only six years, Rabbi Eugene Kohn guided the Congregation through a dramatic period of world Jewish history and tremendous growth of the Baltimore Jewish community.

THE TRANSITION YEARS 1918-1920

With the departure of Rabbi Kohn, the responsibility of leading worship services rested with Rev. Herman Glass. Lay members of the Congregation assisted the cantor and a series of guest speakers presented Shabbat sermons. Glass also supervised the Congregation's school with School Board Chairman Dr. Edgar Friedenwald, Harry Friedenwald's brother. They continued the tradition of holding summer classes, open to any child wishing to attend, at a nominal fee of one dollar per month. The announcement of classes published in the Jewish Comment assured readers that:

The school maintains the same high standards of instruction in the summer as in the winter months and the children are better able to profit by it, as they are free from the pressure of secular studies and come to their Hebrew classes early in the day before they are fatigued.

It is difficult to determine membership growth accurately between 1913 and 1923, but lists of boys becoming bar mitzvah and records of cash receipts reveal many new family names. The expansion of the membership roll was attributable to the association of Eastern European immigrant families with names like Gomborov, Fedder, Rabinovitz, Fineman, Shapiro, Krulewitch, and Rosenbloom. Having achieved financial stability, these first-generation American Jews moved out of East Baltimore neighborhoods and settled uptown. Although the established descendants of German immigrants still controlled the Chizuk Amuno board, the German language had long since ceased to be used in religious services. Adherence to traditional rituals, the use of Hebrew in prayer and school instruction, strong congregational support of Zionism, and the outreach of lay leaders serving communal organizations attracted many new members to Chizuk Amuno. Since the days of Rev. Schneeberger, the Congregation had had a reputation of being outspoken against Russian atrocities, and of welcoming newly arriving Jews. The American-born children of Yiddish-speaking parents attended religious school with the children of families who had lived in Baltimore for more than fifty years. Public lectures, holiday celebrations, and social activities sponsored by the Ladies Auxiliary groups attracted new interest in the Congregation, which was approaching its fiftieth anniversary.

The 1917 Balfour Declaration brought with it the need for administrative guidance in Palestine. Although the British Zionist Commission to Palestine had appointed Dr. Chaim Weizmann to serve as chairman of the multi-national group, Weizmann felt that his presence was needed more as a delegate to the Paris Peace Conference. At Weizmann's request, Chizuk Amuno President Harry Friedenwald was appointed acting chairman of the transition commission charged with designing plans to implement the Balfour Declaration. On January 23, 1919, Friedenwald temporarily turned away from his patients, medical students, and congregational constituents and traveled to Palestine. It would be seven months until he returned to Baltimore. Under Friedenwald's guidance, the Commission coordinated political and administrative affairs between the British Mandatory Power, Palestinian Jewry, and the worldwide Jewish relief efforts in the region. Much of Friedenwald's time was also spent defusing the anti-Semitic hostility of the Turks and Arabs. With great trust in his ability, Henrietta Szold appointed Friedenwald an advisor to the American Zionist Medical Unit in Palestine and asked him to prepare material for the development of a medical department at the Hebrew University. When Supreme Court Justice Louis Brandeis arrived in Jerusalem in June, 1919, Harry Friedenwald spent several days updating the American Zionist on developments in Palestine. The two men traveled together to Paris for meetings at the Peace Conference in late July, before Friedenwald returned home on August 26, 1919.

While Harry Friedenwald was attending to Zionist matters in Palestine, other Chizuk Amuno members were contributing their talents to re-establishing Baltimore's Hebrew College, originally founded by Samson Benderly in 1902, and dormant since his departure in 1910. Primarily intended to be a training ground for teachers, the Baltimore Hebrew College held its first classes on Sunday, November 2, 1919, at Chizuk Amuno's synagogue on McCulloh Street. Five members of the initial Board of Directors were members of Chizuk Amuno – Sadie J. Crockin, Dr. Harry Friedenwald, Julius Levy, Jacob M. Moses, and Israel Silberstein. The college published a memorial tribute to Julius Levy in 1926, which revealed that Levy was not only one of the founders of the institution, but also served five years as its first president.

For close to a decade, various members of Chizuk Amuno had lobbied for the merger of the Federated Jewish Charities and the United Hebrew Charities. William Levy and Louis H. Levin, as president and vice-president of the United, were unsuccessful in 1910. As president of the Federated in 1915, Harry Friedenwald appealed to members to realize that the two communal groups had become closer and developed a fraternal relationship. His remarks were published in the February 19, 1915 <u>Jewish Comment</u>:

> *More and more of us have come to realize that we can no longer speak of "our" institutions and of "theirs," – for "theirs" must become "ours" as "ours" will be "theirs." Let us cease speaking of "uptown" and "downtown" institutions. All who feel their responsibility, who have a sense of communal duty, have long since recognized that for them there is no "uptown" and "downtown" in charity.*

Unfortunately, Friedenwald was also unsuccessful in consolidating the charities during his tenure. M.S. Levy's youngest son, Julius, succeeded Friedenwald as president of the Federated, and in

1918, again sounded a call to merge the Federated and United charities under one banner. Instead of stressing the social benefits of unity, Julius Levy highlighted the financial benefits possible if duplication of administration could be eliminated. This practical approach still failed to convince a majority of the community leaders.

In 1920, social work professional Louis H. Levin spoke to leaders representing agencies in the Federated and United organizations about mutual problems. Alexandra Lee Levin related the story about the dramatic event occurring that day:

> *In an offhand manner he asked, "What would you gentlemen think of having the 'Uptown' and 'Downtown' Charities join forces?" Both sides roared, "Never!" Smiling broadly Louis said, "Hurrah, gentlemen, do you realize that this is the first time that you have ever agreed on any subject?" There was a pause, then someone laughed. The ice was broken. Before they were aware of what was happening, the men began to discuss the pros and cons of a complete community federation.*

An Amalgamation Committee, with representatives of the thirteen Federated charities and the nine United charities, hammered out the details that would formally create the Associated Jewish Charities of Baltimore. Of the twelve men serving on that committee, five of them were Chizuk Amuno members: Julius Levy, representing the Federated Jewish Charities; and Alexander Blumberg, Emil Crockin, William Levy, and Israel Silberstein, representing the United Hebrew Charities. The Maryland Legislature approved the merger on April 16, 1920. Louis H. Levin became the first Executive Director of the Associated Jewish Charities and was credited as the man who accomplished the unification of the Baltimore Jewish community.

The Decision To Move

As enrollment in the Hebrew school increased, it became obvious that the McCulloh Street synagogue would not be large enough to accommodate the growing needs of the Congregation. With its classrooms in the basement of the building, teachers and parents complained about the learning environment of the school. A Ladies Auxiliary journal, printed in March 1920, explained the motivations of the Planning Committee:

> *If we are to make our children loyal adherents of our congregation, it is necessary that the Hebrew school and synagogue be properly located. For these reasons the Chizuk Amuno congregation decided to erect a new synagogue, and after thorough consideration of the matter by the board of directors and the members of the congregation, a site was bought at the north-west corner of Eutaw Place and Chauncey Avenue. This site is admirably adapted for our purpose, being located on a street of the best residential character, and away from car lines. The lot is large, having 106-foot frontage on Eutaw Place, with a depth of 150 feet on Chauncey Avenue. This will permit the erection of a building with abundant light and air on all four sides.*

Announcement was placed in the November 7, 1919 issue of the <u>Jewish Times</u> that Chizuk Amuno intended to build a new synagogue and school. The editor expressed the feelings of the community:

> *No more commendable or noteworthy step has been taken in our Baltimore Jewish community than that which is represented by the project of the Chizuk Amuno Congregation to build a new synagogue and schoolhouse on a scale commensurate with its standing and its broadening activities. The enterprise is applauded by the general Jewish population of the city, not only because it is of a sacred character, but also because it shows a fine readiness to seize an opportunity to serve the Jewish cause as well as the requisite resoluteness and courage to carry the high purpose into execution.*

Chizuk Amuno Congregation had been swept up in the national movement to recast synagogue buildings as multi-purpose synagogue-centers, rather than only as places of worship. Attendance at services had dropped, and there were fears that the younger generation of adults would lose their sense of Jewish life and religious purpose. In an effort to combat assimilation, congregations added social and educational programming to the schedule of religious activities in the synagogue. Services would continue to be traditional, but the laity of Chizuk Amuno envisioned a new synagogue structure designed to promote Judaism by offering each member of the family informal educational programs, clubs, special interest groups, and social functions. The synagogue would be a gathering place and unifying factor for its constituents.

On Sunday, November 2, 1919, close to 400 people filled Lehmann Hall for a dinner to formally announce plans for the Eutaw Street property acquired the previous spring and solicit contributions to the Building Fund. President Harry Friedenwald opened his remarks by reminding those present that Chizuk Amuno had moved twice before, and each time they had *"carried our tabernacles with us and have upheld the dignity and holiness of our faith."* The task of stirring enthusiasm for the appeal was left to Julius Levy, who informed the group that the new school would be capable of accommodating 700 students. Pledges of $75,000 were quickly raised towards the expected minimum cost of $250,000. The November 7, 1919 issue of the <u>Jewish Times</u> printed a list of 150 donors and the amounts each had pledged. To support the building drive, the Ladies Auxiliaries sponsored a very successful Purim dance at Lehmann's Hall on March 8, 1920. Earlier that day, the ladies had treated the school children to a slide show telling the story of Purim. Both activities attracted a large audience.

With plans underway for the new synagogue, the Board of Chizuk Amuno focused its attention on the matter of engaging their next rabbi. Once again the Board turned to JTS for a recommendation.

THE COBLENZ ERA 1920-1948

> *Rabbi Coblenz is doing very well, and stirring up the*
> *dry bones of our congregation. It is livelier than I have*
> *ever known it.*
>
> > Louis H. Levin
> > *Letter to a relative, December 3, 1920*

A small article on page seven of the August 6, 1920 issue of the <u>Jewish Times</u> announced that Chizuk Amuno had procured the services of their third rabbi:

> *Rabbi Adolph Coblens, of Congregation Adath Jeshurun,*
> *Syracuse, N.Y., has accepted the position of rabbi of*
> *Chizuk Emunah Congregation, McCulloh and Mosher*
> *streets, to which he was elected at a special meeting held*
> *last week. He will assume his new duties the first of*
> *September.*

Adolph Coblenz would spend the next twenty-eight years as the spiritual leader of Chizuk Amuno Congregation, guiding them through the relocation of their synagogue, massive internal growth, the horrors of the Shoah, and dramatic ritual changes.

Coblenz had been a classmate of Eugene Kohn at the Seminary and had assumed the Syracuse pulpit vacated by Kohn's older brother, Rabbi Jacob Kohn, in 1913. A letter of recommendation written by the JTS registrar dated March 11, 1919, states:

> *I have known Rabbi Coblenz throughout his student days*
> *in the Seminary and have found him not only an excel-*
> *lent scholar in Jewish subjects, but also well equipped*
> *in general culture. I consider him one of the best ora-*
> *tors that the Seminary has graduated.*

Although he had received his ordination at JTS, the election of Rabbi Coblenz broke the profile of rabbis serving Chizuk Amuno for the previous forty-four years. He was not only the first foreign-born rabbi of the Congregation, but also the first with a non-German family ancestry. Adolph Coblenz was born December 9, 1886 in the port town of Riga, in what was then Kovno Guberniya, Russia and is now considered Latvia. The son of a cantor, the young boy received a traditional Jewish cheder education in Riga before being sent to attend secondary school at the "Realschule der Israelitscherr Religioese Gesellschaf" in Frankfurt-am-Main, Germany. At age seventeen, Coblenz departed Hamburg, Germany aboard the *Furst Bismark* in a second-class cabin with his father and four siblings. The family arrived in New York City on November 13, 1903, and settled in Brooklyn. After graduating with honors in philosophy and literature from New York's City College in 1909, Adolph Coblenz decided to pursue a rabbinical career and entered the Seminary. Reference to Coblenz is made in a letter from the Seminary's Acting President, Dr. Israel Friedlaender, to Dr. Solomon Schechter on sabbatical leave in 1910:

> *The only scholarship which became available...was awarded, after consultation with the Faculty, to Coblenz, who as you know, is very poor and is decidedly a very able student. He promised to be regular in his attendance and industrious in his work.*

The young rabbi served his first congregation from 1913 until accepting the position offered by Chizuk Amuno in the summer of 1920. Rabbi Coblenz delivered a farewell sermon to his congregants, and informed colleagues of his relocation. One of those Syracuse colleagues was Rabbi Hirsh Zaiman of the Anshe Sfard Synagogue, who, in 1918, had assumed the pulpit of his late brother, Rabbi Matthias Tsaimon.

An accomplished speaker, Coblenz quickly gained prominence in Baltimore. Rabbi Israel Goldman summarized Coblenz's personality in his eulogy:

People began to call him a man of Intellect, which he was, for he possessed a profound and well-stocked mind. People began to refer to him as a Scholar, which he was, steeped in learning; as a Philosopher, which he was, for his mind delved into the higher realms of human thought. People spoke of him as a Poet, which he was, for he had great gifts of literary expression. People thought of him as a Linguist, which he was, because he mastered ancient and modern languages. People thought him a Brilliant Conversationalist, which he was, because people young and old delighted to sit and chat with him and enjoy the treasures of his brilliant mind and jolly wit.

Although Chizuk Amuno had a new rabbi, within weeks the Congregation faced a major setback. Only days before Rosh Hashanah, Rev. Herman Glass had taken ill and was unable to serve as cantor for the High Holy Days. Harry Friedenwald used his connections to locate a last-minute substitute – Adolph "Abba" Weisgal.

Hazzan Abba Weisgal

Born on December 13, 1885 in the town of Kikol, in the Russian Empire, Abba Yosef was the first child of Shlomo Weisgal, the town's hazzan-shochet, and Leah Chlast. After bearing five more children, including one set of twins, Leah Weisgal died. Abba was only seven years old. The young child was schooled in a traditional cheder, then supplemented his Talmudic studies by attending a secular school during his teen years. Striking out to follow in his father's footsteps, in 1901, Abba traveled to nearby towns seeking employment as a "Meshorer" – a singer at the cantor's side. In the town of Wloclawek, thirty-five miles from Kikol, Abba was accepted as a member of the synagogue's permanent choir. Under the tutelage of the shul's hazzan, Alexander Ersler, and a local piano teacher, Weisgal learned music theory and Hazzanut. As his skills sharpened, he was elevated to conductor of the choir. In 1903 and 1904, most of Abba's family emigrated to America. Anxious to pursue his cantorial career, Abba set off for Vienna. In his dissertation on Weisgal, Cantor Joseph A. Levine explains:

Vienna was the crossroads between East and West, its synagogue rite joined the melancholy Slavic with its own lighthearted tradition...mournful dirges were juxtaposed with ...bittersweet waltzes.

Added to this mix was exposure to the Vienna Opera and the dramatic intensity of Gustave Mahler. While continuing his cantorial studies and meeting the requirements to become a shochet, Weisgal accepted chorus roles in light operettas.

By 1908, Abba Weisgal was ready to assume a pulpit and accepted a position as Hazzan Sheini of Ivancice, Moravia – a town of five hundred Jews and one synagogue. Although the congregation maintained separate seating for men and women, they allowed the use of an organ and a mixed choir. In December, 1911 Abba married Hungarian Aranka Stricker and applied for Austrian citizenship. As a citizen required to serve in the Austrian military, Weisgal was called into active duty the day Germany declared war on Russia in 1914. Serving in various combat capacities, Abba Weisgal survived the four-and-a-half-year war and returned to live in Ivancice, now considered part of the Czechoslovak Republic. At the urging of his family overseas, Weisgal made the difficult decision to leave economically depressed Ivancice with his wife and two small sons. It took over six months to obtain the United States visa and travel documents that allowed the family to cross Europe and reach the port of Cherbourg, France.

On August 30, 1920, one of New York's Yiddish newspapers, the Morning Journal, printed a lengthy article prematurely announcing the arrival of *"Kantor Adolf Weisgal of Czechoslovakia"* three days before his ship actually docked. Most likely written by his brother Meyer, the article mentioned that Weisgal would be embarking on a tour showcasing his talents as either a cantor or an opera singer. Chizuk Amuno sexton Benjamin Erkes brought the article to the attention of Harry Friedenwald and suggested that he contact Meyer Weisgal, then serving as the editor of the Zionist monthly, Maccabean. The Congregation's president sent a telegram stating that a replacement hazzan was desperately needed for the upcoming holidays.

Chizuk Amuno was searching for a cantor at the peak of a period known as the "Golden Age of Hazzanut" or the "Cantor Craze." Scholar Jonathan Sarna wrote:

> *What the chazan represented...was the ultimate synthesis of the Old World and New – a synthesis most immigrants sought to achieve but few succeeded. The chazan was an ideal role model: observant yet rich, traditional yet modern...in short, a cantorial performance simultaneously served both as an exercise in nostalgia and as living proof that in America the talented could succeed handsomely.*

The arrival of European cantors launched performance tours and guest appearances of cantorial virtuosi throughout the country. As public interest in the great cantors from Europe grew, congregations competed to showcase their talents and entice new members. The possibility of engaging a cosmopolitan cantor propelled the Board to pursue Abba Weisgal.

Meyer Weisgal arranged a meeting at the Hotel Knickerbocker in New York City for a Congregation representative to interview his brother. Leslie Moses, grandson of Chizuk Amuno founder M.S. Levy, traveled to the city for what he thought would be a brief conversation. Abba Weisgal arrived at the hotel wearing a long black coat, gloves, spats, and carrying a walking stick. He proceeded to sing for an hour, then waited while his brother negotiated a fee. When Meyer declared that Abba's services for the High Holy Days through the Sukkot holidays should be worth $1,000 – twice the amount budgeted by the Congregation – Leslie Moses invited the cantor to have a personal interview in Baltimore with the committee.

With less than three days until the holidays, Abba Weisgal arrived by train in Baltimore and was taken to the McCulloh Street synagogue. Cantor Joseph A. Levine continues the story:

The choirmaster, Harry Cooperstein, introduced himself to the candidate. He then took Abba aside and assured him that any mistakes would be overlooked; the object was to run through the entire Ma'ariv service without interruption. This was accomplished, and when Abba concluded the final hymn...he turned, in stovepipe and handlebar mustache and asked "Weiter Fahre"? (shall I continue)? Dr. Friedenwald answered from the back row: "Nicht Notig" (not necessary); he would do.

Harry Friedenwald's decision began a partnership between Abba Weisgal and Chizuk Amuno Congregation that would continue for more than fifty years.

On Erev Rosh Hashanah, September 12, 1920, Rabbi Adolph Coblenz conducted his first High Holy Day service at Chizuk Amuno, joined on the pulpit of the McCulloh Street synagogue by Cantor Abba Weisgal. Weisgal's portion of the service was sung in a modern style. This did not appeal to the Eastern European immigrants in attendance, but Weisgal redeemed himself with a traditional rendition of Kiddush. Over the next week, Chizuk Amuno congregants embraced Weisgal's style and formal manner. Harry Friedenwald discussed the possibility of hiring Weisgal full-time and questioned what the cantor's salary expectation would be. Weisgal asked for $6,000 per year. Friedenwald explained that the rabbi's salary had been set at $4,000, and the Board would not allow the cantor to earn more than the rabbi. Weisgal suggested raising the rabbi's pay.

Cantor Weisgal remained in Baltimore during the intermediate days of Sukkot and joined Rabbi Coblenz at a gathering of school children on October 3, 1920. The Jewish Times noted that *"Refreshments were served and an attractive program was presented, which included storytelling by the Rabbi and singing led by Rev. Weisgal, cantor for the holiday services."* Although the cantor was well received by the Congregation, a single event would create a question in the Board's mind about Weisgal's fitness to serve.

On the Friday evening between Yom Kippur and Sukkot, choirmaster Cooperstein and music committee chairman Ralph Ephraim visited Weisgal at the Altamont Hotel, on the corner of Eutaw Place and Lanvale Street. The evening was warm; the cantor ordered ice water. When the bellhop delivered the water, Weisgal began to reach into his pocket for a tip. Cooperstein grabbed his hand, but the damage had been done. When the Music Committee heard that the prospect handled money on Shabbat, they decided to drop all negotiations. After the holidays, Weisgal returned to the Bronx, not realizing the reason that an offer had not been extended.

Ground was broken on Tuesday, October 19, 1920 for the future home of the Chizuk Amuno Congregation on Eutaw Place. A small mention in the <u>Jewish Times</u> disclosed that the *"magnificent structure"* was budgeted to cost approximately $400,000. The architect of the McCulloh Street synagogue, Joseph Sperry, was selected to design the structure and agreed to a modest fee of $5,000 for his services. He designed the building in the Romanesque-Byzantine style, with more delicate arches than previously used at McCulloh Street. Original plans called for the exterior to be constructed of Maryland granite and included a domed roof. The Mizrach Wall and Ark were to be made from various colored Italian marbles with the remaining three walls of solid oak. As cost estimates steadily rose, the dome concept was abandoned, as were the plans for the Italian marble. When Mr. Hilgartner, owner of the marble company, heard that his $43,000 bid for marble work would not be accepted, he asked the cost of the newly re-designed wooden ark. According to an interview Rabbi Israel Goldman conducted with Mr. Leslie Moses in 1975, Hilgartner was informed that the bid was for $11,500. The non-Jewish businessman responded: *"Your Sanctuary should have only marble. It is an honor for me to build a Holy Ark for a Jewish House of Worship. I will charge you only $11,500 which is the same you would have to pay for a Holy Ark of wood."* Even with these adjustments, the Finance Committee, led by Meyer Abramson, had difficulty obtaining pledges for the mounting costs.

On November 14, 1920, the first combined fund-raising campaign of the Associated was launched. The Jewish Times devoted many pages of its November 12, 1920 issue to promoting the drive, including letters from nine Baltimore rabbis. In the words of newly installed Rabbi Adolph Coblenz, the Associated was *"the living symbol of a community that is morally undivided and indivisible."* The same could be said for Chizuk Amuno. Harry Friedenwald's efforts to create a synagogue community where both German and Eastern European Jews could feel comfortable had been successful. As the Associated served as a common benevolent organization, so Chizuk Amuno had positioned itself as neutral ground attracting both affluent members and intellectual traditionalists of modest means.

In January 1921, as the Congregation approached its fiftieth anniversary, Harry Friedenwald stepped down after serving nine years as president. He would continue to hold the title of Honorary President for the remainder of his life and devote keen attention to the congregation founded by his grandfather. William Levy assumed the top leadership position as well as serving as the chairman of the Joint Committee responsible for the Eutaw Street construction.

Chizuk Amuno Congregation celebrated its fiftieth anniversary on Sunday, April 3, 1921, with ceremonies held in the synagogue on McCulloh and Mosher Streets. Rabbis Coblenz, Schaffer, and Rosenau delivered speeches, along with remarks by Dr. Harry Friedenwald and William Levy. That morning, the Baltimore Sun printed an extensive article highlighting the history of the Congregation, calling it *"an enlightened exponent of traditional Judaism."* Titled "MANY JEWISH LEADERS DEVELOPED IN 50 YEARS BY THIS CONGREGATION," the article described the leaders who had guided it:

> *The congregation has been fruitful in developing leaders of the Jewish community of this city and the country*

and in this way has kept in touch with the development and growth of the Jewish population in Baltimore and the development of Judaism in America. The Chizuk Amuno Congregation is justifyably proud of its large achievements outside of its own immediate sphere of operations and one of the traditions of the congregation is the duty felt by the members to place their services at the command of the city. Inspired by its past record the members hope to contribute in large measure in the future to Baltimore's social and religious forces.

The Sun mentioned that the Congregation had 250 members and additional seatholders, which would mean that there had been substantial growth in membership.

The second stage of Chizuk Amuno's Jubilee Celebration was a fund-raising bazaar sponsored by the Ladies Auxiliaries. Under the leadership of Mrs. Solomon Silverman, the group planned the three-day event for April 4, 5 and 6, 1921 at Carlin's Hall on Reisterstown Road. Sixteen women headed segments of the event including:

Mrs. Jesse Fleischer – Turkish Den
Mrs. Samuel Goodman – Cigar Booth
Mrs. Ralph Ephraim – Apron Booth
Mrs. M. Stulman – Soft Drinks
Mrs. L.M. Hendler – Candy Booth
Mrs. B.W. Hummel – Towel Booth
Miss Ethel Rosenbloom – Men's Furnishings Booth

In the evenings, young people came to the bazaar to hear the dance sounds of Lou Seidenmann's jazz orchestra. A new "Pilot Car" was raffled off. The dedicated efforts of the Women's Auxiliaries brought a $10,000 cash donation to the building fund.

As they looked back over the past half-century, the Congregation also looked ahead. Lay leaders expressed optimistic estimates of membership reaching 500, with increases coming mostly due to interest in the congregational school. From their inception, plans for the Eutaw Street property had always reflected a school building separate from the main synagogue. The purchased lot ran along Eutaw Place between Brooks Lane and Chauncey Terrace. While President William Levy was away from Baltimore for an extended period, the Building and Finance Committees determined that funds would not be sufficient for a separate school building, and that classroom space could be integrated in a single building. Without consulting Levy, the committees sold off half of the parcel. Upon his return, William Levy announced that he would resign as president at the conclusion of his one-year term. Even with the downsizing, the Eutaw Place synagogue cost more than twice the $400,000 estimate to construct.

When the cornerstone laying ceremony took place on June 26, 1921, it was expected that the synagogue would be substantially completed by the High Holy Days later that year. Rev. Herman Glass, suffering from diabetes, had lost his leg to the disease, and was unable to resume his position as hazzan. William Levy instructed Meyer Abramson, Israel Silberstein, and Simon Levin to contact Abba Weisgal and offer him the position at an annual salary of $3,500. Weisgal, frustrated with synagogue politics, had decided to pursue his operatic career. While living in Newark, New Jersey the cantor commuted into New York City for intensive study with Italian and Russian voice coaches. When the invitation from Chizuk Amuno arrived, Weisgal had accepted a contract with the Manhattan Opera Company to be their lead baritone, singing the role of Conte di Luna in an upcoming run of Verdi's "Il Trovatore." After discussing the options with his wife and brothers, Abba Weisgal decided to return to his first love – the synagogue. Accompanied by his brother Meyer, Cantor Weisgal returned to Baltimore and officiated at Shabbat services on August 20, 1921. They both wore silk top hats and tailcoats. Congregation reaction was again very positive, and salary negotiations were settled. Abba Weisgal, now referring to himself as "Adolph," made plans to move his family to Baltimore.

Hoping to attract additional members and seatholders for the coming holiday season, Meyer Abramson placed an announcement in the September 2, 1921 issue of the Jewish Times informing the community that *"one of the highest class cantors in this country"* had been engaged by Chizuk Amuno. Two weeks later, the weekly paper presented an unsigned, full-length article profiling Weisgal containing wild exaggerations and inaccuracies about his European accomplishments, including statements that he had sung at the birthday celebration of the queen of Italy. A handsome photograph of the cantor accompanied the article. In his dissertation, Cantor Levine provides a much clearer picture of Abba Weisgal's abilities:

> *Abba's range was always unusually wide. In his prime he carried a baritonal color from low F to high A; two-and-a-half usable octaves. He was also endowed by nature with a supple musculature which enabled him to execute long rolling cadenzas with amazing ease and speed. Moreover, he could swell or diminish a held tone from either extreme of the dynamic spectrum without any apparent preparation. He could change registrations or resonance adjustments in mid-phrase, with no hesitation or effort. Underlying this impressive vocalism was a rhythmic vitality that surfaced at word-accents and which, for all its percussive vigor, never rent the seamless fabric of his singing.*

The selection of Abba Weisgal was perfectly suited for Chizuk Amuno. He appealed to the older German members because of his fluency in German and his sophisticated, debonair appearance. He was admired by the Eastern Europeans for his Polish style of chanting, which Cantor Levine noted *"recreated for them the illusion of an integrated Jewish lifestyle much like the one they associated with the impoverished Shtetlach of their youth."*

Unfortunately, construction on the Eutaw Place sanctuary was not completed for the High Holy Days beginning on the evening of October 2, 1921. On the first day of Rosh Hashanah, services were held at the McCulloh Street synagogue, but on the second day services were conducted in the partially completed vestry of the Eutaw Place synagogue. Cantor Weisgal often told of how heavy rainfall created flooding in the vestry, forcing the clergy to balance on boards placed as a pathway to the pulpit. Congregants suffered through the service, wading in puddles of water.

Concurrent with the High Holy Days 5682 (1921), Chizuk Amuno issued the first congregational <u>Bulletin</u>. The lead editorial provides a glimpse of synagogue life at the time:

> *The Congregation is experiencing at the present time the thrills of rebirth. The new Synagogue is rising gradually "on the hill" – a citadel of the Jewish spirit, strong and lofty, calling unto us to go up and inherit. Organizations of our young people are now in process of formation; others are planned for the near future. We look forward with anxiety and confidence to the time when we shall have completely organized the Congregation for the Synagogue and the Synagogue for the Congregation.*

Events at Chizuk Amuno paralleled those at other synagogues affiliated with the Conservative Movement. The adult children of Jewish immigrants had flocked to the edge of the city limits to raise their children in suburban neighborhoods and attempted to reconcile traditional Judaism with their American cultural interests. Molding the synagogue to serve the needs of its members was a revolutionary concept. As Jack Wertheimer noted in his essay "The Conservative Synagogue:"

> *Reports on affiliates of the United Synagogue from 1910 to 1920 and during the 1920's consistently highlight the broad range of programs offered, including adult education forums, congregational schools, recreational events, social activities, and auxiliaries for men, women, young adults, and children. Conservative synagogues have not monopolized the concept of the synagogue-center, but they have played a major role in winning wide acceptance for this model of the synagogue.*

On the occasion of completing Chizuk Amuno's relocation to Eutaw Place, the Jewish Times printed a history of the Congregation in their September 22, 1922 edition. Commenting on the new building, the editor mentioned that they had been *"informed that it is the most elaborate Orthodox Synagogue in the United States."* The main sanctuary, including the balcony area, seated 1,500 in individual seats. Acoustical features were state-of-the-art. Vestry rooms downstairs were designed to serve as assembly halls, a Bet Hamidrash, classrooms, boardroom, and offices. Located only one block from Druid Hill Park, the second largest municipal park in the United States, Chizuk Amuno opened its new home in a prime location.

Despite the attractive synagogue, new memberships in Chizuk Amuno stagnated in the early 1920's. Board members discussed methods to increase not only membership, but also attendance at Shabbat services. At Rabbi Coblenz's recommendation, the Congregation instituted Friday Evening Assembly in late 1922. The hour-long service began at 8:00 p.m. and consisted of traditional prayers, psalms, a lecture by the rabbi, and congregational singing. Chizuk Amuno had taken another step toward becoming a synagogue-center, as the traditional family Shabbat evening at home was now available at the synagogue. As noted by Dr. David Kaufman: *"The intensive Jewish home life of the immigrant generation was fast disappearing by the 1920s, as were the organic Jewish communities of areas of first and second settlement."* Adults came to late Friday evening services not necessarily only to worship – they came for social interaction and communal fellowship. Celebration of Shabbat had shifted from the privacy of the home to the public arena of the synagogue.

As the transition to the new synagogue was underway, the seventh president of Chizuk Amuno began his term. Milton Fleischer had previously served as secretary (1898-1910), general trustee (1910-1921), and vice-president (1921-1922) thus accumulating twenty-three years of leadership experience before assuming the top post. Described as a *"peaceable man"* by Rabbi Goldman, Fleischer guided the Board with sound judgement in a very methodical manner. His politeness and sense of integrity earned Fleischer the respect and admiration of the entire community. When not involved in synagogue matters, Fleischer managed the family's successful Liberty Manufacturing Co. – Nightwear Specialists. Milton Fleischer served as President of Chizuk Amuno for the next thirty-one consecutive years, earning him the title, "Dean of Synagogue Presidents."

Formal dedication of the Eutaw Place synagogue took place on Friday December 15, 1922, followed by the first annual "Chizuk Amuno Chanukah Banquet" two days later. The <u>Jewish Times</u> reported: *"The banquet was given for members of the congregation and their wives and certainly gave evidence that there is a strong social as well as a religious spirit binding the members of this congregation."* The tradition of holding a Chanukah banquet would continue for more than three decades.

After the move to Eutaw Place, the Auxiliary changed its name to the Chizuk Amuno Sisterhood, but the mission of the group varied little. As American Jewish women, they assumed the responsibility for safeguarding the future of Judaism by bringing ritual and spirituality into the home, and their household sensibilities into the synagogue. In her essay, "The Special Sphere of the Middle-Class American Jewish Woman: The Synagogue Sisterhood 1890-1940," scholar Jenna Weissman Joselit comments:

> *It was up to the American Jewish woman to see to it that the Sabbath and the dietary laws were observed, the children educated Jewishly, and that the family attended religious services and participated in all manner of Jewish communal activity.*

This cultural characteristic was exemplified in Beatrice (Mrs. William) Levy's charge to members during the 1921 opening Sisterhood meeting:

> *Do we make of our homes sanctuaries, where our children imbibe the ethics and ceremonies so dear to us as*

Mothers in Israel? Do we attend divine Services every Sabbath, so that by our presence in this beautiful House of God, we inspire our children, that they, too, will feel it incumbent to worship with us?

The 1920's brought a serious decline in synagogue attendance. Increased mobility and the need for financial stability caused many men to disregard the observances of their fathers. Women and their children comprised the majority of worshippers on a regular basis. In 1949, Beatrice Levy's daughter, Selma Oppenheimer, recorded remembrances of her mother's term as Sisterhood president. Her stories typify how women of the 1920's strove to manage the synagogue in the same way they managed their homes:

"We always hide some of our funds," confided Mama one day. "If we don't the men take everything we have, and there we are without a penny for our little expenses." Never in those days were contributions donated to outside organizations. Every cent of the dues was hoarded, and only used for the needs of Chizuk Amuno. Mama was the one who proposed starting a building fund for the new school with the moneys realized from card parties and bazaars.

Without voting rights, Sisterhood members registered their opinions by putting action and money behind their words. In 1921, they supported the plan for a marble ark and contributed $10,000 towards its construction. The Sisterhood continued sponsoring Purim banquets and entertainment programs. They provided not only substantial funds, but also nurtured camaraderie among members of the Congregation, as evidenced by the following lyrics sung in the March 20, 1927 Purim Banquet:

To the tune of "Blue Skies"

Chizuk Amuno,
We love our temple of brotherly love.
Coblenz and Weisgal too,

Help to make it worthy for you.
Like to see things go along right
Like to see crowds each Friday night.
Our Rabbi's sermons are a real treat,
Our Chazan's singing cannot be beat.
Oh, Chizuk Amuno,
We love our temple of brotherly love.

It would be decades before a woman would be invited to become a voting member of the Board. For now, the Congregation would only accept Sisterhood help in more traditional ways. Joselit identified various responsibilities of Sisterhoods that grew out of their homemaker role:

> *...equipping the synagogue kitchen...grew out of the Jewish woman's essential talents as homemaker, as did decorating the synagogue...Festooning the alter with flowers, decorating the Sukkah, designing Torah covers and wedding canopies, even operating a synagogue gift shop where members could easily purchase Jewish ritual objects – each was an application of the aesthetic sensibility and taste of the Jewish woman to synagogue life.*

The Chizuk Amuno Sisterhood added to this list of tasks by acting as social hostesses for bachelor Rabbi Coblenz. When weekly study groups assembled at the rabbi's residence for discussions, Sisterhood members took turns seeing that the rabbi's home was presentable and serving refreshments.

Although synagogue attendance dropped, attendance at the synagogue schools surged. From 1922 until 1924, Mordecai Soloff served as principal under the guidance of Board Chairman Jesse Fleischer. As of December 12, 1923, the School Committee reported a total of 265 pupils enrolled in the Hebrew school, Sunday school, and kindergarten. By April 7, 1924, that number had swelled to 326 students. Hebrew school classes met from 3:30-6:30 p.m. Monday through Thursday and Sunday mornings. At the suggestion of the Sisterhood, the Board considered purchasing a second building for school use, and on May 12, 1924, voted to place a deposit on a plot of land at Linden and Chauncey Avenues. Concerned about assuming more debt, the Board decided not to commit to a new building project unless fifty percent of the funds were raised in advance. Julius Levy presented two very generous offers to the Congregation – either to personally pay fifteen percent of the total cost of building a school center or to cover the entire cost of remodeling the existing vestry rooms into additional classrooms. The second option was accepted and two more classrooms were available for students.

At the suggestion of Rabbi Coblenz, young men age thirteen to sixteen formed a new organization within the Chizuk Amuno community – the Junior Congregation. On December 15, 1922, the new Junior Congregation held its first *"Minha"* service at 2:30 p.m. followed by refreshments donated by the Sisterhood. As the boys prepared to follow in the footsteps of their fathers, the <u>Jewish Times</u> declared that *"a new era of religious work has sprung up in the history of us young Jews of Baltimore."* Hebrew School student Paul Fineman delivered an address on the Sedra of Micketz during the second week of Junior Congregation services.

Within the next year, Junior Congregation was redesigned to include the pupils, both girls and boys, of the Hebrew and Sunday schools. Weekly Shabbat services were held at 10:15 a.m. in the synagogue vestry and conducted completely by the children. The group elected officers who occupied seats to the right of the ark. The two seats to the left of the ark were reserved for officers of the Hebrew School Student Council. Records note that about 200 students regularly attended these services in 1924. On January 26, 1924, Rabbi Coblenz invited the Junior Congregation to be guests at the main Shabbat service and preached a sermon prepared especially for the children. Thus began the concept of involving young people in the religious services of adults.

Although no longer involved in weekly synagogue rituals, Rev. Herman Glass continued to maintain his position as respected Cantor Emeritus. After a forty-four year association with Chizuk Amuno, the beloved cantor died on February 8, 1925. Two pages of that week's Jewish Times were devoted to memorializing Herman Glass, and included eulogies by his colleagues. Congregation President Milton Fleischer described his friend's characteristics of *"full-hearted cheerfulness, warm geniality, considerate thoughtfulness,"* and commented on his *"humble devotion to the service of God, his ardent championship of righteousness and the dignity and honor with which he invested his dual office of cantor and teacher."* As they had for Mrs. Schneeberger, the Board voted to grant Mrs. Glass a $300 pension to be paid each year until her death. Cantor Abba Weisgal assured the Congregation that he would strive to be as successful as had his esteemed predecessor.

Cantor Weisgal took a special interest in the youth of the Congregation. He taught music in the Chizuk Amuno schools, and was also engaged by the Board of Jewish Education to teach at all of the religious schools in Baltimore. In a 1926 article, the cantor expressed his objective in instructing children on traditional chants and hymns:

> *This to me, is a labor of love. The little ones are taught the sweet, harmonious and soul-stirring songs. These are never forgotten by them. It serves as their inspiration. When they are caught up later in life – as some of them undoubtedly are – in the welter of existence, the Jewish heritage is forgotten. Then, later, when sober thought supplants loose thinking and a laxity in belief, they return again to the God of their fathers. The songs like Enk Eloihainu, Yigdal, Kodesh, Kodesh, Kodesh, Adon Oldom, come back to their minds like the rush of a tidal wave. Somewhere in their subconsciousness, these beautiful songs have slept and like the oncoming spring burst forth again... We must make them Jews of character proud of their past and hopeful of their future.*

In the fall of 1926, Nathan Kramer was named principal of the schools, and quickly moved to establish more social, cultural, and athletic activities for the students. Miss Kate Fraidin, a member of the first graduating class of the Baltimore Hebrew College, and Miss Sarah Sachs were hired to teach Hebrew school – Fraidin earned $100 per month, and Sachs was paid $83 per month. Unfortunately, many parents felt that lengthy Hebrew school classes every afternoon were interfering with their children's secular studies and extracurricular activities, such as music and dance lessons. Enrollment waned. Reform congregations in Baltimore had cut back the number of hours that students were required to attend classes, causing some Board members to worry that Chizuk Amuno families might change allegiance simply because of Hebrew school requirements. When the School Committee met on June 30, 1927, they reached the decision that:

> *Beginning with the new school year every class shall receive instruction three times a week, and each session shall be of two hours. One group of classes will meet on Sunday, Monday, and Wednesday, and another group on Sunday, Tuesday and Thursday. It was also decided that instead of one hour and a half of instruction, as in the previous year, the Sunday School pupils will learn two hours.*

Cantor Weisgal supervised two Bar Mitzvah classes, each meeting twice a week for one hour. Hebrew school tuition was set at $60 per year, payable $6 per month. Enrollment figures still dropped. As of December 29, 1927, there were ninety-nine boys and twenty-one girls attending Hebrew school, and seventeen boys and sixty-two girls in the Sunday school. The school budget operated on a deficit, and the Congregation was asked to contribute $150 per month for the benefit of the school.

The Young People's League

Lay leaders were concerned about apathy among young adults in the synagogue community, a concern shared by congregations across the nation. In 1921, the United Synagogue organized a network of Young Folk's Leagues designed to provide social interaction for young adults while reinforcing basic Jewish tenets. Chizuk Amuno's chapter, the Young People's League (YPL), was organized on January 13, 1924, and within two years became the largest chapter in the country. Public announcement of the new organization was published in the January 18, 1924 issue of the Jewish Times:

> *Dr. Coblenz delivered an address, in which he outlined the general program of the Junior League's weekly Bible Class meetings. Jewish songs, a short lecture of the light motives of the Bible to be given by the Rabbi, the reading of a current topic, some special musical number, discussion of business in connection with social activities, and the singing of the "Hatukvah" would complete the morning's program.*

Fred Katzner was elected as the first president, a role he would serve until 1927. In his acceptance speech, Katzner reminded his audience to remember their true objective – *"to stimulate and keep alive the interest in our faith and the traditions of our people."*

Each week the YPL presented a variety of programs focusing on cultural, social, dramatic, literary, musical, or athletic interests. Prominent local personalities addressed the weekly Sunday Morning Forum – usually attended by four to five hundred young men and women. The group attracted not only the children of Chizuk Amuno members, but also young adults whose parents were unaffiliated, and those with families belonging to Reform congregations.

YPL members formed men's and women's basketball teams and a bowling team. Participation in an inter-congregational league provided competition and encouraged a sense of fellowship with members of other congregations. The YPL Social Committee organized formal dances usually held at the Belvedere, Emerson, or Southern Hotels, and smaller "mixers" held in the Chizuk Amuno vestry. The first social, held on Saturday, February 15, 1924 at the Esplanade Café, was attended by 150 people. The following morning, Sunday classes were held promptly at 11 a.m., and centered on a discussion of the accomplishments of the late President Wilson and the Russian revolutionary *"Lenine."*

However, not everyone was pleased with the YPL activities. Reminiscing during a visit to Chizuk Amuno in February, 1950, Fred Katzner commented:

> *There were some who frowned upon the Young People's League on the grounds that it was mainly a social organization. It was even referred to by some as a matrimonial bureau. It is true that many couples met here who were later to become man and wife. The charming young lady who is now my wife was introduced to me on the steps of the synagogue following one of our Sunday meetings. I know of no worthier purpose that a youth group can serve than to encourage young Jewish boys and girls to meet in the healthy environment of a synagogue....*

A talented collection of YPL members met every Tuesday evening to draft The Bulletin, their weekly publication. The first issue featured a photograph of Rabbi Adolph Coblenz on the cover, and noted that the rabbi would be *"delivering a most interesting series of addresses every Friday evening between 8 and 9 o'clock."* Edited by Maurice Azrael, Bernard Feiken, Herman Kling, and Leon Lachman, the four-page paper announced coming events, reviewed prior activities, reprinted sermon messages from Rabbi Coblenz, and published short humorous items:

Volume 1, Number 1; February 17, 1924
She – How much are your eggs?
Grocer – 40 cents a dozen, madam, and 30 cents a dozen for cracked ones.
She – Well, crack me a dozen.

Volume 2, Number 13; December 20, 1924
Al Perry – How did you make out in your play the other night?
Al Blum – Great! After the first act they yelled "Fine!" After the second act, they yelled "Imprisonment!"

OrFail

Volume 2, Number 17; January 16, 1925

Sweet spirits of Victory! Our girls' basketball team defeated the Auchentoroly Bible Class team decisively, 34 to 15.

Volume 7, Number 2; February 20, 1927

Now comes our own little Hilda Miller and gets herself engaged to our own "Reds" Abramson. Ain't no use talking, this YPL is a great institution.

Annual YPL theatrical productions ranged from musical comedies and minstrel shows to original plays. Smaller shows were presented at the synagogue, but many plays appeared on stage at the Maryland Theatre on Franklin Street near Howard Street. Following his success with "Banging the Teakettle" in 1925, E. Milton Altfeld wrote "Chopped Trouble (Gehakte Tzarse)" for the YPL to perform in January, 1926. For three successive weeks, the Jewish Times published articles building anticipation for the amateur event:

- *It's going to be the best amateur theatrical production put on in Baltimore by any Jewish organization since the Ark and the Dove sailed up the Chesapeake Bay in 1633.*

- *It's going to be an evening of genuine fun and merriment of a superlative nature. Nothing tawdry, cheap, tinseled with the artificiality of burlesque or buffoonery, but striking comedy of a satirical nature that will stimulate and set one thinking.*

- *Then there is Hugo Weisgal, 13-year-old son of Cantor Weisgal of the Chizuk Emuno Synagogue, displayed histrionic talent of a high order. He has assurance, a self-possession that would do justice to many a professional. His sangfroid manner coupled with his sweet singing voice bids fair to inspire his audience and bring him tumultuous acclaim.*

Over forty members of the YPL appeared on stage, including featured roles played by Albert Blum, Rosalee Nathanson, Miriam and Jack Sirasky, Lenny Trout, and Rebecca Melnicove. The YPL shows created lifelong bonds between friends that would inspire many members to remain active leaders of Chizuk Amuno in the decades to come. Milton Altfeld became a prominent attorney and served as a Maryland State Senator. His creative talents passed from the YPL to the emerging Chizuk Amuno Brotherhood.

First mention of forming a Chizuk Amuno Brotherhood is noted in the Board minutes of April 27, 1921: *"consider the organizing of a young men's Brotherhood in our Congregation as the need for such an organization was felt for a long time."* In 1925, the Brotherhood was formally organized under the leadership of Charles Abramson. After experiencing difficulties, the group was reorganized through the efforts of Leslie Moses, grandson of M.S. Levy. In November, 1927 twelve men met for dinner and a lecture delivered by author Herman Bernstein at Moses' home. The men discussed rejuvenating the Brotherhood and elected Leslie Moses as president, Charles Abramson, vice-president, William Schimmel, secretary, and Solomon Rogers, treasurer. From that date forward, the Chizuk Amuno Brotherhood sponsored a variety of educational, cultural, religious, and fund-raising programs aimed at strengthening fellowship between the men of the Congregation and providing financial support for synagogue projects.

Chizuk Amuno members continued to be a guiding force in the development of Baltimore's charitable institutions. In 1921, while serving as Executive Secretary of the Associated, Louis H. Levin organized the Jewish Children's Society of Maryland by consolidating the Hebrew Orphans Asylum and the Hebrew Children's Sheltering and Protective Association. Long-time friend Dr. Edgar Friedenwald joined Levin in the campaign to stress educational priorities for homeless children. Friedenwald served as the chairman of Chizuk Amuno's School Board from 1912 until 1923, and held the position of chief of pediatrics at Hebrew Hospital. The men reviewed plans for a new children's home, to be located in the Mt.

Washington area of Baltimore, which would include playgrounds, orchards, and a vegetable garden.

Unfortunately, Louis Levin became ill a year later and died on April 21, 1923, at age fifty-seven. Reaction by the Jewish community was swift and intense. Levin's sister-in-law, Henrietta Szold, was visiting New York from her home in Palestine and arrived in Baltimore hours before Levin's death. Alexandra Lee Levin reprinted a letter Szold sent to her sister, Rachel Jastrow, who had been unable to attend the funeral:

The Baltimore community is sharing Bertha's grief as though it...had suffered a personal loss. The services were simple enough, only psalms and a traditional prayer. Bertha had requested...the rabbi of Louis' congregation not to pronounce a eulogy. But the community as a whole begged her to allow Mr. Sydney Nyburg to speak in its name. With noble simplicity he described the love of the community for Louis, almost as though he were a son speaking of his father, between whom the generations had created a bridge and in no ways a gulf. At the end he pronounced a pledge for the community, that it would remain in the path in which he had set its feet, faithful to his enlightened ideas and ideals.

On April 24, 1923, an editorial printed in the Morning Sun expressed how Levin's death had affected the entire field of charitable activity in Baltimore and that *"the Associated Jewish Charities is, in a sense, a memorial to his personality, ability and character."* The most permanent acknowledgement of this prominent Chizuk Amuno Board member's efforts came shortly after his death. At its dedication on September 30, 1923, the children's home that Levin had envisioned was named "Levindale." In the last few years of Louis Levin's life, he and Edgar Friedenwald had gradually placed many of the children living in the orphan asylum into foster homes. In 1929, the final placement was made, and the buildings of Levindale became the Hebrew Home and Infirmary for the Aged.

Since the founding of the United Synagogue of America in 1913, Chizuk Amuno had sent a representative to each Annual Convention. In April, 1926 the Congregation played host to the Fourteenth Annual Convention and its 1,000 delegates from 200 organizations. Several pages of the April 16, 1926 issue of the <u>Jewish Times</u> were devoted to welcoming the arriving delegates and informing the community of their goals. Chizuk Amuno president Milton Fleischer served as chairman of the convention's Executive Committee, and greeted the delegates to the opening session held at the Hippodrome Theatre. Fleischer stressed adherence to traditional teachings in his remarks, saying:

> *We must know our Judaism, its message and significance. We must absorb ourselves into the comprehensive sources of Judaism and obtain renewed inspiration and a proper sense of the true values of Israel's spiritual heritage...Only by holding fast to the ancient moorings can we continue to be a civilizing force in the progress of mankind.*

Meetings were held at the Emerson Hotel and Chizuk Amuno synagogue. Women's League members gathered to focus on what their national president Mrs. Charles Hoffman termed, *"the Jewish woman, the Jewish child, the Jewish home and the Jewish future."* Sponsored by the combined support of the Sisterhoods of Chizuk Amuno, Shaarei Tfiloh, Shaarei Zion, Beth Tfiloh, and Har Zion Congregations, the women delegates were treated to a reception and tea in their honor. On the final day of the conference, hundreds of delegates boarded chartered trains and traveled to the White House for a reception with President Calvin Coolidge, and a sightseeing tour of the Capitol.

Sale Of McCulloh Street Property

It took two years to find a buyer for the McCulloh Street synagogue. On February 12, 1924, the Board executed a Deed of Sale transferring the building to Robert J. Young for the price of $50,000, payable six thousand dollars at the time of settlement and the balance in mortgage debt. Young signed a letter to the Congregation clearly stating his intended use of the building:

> IT IS HEREBY AGREED that the property situated on the Northeast corner of Mosher and McCulloh Streets, which I have contracted to purchase, will not be used by me as a place of public worship or stable. It is my intention to use this property as a music hall, and I hereby agree to the aforegoing use for this property.

Real estate agent J.C. Martien graciously donated his commission of $681.25 back to the synagogue.

Unfortunately, Young's plans for a music hall fell through within weeks of settlement. The owner of several orchestras in the United States and Europe, Young had planned to combine them in Baltimore, forming a symphony orchestra of African-American musicians. The Baltimore Sun of May 12, 1924 announced the disappointing news: "Negro Buys Temple – Drops Music Plans – Use of Building Uncertain." Later that year, Young resold the McCulloh Street property to the Metropolitan Baptist Church. When quarterly payments due to Chizuk Amuno became delinquent, the Congregation was strapped for cash to pay their own Eutaw Street mortgage. The Board was periodically forced to delay payment of interest to holders of their 6% Gold Second Mortgage Bond coupons. In the following years, several members who had purchased these bonds returned them to the Congregation as gifts. Board member Julius Levy donated $6,000 worth of Gold Bonds in December, 1924. To assure the bank that the outstanding debt of Chizuk Amuno had been reduced, retired bonds were taken to the Maryland Trust Company and cremated in the presence of witnesses. By June 15, 1925 the total debt due to banks and bondholders had swelled to $185,000.

State Senator Harry O. Levin and Mr. Reuben Oppenheimer, Esq. were invited to attend a Board meeting on November 21, 1927 when it was decided to *"take out a decree against Robert J. Young and Harry W. Young but not advertise this action, less results are obtained."* Three weeks later, Oppenheimer reported that he had negotiated an arrangement with the bank not to foreclose on the Mosher and McCulloh Street property. Chizuk Amuno's involvement with their prior synagogue property ended in 1939 when the Hopkins Bank notified the Board that it was foreclosing on the Metropolitan Baptist Church.

Chizuk Amuno was not the only synagogue struggling under the burden of mortgage debt. Elaborate synagogues were under construction in major Jewish communities throughout the country as lay leaders postulated that lavish synagogues and renown cantors would lead new members to their doors. However, these projections proved erroneous as the flow of Jewish immigrants from Eastern Europe was virtually halted in 1924. Anti-Semitic comments from influential people, such as industrialist Henry Ford, and the activities of the Klu Klux Klan, incited the public to fear the invasion of immigrants into the American workplace. Congress reacted by passing the Johnson Immigration Act, severely restricting the migration of Jews from Eastern European areas and quashing any chance for further dramatic growth in the Jewish community.

Much needed financial support came from sizable gifts granted to the Congregation in the form of legacies. As the years passed, older members died but remembered Chizuk Amuno in their wills. Many less wealthy congregants established memorial funds for their deceased parents, spouses, and children to assure that someone would recite Kaddish for their family members. The names and yahrzeits of loved ones were recorded in the permanent Chizuk Amuno Memorial Book for a fee of $100. Other contributions included 200 prayerbooks from Abraham Cummins, a piano from the YPL, and $1,000 provided by the Sisterhood's 1927 Purim banquet.

One of the most generous bequests was that of Julius Levy, youngest son of Chizuk Amuno founder M.S. Levy, and a devoted member of the Congregation. At age fifty-eight, Levy's death on November 22, 1926 was a shock to the entire Baltimore community. An astute businessman, Levy had recently been elected president of the National Association of Men's Straw Hat Manufacturers and actively served on the boards of several banks, The Baltimore Museum of Art, Baltimore Hebrew College, Mount Pleasant Sanatorium, and The Associated Jewish Charities. His dedication as a builder of Baltimore's Jewish communal organizations was legendary. Besides liberal donations to many causes, Levy's will stipulated that $25,000 was to be applied to the unpaid mortgage balance of Chizuk Amuno.

After the synagogue construction frenzy of the 1920's, Baltimore's Jews no longer assembled for community events at privately owned locations such as Lehmann's Hall, but rather convened for public rallies and memorials at synagogues. One of the most elaborate complexes, Chizuk Amuno was frequently asked for permission to use their assembly rooms. On Wednesday, April 1, 1925, a citywide celebration was held in the Chizuk Amuno auditorium in honor of the dedication of the Hebrew University of Jerusalem. Dr. Harry Friedenwald had been instrumental in the establishment of the institution as had Abba Weisgal's brother, Meyer. Hadassah chapters, Zionist groups, and agencies of the Associated Jewish Charities were among those requesting use of rooms. Chizuk Amuno also hosted the 1929 Community Thanksgiving Service, held in conjunction with the Madison Avenue Temple (Baltimore Hebrew), the Eutaw Place Temple, and the Bolton Street Temple. With each event, Chizuk Amuno reinforced its reputation as one of the most notable congregations in Baltimore.

Introduction Of Ritual Changes

The need to bolster membership levels prompted the Board to consider minor changes to the rituals of Chizuk Amuno. Few members still had first-hand memories of the strict ritual interpretations that the founders established sixty years earlier. Surprisingly, it was William Levy, son of founder M.S. Levy, who made the suggestion at the Annual Meeting in December, 1928, to have more prayers recited in English. A new Ritual Committee composed of the rabbi, cantor, and three Board members was established *"for the purpose of suggesting changes in prayers at our services."* Over the next two years, those changes included limiting each Torah reader to one *"Mi Sheberach and El Mole Rachamin"* and limiting the rabbi's sermons to thirty minutes and *"his address to Barmizva Boys to five (5) minutes."* Time concerns also prompted the suggestion that Shabbat services begin at 8:30 a.m. (instead of 8:00 a.m.), the Ashrei be read in either English or Hebrew, the Prayer for the Government be omitted, and *"when pressed for time, the silent reading of Mussaf eliminated."*

In 1924, the Board approved conducting the Yizkor service in English and in 1931, the Ritual Committee suggested that the names on the memorial lists be read aloud only three times a year – Yom Kippur, Pesach and Shavuot – eliminating the fourth reading on Sukkot. Rabbi Coblenz wrote a touching Meditation to be recited during the Memorial Service on Yom Kippur. His work, "On Wings of Memory," remains as the title of the annual memorial volume printed at Yom Kippur.

The Board rejected one recommendation for ritual change before it was presented to the full membership for vote. Discussion at the March 9, 1931 Board meeting focused on allowing mourners to remain standing at their seats while Cantor Weisgal led them in reciting the Mourner's Kaddish. The proposal failed to pass and the tradition of having mourners assemble at the foot of the bimah to recite the prayer was continued. It would remain the procedure until the change was adopted in November, 1945.

To enhance the cohesiveness of the service, the Congregation decided to promote the use of one common prayerbook – the London edition of the Adler Machzor. Worshippers, accustomed to using their own books during services, were informed that copies of the prayerbook could be purchased through the synagogue office. In 1933, Milton Fleischer, Herbert Levy, Samuel Hoffberger, and Jacob I. Hamburger established an inventory of prayerbooks, each donating twenty-five copies to the synagogue in memory of their loved ones. Sexton Benjamin Erkes was instructed to place the books *"for public reach"* and to *"see that they are collected after use."*

A major change in the Congregation's organizational structure was instituted in 1934 as the positions of sexton and secretary were redefined. In May 1933, Benno Hummel, Secretary of the Congregation for the past twenty-three years, died suddenly. Three months later, Joseph Weinstein was engaged to serve as secretary for a six-month probationary period that ultimately led to a twenty-two year position with Chizuk Amuno. In May, 1934 Benjamin Erkes, sexton for the previous twenty-six years, submitted his resignation letter in which he stated:

> *I am not leaving the cong. for materialistic motives but purely for idealistic – to live in Eretz Israel – the practical expression of our synagogical service. Sorry as I am to part with you, I nevertheless can't ignore the call within me to come to the embraced arms of our Holy Land. May God bless you and enable you to continue to work for the spiritual values of Israel, our land and our Torah.*

Before a replacement sexton was hired, the Board debated whether handling the finances, collections, and care of the synagogue was a full-time job. Joseph Weinstein agreed that these would be his responsibilities and that the sexton would be engaged to *"take care of matters pertaining to the religious life of the Congregation only. This man should also be the Baal Shachrith on the High Holidays and should know how to Leinen."* After interviewing six candidates, the Committee recommended that Hyman Bassan be elected *"to attend to all religious functions"* beginning on July 1, 1934 at an annual salary of $900. Bassan would remain with Chizuk Amuno as sexton for more than thirty years.

The School Board, now headed by Isaac Potts, struggled to maintain enrollment levels in the Sunday and Hebrew schools. Aware

LEADERS OF OTHER YEARS

Judah Rosewald
President, 1871—1879

Jonas Friedenwald
President, 1879—1892

Dr. Aaron Friedenwald
President, 1892—1902

Michael S. Levy
President, 1902—1911

Rev. Herman Glass
Cantor—1878 to 1921
Cantor Emeritus—1921

Dr. Harry Friedenwald
President, 1911—1920

William Levy
President, 1921

Dr. Henry W. Schneeberger
Rabbi, 1876—1912
Rabbi Emeritus—1912

Dr. Eugene Kohn
Rabbi, 1912—1918

Adolph Coblenz
Rabbi, 1920—

Page from 75th Anniversary commemorative program, 1946

Top left to right: Program from Consecration of Synagogue, 1876; Renovated synagogue on Lloyd Street. Bottom: Congregation sanctuary, Lloyd Street.

Clockwise from top left: Bet Hamidrash cash receipts ledger, 1887; Entry from minute book, April 1872; Rev. Dr. Henry Schneeberger.

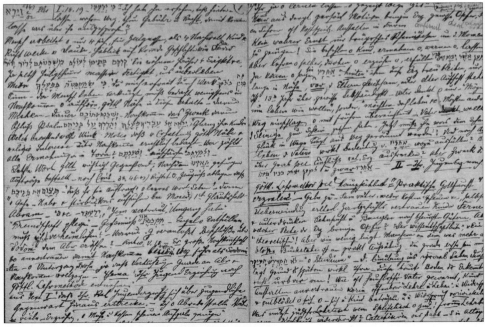

Top: Dr. and Sarah Schneeberger and family.
Bottom: Dr. Schneeberger's handwritten sermon notes.

Top left to right: Religious school award, ca. 1885; Receipt for tuition payment, 1902. Bottom: Program from Jonas Friedenwald's birthday tribute, 1891.

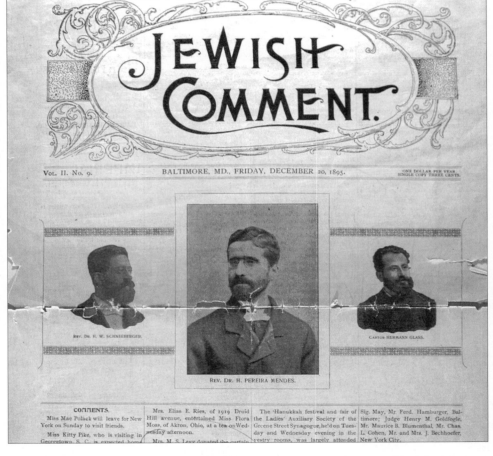

This page top: Synagogue at McCulloh and Mosher Streets, 1910. This page bottom: *Jewish Comment* issue dedicated to McCulloh Street synagogue, 1895. Facing page top: Men's seating assignments, 1916 and 1917; Facing page bottom: Women's seating assignments, 1916 and 1917.

Gent's

LEFT 1916

Bench 1917

Bench	#	1917		1916	
1	1				
	2				
	3				
	4				
	5				
3	1	A. S. Oppenheim	W	A. S. Oppenheim	W
	2	M. Robinson	W	S. Seidman	W
	3	L. Nathans	W	J. Tamboro	W
	4	Israel Tamboro	W	Chas Schueberg	F
	5	Isaac Tamboro	W	Sieg Schussberger	F
5	1	M. Goldberg	W	Meyer Goldberg	W
	2	M. Ruben	W	S. Seidman	W
	3	Sidney Seidman	W	Jos Levy	W
	4	A. Löwenberg	W	Chas Seidman	W
	5	Alfred Löwenberg	W	Sidney Seidman	W
7	1	M. Brownstein	W	M. Brownstein	W
	2	J. Brownstein	W	J. Brownstein	W
	3	L. Seidman	W	Max Bernstein	W
	4	L. Seidman	W	Jsc Shapiro	W
	5	Chas Seidman	W	H. Cantz	W

Gents

Right 1916

Bench 1917

Bench	#	1917		1916	
2	1	H. W. Finkenwald	—	H. W. Finkenwald	—
	2	B. B. Finkenwald	—	B. B. Finkenwald	—
	3	Isaac Raffel	—	Isaac Raffel	—
	4	Jacob M. Raffel	—	Jacob Raffel	—
	4	"	BL	Jacob Raffel	BL
4	1	E. Wolfram	—	E. Wolfram	—
	2	L. Wolfram	BL	L. Wolfram	BL
	3	Joe S. Moses	BL	Joe S. Moses	B.
	4	A. S. Weinberg	—	A. S. Weinberg	—
	5	J. L. Weinberg	BL	J. L. Weinberg	B.
6	1	Benj. Fleischman	BL	Benj. Fleischman	B
	2	Silas Fleisch	BL	Silas Fleisch	B
	3	Isaac Rotz	BL	M. Greenblatt	
	4	A. B. Hirschman	—	"	E
	5	A. B. Hirschman	BL	" "	
8	1	A. Jacobs	BL	A. Jacob	B.
	2	A. Jacobs	BL	A. Jacob	B.
	3	J. Freedman	—	A. S. Hirschman	
	4	F. S. Sachs	—	" "	B.
	5	Simon Lennon	BL	"	B

16

Ladies

Left

First Row

Bench	#	1917		1916	
1	1	Mrs H. W. Schussberger	F	Mrs H. W. Schussberger	F
	2	" H. Clar	F	" H. Harri	F
	3	" E. Kohn	F	" E. Kohn	F
	4	" S. Neuberger	—	" S. Neuberger	—
7	1	Mrs E. Wolfram	—	Mrs E. Wolfram	—
	2	" E. Eilau	BL	" E. Eilau	BL
	3	" Jae S. Moses	BL	" Jae S. Moses	BL
	4	" E. H. Friedl	—	" E. H. Fried	—
13	1	Mrs A. Harris	—	Mrs A. Harris	—
	2	Miss Hannah Harris	BL	Miss Hannah Harris	BL
	3	Mrs R. Bernstein	—	Mrs R. Bernstein	—
	4	" S. Wolman	—	" S. Wolman	—
19	1	Mrs Max Cohen	BE	Mrs Max Cohen	BE
	2	Miss Bertha Cohen	—	Mrs Ch. Abramson	—
	3	" M. Wyman	BL	" M. Wyman	BL
	4	" M. Ortz	BL	" M. Ortz	BL
25	1	Mrs M. Pincus	—	Mrs M. Pincus	—
	2	" A. B. Hirschman	—	" A. B. Hirschman	—
	3	" Philip Lewin	—	" Ph. Lewin	—

17

Ladies

Right

First Row

Bench	#	1917		1916	
2	1	Mrs Milton Fleischer	—	Mrs Milton Fleischer	—
	2	" Miss Fleischer	—	Miss Fleischer	—
	3	" Emile Clarke	—	Bertha Blumkleim	BL
	4	" Blau Hummel	—	" Blau W. Hummel	—
8	1	Mrs B. Ottman	—	Mrs B. Ottman	—
	2	" H. Finkenwald	—	" H. Finkenwald	—
	3	" E. B. Finkenwald	—	" E. B. Finkenwald	—
	4	" A. Finkenwald	—	" A. Finkenwald	—
14	1	Mrs Fanny Rosenfelt	—	Mrs Fanny Rosenfelt	—
	2	" Max Sketch	—	" Max Sketch	—
	3	" Mamie E. Hecht	—	" Mamie E. Hecht	—
	4	Miss Celia Rosman	—	Miss Celia Rosman	—
20	1	Mrs Isaac Epstein	—	Mrs Isaac Epstein	—
	2	" Julia Levy	—	" Julia Levy	—
	3	" William Levy	—	" William Levy	—
	4	" Rose Moses	—	" Rose Moses	—
26	1	Mrs Jacob Levy	BL	Mrs Jac. Levy	BL
	2	" Ralph L. Epstein	—	" Ralph L. Epstein	—
	3	" Mrs B. H. Finkenwald	—	" B. H. Finkenwald	—

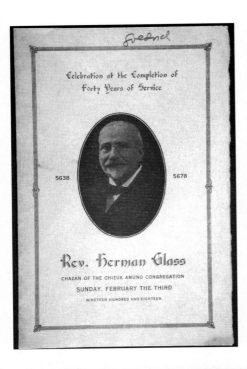

Celebration at the Completion of
Forty Years of Service

5638   5678

Rev. Herman Glass

CHAZAN OF THE CHIZUK AMUNO CONGREGATION

SUNDAY, FEBRUARY THE THIRD

NINETEEN HUNDRED AND EIGHTEEN

Chizuk Ammo Congregation

+

INSTALLATION SERVICES

OF

Rabbi Eugene Kohn

+

FRIDAY, SEPTEMBER 6, 1912

8.15 P. M.

Program

1. (מה טובו) "How goodly are thy tents, O, Jacob!" . . . . Rev. H. Glass
2. Installation Address . . . . Solomon Schechter
   Prest. of the Jewish Theological Seminary, N. Y.
3. Sermon—ובחרת בחיים "And thou shalt choose life" . . . . . Rabbi Eugene Kohn
4. Address . . . . Rabbi Jacob Kohn
   Of New York
5. Address . . . . Rev. Dr. H. W. Schneeberger
6. (יגדל) "Extolled be the living God" . . . . . . Rev. H. Glass and Congregation

On Sabbath morning, September 7th, the Sermon will be delivered by
Rabbi Charles I. Hoffman, of Newark, N. J.

Facing page clockwise from top left: Program from tribute to Rev. Herman Glass, 1918; Program from Rabbi Eugene Kohn's installation, 1912; Inside of program from Rabbi Eugene Kohn's installation. This page top: Synagogue at Eutaw Place and Chauncey Avenue; Bottom: "Festival of Synagogue Music," Eutaw Place synagogue, 1954.

Chizuk Amuno Celebrates Tenth Anniversary of New Synagogue

Banquet and Entertainment in the Vestry, Monday, May 23; History of Congregation to be Dramatized; Rabbi Elias Margolis of Mt. Vernon, N. Y., to Deliver Address

Congregation Chizuk Amuno will gather in the vestry of its synagogue on Monday, May 23, at 6.30 in order to celebrate the tenth anniversary of its occupancy of the new synagogue on Eutaw Place and Chauncey Avenue by means of a banquet followed by appropriate entertainment.

This anniversary marks the passing of sixty-one very eventful years in the history of Congregation Chizuk Amuno. The history is the record of a growth from small but vigorous beginnings to a position of representative distinction in the community of

Chizuk Amuno Synagogue

ADOLPH J. WEISGAL, Cantor

RABBI ADOLPH COBLENZ

Baltimore and, indeed, of American Israel.

Chizuk Amuno originated in 1871 in a secession by a few vigorous, staunchly traditional minded personalities from the Baltimore Hebrew Congregation of which, until then, they had been members. The cause for this secession was the introduction by the Mother Congregation of innovations in the service which the uncompromising traditionalism of these inflexible men could not accept. On April 2, 1871, Mr. Jonas Friedenwald called a meeting in the Beth Hamidrash at Exeter Hall. At this meeting Chizuk Amuno was organized. It is certainly not without interest to preserve the memory of those men who constituted the Chizuk Amuno Congregation at its inception. The following men were present and started this new congregation:

Isaac Arnold, Simon Altmyer, Jacob Behrends, Samuel Bergman, Raphael Berliner, Jonas Friedenwald, Joseph Friedenwald, Isaac Friedenwald, Moses Friedenwald, Asher Heilner, H. S. Hartogensis, Philip Hersberg, Tobias Harts, Morris Levy, Samuel Neuberger, Herts Oppenheimer, Nathan Oppenheimer, Judah Rosewald, Moses Rosenthal, Benjamin Stern, Benjamin Simon, Samuel Sondheimer, Marcus Weil.

At this same meeting the officers of the new congregation were elected. They were: President, Judah Rosewald; vice-president, Jonas Friedenwald; treasurer, Tobias Harts; secretary, Mr. H. S. Hartogensis.

In 1876 the congregation removed to its home on Lloyd Street, where it continued to worship for almost 20 years.

The synagogue on McCulloh and

MILTON FLEISCHER, President

Mosher Streets was dedicated in 1895, and remained the home of the congregation until the present building was erected on Eutaw Place and Chauncey Avenue in 1921.

The spiritual leadership of the congregation was in the care of the Rev. Dr. Henry W. Schneeberger, who was rabbi of the congregation from 1876 until his death in 1916. He was succeeded in 1912 by Rabbi Eugene Kohn, who in turn was succeeded in 1920 by Rabbi Adolph Coblenz.

The first cantor of the congregation was Rev. Mr. Heilner. In 1881 Cantor Herman Glass became the Chazan of Congregation Chizuk Amuno. He ministered for 43 years until his decease in 1925. In 1921 he was succeeded by the present cantor, Adolph J. Weisgal.

In the course of the years as the activities of the congregation expanded there was organized a daily Hebrew and Sunday School, a Sisterhood, a Brotherhood and a Young People's League. There were also added new activities within the range of congregational work; the Friday Evening Assembly, the institution of having a

scholar learn at the services in the Beth Hamidrash, morning and evening. The last addition to the program of congregational activities is the organization of a Sisterhood Cultural Group which has taken place this year.

The present officers of the congregation are: Milton Fleischer, president; Siegfried Neuberger, vice-president; Charles Katz, treasurer; Benno Hummel, secretary. The Board of Directors of the congregation consists of the above officers and the following: Ralph L. Ephraim,

BENNO HUMMEL, Secretary

Samuel H. Hoffberger, William Katz, Samuel Levy, Isaac Potts, Kauffman Waskins, Maurice Robinson, Herman Scherr, I. William Schimmel, Israel Silberstein, Morris Stulman.

Congregation Chizuk Amuno has throughout its career of distinction remained a fortress of Traditional Judaism and has been prominently identified with all important endeavors—both local and national in scope that make for social betterment—for the enlargement of Israel and for the deepening of our sacred faith.

The celebration Monday night will

include as its major features a dramatization of sister years of Chizuk Amuno history, followed by an address given by the famous Rabbi Elias Margolis of Mt. Vernon, N. Y.

Prologue

Fred E. Katzner .... Milton Fleischer, Pres.
Millard Jeffries .... Bernard Mehldove.
Pres., Y.P.L.

First Episode

William Feld .... Rabbi Abr. Hoffman
Michael J. Bronstein .... Martin L. Strauss
Hugo Weisgal .... Meyer Stein
Benjamin Feiken .... Aaron Frank
Nathan Harris .... Jacob Rice
M. M. Slatkin .... Jonas Friedenwald
Benjamin Katzner .... Moses Wiesenfeld
I. Wm. Schimmel .... Judah Rosewald
Aaron Borden .... Simon Rosenfeld
Benjamin Katzner .... Rabbi H. W. Schneeberger

Modern Episode

M. M. Slatkin .... Milton Fleischer
Hugo Weisgal .... Siegfried Neuberger
Benjamin Feiken .... Charles Katz
Michael J. Bronstein .... Isaac Potts
William Feld .... Benno W. Hummel
David Kirtland .... Israel Silberstein
Aaron Borden .... Herman Scherr
Nathan Harris .... Ralph Ephraim
I. Wm. Schimmel .... I. Wm. Schimmel
Sam Moore .... Sam Levy
.... Sam, the Janitor
.... K. Waskins
Director, David N. Fleck

"Help your wife," says John Miller, the famous domestic expert; "when she mops up the floor, mop up the floor with her."

CHARLES KATZ, Treasurer

Jewish Times, 1932

THE CHIZUK AMUNO CONGREGATION

EXTENDS THIS INVITATION TO YOU AND YOUR FAMILY

TO BE PRESENT AT

THE DEDICATION CEREMONIES

OF THE

RABBI ADOLPH COBLENZ MEMORIAL PULPIT

TO BE HELD AT THE

OPENING LATE FRIDAY EVENING SERVICE

FRIDAY, NOVEMBER 3, 1950, AT 8:15 P. M.

AT THE SYNAGOGUE

EUTAW PLACE AND CHAUNCEY AVENUE

Clockwise from top: Meeting of trustees, Eutaw
Place, 1946; Invitation to Coblenz Memorial Pulpit
dedication, 1950; Coblenz Memorial Pulpit, Eutaw
Place.

BROTHERHOOD DINNER
TO
MILTON FLEISCHER, PRESIDENT.
APRIL 7, 1930.

CHIZUK AMUNO BROTHERHOOD
Presents the
EUTAW PLACE SCANDALS

Conceived and Produced by
FRED E. KATZNER AND ALVIN NEUBERGER

Directed by
MORTIMER MURRAY SLATKIN

Dances by ETTA STULMAN

Costumes designed by ADRIENNE

Orchestra under the direction of LOU SEIDENMAN

ACT I

1. OVERTURE
2. "WE KNOW"
   Sung by Bobby Louise Cook
   of Lou Becker's Penthouse
   Lyrics: Buff Elias
   Music: Lou Seidenman
3. "COLLEGE RHYTHM"
   Danced by
   Etta Stulman and Manny Fine
   and the Young Ladies
4. THREE SKITLETS
   by Fred E. Katzner
   a. At the Zoo
   b. At the Back Door
   c. At Home
   Played by
   Rena Frieman, Sophia Kaufman,
   Jack Willen, David Kurland, Hilda
   Preissman, Harold Kropman, Mignon Bank, Buff Elias
5. "YOU'RE A LAWYER"
   Goldman ....Max Shavrik
   Pincus, his lawyer......Nathan Harris
   Policeman ....Fred Sapperstein
   1st Judge...................Buff Elias
   2nd Judge..............Alan Klompus
   Warden ....Jack Willen
   Wife ....Sophia Kaufman
6. "QUARTET FROM EUTAW"
   Samuel Harfeld
   Irvin Levin
   Hugo Weissgall
   David Kurland
7. A TOUCH OF COLOR
   Danced by
   The Night Hawk

8. EVELYN LANE
   In a
   Cycle of Songs
9. "WHILE ROME BURNS"
   Bob ....Murray Slatkin
   Ed ....Alan Klompus
   1st Fireman ....David Kurland
   2nd Fireman ....Nathan Harris
   Bell-Boy ....Harold Kropman
10. KEN LANE and EDYTHE CARRALL
    Those Eccentric Dancers
    Direct from the Fox Studios
11. "BLACK AND WHITE"
    WFBR Radio Artists
    Sarah Stulman   Selma Tiefenbrun
12. "29"
    The Broker............Murray Slatkin
    Bill Webb...............David Kurland
    Boy ....Harold Kropman
13. DON CARLOS
    Noted Operatic Tenor
    Accompanied by......Sarah Stulman
14. "FOR ALL WE KNOW"
    Prologue
    Mitzi Salit, Helen Glasser,
    Carolyn Cohen
    Mother ....Ruth Finkel
    Son ....Alan Klompus
    Girl ....Mignon Bank
    Father ....Fred Sapperstein
    Maid ....Sophia Kaufman

INTERMISSION

ACT II

1. HERBERT SOKOLOVE
   Violinist Extraordinaire
2. "THE PRIDE OF THE SOUTH"
   Jasper ....Jack Willen
   The Colonel.............David Kurland
   His Wife..................Mignon Bank
   His Daughter..........Rena Frieman
   Her Suitor...............Jerry Schloss
   Caras ....Nathan Harris
   Martin ....Fred Sapperstein
3. EVELYN CALMEN
   In
   Soft-Shoe Stepping
4. ALMA METCALFE
   Songs With a Violin
5. "THREE MORE SKITLETS"
   a. Buy American
   b. My Error
   c. True To The End
   Played by
   Alan Klompus, Fred Sapperstein,
   David Kurland, Max Shavrick, Buff
   Elias, Selma Berkow, Harold Kropman.
6. "MOOD INDIGO"
   Danced by
   Etta Stulman
   and the Young Ladies
7. "THAT EUTAW QUARTET"
   More Harmony

8. "THE FIRE-FIGHTERS"
   By Buff Elias
   The Chief...........Fred Sapperstein
   Schwitsky ....Buff Elias
   Kibitzer ....Max Shavrick
   Shleppermean ......Harold Kropman
   Lapides ....Jack Willen
9. BOBBY LOUISE COOK
   Lovely Singer of Songs
   From Lou Becker's Penthouse
10. JEAN SAVAGE
    Youthful Rhythm
11. THE INEVITABLE BED-ROOM SCENE
    (At Last)
    by
    and Fred E. Katzner
    Prologue
    Sylvia Stark, Carolyn Cohen, Helen
    Glasser, Mitzi Salit, Eppie Bernstein,
    Mindel Kaufman.
    Wife ....Hilda Preissman
    Son ....Buff Elias
    Husband ....David M. Kurland
    Lazarus ....Max Shavrick
12. DON CARLOS
    With
    Sarah Stulman at the Piano
13. CAFE DE SCANDALLES

FINALE

THE YOUNG LADIES

Eppie Bernstein	Rosalind Kolan	Selma Tyser
Carolyn Cohen	Selma Marks	Jane Schwartz
Helen Glasser	Ethel Miller	Sylvia Stark
Mindel Kaufman	Mitzi Salit	Tootie Weinstock

Stage Manager...ALAN KLOMPUS
Assistant Stage Manager..................BERNARD NACHLAS
Scenic Manager..............................BERNARD ARONSON
Property Manager..............................HAROLD PRISSMAN
Assistant Property Manager..........J. NORMAN MUNAKER
Wardrobe Master..................................JOEL COOPER
Assistant Wardrobe Mistress....................FERN OLINER

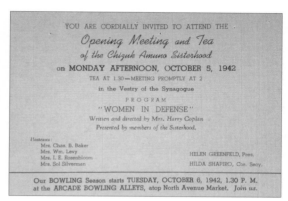

YOU ARE CORDIALLY INVITED TO ATTEND THE

Opening Meeting and Tea

of the Chizuk Amuno Sisterhood

on **MONDAY AFTERNOON, OCTOBER 5, 1942**

TEA AT 1.30—MEETING PROMPTLY AT 2

in the Vestry of the Synagogue

PROGRAM

"WOMEN IN DEFENSE"

Written and directed by Mrs. Harry Coplan

Presented by members of the Sisterhood.

Hostesses
Mrs. Chas. B. Baker
Mrs. Wm. Levy
Mrs. I. E. Rosenbloom   HELEN GREENFELD, Pres.
Mrs. Sol Silverman   HILDA SHAPIRO, Cor. Secy.

Our BOWLING Season starts TUESDAY, OCTOBER 6, 1942, 1.30 P. M.
at the ARCADE BOWLING ALLEYS, atop North Avenue Market. *Join us.*

Facing page top: Brotherhood dinner, Eutaw Place, 1930; Bottom: "Eutaw Place Scandels," 1935. This page clockwise from top left: Ticket to "Night of Fun," 1943; Announcement of Sisterhood meeting, 1942; Cast of Sisterhood play, 1940s.

Your
Shule and
Your
School

The Chain Must Remain Unbroken

GIVE YOUR CHILD
A JEWISH EDUCATION

in the

CHIZUK AMUNO SCHOOL

EUTAW PLACE *and* CHAUNCEY AVE.
BALTIMORE, MD.

Hebrew School re-opens Tuesday, September 3, 1940
Sunday School re-opens Sunday, September 8, 1940
REGISTRATION: SEPTEMBER 3 to 15, 1940

Top: School promotional pamphlet, 1940;
Bottom: Faculty luncheon honoring Sarah Sachs,
Eutaw Place, 1943. Facing page top: Nursery
school class, School Annex on Eutaw and
Whitelock Streets; Bottom: Religious school
class, Enslow Avenue, 1952.

Top: *Bulletin* announcing Rabbi Israel M. Goldman's selection, 1948; Bottom: Rabbi Goldman's personal work book, 1948.

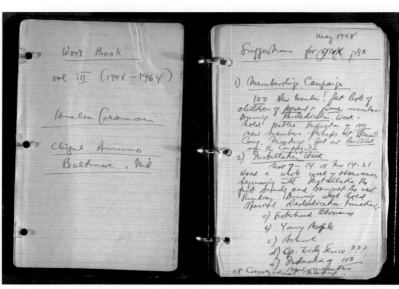

that some families sent their daughters to Reform congregational schools, attracted by their Confirmation Services, the Board discussed the possibility of holding similar services for the graduating girls of the Sunday School. Rabbi Coblenz strongly supported this idea, commenting at a Board meeting on May 12, 1930 that it would encourage girls to continue studying into their teen years. The Sisterhood handled the arrangement for Chizuk Amuno's first Confirmation Service held on June 2, 1930, the first day of Shavuot, before the singing of Ein Ke-elohenu. Nine girls participated in the short service. In 1935, requirements for confirmation were refined to include regulations that the girls must be fourteen and have attended Chizuk Amuno schools for at least two continuous years prior to confirmation.

Generous patrons, including Solomon Rosenbloom, continually made directed contributions to cover financial shortfalls in the religious schools. The Sisterhood and Congregation joined together to fund the balance of the school deficit. On May 19, 1931, the School Board met to discuss the qualifications of a candidate for principal. Dr. Louis Kaplan had recommended Hymen Saye, a teacher at the Baltimore Talmud Torah. Rabbi Coblenz supported the recommendation, reporting *"Mr. Saye to be a gentleman of 26, Hopkins pupil with executive ability and the type of man which should appeal to our children attending school."* Offered a salary of $1,800, Saye began his tenure as religious school principal on September 1, 1931 – a role he would serve for the next forty years.

As the country headed towards depressed economic conditions, Chizuk Amuno faced mounting financial concerns. Members suffering business reverses found it necessary to suspend their support of congregational fund-raising. In September, 1930 Meyer Abramson petitioned the Board in writing for a reduction of his membership dues and seat rental fees, ending his letter with the comment, *"I have always worked very hard for the schule, and my heart is still with it one hundred per cent."* With annual dues set at $56 and membership wavering around 180, it became increasingly difficult to meet the expenses of managing the synagogue. At the Semi-Annual Congregational Meeting on June 9, 1930, the following annual salaries were approved:

Rabbi Adolph Coblenz as Rabbi & Lecturer at $6,500
Rev. Adolph J. Weisgal as Cantor & Bal Koreah at $5,000
Benjamin Erkes as Sexton & Collector at $1,400 and 10% Commissions on all collections given to him by the Secretary
Benno W. Hummel as financial & recording Secretary at $1,200
The Choir shall be retained at a salary of $3,000

In April, 1932, recognizing that the Congregation was in dire financial straits, Coblenz and Weisgal voluntarily offered to reduce their salaries by ten percent. The Board accepted their offer, but at a meeting only one month later discussed the need to cut salaries even further. The rabbi's contract was renewed at $5,000, the cantor's contract at $4,000, the sexton's at $1,000, and the secretary's at $900. At the May 9, 1932 Board meeting, President Fleischer issued an emergency call for cash:

In order to pay our monthly payroll, the following sums were advanced:

Milton Fleischer $250
Isaac Potts $150
Ralph L. Ephraim $100
Charles Katz $100
Wm. Katz $100
Herman Scherr $50
Samuel Levy $50

In order to gather pledges, the Board decided to sponsor a banquet in honor of the tenth anniversary of the Eutaw Place synagogue. The May 23, 1932 dinner was followed by a satirical play written by Fred Katzner depicting the history of Chizuk Amuno from 1871 to

1932. An article printed in the <u>Jewish Times</u> of May 20, 1932 summarized the history of the sixty-one-year-old congregation, calling its current status *"a position of representative distinction in the community of Baltimore and, indeed, of American Israel."* Rabbi Elias Margolis of Mt. Vernon, New York delivered the keynote address.

Cantor Weisgal served as the head of the Membership and Seating Committees and canvassed the neighborhood in search of unaffiliated Jews. He was intimately involved with the inner workings of the Congregation and sincerely interested in its success. Attached to the Minute Book is a letter dated September 16, 1930, in which Weisgal humbly proposed changing the process of collecting unpaid amounts from members and seatholders. At the time, collection efforts consisted of a series of progressively threatening letters. Weisgal commented that members became insulted by the dunning system and resigned in anger. He suggested that a committee be sent to make a personal appeal for the balance due. If a resignation was received, Weisgal recommended sending the same committee to discuss the reasons for the resignation and attempt to have the member reconsider his decision. In closing, the cantor offered an apology *"if I by any chance have overstepped my rights in offering these suggestions."*

Increased sensitivity was not enough to overcome the economic effects of the Depression. Long-standing members petitioned the Board for special allowance in order to maintain their affiliation. In August, 1933 Morris Stulman requested permission to pay $50 per year for his four seats instead of the standard $28 per seat until *"business conditions improve."* Young adults were not joining in sufficient numbers to offset the deaths of older members. Membership figures plummeted from 188 in 1926, to 140 as of June, 1934. Attendance at services and enrollment in the religious school dropped significantly. Once again, the Sisterhood was summoned by the Board to urge their husbands, grown sons, and daughters to attend services. An atmosphere of general apathy settled over the Congregation. Annual Purim and Chanukah Banquets were still orchestrated by the Sisterhood and Brotherhood, but attendance at Junior Congregation services had slipped to an average of twenty-five. In an effort to arouse spiritual devotion in 1934, Rabbi Coblenz requested that the Board approve the continuation of Friday Night Assemblies, which had been suspended to save money. To assess interest, members and seatholders were surveyed – eighty-five percent did not bother to respond.

Although the Board was quick to ask for Sisterhood support, they rarely accepted advice from the women. On October 21, 1935, the Board read a letter from the Sisterhood making the following suggestions:

- *Bookracks be installed in the last two benches on both sides of the ladies section*
- *Ventilators be placed in the windows of the main auditorium*
- *Amplifiers be installed*
- *Children's services be held on the High Holidays in the Vestry*

As could be expected, the Board announced their decisions that:

- Bookracks would *"be taken care of in due time"*
- A committee would investigate the matter of ventilators
- Amplifiers were *"unnecessary in our synagogue, and would be undignified to our services,"* and
- A children's service *"would be impractical, uneducational and that it would create a lot of commotion to the services of the synagogue"*

Frustrated with their lack of influence, the women decided to seek a position on the Board of Trustees. Their formal request for Board representation was read into the minutes of March 22, 1937. Discussion ensued and the decision was reached that *"since the Constitution does not provide for such a representative,"* the request would not be granted. Six years would pass before the Sisterhood repeated their request for Board appointment. Meanwhile, they would have to be satisfied with two seats on the School Board.

The Brotherhood advocated a second tier of membership to stimulate affiliation. On November 8, 1937, Board member Isaac

Potts introduced a motion to create a Junior Membership at the Board meeting. Dues of $25 would entitle a Junior Member to one seat, but no voting privileges. This discounted membership was only open to Brotherhood members, unmarried men under thirty-five and married men under thirty. The motion passed unanimously.

Heading Towards War

Rabbi Coblenz often spent his summer vacations traveling throughout Europe or the Middle East. The Chizuk Amuno archives holds a letter written to a colleague after the rabbi vacationed in Europe in 1932. Ironically, that letter was addressed to Coblenz's future replacement, Rabbi Israel Goldman of Providence, Rhode Island:

> *I have just returned from Europe, about which I can say very little that is gladsome or happy. The shows were rotten – the sermons, if possible, worse – conditions generally punk, but the beer was good, and where there is good beer, there is hope.*

Unfortunately, conditions in Europe soon worsened well beyond "punk" as the National Socialist Party gained control of Germany in March, 1933. When the Nuremberg Laws restricting the civil and political rights of Jews were passed in 1935, the Jews of America could not help but ponder their own experiences with anti-Semitism in the past decade. Jewish enrollment at major universities had been limited as had enrollment in medical and law schools. Restrictive immigration acts passed in the 1920's remained intact as anti-alien sentiment grew with the Great Depression. In his book, The Politics of Rescue, Professor Henry L. Feingold comments on the psychological climate of the times:

> *Insecurity generated by the spread of virulent anti-Semitism abroad and at home was a prime ingredient of American Jewish life in the 1930's. ....Jews became aware that by example and by offering funds and leadership,*

the Nazi Party had succeeded in sparking a wave of do-
mestic anti-Semitism, which, when combined with the so-
cial tensions generated by the Depression, might undo
their hard-won gains.

Realizing that strong American Jewish identity was an essential factor in combating growing anti-Semitic attitudes, Rabbi Coblenz
used the pulpit to stress the need to maintain religious and cultural
bonds with fellow Jews around the world.

Re-emerging into the spotlight, Dr. Harry Friedenwald spent
tremendous energy attempting to raise awareness of the pending di-
saster in Europe. Friedenwald was instrumental in organizing the
Baltimore branch of the American Jewish Congress in its efforts to
protest injustices in Germany. Although the seriousness of the situation was reported in the New York newspapers, the Baltimore press
carried little coverage of actions against the Jews of Europe. Only
after Friedenwald and three others met with Sunpapers publisher
Hamilton Owens in April, 1933 did the paper begin publishing bits
of information. The following month Friedenwald addressed a group
of seven hundred leading bankers, industrialists, and professionals
to convey his perspective on the German situation as he had learned
it from correspondence with leading physicians and scientists in
Europe. He urged anyone who would listen to lobby Congress to
allow ten thousand Jewish children from Germany to immigrate to
the United States.

Chizuk Amuno continued its staunch support of Zionist activities. After a 1934 trip to Palestine, Coblenz delivered a stirring High
Holy Day message entitled, "The Wailing Wall and the Singing Wall"
in which he compared the suffering of centuries with the walls being
built for new homes and schools in Tel Aviv. Harry Friedenwald's
daughter, Julia Friedenwald Strauss, traveled to Palestine with her
father in May, 1935 and visited with Henrietta Szold, learning about
Hadassah's efforts to build a medical center connected with Hebrew
University. Julia Strauss was also interested in Szold's plans to save
the children of Nazi Germany. Within the year, Julia and her husband, Meyer Strauss, adopted two teenage brothers from Chemnitz,

Germany named Siegfried and Manfred. More than forty years later, Sigi Strauss would become the fifteenth president of Chizuk Amuno Congregation.

On December 21, 1935, the Baltimore Chapters of Hadassah joined together at Chizuk Amuno to celebrate the seventy-fifth birthday of Henrietta Szold. The <u>Jewish Times</u> previewed the celebration in their December 20, 1935 issue:

> *The exercises will be opened with Havdalah by Cantor Adolph Weisgal. Mrs Myer Strauss [Julia Friedenwald Strauss], president of Senior Hadassah, will then extend the greetings of the organizations. Dr. Harry Friedenwald will deliver the main address which will be an estimate of Miss Szold's place in Jewish and Zionist life, while Mrs. Emil [Sadie] Crockin will give some intimate reminiscences of her association with Miss Szold. The birthday blessings will be pronounced by Rabbi Adolph Coblenz...The program will conclude with the lighting of the Chanukah candles by Mrs. Louis H. Levin [Bertha Szold Levin] and the singing of Mooz Tsur by all assembled.*

Harry Friedenwald returned to Europe in the summer of 1936, receiving updates on conditions in Germany and Palestine from Chaim Weizmann, Felix Frankfurter, and his old friend, the Chief Rabbi of Great Britain, Joseph H. Hertz. Speaking to the delegates at the World Jewish Congress in Geneva, Friedenwald introduced a Declaration of Principles that was adopted by the group. Back in Baltimore, Friedenwald joined with other prominent families to secure visas for refugee families struggling to leave Germany.

On May 11, 1936, the field director of the Hebrew Immigrant Aid Society (HIAS) discussed his agency's mission with the Board and requested that Rabbi Coblenz make an appeal for support on the second day of Shavuot. The request was granted. Rabbi Coblenz presented a similar appeal on behalf of HIAS in May, 1937. Cantor Weisgal was deeply involved with the resettlement of German Jewish refugees in Baltimore, using his charm and network of contacts to find them homes and employment. In his dissertation, Cantor Joseph Levine noted that every Friday night the Weisgals hosted the *"Austrian Invasion"* at their home on Chauncey Avenue.

Care for the newest immigrants included providing for their education. Minutes from the May 4, 1938 School Board meeting report that *"German refugee children will be taken into the School free as long as the School facilities permit."* When the Council of Jewish Women requested use of Chizuk Amuno classrooms for "Americanization Classes" during the summer of 1938, the Board graciously agreed. The sessions were held two afternoons and two evenings a week and continued through the following year. Member J. Louis Rome served as chairman of the Refugee Scholarship Fund, established to sponsor German students to study in the United States.

Several additional rows of seats were placed in the synagogue to accommodate the needs of the refugees during the High Holy Days of 1938. With his excellent command of languages, Rabbi Coblenz was approached to lead an auxiliary service in German. The Board disapproved of religious services with German overtones, but agreed to permit Coblenz to deliver lectures in German. The Jewish Times of April 21, 1939 printed a public announcement of the assembly, commenting that the purpose was:

> *...to afford an opportunity of religious instructions and edification to those of our brothers and sisters who have recently come here from Germany, who have not acquired the English language, and who thus are left without spiritual sustenance.*

These assemblies were well attended and continued for several years.

As the Roosevelt Administration briefly loosened immigration policies after Kristallnacht in November, 1938, Chizuk Amuno's synagogue became hectic with efforts to provide for those few Jews who managed to escape. The vestry was used as a Reception Center to process refugees after arrival at the port of Baltimore. The United Synagogue urged member congregations to consider aiding German refugee rabbis by offering them jobs. Although the Congregation was struggling with financial difficulties and membership had decreased to 160, the following motion proposed by Max Reiser is recorded in the Minute Book on November 14, 1938:

Resolved that the Chizuk Amuno congregation, Eutaw Place & Chauncey Avenue, Baltimore, Md. engage Rabbi Mordke Gerstel of Vienna, Austria, Ober Augarten str. 46, for a period of two years beginning with February 1, 1939 at a salary of $1500.00 per year. Rabbi Gerstel is to act as assistance to Rabbi Adolph Coblenz and to perform all Rabbinical functions at the synagogue.

The motion passed and Solomon Rogers was appointed to handle all legal formalities. Obviously the offer of employment was a façade, merely documentation to meet requirements for valid immigration. On January 9, 1939, the Board reviewed a letter from Rabbi Gerstel acknowledging that he had received the affidavit of employment and thanking the Congregation. The last mention of Rabbi Gerstel appears in the minutes of July 31, 1939:

A letter was received from the State Department in reference to Rabbi Mortka Gertzel who is now in Palestine on his way to the United States. The State Department suggests that Rabbi Gertzel apply to the Consul General in Jerusalem who in turn will communicate with the Consul General in Vienna regarding his visa.

In September, 1939 Hitler's army invaded Poland and for Jews, escape from Europe was nearly impossible.

In support of the local United Jewish Appeal campaign, Rabbi Coblenz wrote an editorial that appeared in the November 24, 1939 issue of the <u>Jewish Times</u>. Entitled, "The Cry That Pierces the Night," the article illustrates the rabbi's passionate support of the Zionist cause and provides insight into the content of his sermons:

The word "blackout" has come to the fore since the out-

break of the present war and I know of no other word that so completely describes the condition of our people in Poland and elsewhere in Central and Eastern Europe. It is as though the brimming vitality of three and one-half million Jews in Poland were suddenly, crushed out by some sinister and irresistible juggernaut rolling over them. Whatever light, spiritual or material, the sheer existence of this great community represented, that light went out suddenly, violently choked, by a heavy mass of blackness, stark, palpable, grim, that settled upon it and all around it. Life and light went out all of a sudden...

In the last few years the lights went out in quick succession for German Jewry, Austrian Jewry, Czechoslovakian Jewry, and now Polish Jewry. And out of all this blackness emerges one sign, that life is still throbbing beneath – the outcry from millions of crushed hearts, piercing the night: "Brothers in America, we are sinking fast. You are our only help!"

...Palestine is the great light that the Jewish people are kindling today to relieve the darkness of Europe.... Suffice it to say that the physical fact of Jewish Palestine offering in this black hour, a home, immediately, to great masses of the Jewish people is overwhelming and incontrovertible. The appeal is addressed to a United American Israel for the salvation of the Jewish people. The imperious challenge of this tragic hour comes to us: Save the remnant of our people, if there is to be a remnant!

As the 1930's drew to a close, members of Chizuk Amuno were focusing on the major issues facing American Jews – spreading worldwide anti-Semitism, the struggle to establish a Jewish homeland, and the assimilation of second-generation American Jews. The 1939 annual Chanukah Banquet included a pageant by the Sisterhood entitled "My Country 'Tis," reflecting the strong patriotic spirit prevalent at the time. Member Ichel Folick *"presented 500 Benchlach (Grace After Meals Booklets) to the congregation"* but, unfortunately, everyone took them home as souvenirs of the evening. Folick graciously agreed to donate another 500 copies.

On January 21, 1940, a mass demonstration held at the Lyric Theatre attracted over 5,000 people to hear Dr. Chaim Weizmann, president of the Jewish Agency for Palestine. The event opened with Cantor Weisgal singing "America" followed by introductory remarks by Dr. Harry Friedenwald. Hoping to enlist aid for Zionist efforts, Weizmann excited the crowd with assurances that there were no disputes between the Joint Distribution Committee and the United Palestine Appeal. The following week, Chizuk Amuno hosted a lecture featuring Dr. Nachum Goldman, Chairman of the World Jewish Congress, and Rabbi Maurice L. Perlzweig, Chairman of the British Jewish Congress. Rabbi Coblenz was elected president of the Baltimore Zionist District the following year and would serve in that position throughout the war years.

In June, 1939 in an effort to centralize all youth activities, the Board established a "Youth Board" under the advisorship of Hymen Saye. Representatives from the Chizuk Amuno Junior and Senior Discussion Groups, Youth Group, and Young Peoples League participated. To promote synagogue attendance, Rabbi Coblenz declared that one Shabbat would be designated as *"Youth Shabbos"* when the young people of Chizuk Amuno would conduct the complete service. The Jewish Times of April 12, 1940 heralded the next day's Youth Shabbat as *"an extraordinary event in the life of Chizuk Amuno."* The Sisterhood sponsored a Kiddush after services in honor of the occasion.

Although the young men of the Congregation were allowed to assume religious responsibilities for a portion of the service, Sisterhood members were not. There had been a Sisterhood Shabbos in 1939, but the president was allowed only to address the worshippers from her seat. At the Board meeting on March 18, 1940, Milton

Fleischer announced that March 31 would be designated as Sisterhood Shabbos, and that *"Mrs. I.E. Rosenbloom would like to address the Congregation from the pulpit."* After considerable discussion, it was decided that Flora Rosenbloom could speak from the pulpit – after the benediction. Waiting another year, the Sisterhood changed their request in 1941, asking the Board's permission for Flora Rosenbloom to speak <u>before</u> the closing prayer. The decision was deferred to the judgment of Rabbi Coblenz, who ruled in favor of the women.

The annual Brotherhood Shabbat service also began in 1941. Participating in the March 1 service were J. Max Abramowitz, Edward Shalowitz, Jack Mark, Nathan Harris, and Alvin Neuberger. Fred E. Katzner delivered the sermon and Marvin S. Plant was responsible for leading the rabbi's English readings. By 1941, the Brotherhood was sponsoring a Boy Scout troop, father-son evenings, monthly public guest lectures, and formal men-only banquets. Rabbi Coblenz also hosted a Brotherhood study group at his home on the second Thursday of each month.

Rabbi Coblenz approached the High Holy Days of 5701 (1940) challenging his congregants to dedicate themselves to the *"spiritual unity of mankind."* Ads in the <u>Jewish Times</u> listed dates when the Chizuk Amuno Seating Committee would be available to arrange holiday seat rental and noted that the Seating Committee would be present all day on October 2, 1940 – Erev Rosh Hashanah. Anxious to maximize attendance, Rabbi Coblenz began Selichot Services at 11:30 p.m. instead of the traditional 6:00 a.m. starting time. Cantor Weisgal continued the service at midnight accompanied by the Chizuk Amuno Choir. The late service drew over 300 people, an exceptional attendance given the fact that membership stood at 180. Coblenz and Weisgal wrote a special edition of the Selichot Service, printed with the English translation alongside the original Hebrew text. The booklet, which also contained an introduction to the service explaining its history and significance, was registered with the Library of Congress and received a copyright.

A significant innovation was introduced in 1940, when loud-speakers were installed in the synagogue. The Board had ignored the Sisterhood's request for amplifiers in 1935, but now thought it prudent, subject to the approval of the rabbi. For an opinion on the question, Coblenz turned to his colleague at Beth Tfiloh, Rabbi Samuel Rosenblatt, who had researched the same question years earlier. Rosenblatt responded that leading Orthodox rabbis had indicated that it was permissible to use an electronic amplifier so long as it was permanently attached and not operated when the Shofar was sounded. The Brotherhood and Sisterhood shared the $600 cost with the Congregation.

The War Years

Only eight men affiliated with Chizuk Amuno were noted as *"Men in the Army"* when the High Holy Days of 5702 (1941) began on the evening of September 21. Rabbi Coblenz's thoughts were published in the monthly <u>Bulletin</u>:

> *Now the saddest and most disappointing aspect of the condition of the world today undoubtedly consists in the fact, that the volcano of evil, ever-present and ever-active in all periods of history, has recently thrown up the lava of universal demoralization with such fury and is such bulk as to overwhelm the entire landscape of the Human and to threaten the complete extinction of all that is left of decency and elementary civilization on earth.*

An emotional service on Yom Kippur underscored the rabbi's remarks as Arthur Lindner of Heilbrunn, Germany, presented the Congregation with a Sefer Torah that he had brought with him to America. The scroll, which had been stabbed in several places, had been rescued from a German synagogue on November 10, 1938 – Kristallnacht.

With the advent of war in Europe, the Sisterhood temporarily redirected its attention from congregational matters to the support of fellow Jews worldwide. Used clothing drives were organized under the "Bundles For Britain" campaign, and a dedicated Sewing Group met weekly in the vestry to make clothes for the Red Cross. Adapting to the growing war, Sara S. Cantor, chairman of the Sisterhood Culture Group, encouraged members to attend Hebrew language courses taught by Hymen Saye or the Sisterhood's weekly cultural lectures. Cantor wrote: *"With the decline of European Jewry, the American Jewess has the responsibility of fostering and furthering Jewish culture. Let us rise to this opportunity."*

The events of December 7, 1941 suddenly thrust the United States, along with Chizuk Amuno, into the war effort. At the first Board meeting held after the U.S. officially entered the war, a letter was read from Cantor Weisgal asking if the Congregation would object if he joined the *"home guard."* Rabbi Coblenz also requested permission to participate in national defense. The Board agreed that the clergy could register for civilian defense but added that the men could not volunteer for any activity that would draw *"them away from their duties in the synagogue."* At the suggestion of Charles Katz, the Board decided to purchase American and Maryland flags to be positioned on either side of the pulpit. Six months later, these flags were joined by a Zionist flag on the bimah. The Sisterhood presented a Service Flag to the Congregation at Shabbat services on May 30, 1942. Blue stars were added onto the field of white to represent each Chizuk Amuno family member in active military service. A bronze plaque, donated by Mr. and Mrs. Louis Weinberg, recorded the names of those young men and women. By the summer of 1944, that list had grown to 177 names.

Milton Fleischer assumed the role of heading the Emergency Committee and reported full cooperation with the local Red Cross and Baltimore Committee for Civil Defense. The synagogue was prepared for possible blackout measures, and the building insured under War Risk and Bombardment coverage. It was officially classified as a Civil Defense Air Raid Shelter and the Red Cross Headquarters for Zone 13A. On October 14, 1942, the Red Cross Canteen Unit began using the vestry every Wednesday to serve lunch to workers and volunteers. Committees were formed to solicit sales of war bonds and stamps. Several members donated bonds to the Congregation and the Board voted to reinvest the savings of the Congregation in defense bonds.

To protect against any negative public reaction hinting of anti-Semitism, Rabbi Coblenz suggested keeping a register of Chizuk Amuno war statistics. In the <u>Bulletin</u> of April, 1942 Coblenz explained that the information would be useful to the American Jewish community to *"combat slanderous charges that are likely to be made against the Jewish people, as happened, for instance, at the end of the last war."* A system of index cards recorded pertinent information on every adult and child of the Congregation who had joined the defense forces. The synagogue office carefully maintained a record of the Red Cross activities Sisterhood members were involved with and of all classes conducted at the synagogue related to the war effort.

As more men were drafted into service, the women of the Chizuk Amuno Sisterhood joined with American women around the country to aid civilian defense efforts and raise the spirits of servicemen and women. Ethel Cordish, chairman of the Defense Committee, organized knitting groups to supplement sewing efforts, Red Cross nutrition classes, blood drives, and the Victory Book Campaign. The "Sisterhood News," published in the Congregation's <u>Bulletin</u>, urged members to join in the war effort:

> *Save your silk and nylon stockings. It is hard to have to give them up since they are scarce. However, from those that are discarded, the government makes silk bags for powder.*

> *Save the fats in your kitchen. Instead of sending it down the drain, send it to the Axis in form of vital oil needed for ammunition.*

Dances and other entertainment were arranged by the Sisterhood to provide local servicemen with needed emotional support. Box lunches were packed and distributed to nearby military units before the men were shipped out. A note, received from a group of Navy recruits in late summer 1942, thanked the women for their courtesy:

> *...thank your organization for the box lunches and the good wishes that went with them. I am sure that the boys and myself are very glad of the opportunity we have to fight for a country which is made up of such fine people as you have shown us you are...Thank the committee, who were very efficient, yet very friendly, and very instrumental in making our last impressions of Baltimore very happy and thankful ones. And who also aided in the goodbyes and farewells for those of us who had no mothers, sisters, wives, or sweethearts to say goodbye to us.*

Certain Sisterhood activities continued as usual during the war years. The bowling league still played at the Arcade Bowling Alleys atop the North Avenue Market. Women still volunteered to be "mothers" for Jewish students at Baltimore's Goucher College, decorated the sukkah for Sukkot and the sanctuary for Shavuot, and co-sponsored the annual Chanukah Banquet in conjunction with the Brotherhood. The creative talents of the Sisterhood were showcased in October, 1942, as members presented "Women in Defense" at their opening meeting. The musical, written and directed by Fannie Coplan, featured the women dressed in military uniforms representing the various branches of the armed services:

> *To the tune of "Marine Hymn"*
>
> *We held a Bundles for Britain Day*
> *We helped the U.S.O.*
> *To man our booths for Bonds and stamps*
> *Surely kept us on the go———*
>
> *Blood donors, too, we all became*
> *The midnight lunches, too*
> *There was no job too big or small*
> *For our sisterhood to do———*

From the moment America entered the war, Rabbi Coblenz devoted his attention to maintaining the morale of his congregation and lifting the spirits of those members of the Chizuk Amuno family serving their country. In his first <u>Bulletin</u> column printed after the attack on Pearl Harbor, Coblenz encouraged the community to guard against the extreme attitudes of hysteria and cocky indifference. As though coaching his team in the big game, Coblenz emphasized that faith in the cause would *"keep our minds free from confusion, our emotions balanced, our wills steady and our morale firm."*   The continuing program of congregation activities was touted as an important factor in maintaining morale during the crisis. Under the banner headline *"It Is There For You,"* the <u>Bulletin</u> suggested that readers attend:

- *Weekly class in Midrash conducted every Shabbat afternoon with a passage expounded and interpreted by the rabbi, or*
- *Monday morning sessions of the Sisterhood's course in Jewish culture tracing the history of Jews from ancient times, or*
- *Series of lectures analyzing the reaction of Jews in critical times in history conducted every other Thursday at the rabbi's home under the auspices of the Brotherhood.*

By October 1942, the list of programs had grown to include courses in Hebrew, Biblical and Rabbinic literature, the story of the prayerbook and *"other courses as an essential part of our program of adult education in our synagogue."* A novel approach to providing instruction was implemented as laymen of the Congregation were invited to teach courses. Enrollees were assured, however, that the *"program of study has the guidance and supervision of the Rabbi."* Classes were open to both men and women.

As the men of Chizuk Amuno were drafted into military service, parents and friends of servicemen were asked to submit the name, rank and unit of their loved ones to the synagogue office so that Rabbi Coblenz could correspond with them personally. Copies of the <u>Bulletin</u> carried prayers of the Congregation – *"May the Angel of Peace guard them and may they come back safe and sound into a liberated world when peace may reign for the future generations."* Occasionally, a letter would arrive from a soldier:

Dear Friends:

Just a note to let you know that although I may be many thousand miles away, my thoughts are still with my friends back home. I have often thought about Chizuk Amuno, and my association with the Synagogue since early childhood. I have longed many times to be in a Saturday morning service. Our facilities are limited and being of a minority religion I am obliged to pray in silence. However, I know my prayers are heard. We have no fear because God is on our side. Kindest regards,

Lieut. Stanley J. Robinson

To fortify the spiritual foundation of the servicemen, the Congregation sent 175 pocket-sized prayerbooks, covered in steel, to members of the Chizuk Amuno family in the armed forces. Sent as a Passover gift in April, 1944, the books were accompanied by a message of support and a prayer for their safe return. Over sixty letters of appreciation were published in the <u>Bulletin</u>, each expressing not only gratitude, but also the warmth of their recollection of happier times spent at Chizuk Amuno.

Hints of the atrocities occurring in Europe became public knowledge in late 1942, sparking a resurgence of synagogue attendance as people struggled to cope with devastating news reports. The holiday of Purim offered Rabbi Coblenz the opportunity to address the overwhelming despair expressed by his members. Linking Esther's plea of, "How can I look on and behold the extermination of my kindred?" with the current situation, Coblenz stressed the profound sense of kinship within the Jewish faith. Providing what would turn out to be premature hope, the rabbi concluded his message as follows:

*And this is perhaps symbolic of the mood in which the
Jewish people are celebrating Purim this year: on the
one hand, a sense of despair at our helplessness to save
the millions of our brothers yonder, and on the other hand,
a sense of great relief at the realization that the worst is
probably over, and that together with the rest of the world
our people too are definitely moving toward the light.*

Shocking news of the war coupled with the comforting messages of the rabbi stimulated a steady growth in congregation attendance and affiliation. Each year at the Annual Congregation Meeting
in December, membership figures were recorded in the Minute Book:

1937   160 members
1938   163 members
1939   168 members
1940   178 members
1941   184 members
1942   197 members
1943   220 members
1944   240 members
1945   260 members
1946   356 members

The Sisterhood boasted a membership of 600 women in January, 1944. The Seating Committee had to turn down 300-400 requests for High Holy Day seats each year beginning in 1943.

As a result of increased membership, the financial position of
Chizuk Amuno improved considerably – both from dues and additional offerings. The Congregation was also the recipient of large
legacies after the deaths of several prominent members. Long-standing member Solomon Rosenbloom willed $3,000 to Chizuk Amuno,
and Board member Ephraim Macht designated that $10,000 of his
estate be used to build an assembly hall at the Eutaw Place synagogue. Gifts in honor of birthdays, recovery from illness, and in

memory of loved ones included sets of machzorim, siddurim, chumashim and taleisim.

Slowly, but steadily, the Board made additional payments against the principle due on the outstanding mortgages. Holders of the Gold Second Mortgage Bonds were requested to donate them back to the Congregation, and a Committee to Liquidate the Mortgage was established under the leadership of Samuel H. Hoffberger and his co-chairman, J. Benjamin Katzner. Pledges and cash contributions were solicited with hopes that the entire debt of Chizuk Amuno could be cleared by December 31, 1942. An appeal for the final few thousand dollars, made at the Chanukah Banquet on December 6, proved successful. Announcement was made at the December 14, 1942 Board meeting that the goal had been reached, and President Fleischer thanked members of the committee *"for their vision, foresight and generosity in liquidating the mortgage of our synagogue."* The first page of the March 1943 <u>Bulletin</u> carried the headline, "Important Congregational Announcement" in bold type. Along with a photograph of Samuel Hoffberger was an Honor Roll listing the names of 109 individuals and families whose contributions, along with those made by the Brotherhood and Sisterhood, had relieved the Congregation of the Eutaw Place debt after twenty-two years. The prosperity of the Congregation during the war years also facilitated plans for two major projects – building the much-needed school annex and establishing a congregational cemetery.

One issue of constant concern to the Sisterhood and Brotherhood was the adequacy of classroom space. When concerns were brought to the Board's attention, they were discussed, but no action was taken. On April 9, 1938, Sisterhood President Nellie Baker presented the Congregation with a $500 check in honor of the Sisterhood's fiftieth anniversary. The women specifically directed that the funds be used to establish a special savings account for the construction of a synagogue "Community Center" to be constructed after the war ended. A special Board meeting was convened on October 31, 1938, to discuss once again the *"grave necessity of a School Center"* and select a committee to locate a possible site. Three years passed, and the School Center Fund increased with donations. On October 31, 1941, Hyman D. Caplan reported that a large house located at 2401 Eutaw Place at the corner with Whitelock Street was for sale. The Board approved purchasing the property for $13,500 but would delay using it for classroom space for more than seven years.

After the liquidation of the synagogue mortgage in 1942, the Congregation felt financially secure enough to enter another building campaign. Milton Fleischer's address from the pulpit on Yom Kippur 5704 (1943) included an announcement of a $125,000 campaign to build a new "School Centre." The December, 1943 <u>Bulletin</u> devoted its full front page to the new campaign and published photographs of the committee's co-chairmen, Charles Katz and J. Benjamin Katzner, and committee treasurers Samuel Hoffberger and Isaac Potts. Members were solicited privately for the privilege of dedicating a room in the proposed building to a loved one. As recorded in the Minute Book of November 15, 1943:

> *The plan is to have an assembly hall, a library at $7500.00, 15 classrooms at $3000.00 each, 5 tutorial rooms at $1500 each, a lounge at $5000.00, a gymnasium at $5000.00, a kindergarten at $5000.00 and an arts and crafts room at $3500.00.*

Rabbi Coblenz strongly supported the building campaign. He reminded members that Chizuk Amuno was *"the only large Congregation without adequate facilities for a school."* In an emotional appeal, Coblenz stressed that the children must learn to associate Judaism *"not with narrow quarters and dim basements...but with largeness and freedom and sunlight."* Over the next few years, friends of the Congregation made generous contributions to the building fund, as did the Brotherhood and Sisterhood. The parents of the 1943 Confirmation Class contributed $100 to the fund in lieu of holding a public reception for their daughters. By December, 1945 cash and pledges for the School Center totaled close to $90,000 – still short of the minimum $125,000 necessary to develop the center.

Arlington Cemetery

Ironically, one indication of a congregation's growth is their need for burial grounds. Purchasing cemetery lots could be considered a commitment by the member to stay affiliated with the congregation over his lifetime. The first synagogue cemetery in Baltimore, located on Belair Road, was purchased by Baltimore Hebrew Congregation in 1832. By 1871, large cemetery properties were owned by the Eden Street Shul, Har Sinai, and Oheb Shalom. During the Congregation's first seventy years, most Chizuk Amuno members were buried at Hebrew Friendship Cemetery or the Belair Road cemetery.

At a Board meeting on August 10, 1936, Israel Silberstein proposed that the Congregation establish a cemetery of its own, but two months later the Board decided to *"abandon"* the idea. Silberstein died in August, 1938 before any progress had been made on his proposal. Interest in a cemetery, however, did not diminish. In May, 1940 the Brotherhood requested that the cemetery issue be reopened and offered their assistance. A committee was appointed to investigate the possibility of acquiring the Hebrew Friendship Cemetery, which, after the dissolution of the Eden Street Shul in 1902, was managed by an independent corporation. Negotiations broke down six months later and a new Cemetery Committee, led by Max Fish, was instructed to search for grounds suitable to develop for burials.

Fish and his committee investigated several possible cemetery sites, only to find that they lacked proper zoning certification. Finally, the group located one hundred acres on Rogers Avenue that would suit their purpose. On November 9, 1944, a special meeting of the Congregation was called for the purpose of ratifying the $50,000 purchase. Although there was general consensus that a cemetery was needed, some members questioned the advisability of assuming a new mortgage when they had recently liquidated the Eutaw Place debt. Twenty men pledged a total of $29,500 in no-interest loans towards the purchase, which would be refunded when Chizuk Amuno received final zoning approval for cemetery development and mortgage funds.

Less than two months later, long-standing member Ephraim Macht died. He was touted in the press as one of the *"foremost Jews of Baltimore,"* having committed his time and money to many communal organizations. At the request of the family, the Board agreed to allow Macht's funeral service to be held in the synagogue on December 20, 1944. The Board determined that any member could use the synagogue for a funeral service if the body was brought in immediately before the memorial service and taken for burial immediately after.

Louis Zusman, formerly a resident of Levindale, has the distinction of being the first person interred in the congregational cemetery on June 10, 1945. Formal development of eighteen acres of the grounds was contracted to the Gott Construction Company for just under $42,500. Work on paving roads and walkways began in December 1945. Naming the new cemetery was a matter of great discussion among the committee members. At their suggestion, the Board voted to name the burial grounds with a reference to the geographic community in which it was located. The Arlington Cemetery of the Chizuk Amuno Congregation was officially dedicated on Sunday afternoon, October 27, 1946 – two weeks later than planned due to excessive rain. Rabbi Coblenz commented that the new cemetery grounds were not only beautiful in a landscaping sense, but also in a *"subduing, quieting, heart-soothing nature."* Cemetery Committee Chairman Max Fish, concluded his dedication remarks by saying: *"This place will not be called a 'bet hakvotim' – a graveyard, but a 'bet hachayim' – a House of Eternal Life."*

Sales of lots began with a glossy brochure mailed to members touting the cemetery's convenient location, *"only twenty minutes' drive from heart of the city,"* and solicitations printed in the <u>Bulletin</u>:

Have you provided for the future?
Arlington Cemetery
For information call
Bernard or Harold Manekin
SAratoga 7725

Bernard Manekin, Charles Katz's son-in-law, accepted a job as sales manager along with his brother, Harold. Lots were priced according to their proximity to the walkway, with prime locations costing $125. Graves in the center area, "Section Z," were sold at a premium price of $175 in plots of not fewer than six graves. The first annual Memorial Service was scheduled to be held at Arlington Cemetery on Sunday morning, September 7, 1947, but serious illness forced Rabbi Adolph Coblenz to postpone the service. Two weeks later, with Coblenz still hospitalized, Cantor Abba Weisgal conducted the service joined by Rabbi Charles Rubenstein.

During the prosperous years preceding the Depression, the Baltimore Jewish community continued to evolve as families began moving outside of the urban area. In 1919, Orthodox Jews formed the Shaarei Zion Congregation and built the first synagogue on Park Heights Avenue, just north of Druid Hill Park. Wealthy professionals and businessmen purchased homes in the northwest corner of the city, not far from The Suburban, a German Jewish social club. Orthodox Shearith Israel Congregation was the first existing congregation to react to the geographic shift, breaking ground for the suburban branch of their synagogue in 1924 at Park Heights and Glen Avenues. As the price of housing became more affordable, the Jewish population in the uptown neighborhoods increased. Another Orthodox congregation, Beth Jacob, formed on Park Heights and Manhattan Avenues in 1938. Reform congregation Har Sinai established a suburban branch on Park Heights and Strathmore Avenues in 1938, and moved their religious school uptown. Five years later, Baltimore Hebrew Congregation dedicated their new administrative and school facilities at Park Heights and Slade Avenues. Jewish migration to the suburbs also gravitated westward to the Forest Park/ Walbrook area of the city. In 1921, the Beth Tfiloh Congregation was organized to serve the Orthodox community residing in that growing area, joined in 1926 by Tifereth Israel. Both congregations built synagogues on Garrison Boulevard.

The plethora of traditional synagogues composed of Jews from both German and Russian backgrounds forced a polite competition for members. With multiple options available, synagogue membership became a "buyer's market." No longer could congregational boards dictate strict rules of conduct enforced by threat of fines. Disgruntled members would simply join another synagogue. This competition, coupled with a fear for the future of Judaism, caused the Chizuk Amuno Board to contemplate changes unlike any that had been considered over the prior seventy-five years. Just as the influx of Russian immigrants had dictated adjustments in the synagogue community years earlier, so the socioeconomic forces of twentieth century America dictated additional adjustments both in ritual practice and administrative management of the synagogue.

The Board spent many hours discussing the dilemma of attracting new members while retaining existing ones. Cognizant of the growing clamor for ritual changes and a more contemporary environment, the Board approached member Isaac Potts to prepare a paper on *"the future of our synagogue."* Presented at a Board meeting on March 13, 1944, the "Potts Paper" provoked much discussion and spurred the formation of the Future of the Synagogue Committee chaired by Joseph Davidson. Potts recommended several changes centered on three major points – more English in the service, shortening the length of Shabbat and holiday services, and mixed seating. There was no question of Potts' dedication to Chizuk Amuno or his commitment to Judaism. His comments were intended to strengthen both.

Within months a new committee was formed to address some points of the Potts Paper. Chaired by J. Benjamin Katzner, the *"Committee on the Readjustment of the Yom Kippur Memorial Services and Mi-Sheberachs"* investigated both the logistical problems of the

Yizkor Service and the financial benefits of the existing *"Shenodaring"* system – offering donations during the service. Chizuk Amuno clung to the tradition of having congregants line up to ascend the bimah one at a time to recite a memorial prayer. During the prayer, members would pledge a contribution to the synagogue in memory of their loved ones. Although the procedure took hours and destroyed the solemn atmosphere of the service, it did generate substantial funds for the annual budget.

Katzner poured over the financial records of the Congregation searching for a method of eliminating the offerings while still collecting the revenue. By calculating each member's previous contributions, Katzner devised a method asking members and seatholders to sign pledge cards that would replace all offerings tendered during the year for aliyot and mi-sheberachs. On the card the member would include the names of all departed family members, which would be printed in a special "Sefer Hachayim – Book of Life" distributed on Yom Kippur. The rabbi would read aloud the names of all those listed in the perpetual Memorial Book of Chizuk Amuno. These pledges were in addition to the annual $56 dues and seat rental charges. The Board accepted Katzner's recommendation with appreciation and informed the Congregation of the new system in July, 1946. Records disclose that $7,500 was collected from offerings in 1944, but only four months after the elimination of the old system, Katzner reported that 320 pledge cards had been returned with pledges totaling $22,200.

The officers and clergy of Chizuk Amuno were re-elected for one-year terms every December at the Semi-Annual Congregational meeting, while members of the Board of Trustees were elected for a two-year term. The trio of President Milton Fleischer, Vice-President Siegfried Neuberger, and Treasurer Charles Katz led the Congregation as a team for twenty-two years until December, 1944, when Katz decided to step down and concentrate his attention on chairing the School Building Fund campaign. Neuberger, then age eighty-five, served until his death eighteen months later. Stepping into the position of treasurer was J. Benjamin Katzner – the designer of the pledge system and a past president of the Brotherhood and now dormant Young Peoples League.

The Chizuk Amuno Brotherhood and Sisterhood cooperated to jointly sponsor many social, cultural, and fund-raising projects including banquets, plays, and "Night of Fun" benefits for the War Service Fund. Good-natured competition existed between the women's and men's bowling leagues. The men, bowling weekly at the King Pin Alleys on Reisterstown Road, challenged the women to a match on February 14, 1945. The Bulletin reported the results:

> *The men spotted the women 8 pins each game. The men's A team beat the women's A team, but the women's B team was victorious over the men's B team, without the spotted points. When the final score was totaled, the Sisterhood league was victorious. The evening was such a success that the Brotherhood asked for a return match.*

Although members of the men's bowling league appreciated the women's skills in competition and organization, the Board of the Congregation continued to ignore the Sisterhood's requests for representation.

The additional responsibilities assumed by women during the war years exposed them to decision-making roles and bolstered their sense of self-confidence in administrative situations. In a letter dated December 3, 1943, Sisterhood president Florence Rogers informed Milton Fleischer of a motion proposed by Beatrice Levy at the Sisterhood Executive Board meeting on November 29. The women had unanimously approved the motion to request that two members of the Sisterhood be appointed to the Board of Directors, thus repeating their original request made in 1938. Supporting their position, the letter continued:

> *The Sisterhood now has a membership of about 600 women. We believe the Sisterhood is a vital force in ob-*

> *taining many new members for the Synagogue. The Sisterhood is interested in every phase of Congregational association. The religious services, the educational program, the cultural work, and even the financial condition of the Synagogue is a matter of keen interest to the Sisterhood...*

> *In these modern times, when women are being appointed to many governmental positions of importance throughout the country, we feel that our Synagogue could keep abreast with the times. A woman's point of view in many instances, especially in regards to home, children, and Congregation, could be very helpful if expressed at the proper time, for even the men to make decisions.*

Once again, the Board deferred discussing this matter until Rabbi Coblenz could be consulted as to his opinion.

Coblenz stated his position in a letter read at the January 17, 1944 Board meeting. In his response, the rabbi referred to three situations – Deborah, the prophetess acting as a Judge in Israel, Queen Salome Alexandra, ruler of the Jews during the Maccabean dynasty, and modern-day women serving as heads of charitable institutions:

> *The above instances will clearly prove that at least there is no outright and inflexible opposition on the part of the Jewish spirit to the participation of women in running the affairs of Jewish life.*

> *It is therefore my opinion that there can be no objection to the admission of representatives of the Sisterhood to the Board of Directors of our Synagogue with the understanding, however, that they are to abstain from voting, especially on all purely religious matters.*

Rather than accept their rabbi's scholarly opinion, the men decided to gather the opinions of *"authorities of the Jewish Theological Seminary in the matter."*

Letters of response from Dr. Louis Finkelstein, president of the Seminary, and Dr. Louis Ginzberg, Professor of Talmud, were read into the minutes of February 14, 1944. Ginzberg commented that *"according to my opinion, there is not the slightest objection to having women on the board of a Synagogue."* He even went further and maintained *"that Maimonides would have no objection...."* Finkelstein agreed with Ginzberg's position, adding that there was no objection to women voting on any issues presented to the Board. Interestingly, he concluded with the disclaimer, *"Of course, religious issues should be decided by the Rabbi of the Congregation on the basis of Jewish law, and would not come before a lay board for its decision."* Of great concern to the Seminary was the trend of lay leaders changing ritual practices without regard to halakhic standards. With no Talmudic basis to deny the Sisterhood's request, Executive Secretary Joseph Weinstein sent Florence Rogers a letter informing her of the Board's resolution:

> *Resolved that the President of the Sisterhood and the President of the Brotherhood, ex-officio be invited to attend the meetings of the Board of Directors of the congregation and participate in the deliberations of the Board without the privilege of voting.*

There is no evidence that the Brotherhood had ever formally requested a Board position.

Sisterhood President Florence Rogers and Brotherhood president Joseph Davidson officially attended their first Board meeting in March, 1944. The women were pleased to finally have representation, but deeply disappointed to be refused voting rights. They wrote to the Board again, stressing that their representative should have the same rights as all other Board members, and requesting that any constitutional changes should be made promptly and *"not allowed to drag on indefinitely."* In closing, the Sisterhood stated their opinion that *"it will be of great benefit to the congregation that it accede to the modern trend of equality of women's privileges to have not only representation, but of voting rights."* Given these expressions

of early feminism, it is ironic to note that the president and corre-
sponding secretary signed their names as was typical at the time –
Mrs. Sol Rogers and Mrs. Joseph Kolodny – without their own given
names. A constitutional amendment was passed at the Special Congregational Meeting on March 11, 1946, that enlarged the Board of
Trustees to include the presidents of the Sisterhood and Brotherhood,
along with the chairmen of the Cemetery Committee and the School
Board. The first hurdle towards synagogue equality for women had
been cleared.

Not all changes were adapted painlessly. Differing opinions
among Board members prompted the decision to poll the membership as to their thoughts on a variety of questions. On May 21, 1945
questionnaires were sent to members, seatholders, and their wives –
"one questionnaire to each individual man and woman." A cover
letter explained that the poll was being conducted in conjunction
with the approaching seventy-fifth anniversary of Chizuk Amuno.
*"We are sending out the enclosed questionnaire in order to get your
views on what will best satisfy our religious and educational needs
both now and for our children, as far as we can visualize them for
the future."* The one-page survey requested opinions on increasing
attendance at the Shabbat service and focused on the issues of shortening the service, introducing more English, including a more active
lay participation in the service, and seating women and men together
in mixed pews.

The June, 1945 issue of the <u>Bulletin</u> reminded readers to complete their surveys and return them quickly. It also addressed the
anxiety of those questioning the true motivation behind the survey:

> *It is not the intention of Chizuk Amuno to adopt doc-
> trines of reform Judaism, or ever in the future to become
> a REFORM TEMPLE. For quite some time, however,
> various suggestions were made by some of the younger*

members to make our services more attractive to the younger generation, so as to enable them to get greater spiritual value out of the services, without deviation from traditional Judaism. The board, therefore, considering these views of the members, has decided to send out this most important questionnaire.

Approximately 220 replies were received from member families representing an impressive fifty percent response rate. Seatholder families returned 230 replies representing a one-third response rate. Results indicated some preference for introducing more English into the service, but not shortening its duration. Thoughts on allowing lay involvement in ritual services were split equally, as were opinions on mixed seating. In light of the inconclusive results, the Board decided to call a special meeting of the male members of the Congregation for the purpose of discussing the major points of the Potts Paper. The Sisterhood immediately reacted to their exclusion from such a meeting in a letter to the Board on November 1, 1945, signed by Bernice Kolodny, President:

Although we are told no definite action will be recorded at this meeting, and that it will only take the form of a discussion, we respectfully request that the wives of the members be invited to participate. The issues involved are of great significance in the Synagogue life of our families and we believe the woman's point of view is vital and important.

The Sisterhood petition was approved, and the wives of members were invited to attend the November 26, 1945 meeting.

Sensing the importance of the November special meeting, Milton Fleischer agreed to have a professional secretary record a transcription of the event. Fleischer served as moderator with Isaac Potts, and attorney Joseph Fax representing the opposing positions. In his opening statement, Potts stressed the point that Judaism is a living organism, subject to change, modification, and adjustment. On the issue of mixed seating, he remarked:

*Woman has achieved in modern times in every walk of
life and among all nations of civilization a status equal
to that of man, and I know that woman will not tolerate
being relegated to the sides and rear very much longer.
Woman is coming to be more and more a dominant influence in the life of the Synagogue and the community at
large. Thank goodness for that.*

Potts closed with a reference to the increased competition between congregations to maintain membership levels. Joseph Fax
based his argument against ritual changes on maintaining the biblical traditions of our forefathers.

Questions and comments from the audience indicate just how
much tension there was over the issues of mixed seating and use of
English in the service:

*Mr. Rand: God could hear us in English as well as in
Hebrew, and so if we use more English we could get our
children interested, more interested in our religion and
Faith, and probably get them to come to Shule.*

*Dr. Isidore Siegel: I should think, Mr. Potts, that if all
these people here this evening would make it their business to come to every Shabbos, wouldn't that be one of
the greatest inspirations for the children to come with
them?*

*Mr. Fax: If the future of Jewish education depended on
the people sitting here before me, the future is very dis-
mal. If the future of Judaism or Jewish education depended on you people, it is black indeed.*

Notable among the comments made by members was a question by Charles Santry to Isaac Potts about the possibility of education for adults:

*I believe that the crux of the matter has been the educa-
tion that most of us have neglected to have as far as*

Hebrew, and I wonder if it wouldn't be possible for my sons, and the sons of the fathers here, for this congregation to establish some schooling that would definitely teach them this learning?

Potts, who also served as the chairman of the School Board, responded:

I think it is hardly possible. The period of time it would require to educate older people and young people—even if you did, it would have to be adjusted into the present American picture of life, and if you do not do that you are just beating your head against the wall.

The evening ended with Milton Fleischer promising that there would be more discussion on the issues before a final vote was taken.

    As the final days of the war approached, the Chizuk Amuno community formed post-war committees to aid in the rehabilitation of soldiers and the resettlement of refugees. The Sisterhood collected phonograph records and craft items for use by therapists at military hospitals. The Brotherhood/Sisterhood joint War Service Fund furnished and decorated the Day Room at Fort Meade, held a Chanukah party at the Aberdeen Proving Grounds, arranged a bingo party at Fort Howard, and cooperated in a campaign to collect cartons of used clothing to send to Europe. At the request of the B'nai B'rith organization, members donated religious articles to be sent to the Jewish community surviving in Rumania. One of the most touching post-war events was the May 20, 1947 marriage of two Holocaust survivors in the Eutaw Place synagogue. Five Chizuk Amuno families sponsored the wedding and reception of Mordecai Friedel and Esther Schmulowitz.

Chizuk Amuno Congregation celebrated the twenty-fifth anniversary of Rabbi Coblenz's spiritual leadership with a weekend of activities in 1945. A gala banquet attended by over five hundred people was held at The Alcazar on Thursday evening, December 6, featuring Dr. Louis Finkelstein, President of JTS, as guest speaker. Cantor Weisgal kindled the Chanukah lights and led the audience in singing "Mo'oz Tsur" in Hebrew and English. Through the generosity of Coblenz's many friends, L. Manuel Hendler presented the rabbi with a "purse" of $7,500 – remarkable considering his annual rabbinic salary of $6,450.

Prominent Orthodox and Reform local rabbis, including Samuel Rosenblatt, Abraham Shaw, Abraham Shusterman, Morris Lazaron, Nathan Drazin, and Israel Tabak participated in the Shabbat morning service which drew a reported 1,000 people. Milton Fleischer introduced JTS professor Rabbi Max Arzt, who delivered the "Anniversary Sermon." On Sunday morning, the children of the religious schools gathered at a special assembly to honor their rabbi. Tributes to Coblenz printed in the Jewish Times covered more than two pages of the December 14, 1945 issue and included accolades from Governor O'Conor, Mayor McKeldin, judges, communal leaders, and colleagues. An editorial summarized the thoughts of many:

> *By his profound learning, his love of man, his emphasis on the ethical life and by his special love of K'lal Yisroel, Rabbi Coblenz has brought to its highest flowering the quality which our community has come to look upon as a requisite for a rabbi and a teacher in Israel...Rabbi Coblenz has used his gifts and abilities in the furthering of every communal cause of importance. His Congregation Chizuk Amuno benefited by his guidance over the past quarter century and through his leadership has achieved recognition as one of the important congregations in America.*

Unfortunately, Adolph Coblenz's health soon rendered him unable to continue his services to the Congregation. Illness had occasionally forced him to cancel lectures and appearances, but it was not until June, 1946 that the records of the Congregation indicate the seriousness of his condition. In a letter to Isaac Potts, Dr. Milton Sherry described his care of Rabbi Coblenz that had begun in 1939. The doctor concluded that there was now evidence of progressive heart disease and strongly suggested that the rabbi discontinue his normal activities. At the Semi-Annual Congregational meeting on June 27, 1946, Herbert Levy introduced a motion to hire an associate rabbi to relieve Rabbi Coblenz of his official duties and to continue Coblenz's current salary as a pension paid throughout his lifetime. The resolution passed unanimously, and the Committee on Engaging an Associate Rabbi was formed. Fleischer traveled to New York to discuss recruitment with the administrators at JTS and with noted Rabbi Stephen Wise.

Although Coblenz continued to write articles for the Jewish press and conduct classes for the Brotherhood in his home, it soon became obvious that hiring an associate rabbi would not be sufficient. On April 14, 1947, the Board agreed to recommend that Rabbi Coblenz be elevated to Rabbi Emeritus and a new rabbi be hired for the Congregation. Interviewing began immediately. Rabbi Isaac Klein of Springfield, Massachusetts traveled to Baltimore to meet with the Board on April 21, 1947, and Rabbi Jacob Agus of Dayton, Ohio met the Board on May 19, 1947. Fleischer traveled to interview rabbis in Cleveland, Florida, and New York. Rabbi Max Arzt served as guest rabbi for the High Holy Days of 1947, and Dr. Louis L. Kaplan officiated at Sukkot services.

Issues of rabbis and mixed seating were temporarily set aside as Chizuk Amuno prepared to celebrate its seventy-fifth anniversary in December, 1946. The Jubilee celebration also marked the twenty-fifth year of Milton Fleischer's presidency and twenty-five years of Cantor Weisgal's service to the Synagogue. In recognition of Dr. Harry Friedenwald's significant contribution to the perpetuation of Chizuk Amuno, he was named Honorary Chairman of the event.

Shabbat morning services on December 21, 1946 featured Rabbi Harry B. Kellman of New Jersey delivering the sermon, assisted by Cantors Henry Cooper and Hillel Lipsicas. Representatives from the Brotherhood and Youth Center also participated in the service.

The Anniversary Banquet was held on Sunday evening, December 22, 1946, at the Alcazar. The commemorative program opened with a four-page history of the Congregation's first seventy-five years, followed by photographs and short biographies of Weisgal and Fleischer. An original skit by Fred E. Katzner, "Chizuk Amuno Marches On," presented a humorous look at the shul's history. Committee Chairman Lester Levy acted as Toastmaster and presented Fleischer with a war bond on a silver tray for the School Center Fund. Weisgal was honored with a $7,500 cash gift donated by his many friends in the Congregation and in the community. The cantor's popularity had spread well beyond the synagogue as he made frequent appearances in concert with the Young Men's Hebrew Association (YMHA) Choral Society, at United Synagogue regional meetings and in programs sponsored by the Jewish Educational Alliance. The personable cantor coached many of the actors starring in satirical Brotherhood and Sisterhood plays and the local Yiddish Theater group.

Capturing the significance of celebrating seventy-five years of existence, Rabbi Coblenz's remarks were published in the December 1946 Bulletin:

> *We have sought to be a bulwark to strengthen Judaism among ourselves and in the community.... We thank God for the opportunity to serve our Faith, our people and our community, and we pray that He may continue His favor unto us and permit us to go forward in scope of service and in intensity of faith and understanding to new achievements of the spirit in the Cause of our people, which is the Cause of God.*

At the suggestion of the Jubilee Arrangements Committee, the Congregation sponsored a grove of one thousand trees in Palestine in the name of Chizuk Amuno.

Although Chizuk Amuno celebrations were joyous, an undercurrent of dissatisfaction ran through the Congregation. Letters of resignation cited the absence of mixed seating as the reason for separation. Manuel Schneider's letter, read into the minutes of September 18, 1947, typifies this attitude:

> *For many years I wanted to worship in a conservative synagogue where I could sit together with my family, but, at the same time, adhere to traditional Judaism. I left Beth Tfiloh Congregation and became a member of the Chizuk Amuno Congregation hoping that here I would find what I crave for. Unfortunately, Chizuk Amuno, the way it is set up today, did not give any answer to my spiritual desires. I am therefore joining the new conservative Synagogue – Beth El Congregation, and I am very sorry that I have to sever my association with your congregation.*

Beth El Congregation, established in 1947, immediately affiliated with the United Synagogue and publicly announced that they were a Conservative congregation. Chizuk Amuno had been intimately involved with the Conservative Movement since its inception. They were active in their support, but nonetheless, remained formally known as "Orthodox." According to sociologist Marshall Sklare, mixed seating was the *"most commonly accepted yardstick for differentiating Conservatism from Orthodoxy."*

The issue of allowing women and men to sit together, also known as "family seating," was the most acrimonious dispute in the history of the Congregation. It epitomized the changing climate of the synagogue as it struggled to mature in post-war America. As stated by Jonathan Sarna in his essay, "The Debate over Mixed Seating in the American Synagogue:"

> *Behind wearisome debates over how sanctuary seats should be arranged and allocated lie fundamental disagreements over the kinds of social and religious values*

that the synagogue should project and the relationship between the synagogue and the larger society that surrounds it.

...mixed seating is a ramified and multifaceted issue that clearly reflects the impact of American values on synagogue life, for it pits family unity, sexual equality, and modernity against the accepted Jewish legal (halachic) practice of sexual separation in prayer.

Within the debate over mixed seating was the issue of elevating the status of women and their right to ritual equality in the synagogue. The resolution of the question would ultimately represent the defining moment in Chizuk Amuno's journey toward religious modernity.

By 1947, the overwhelming majority of Conservative congregations had adopted mixed seating decades earlier. In his High Holy Day remarks at Chizuk Amuno, Rabbi Max Arzt revealed that out of approximately four hundred congregations affiliated with the United Synagogue of America, only four still maintained separate seating. Chizuk Amuno was one of the four. Sensing that the issue of mixed seating would soon come to the forefront, Chizuk Amuno members who supported the change quietly launched a campaign to enroll as members those sympathetic to their position. In order to effect a change in ritual, the support of greater than ninety percent of the membership would be needed. Actions and reactions of the Board and membership during the fall of 1947 were emotionally charged as each side felt that they had the best interest of Chizuk Amuno at heart. To make matters even worse, Baltimore's Orthodox community soon jumped into the fray.

On September 18, 1947, the Board reviewed the position stated in 1921 by the Rabbinical Assembly's Committee on Jewish Law. That body, led by Dr. Louis Ginzberg, declared that gallery seating was unnecessary, but that separate seating had been a Jewish custom for over two thousand years and should not be taken lightly. The Board decided that a resolution adopting mixed seating would be presented at their next meeting.

Before that scheduled meeting could take place, a committee consisting of Herbert Harris, Joseph Fax, Samuel Sakols, and Louis Cordish requested a special meeting with the Board, which was held on October 5. Assuming that the session would serve as a forum to work out an amicable solution to the dispute, the Minute Book recorded that the Board was *"greatly disappointed"* when Joseph Fax stood and quoted Article II of the Chizuk Amuno Constitution as follows:

> *The ritual of our service shall be in accordance with traditional Judaism and the custom of Orthodox Israelites. No alterations whatsoever shall be made in the prayers, ceremonies or customs as long as ten per cent of the members of the Congregation present at the meeting oppose it.*

After reciting the section, Fax turned to the Board saying: *"Gentlemen, this is all we have to say. I beg of you not to violate any portion of the above section of the Constitution."* At that point, the committee of four walked out of the meeting.

Hoping to resolve the dispute with a compromise plan, five Board members met with the minority group on October 13, 1947. The Board suggested the possibility of a second service held downstairs for those wishing separate seating, or a segregated section in the balcony of the synagogue. After over three hours, no agreement could be reached. Milton Fleischer appointed J. Benjamin Katzner, Albert Esterson, and Irving Grant to bring about the *"change under consideration."* The men enlisted the services of Chizuk Amuno members Judge Joseph Sherbow and Herbert Levy, both widely respected attorneys, to draft an appropriate resolution. To assess the level of support for family seating, postal cards were mailed to each member requesting that they indicate their position for or against any such change.

As expected, rumors of the proposed change in seating quickly spread through the Baltimore Jewish community. Unlike Beth El, which had declared itself Conservative from its inception, Chizuk Amuno had spent the past seventy-five years as an Orthodox congregation. For decades, the Council of Orthodox Rabbis had repeatedly invited Chizuk Amuno to join their association, but the Board had always respectfully declined, citing their affiliation with the United Synagogue of America. The Council was appalled to learn that Chizuk Amuno, a congregation they considered to be one of their own, was contemplating mixed seating. Metaphorically, in the minds of the Orthodox clergy, Beth El was a non-observant neighbor, but Chizuk Amuno was a sister about to intermarry. In a full-page advertisement published in the October 17, 1947 issue of the Jewish Times, entitled "A Call to Loyalty," the Council boldly cited that riding on Shabbat, mixed seating, and instrumental music during services were violations of Jewish Law. The ad warned Jews not to undermine the synagogue, which serves as the *"only effective spiritual fortress we have in our struggle for Jewish survival."* Although Chizuk Amuno was not mentioned by name in the indictment, the ad was a thinly veiled effort to lobby voting members of the Congregation to oppose mixed seating.

Ignoring the public intrusion into internal synagogue matters, the leadership of Chizuk Amuno briefly turned their attention to the annual campaign for support of JTS. Lester Levy chaired the $100,000 drive launched on October 30, 1947, at a dinner sponsored by the Baltimore Friends of the Jewish Theological Seminary. Although the dinner was held at Chizuk Amuno, several members of the Beth Tfiloh Congregation joined in their support and volunteered as co-chairmen of the campaign. The strength of the long-standing relationship between Chizuk Amuno and the Seminary would be of great assistance as the vote on mixed seating approached.

With a guest rabbi on the pulpit for Shabbat services on November 15, 1947, Milton Fleischer delivered an emotional message. His passionate plea for *"peace and harmony in this congregation"* reflects the tension that must have permeated the community:

> *Certain statements have been circulated both within our congregation, and throughout the city- - that we intend to install an organ, that we will have shicksas singing in*

*the choir and that we are going to worship with our hats
off. Permit me to say the circulation of such false statements have caused a disturbance in the minds of certain
people, and have actually instilled fear in their minds.*

Fleischer proceeded to dispel these rumors and reassure the
worshippers that Chizuk Amuno would *"always remain Conservative, same as it is at the present time."*

Three days later, Fleischer and Katzner traveled to New York
for a meeting with seventy-five-year-old, Talmudic scholar Louis
Ginzberg. Armed with survey data that approximately eighty-five
percent of the congregants favored the change, the men questioned
Ginzberg about any written prohibition against mixed seating. Anticipating that the minority would want to see Ginzberg's opinion,
Fleischer requested a written response from the scholar.

Ginzberg's two-page letter of December 2, 1947 briefly reviewed the two-thousand-year tradition of separating the sexes in
the synagogue. He commented that separate seating had become a
cherished tradition, although the *"original reason for its existence
had lost its validity."* Concluding that there was *"no written prohibition against the mixing of the sexes during worship,"* Ginzberg
also noted, however, that separate seating was established custom.
Sensing that his response would not provide the definitive answer
that the Chizuk Amuno Board wanted, Ginzberg added: *"I am sure
that my answer will find favor with neither faction of your congregation."* He was correct. The same day Fleischer received Ginzberg's
response he again wrote for clarification:

*The request of the majority has been a constant one for
the past ten years, and has culminated in a demand which
carries the threat that unless the change is instituted,
many of those now affiliated will leave our Congregation. To put the situation before you as it actually exists,
I can say that we are faced with disintegration.*

*I know it is an imposition on your time and your health
to bring you into this controversy, yet in the interest of*

our unity we must ask you to make this sacrifice and advise us.

An unnamed member of the minority group had threatened Fleischer with court action if the Board insisted on pursuing a change to family seating.

Dr. Ginzberg's next letter of December 5, 1947, outlined the major point of his position – that the custom of separate seating originated *"to emphasize Jewish opposition to the Pagan immorality which held sway over the idolatrous neighbors of the old Hebrews like the Phoenicians and Assyro-Babylonians."* Ultimately, Fleischer's decision to let the conflict come to a vote was based on Ginzberg's final point: *"If conditions of a congregation are such that continued separation of family units during services presents a great danger to its spiritual welfare, the minority ought to yield to the spiritual need of the majority."*

Armed with the Ginzberg letters, Fleischer convened a Board meeting on December 10, 1947. As the president had expected, Joseph Fax presented a petition signed by thirteen opponents requesting that Professor Louis Ginzberg *"be asked for an opinion on the Din of seating both sexes together during services."* Surprising Fax, Milton Fleischer reported that the committee had already contacted the scholar and proceeded to read aloud the series of correspondence with Ginzberg. Joseph Sherbow and Herbert Levy arrived at the Board meeting and presented their proposed motion. The attorneys suggested that the motion first be passed by the Board, and then submitted to the membership of the Congregation at a special meeting. The resolution was adopted by the Board with only one vote – that of Ichel Folick – cast against it. A week later, letters were mailed to each member, notifying them of the Semi-Annual Congregation meeting scheduled for Monday, December 29, 1947. Attached was a copy of the Sherbow/Levy proposal instituting family seating at Chizuk Amuno. A small reminder about the meeting was published under the banner, "Chizuk Amuno Events" on page twenty-five of the December 12 issue of the Jewish Times.

In a last-minute effort to denounce the opinions of JTS faculty, a paid advertisement appeared in the <u>Jewish Times</u> on December 26, 1947 with the bold headline, *"AN EDITORIAL from THE JEWISH SPECTATOR."* The lengthy article viciously attacked JTS president Louis Finkelstein, citing him as *"an ally and collaborator of Christian missionaries"* and *"unfit to preside over the Jewish Theological Seminary."* Readers were encouraged to stop their support of the Seminary and demand the removal of Finkelstein.

Although the historic meeting was scheduled to begin at 8:15 p.m., the Minute Book notes that actual starting time was 8:40 p.m. The crowd was estimated at over five hundred, forcing the group to assemble in the main sanctuary of the synagogue. Milton Fleischer began the proceedings according to strict parliamentary procedure, then introduced Max Fish, chairman of the Cemetery Committee, to say a few words. The Minute Book parenthetically notes that due to the large crowd present, Fish *"was desirous of acquainting them with the facts appertaining to our cemetery"* – a sales pitch. The next order of business was the report of the Nominating Committee chaired by Albert Esterson. Milton Fleischer was unanimously re-elected to serve his twenty-seventh term as president of the Congregation. Concluding the routine business portion of the meeting, Fleischer turned the meeting over to Katzner who firmly stated the rules for discussion.

Milton Fleischer was the first person to speak, breaking the tension of the moment by saying: *"First of all, I desire to thank the ladies and gentlemen who have relinquished their tickets for tonight's symphony. The large attendance we have here tonight makes it seem to me as though it might be Yom Kippur."* The president reviewed the events leading to the evening's meeting, noting attempts to reach an amicable compromise with the minority group. The Fleischer – Ginzberg series of correspondence was read aloud, followed by a reading of the proposed resolution. Before Katzner recognized speakers from the floor, he read an emotional statement from Rabbi Adolph Coblenz:

I have not words to express my grief and my anxiety over the fact that the condition of my health has not permitted me during these past months to be with you and to share with you in the labor, the effort, the problems, the joys and concerns of our congregational life. And that even tonight, at this most crucial and decisive meeting, I must content myself with sending you a written opinion while being forced to stay away from you. I assure you that my spirit and my emotions, as well as my mind, are with you tonight, as they have been over the past so very long months.

Coblenz's letter repeated many of the points included in Ginzberg's opinion and ended with a definitive statement:

In view of all of the foregoing, and particularly because there is no written law of our tradition prohibiting mixed seating, at Jewish religious services, I want to express myself as strongly urging the proposal. The voice of the majority should prevail, and especially when the majority is so overwhelming.

Five members – Herbert Harris, Meyer Zuravin, Harry Morris, Yale Merrill, and Edward Shalowitz – spoke for the minority position. Isaac Potts, then Beatrice Levy (widow of William Levy) spoke for the majority. Judge Joseph Sherbow spoke last, assuring the crowd that his words were neither on behalf of the majority or minority, but simply from a heartfelt interest in the future of Chizuk Amuno.

Members of Chizuk Amuno then voted on the proposal, and the tally announced – 284 votes for the resolution and twenty votes opposed. Telegrams and letters had been received from twenty-six additional members stating that they would have voted for the change. A call for unanimous consent was defeated as six men stood up in a final show of opposition to mixed seating. Stories still circulate that some opponents were offered rides to the synagogue, then driven around the city until after the vote was taken.

Rather than publishing a featured article on the momentous vote at Chizuk Amuno, the <u>Jewish Times</u> simply noted the change of practice on page thirteen of its January 16, 1948 issue:

*In accordance with the resolution adopted by the Con-
gregation at the general meeting of the membership held
on Monday, December 29, to institute mixed seating (family pews), the Board of Directors decided to set Saturday
as the date when men and women will begin to sit together in the Synagogue during the services. The seating arrangements are temporary, and all worshippers
may sit anywhere they desire, until permanent reassign-
ments will be made.*

Rabbi Max Arzt returned to Baltimore to conduct the historic January 24, 1948 Shabbat service with a mixed seating audience.

Repercussions from the seating change were swift. In a one-line letter dated the day after the vote, Joseph Fax informed the Board that his pledge for 1948 would be ten dollars instead of one hundred dollars. A second letter was much more upsetting to the Board. Under the auspices of the Chizuk Amuno Beth Hamidrash Association, Rabbi Michael Eliezer Forschlager had taught Mishna and Talmud every day between Mincha and Maariv for over twenty-five years. A well-respected scholar in the community, Forschlager felt forced to sever his connection in light of the decision. His remarks under-score how the mixed seating debate served to divide the Orthodox and Conservative communities and the emotional strife that division created:

*I wish to remark here another fact that the people who
appealed to me most by their Jewishness, piety and nobility of character I found at Chizuk Amuno. I further
know that every person with whom I came in close contact in Chizuk Amuno showed me in all respects great
honor, while I think that, with His help, I attended to my*

duties faithfully and to the best of my abilities. I was most gratified with my position, as any person should have been, to be in daily contact with you. I believe that everyone in the Shul understands my feelings, that I am forced to take this step, much as it grieves me. It hurts me to leave the Shul and these fine people of noble hearts overflowing with infinite goodness and friendship.

Max Abramowitz and William Greenfeld were appointed to meet with Rabbi Forschlager and attempt to convince him to reconsider his resignation. Although their efforts failed, the Board voted to pay the rabbi for the month of January, 1948 – then accepted his resignation with regret.

The reaction of the Council of Orthodox Rabbis (Vaad Harabonim) was much less civil. One week after the first mixed seating service at Chizuk Amuno, an article appeared in the Jewish Times written by Rabbi Manuel Poliakoff entitled *"In the Name of Truth."* The author lambasted the Conservative Movement and offered to "expose the intentional falsehoods employed by these men in their desperate struggle to gain a foothold in our community." Supporting his position that Conservative Jews seek to destroy traditional Judaism, Poliakoff ended with the warning: *"So beware of Conservatism; do not add hypocrisy to apostasy."* Unfortunately, Chizuk Amuno's relationship with the Orthodox clergy of Baltimore would get much worse before it improved.

A seemingly simple decision by the Board on February 2, 1948 may have been the most symbolic expression of their embrace of Conservatism. Secretary Joseph Weinstein questioned the Board about the synagogue's listing in the city's telephone book and Hotel Church Directory. They unanimously decided that the name of Chizuk Amuno, currently listed among Orthodox congregations, be removed and relocated under the heading, "Conservative."

THE GOLDMAN ERA 1948-1976

What impresses you most about Dr. Goldman, aside from his record and achievements and accomplishments is his warm-hearted and informal conversational approach. He talks with you as if he has all the time in the world. He has an approach...which should gain the personal friendship of anyone with whom he may come in contact.

Maurice R. Shochatt
"Monumental Sidelights"
<u>Jewish Times</u>, *November 5, 1948*

Final settlement of the mixed seating controversy allowed the Board to focus on their next major decision – hiring a new rabbi. Many rabbis had substituted at Shabbat and holiday services for the ailing Rabbi Coblenz, and could have been considered candidates for the position. Surprisingly, Chizuk Amuno's fourth rabbi, Rabbi Israel M. Goldman, never preached from the Baltimore pulpit before formally starting his employment.

By late 1947, Rabbi Goldman was nationally known among the Conservative community. He had written several articles that had appeared in the local Jewish press, even though he served a congregation in Providence, Rhode Island. There is no mention of Goldman in the minutes before February, 1948 however, letters in the Chizuk Amuno archives indicate that Board member Isaac Potts had approached the rabbi several months earlier about relocating to Baltimore. Years later, Israel Goldman commented to family members that he would not have seriously considered a move to Baltimore until Chizuk Amuno settled their mixed seating debate. Goldman quietly slipped into town on January 14, 1948 for an undocumented interview with selected Board members at the home of

Isaac Potts. In a letter dated January 8, 1948, confirming the trip, Goldman wrote:

> *I am very glad that I shall be arriving in Baltimore a little earlier for I so much want to call on my esteemed colleague, Rabbi Coblenz and, if possible, I should also like the pleasure of visiting the Synagogue in which he has ministered with such devotion and distinction for so many decades.*

At the January meeting, Rabbi Goldman asserted that he did not want to be known as a candidate for the position. Privately, however, he let Potts know that he would consider an offer if it constituted a promotion from his present pulpit.

When the Board convened on February 2, 1948, Potts, Chairman of the Rabbi Committee, reported on the interview with Dr. Israel Goldman, reviewing his educational and professional achievements. The committee's report included comments about the rabbi's personal characteristics:

> *In person he is tolerably attractive, has a pleasant manner, a positive personality, very definitely that of a leader. He speaks Hebrew and is familiar with sources. I have the statement of Rabbi Finkelstein that he is an able speaker, with a good vocabulary, poise in the pulpit, an adequate knowledge of sermon material, and an ability to integrate into his sermons his texts so that they are readily understood by the average congregation.*

In an effort to convince Board members that Goldman was a distinguished choice, Potts concluded with the remark: "*I was told that if one disregards the five nationally famous rabbis, such as Solomon Goldman and Milton Steinberg, that Rabbi Goldman ranks very high in the next grouping.*" Discussion about Israel Goldman was very positive, although in a written statement, Albert Esterson expressed his opinion that perhaps "*a younger man would be preferable.*" The Board unanimously decided to offer Goldman the pulpit of Chizuk Amuno at a salary of $13,500 per year.

Rabbi Goldman and his wife, Mildred, traveled to Baltimore on February 5, 1948, to discuss contract provisions. The rabbi requested that the Congregation contribute to a retirement fund established by the Rabbinical Assembly, and purchase a home for his family to rent. Six days later, the Board approved these stipulations and the Rabbi Committee was instructed to draft the necessary formal documents. Irving Grant, Hyman Caplan, and Bernard Manekin were appointed to secure a home for the Goldman family.

Rabbi Goldman received two letters at his Rhode Island home dated February 12, 1948. The first, from the president of the Chizuk Amuno Congregation, informed him that the Board had unanimously elected him to their pulpit. *"With this call we present to you a new field for your varied abilities, certain, that you will be glad to share your God-given talents, with our large community, and thus, spread your enlightening influence over a greater section of our country."* The second letter, from Isaac Potts, complimented Goldman on his "charming" wife. *"It is a lot of satisfaction to be able to tell you that the women who met with Mrs. Goldman were more than favorably impressed."*

A special congregational meeting was held on March 2, 1948 to approve the Board's selection. In addition to reading the committee's recommendation, Fleischer also read resolutions from Temple Emanu-El in Providence releasing Goldman from his contract, and a letter from Rabbi Coblenz. Dispelling any doubts that he hoped to actively resume his congregational responsibilities, Coblenz endorsed the selection of his colleague, and accepted the status of Rabbi Emeritus. As expected, the vote was again unanimous.

Late in life, Rabbi Goldman began a handwritten draft of his autobiography with the words:

My father's name was Moshe Yaakov ben Yitzchak Dov. My mother's name was Hannah Ziese bas Yisroel Mordechai. I was born on Purim in the Polish town of

Prushnitz [Przasnyz] *not far from Warsaw. My father
was a Russian soldier for 4 years and was most scrupulously observant. He wore his tefillin daily and kept
strictly kosher...*

As thousands of others had done, Goldman's father traveled to
America before sending for his wife and two young children in May
1910. Israel Goldman arrived in New York on the *S.S. Finland* and
was listed, along with his mother and sister, Sarah, on the manifest
of passengers by their original family surname – Guzawacka. The
family initially settled on the Lower East Side and adopted the name
"Goldman." It was not until 1926 that the man known on government documents as "Max Guzowacker" became an American citizen, and legally changed his name to Israel Max Goldman.

As a young boy, Goldman attended public schools and the
neighborhood Hebrew school. Inspired by influential teachers, he
continued his Jewish education and assumed leadership positions in
Jewish youth organizations. Upon high school graduation, Goldman
enrolled both at the City College of New York and the Teachers Institute of JTS. After two years, he was summoned to the office of
Dr. Samson Benderly, head of the New York Board of Jewish Education. Benderly, who had previously served as the first principal of
the Chizuk Amuno Hebrew School, lobbied Goldman to devote his
future career to the field of Jewish education. Although fascinated
by the thought, he felt a calling to become a pulpit rabbi and enrolled
at the Seminary. While attending the last two years of his rabbinical
training, Goldman also completed a Master's Program in Philosophy at Columbia University.

In 1925, prior to receiving his ordination, Goldman was recommended to the fledgling Temple Emanu-El Congregation in Providence, Rhode Island to officiate at their first High Holy Day services.
Delighted with Goldman's professionalism and his eagerness to become involved in the establishment of a new congregation, the Conservative congregation hired him immediately after his June 6, 1926
ordination. It was in Providence that Goldman refined his interests
in adult education. He established the Institute of Jewish Studies for

Adults in 1929, and organized a series of Jewish cultural events including art exhibits and historical lectures. Continuing his own education, the rabbi was awarded the degree of Doctor of Hebrew Literature from the Seminary in 1937.

Plans to develop a National Academy for Adult Jewish Studies were unveiled at a convention of the Rabbinical Assembly in 1940. Dr. Louis Finkelstein recruited Rabbi Goldman to serve as the organization's first director – a volunteer position that he held for fourteen years. The JTS chancellor also invited Goldman to become the president of the United Synagogue of America, but the rabbi declined the invitation. After serving various leadership roles in the Rabbinical Assembly, Goldman was elected president of the Assembly in 1946. A year later, he traveled 10,000 miles touring Jewish communities from San Diego to British Columbia assessing the region's level of spiritual and religious awareness. As a result of that tour, the Conservative leadership offered him the position of Provost at the West Coast University of Judaism. This position was also graciously declined. Israel Goldman always knew in his heart that he was destined to be a congregational rabbi.

With Rabbi Goldman's formal acceptance completed, Fleischer was anxious to publicly announce that as of August 1, 1948, Chizuk Amuno would be led by a new rabbi. Executive Secretary Joseph Weinstein coordinated the distribution of news releases to local newspapers and Jewish press nationally. Goldman's photograph appeared on the cover of the March 5, 1948 <u>Jewish Times</u>, accompanied by a full-page story devoted to the announcement of his appointment. A biographical sketch of Goldman's life and a reprint of his acceptance letter were printed in the April, 1948 <u>Bulletin</u>. The rabbi's words echoed his hopes for the future:

> *The enlightened spirit and zeal of its lay-leadership, the pride and consecration of its general membership, the devotion and dedication of its talented staff, and above*

all its time-honored traditions which link modernity to eternity in Jewish religious life, are all absolute guarantee of the bright horizons towards which this historic Congregation is moving.

I shall strive to weave my own life into the fabric of Chizuk Amuno, into the texture of its auxiliary organizations, and more especially into the lives of its men, women, young people, and children.

The Baltimore Jewish community was taken by surprise. In a letter to Goldman dated March 14, 1948, Weinstein commented, *"I want to tell you that the news of your election...has already stirred the entire Jewish community of Baltimore and everyone is talking about and looking forward to a dynamic Rabbinical leadership in Chizuk Amuno."* Letters, telegrams, and calls of congratulations poured into the Goldman home. Among those writing were Cantor Weisgal, Hymen Saye, church leaders, colleagues around North America, and communal leaders.

The Congregation could not delight in its accomplishment very long, as repercussions from the mixed seating change continued to explode. Just two weeks after Goldman's election, the <u>Jewish Times</u> printed a pronouncement by the Council of Orthodox Rabbis, condemning Chizuk Amuno for *"desecration of the Sanctity of the Synagogue"* by introducing family seating. The rabbis warned that the Conservative movement was wantonly discarding hallowed traditions. Segregation of the sexes during worship was once again termed *"a strict requirement of the law and tradition of Israel"* by the Council. The advertisement proclaimed, *"NO JEW MAY WORSHIP IN A SYNAGOGUE WHERE THIS SACRED PRINCIPLE IS BEING VIOLATED."* Milton Fleischer wrote to Goldman, informing the rabbi of Chizuk Amuno's position in dealing with the inflammatory article:

Do not let this get you – nothing to worry about, for I believe it is simply a "face saving" matter – as some of the "orthodox"(?) Rabbis are apparently afraid that some

*of their congregants may endeavor to bring about a con-
servative change. We feel it will be a part of wisdom on
our part to entirely ignore the article, for we believe
"they" would welcome a reply in order to start a controversy.*

Fleischer received similar advice from Rabbi Max Arzt:

*The latest exhibit of the zealots of Baltimore proves con-
clusively that you are dealing with 14th century minds.
To answer them means to give them status, which they
do not deserve....Those who seek to promote their views
through paid advertisements will soon learn that Chizuk
Amuno will ever remain an impregnable citadel of the
living tradition of Judaism.*

Vicious letters attacking Conservatism continued to appear in
the local Jewish press through the subsequent weeks. It was amidst
this tension that Rabbi Goldman's involvement at Chizuk Amuno
began.

Although his term was not officially to start until August 1,
Goldman immediately began preparing for his new position. On
April 1, 1948, Israel and Mildred Goldman visited Baltimore to tour
the synagogue, the city, and their future home. The rabbi met with
the nine young ladies of the confirmation class, and the Ritual Committee. These meetings led to a flurry of correspondence between
Goldman and members of the synagogue community as he formulated his ambitious plans for the future of Chizuk Amuno.

Preserved in the rabbi's private *"Work Book Vol. III (1948-
1964),"* are notes listing suggestions he planned to implement. The
first pages, dated May 1948, exhibit the attention to detail that would
continue to mark Goldman's style of management:

1) *Membership Campaign – 100 new members! Get lists of children of present & former members. During   Rededication
   Week hold public induction of 100 new members*
2) *Installation Week – hold a whole week of observances beginning with Installation the first Sunday and Banquet the*

next Sunday. During the week hold special Rededication functions

3) Institute of Jewish Studies

4) Hebrew lettering on Stationery

5) Weekly or bi-weekly Bulletin

6) Membership record card

7) Send out Rosh Hashana greeting cards

8) Wedding anniversary cards

9) Men's Club – Laymen's Institute in winter, Community Service Award

10) Sisterhood – Mother & Daughter Sabbath, J. Ceremonial Art program

11) BMB & BMS [bar mitzvah Brotherhood and Sisterhood]

12) Branch School with bus service

13) School Board – double enrollment, re-organize

14) New prayer books – Silverman for H.H.

15) Hertz Bibles

16) Y.P.L. & misc. Youth activities – alumni et. al.

17) Friday Eve Services – forums, Choral Society

18) Shabbos A.M. Services – more cong. singing, new melodies

19) Shabbos Afternoon – study period, group singing

20) "House Gatherings" – a chain of them, make a social evening of it but also give a brief talk & discussion, cover the entire cong.

21) Certificate for Naming new born children

22) Rabbis Special Fund

23) Dedicate new pulpit in honor of Coblenz

24) Womens Institute of C.A. – 6 or 7 sessions

25) Mr. & Mrs. Club

Speaking at a memorial service for his colleague in 1979, Rabbi Joel H. Zaiman reflected: "*Israel Goldman loved beginnings. More than any rabbi I have ever known, he loved reciting the Shehecheyanu blessing.*" Even as Rabbi Goldman's Providence congregation hosted a lavish series of testimonial and farewell events, his excitement over a new beginning at Chizuk Amuno was evident.

The summer of 1948 was hectic for the lay leaders of Chizuk Amuno as they prepared not only for a new spiritual leader, but also for the first holiday session with mixed seating. The Committee on Reassignment of Seating polled members by mail as to the number of seats the family needed. Noted in red on the bottom of the card was the warning, *"NOTE: Seats will be assigned on a mixed-seating basis unless you specify otherwise."* Every effort was being made to satisfy the remaining dissenters. As responses were received, the committee faced a dilemma – there were 1,100 requests from members for seats and only 1,000 seats available on the first floor. To accommodate the shortage, a new dues structure was proposed. Dues were raised from $56 to $65 and included two seats per member on the main floor. A member also had the option of paying dues of $40 (and a minimum $10 pledge) to receive two seats in the balcony. Seatholders were strongly encouraged to become full members. Extra seats for the High Holy Day services were sold to the public at prices that varied with the location of the seat. A few long-time members challenged the Board's authority to reassign their seats. Formal deeds had been issued to them when the Congregation moved to the Eutaw Place synagogue. Thankfully, settlement was reached before any of these disputes reached formal litigation.

Following Rabbi Goldman's suggestion, the Divine Services Committee agreed that the Silverman Machzor, used by most other Conservative synagogues, be adopted by Chizuk Amuno for the coming High Holy Day season. On July 20, 1948, the Board unanimously approved the purchase of 1,600 books. By the fall, the cost of all of the new machzorim had been covered by pledges from members. Decision to purchase a substantial number of *"Hertz Chumoshim for the Synagogue"* was reached in November. Rabbi Goldman felt that if each worshipper had a copy, they would be more comfortable following along, either in English or Hebrew, during the Torah and Haftorah readings.

On August 24, 1948, the Goldman family, including young daughters Anna and Tobie, moved into their new home at 2444 Eutaw Place. The three-story house included a remodeled library built to the rabbi's specifications. Members of the Board, staff of the Congregation, and other selected guests were invited to a formal "Consecration of the Home" service in November to witness the "Ceremony of Affixing the Mezuzah" at the Goldman home. The Baltimore press interviewed the new rabbi upon his arrival, and published Goldman's thoughts on the role of Conservative Judaism. The September 13, 1948 edition of The Evening Sun quoted his first sermon at Chizuk Amuno:

> *The greatest task for American Jewry now is to develop itself qualitatively. Having grown in size, it must now grow in depth. Having excelled philanthropically, it needs now to mature intellectually. Having served as a material granary, to feed world Jewry, it must now provide a spiritual storehouse to nurture its own soul.*

Just as Israel Goldman had proposed six months earlier, official installation ceremonies took place during the November 14-21, 1948 "Rededication Week." Engraved invitations welcomed the community to varied events, which included a youth rally, Sisterhood and Brotherhood celebrations, inaugural Friday night services, a school pageant entitled, "Strengthening of Faith," community Shabbat service, and an elegant banquet at the Lord Baltimore Hotel. The November 12, 1948 issue of the Jewish Times published seven pages promoting the events, and commented on Goldman's future in their editorial column:

> *Dr. Goldman has already proved that he is vitally concerned with dynamic rather than static religion. It is his contention that the Jewish way of life, be it religion, culture, education, history, etc. is vital enough to offer spiritual nourishment on a year-round basis rather than the*

three-day prescription adopted by too many of our breth-
ren. That accounts for why so many educational pro-
grams for the benefit of old and young are about to be
added to the sphere of activities at Chizuk Amuno.

As in prior years, prominent members of the Conservative movement were invited to participate in the installation of a Chizuk Amuno rabbi. Dr. Louis Finkelstein, president of the Jewish Theological Seminary, delivered the installation address and conferred the charge to the rabbi. The executive director of the National Young People's League spoke at the Monday evening Youth Rally, and the president of the National Women's League addressed the Sisterhood's Tuesday afternoon celebration. Dr. Solomon Grayzel, renowned Jewish historian and editor of the Jewish Publication Society, was the principal speaker at the Brotherhood's Wednesday evening celebration. Special invitations to the lectures were issued to members of the Beth El and Beth Tfiloh Sisterhood and Brotherhood. Chizuk Amuno made obvious efforts to reconcile with portions of Baltimore's Orthodox community. Rabbi Samuel Rosenblatt of the Beth Tfiloh Congregation, Rabbi Benjamin Axelman of the Petach Tikvah Congregation, and Rabbi Uri Miller of the Beth Jacob Congregation all participated in Rabbi Goldman's installation ceremony.

As promised, one hundred families were presented at the November 19, 1948 Friday evening service to be installed as new members of Chizuk Amuno Congregation. They accepted the charge by Rabbi Goldman to *"be loyal to the teachings of the Synagogue and uphold them by your prayers, your presence and your service."* Although many of the new members had previously been seatholders, the public announcement that one hundred additional families were now associated with the Congregation was perceived to indicate tremendous growth. The rabbi continued to set a goal of one hundred new members for each of the years to come.

The Installation Banquet reflected Goldman's prior involvement with interfaith relations. Judge Joseph Sherbow served as Toastmaster for the evening, introducing the executive director of the

National Conference of Christians and Jews, the Methodist minister serving as president of the regional Council of Churches, and a representative of the Archdiocese of Baltimore. The Governor of Maryland and Mayor of Baltimore were also present to convey their greetings. Dr. Israel Herbert Levinthal of the Brooklyn Jewish Center and Senator J. Howard McGrath of Rhode Island delivered the keynote addresses.

One prominent member of the Chizuk Amuno community was not able to attend the festivities due to poor health. In a note to Rabbi Goldman dated September 6, 1948, Dr. Harry Friedenwald welcomed the rabbi, and provided some personal insight into the seventy-six-year-old congregation:

> *It is the congregation which was called into being, chiefly by my Grandfather and to which my father was devoted until his death. It was the Congregational School which I attended. I was married in its Synagogue and for a number of years I followed in the steps of my father & grandfather as president. I need not tell you that I am deeply interested in the Congregation. It is my wish that it will thrive under your leadership and serve as a bulwark of Judaism and Jewish life.*

Goldman was quite impressed when he visited the elderly Friedenwald. Decades later, the rabbi researched the Friedenwald family story, and frequently referred to their public accomplishments and dedication to Chizuk Amuno in sermons. In 1964, Goldman recognized the centennial anniversary of Harry Friedenwald's birth with a special address on the first day of Sukkot.

For the first time in its history, Chizuk Amuno had hired a rabbi with not only scholarly achievements, but also with decades of proven professional experience and a national reputation. This maturity facilitated the shift in ritual authority that the Conservative movement advocated. The United Synagogue of America asked every member congregation to accept the rabbi as the *"authority on all matters of Jewish law and practices and as the interpreter of the decisions rendered and principles established by the Committee on Jewish Law and Standards of the Rabbinical Assembly."* In the past, the Board or Divine Services Committee proposed new programs and ritual changes, and then consulted the rabbi as a courtesy. Milton Fleischer was serving his twenty-sixth year as president in 1948, and spending more time traveling away from Baltimore. The new generation of lay leaders had not been schooled in the traditional "cheder" manner of their fathers and grandfathers, and welcomed the strong spiritual leadership of Rabbi Goldman.

Many of the rabbi's initial changes to established Chizuk Amuno rituals and procedures were aimed at increasing lay participation in worship and synagogue activities. The Torah reader was turned to face the worshippers rather than the Ark. Standing committees were established, and the chairperson of each committee was granted a position on the Board. The School Board was enlarged to include twelve additional members. A constitutional amendment restricted trustee positions to a two-year term, and set a maximum two-consecutive-term limit. Dramatic readings, music, and a candle lighting ceremony were added to the girls' confirmation service.

Raising the standard for religious education of children was also on Rabbi Goldman's agenda. On April 4, 1949 the Board adopted new *"Requirements for Bar Mitzvah."* Although parents were strongly urged to provide six years of Hebrew education for sons prior to their becoming a bar mitzvah, the rabbi realized that some families delayed starting their children's religious education. Phased in over a three-year period, the following minimum standards were established:

> *A Bar Mitzvah certificate will be issued only to a boy who has completed a minimum of three years in our Hebrew School or its equivalent in addition to attending for approximately six months the two Bar Mitzvah courses...*

All Bar Mitzvah candidates must be examined every three months and one month prior to Bar Mitzvah by the Rabbi and certified by him.

During the year preceding their becoming a bar mitzvah, the boys met as a class with Cantor Weisgal four afternoons a week. Attendance at every Shabbat morning service during that year was also a compulsory requirement.

Less than one month later, the Board unanimously passed another resolution intended to strengthen the educational program for boys. Young men were encouraged to continue their formal learning for three years after becoming a bar mitzvah by studying with the girls of the confirmation class. In June, 1951 three boys, Jerry Blum, Eugene Klompus, and Rodney Plotkin joined seven girls for the first coed confirmation service. The women lighted Shabbat candles and recited biblical passages before the Kabbalat Shabbat service, while the young men received parts in the evening service. To encourage these young people to continue their involvement with Chizuk Amuno, the Bar Mitzvah Brotherhood was formed in 1950. The young men met every Sunday at nine for services, followed by breakfast and discussion.

The Baltimore Jewish Council estimated the city's Jewish population in 1947 to be approximately 80,000. The generation reaching adulthood in the late 1940's continued the pattern of leaving intensely urban areas. They migrated to the suburbs, hoping to raise their children in single-family homes nestled among green lawns and open areas. This shift out of the ethnic neighborhood surrounding the synagogue gave rise to a new dilemma. As expressed by Jack Wertheimer in his essay, "The Conservative Synagogue":

Having been raised in densely populated Jewish enclaves where identification with Jewishness, if not necessarily Judaism, was taken for granted, they now found themselves in far more integrated neighborhoods that provided no natural outlet for Jewish identification.

Members sought the fellowship of the synagogue community as a surrogate for the eroded sense of a communal neighborhood.

To promote fellowship among members, Rabbi Goldman insisted that the <u>Bulletin</u> be printed on a weekly basis. This would enable congregants to be constantly aware of the worship service schedule, synagogue activities, news of contributions, and the rabbi's planned sermon topic. Goldman also used the newsletter to convey a personal message and extend an offer of pastoral counseling. The <u>Bulletin</u> often printed the message: *"The Rabbi would appreciate being advised of any congregant to whom he may be of service in any way."*

Although attendance at Shabbat services had decreased, participation in Sisterhood, Brotherhood, and Youth Center activities remained strong. In 1948, J. Max Abramowitz proposed the idea of the Brotherhood holding Sunday morning breakfast minyans followed by a discussion on Jewish topics. With all available rooms occupied on Sundays by the school, the Brotherhood petitioned the Board for access to an unfinished basement room. The group used their own funds to convert the space into a *"club room where it would be possible to hold these Sunday morning get-to-gethers."* I. C. Rosenthal personally supervised the remodeling project and the first Brotherhood Breakfast Minyan was held October 10, 1948, with forty-five men in attendance.

Educational opportunities also brought adult members together as a community. Goldman established the Women's Institute of Chizuk Amuno within his first three months in Baltimore. Two courses began on Wednesday, October 20, 1948, with an enrollment of over 200 women. "Words and Music of the Prayer Book" was taught by Rabbi Goldman and Cantor Weisgal, and "Eight Easy Lessons in Reading Hebrew" by Mildred Goldman. In subsequent years, courses explored topics on Jewish art, parenting skills, and holiday celebrations. The one-dollar enrollment fee also entitled the participant to complimentary coffee and dessert after class.

Delighted with the success of the women's courses, in the winter of 1949 the rabbi established a series of adult courses open to both men and women. The Institute of Adult Jewish Education at Chizuk Amuno offered classes in Hebrew, Mishna, Jewish Literature, and American Jewish History. At the March 7, 1949 Board meeting, Rabbi Goldman reported that *"our Institute has met with great success and that, at present, there is a paid enrollment of 540."* As the annual event continued, curriculum expanded, and prominent scholars appeared as guest lecturers. By 1955, the Adult Institute included lectures on the great masters of Jewish music, interfaith relations, marriage, and a film forum.

As the first year of Israel Goldman's tenure drew to a close, he initiated one more form of adult education – the Weekend Laymen's Institute. Sponsored jointly by the Brotherhoods of Chizuk Amuno, Beth El, and Adas Israel of Washington, D.C., the four-day retreat was held May 23-26, 1949. Thirty-six men gathered at Camp Wohelo, located atop the Blue Ridge Mountains of Pennsylvania. As explained by Rabbi Goldman, the mission of the *"vacation Institute"* was two-fold:

> *To afford you a Jewish cultural program under outstanding Jewish scholars so as to enrich the store of your Jewish knowledge and to equip you for more effective Jewish living and leadership; and to offer you a vacation program for wholesome and healthful recreation in a beautiful mountain camp.*

Addresses by keynote speakers, study sessions with Rabbis Goldman and Beth El's Rabbi Agus, round table discussions, worship services, and nightly campfires served to strengthen fellowship among those present. Winter "reunions" were held at the synagogue to share feedback on the experience and make plans for the following season. In 1959, eighty-nine men attended the twelfth annual Laymen's Institute.

The Congregation's close association with JTS and Israel Goldman's reputation enabled them to attract prominent Jewish personalities to lecture at Chizuk Amuno. On December 16, 1951 Professor Martin Buber, of the Hebrew University of Jerusalem, spoke on "Judaism and Civilization" to a packed crowd. Occasionally, a special Sabbath Institute was held during the year, showcasing a noted scholar. Dr. Abraham Joshua Heschel, Professor of Theology at JTS, joined the Congregation for the weekend of November 18, 1955. He delivered two addresses – "The Spirit of Judaism" at the late Friday night service, and "Faith In The Living God" at a Supper Party following Havdalah services Saturday evening. Other visiting scholars during the early 1950's included Dr. Robert Gordis of JTS, Dr. Abraham A. Neuman, president of Dropsie College, Dr. Salo Baron of Columbia University, and Dr. Marshall Sklare of Brandeis University.

In early 1949, a study commissioned by the National Jewish Welfare Board reported demographic information about the Baltimore Jewish community. Rabbi Goldman requested an interpretation of that data from the chief statistician of the city's Department of Vital Records. In his letter of April 11, 1949, Dr. Thureber Fales noted several demographic characteristics of the area surrounding the synagogue:

- *higher percentage of adults over 65 than the average of the entire city*
- *smaller percentage children under age 15 than average*
- *among the highest rental fees in the city*
- *more than double the average proportion of population in the upper social economic groups*

Based on these findings, Fales expressed his opinion that *"the area will remain for the next ten to fifteen years socially and economically very much as it has during the last twenty years."*

At the Board's request, Joseph Weinstein conducted a formal survey of Chizuk Amuno members gathering similar demographic information. Five hundred members and three hundred seatholders were contacted. An analysis of the 1949 results reveals the extent of the Jewish migration to the suburbs:

- 357 affiliated families had a total of 525 children
- of the families with children, 203 lived in the Eutaw Place area, the balance of 154 families lived in Upper Park Heights and Forest Park areas
- approximately 30% of school age children did not enroll in Chizuk Amuno schools or youth center activities

Relying on these facts, the Board determined to fully develop the School Center nearby the existing synagogue, rather than relocate the Congregation.

Expanded membership brought increased enrollment in the Congregational schools. The destruction of European Jewry motivated families to assign increased importance to the religious education of their children. Parents and grandparents strove to instill a sense of Jewish consciousness into their school-age children by sending them to Hebrew school. They hoped that their youngsters would carry Judaism into the next generation.

Synagogue classrooms were stretched to capacity. The property at Eutaw Place and Whitelock Street (2401 Eutaw), purchased by the Congregation in 1941, had been maintained as rental apartments. As tenants on the first floor moved out, remodeling activity began. On March 27, 1949 the Chizuk Amuno Annex Building was dedicated with a brief program and a formal "Presentation of the Keys" ceremony. The additional space for 150 students was immediately put into use. Six months later, children's services for the High Holy Days were conducted in the Annex. On September 12, 1949 the School Center doors opened for the first class of the Chizuk Amuno Daily Hebrew Nursery School.

As a member of the Board of Jewish Education, Chizuk Amuno cooperated in an advertising campaign to encourage religious school enrollment. Announcement of session starting dates appeared before each semester. A committee, composed of PTA mothers, embarked on an Enrollment Campaign and personally contacted families with school-age children. Concerned that parents would elect to send their children to the afternoon school that was closest to their homes, the School Board decided to provide a system of transportation to the Hebrew and Sunday schools. Messages in the <u>Bulletin</u> reminded parents that *"we are now providing quick and safe service by means of the Yellow Cab Company."* In September, 1951 transportation problems eased slightly as Mr. and Mrs. Milton Schwaber presented the Congregation with a new station wagon in honor of their twenty-fifth wedding anniversary. By 1955, the *"fleet of station wagons"* had grown to five.

When discussing the welfare of the Congregation at the June 6, 1949 Board meeting, Rabbi Goldman cited the possibility of enhancing the musical portion of the service. Anxious for increased congregant involvement, the rabbi proposed hiring a music director to coordinate musical programming:

> *At present we have a fine Chazin, but no musical activities whatsoever. For a congregation of our type, it behooves us to have a permanent choral society, a good choir, congregational singing, both at the Friday Evening Services and Saturday mornings.*

Goldman suggested Hugo Weisgall, son of Cantor Abba Weisgal, for the position. Weisgall, who had altered the spelling of the family surname to aid in its proper pronunciation, was a prominent composer and conductor. He had studied at the Peabody Conservatory of Music, the Curtis Institute in Philadelphia, and held a doctoral degree in German Literature from Johns Hopkins University.

The Board clearly defined Dr. Weisgall's charge as Director of the Chizuk Amuno Choral Society. The first choir of male and female voices was to have a target membership of fifty, and be comprised of volunteers from the Congregation and community. Although the mixed group provided choral music and led congregational singing at the late Friday service, they did not sing at Shabbat morning services. Four male choir members, led by Harry King, were compensated for accompanying the Shabbat service. The Society presented special programs at Brotherhood, Sisterhood, and Congregational meetings when invited, and participated in citywide events during Jewish Music Week. A small budget was granted to purchase sheet music.

Notice of the new Choral Society appeared in the Bulletin of September 30, 1949. Interested members were encouraged to attend the first meeting of the Society on October 6. After only three rehearsals, the *"Vested Choir of Forty Voices under the direction of Dr. Hugo Weisgall"* made their first public appearance during late services on Friday evening, November 11, 1949. Over seventy-nine years had passed since Jonas Friedenwald had founded Chizuk Amuno, protesting plans for a mixed choir at Baltimore Hebrew Congregation.

During his tenure as choral director, Hugo Weisgall continued to expand his musical talents. He composed and directed operatic scores, and founded the Baltimore Chamber Arts Society in 1951 and the Hilltop Musical Company in 1952. In 1951, Weisgall was selected to become the chairman of the faculty at the newly established cantorial school at JTS, a position he held for forty-six years. His responsibilities included designing the curriculum of the school and implementing the musical facets of the program. In his essay, "Music at JTS," Neil W. Levin comments that Weisgall, as the heir to a European cantorial lineage, was perfectly suited for his role:

> *His breadth of cultural background, musical as well as literary intellect, Jewish musical sensibilities and commitment, and vast western musical knowledge and activity, taken together, embodied some of the basic historical principles of the Seminary.*

Under Weisgall's guidance, the curriculum centered around the concept of *"hazzanut as a vital musical-liturgical tradition governed by its wider context of diverse genres, forms, styles, and periods that compose the aggregate Jewish music tradition."*

On June 5, 1951 the Congregation hosted a dinner in honor of the Choral Society in the vestry of the synagogue. Members performed an original skit, mocking their Thursday evening rehearsals. A song, with lyrics by Lil Forman, concluded the program:

To the tune of "Some Enchanted Evening"

Every Friday evening
Fourteen weeks together,
We don't let the weather
Keep us away.
Paul hands us our music,
Looks out for who's late,
And we go marching out on time,
Five after eight.

Hugo's nearly frantic,
Marty isn't here.
Pop forgot his tuning fork,
And Dorothy's nowhere near.

So on Friday evening,
In all kinds of weather,
We'll be there together
With Hugo guiding us through.
Elohim Hashibenu,
Yigdal, Ma Navu,
To you, Hugo, thanks
A million thanks to you.

Even after moving his family to New York in 1960, Cantor Abba Weisgal's son returned to Baltimore for each Jewish holiday to conduct the synagogue's choir.

As the Board looked toward the High Holy Days of 5710 (1949), it was obvious that there would not be sufficient seating available in the main sanctuary to accommodate the demand for tickets. Although many families had moved from the immediate area, the desire to remain affiliated with Chizuk Amuno was strong. Even with a separate service for children, there would not be enough seats for adults. The first auxiliary service, with a capacity to seat three hundred, was planned for the vestry of the Eutaw Place synagogue. Advertisements placed in local papers announced that the synagogue could now provide High Holy Day seats to the community for a price as low as six dollars. Rabbi Goldman insisted that the *"services downstairs will be the same as upstairs, with the same manner of worship, and the same seating arrangements."* There would be no misunderstanding that family seating was now the only option available at Chizuk Amuno.

Rabbi Jacob Kabakoff of New York was engaged to lead the auxiliary service accompanied by Rev. Nathan Vainstein as cantor. Unfortunately, the selection of Vainstein proved to stir another debate with the Orthodox community. The cantor, who made his living as a schochet (ritual slaughterer), received a threatening letter from the Council of Orthodox Rabbis of Baltimore, which was translated into English by Rabbi Goldman. The letter warned Vainstein that if he dared to *"violate the authority of those whose words are like living coals of fire"* by officiating in a congregation with mixed seating, the Council would revoke his certification as a schochet. Vainstein yielded to the pressure, and Kopel Weinstein was contracted to serve as cantor.

Sadly, Rabbi Emeritus Adolph Coblenz passed away shortly after the holidays. In New York for his nephew's bar mitzvah, Coblenz died on Shabbat Noach, Friday, October 28, 1949. Several representatives of JTS and the Rabbinical Assembly attended a family funeral held the following evening. The body was transported to Baltimore, where Rabbi Goldman conducted a formal funeral on Sunday, October 30, 1949, in the sanctuary of Chizuk Amuno. Over 1,500 people attended the afternoon service, including prominent clergy, distinguished communal workers, civic leaders, the Governor and Mayor. Members of the Board and Brotherhood joined other dignitaries in serving as active and honorary pallbearers. The November 4, 1949 issue of the Jewish Times featured a photograph of Rabbi Coblenz on the cover and printed numerous tributes.

Weeklong Shiva services were conducted at Rabbi Coblenz's home – each followed by a study period led by various rabbis. In recognition of his service to the Congregation, the Board approved several tributes to Coblenz. A Memorial Service was held, after the period of Sheloshim, on December 4, 1949. Engraved copies of Rabbi Goldman's eulogy for his colleague, entitled "A Man Who Walked With God," were distributed. At Goldman's express wish, the late rabbi's chair on the bimah was draped in black and remained empty for a year. A grove of one thousand trees was planted in the Jewish National Fund Forest in Israel in memory of the rabbi. The Sisterhood permanently endowed the "Rabbi Adolph Coblenz Memorial Scholarship" for students attending the Seminary.

As a permanent memorial, a marble pulpit was carved in Carrara, Italy matching the Italian marbles in the Eutaw Place sanctuary. Contributions from over six hundred people funded the Rabbi Adolph Coblenz Memorial Pulpit, which was dedicated during the Friday evening service on November 3, 1950. Twenty years later, the personal library of Adolph Coblenz, comprised of over three thousand books, was shipped to the Seminary Student Center on the campus of the Hebrew University in Jerusalem. On August 17, 1970 members of the Chizuk Amuno Youth Pilgrimage unveiled a bronze plaque dedicating the Rabbi Coblenz Library.

Rabbi Coblenz left instructions stating his wish to be buried in Israel. Due to the unexpected timing of his death, temporary internment took place at Chizuk Amuno's Arlington Cemetery. In late 1950, Coblenz's brother wrote to the Board requesting that the rabbi's remains permanently rest in the Baltimore cemetery, *among the people to whom for more than a quarter century he was so intensely devoted.* Chiseled into the marble slab covering his grave are the words:

Rabbi Chizuk Amuno Congregation
1920-1949
Servant of God
Lover of Israel
Teacher of Torah

Forecasting future increases in youth activities, the Board appointed a Planning Committee to investigate options for additional space. Estimates of the cost to construct an addition adjoining the first floor of the Annex proved too expensive, and the idea was abandoned. On June 27, 1950, the Board approved a two-step expansion. First, the second floor of the School Center would be remodeled. Second, a committee would be appointed to locate and *"purchase a plot of ground in the suburbs for the future."*

Remodeling of the entire School Center occurred during the spring of 1951 under the watchful eye of David Kleinman. Costing less than $15,000, the building now housed eleven *"sunlit, airy, and newly painted classrooms."* The <u>Bulletin</u> also boasted: *"all the floors are covered with asphalt tile and all the ceilings have new electric fixtures."* Building inspectors had ruled that the third floor could not be used for classrooms, so it was designed to accommodate the school library and a youth lounge. Two apartments were partitioned at one end of the third floor and made available to the couples providing janitorial services to the Congregation. A playground, enclosed by a fence, was constructed behind the building.

Two other remodeling projects began in the spring of 1951, as the main sanctuary received much needed maintenance, and the vestry of the synagogue was enlarged and redecorated. Redecoration of the main sanctuary included painting the interior bricks and cleaning the ceiling. Eliminating the classrooms on either side of the basement allowed the formation of one large assembly hall – *"airy, comfortable, beautifully illuminated, and artistically redecorated."* The downstairs kitchen facilities were also enlarged and equipped with new appliances. Funding for the improvements was provided by a $3,500 gift from the Sisterhood and a sizable legacy bequeathed by Ephraim Macht. On November 23, 1951, the new Ephraim and Annie Macht Assembly Hall was formally dedicated after the Friday night service.

With the space added by the School Center building, Rabbi Goldman continued to introduce new programming ideas. Youth activities at the synagogue quickly expanded in the early 1950's. The weekly <u>Bulletin</u> alerted families to the spectrum of clubs available – Girl Scouts, Cub Scouts, Boy Scouts, drama, orchestra, dance troupe, camera, art, arts & crafts, Palestine dancing – and the basketball and ping pong athletic teams. High School students in the Senior Supper Club gathered monthly to hear guest speakers, view films, and be delighted with occasional accordion recitals and hay rides. Monthly cultural programs and dinners attracted young adults to the YPL meetings. The YPL Spotlighters drama group presented original plays and musicals to packed houses. The <u>Bulletin</u> of June 22, 1951 reported that *"nearly 500 young people of all ages were enrolled in the many clubs and activities of our Youth Center."*

When they were not raising funds to support the synagogue or engaged in adult learning, the Brotherhood and Sisterhood arranged social activities aimed at promoting unity within their groups. Sisterhood meetings, always held at mid-day, were preceded by "tea." Many women participated in Sisterhood plays and the bowling league. Occasionally, the Brotherhood's evening meetings were announced as "Stag" – no women allowed. One such meeting, held on November 8, 1950, promised men:

> *...a grand get-together of Brotherhood members for a nite of real enjoyment.*
>
> *There'll be tables set up for all you who want to play Gin Rummy, Canasta, Poker, Bridge, or Black-Jack! There'll*

be free beer, pretzels, hot dogs, smokes – all you want.
And, there'll be a couple of "special surprises" that we've
got in store for you. So take the night off and take the
cares off your mind in the friendly, jolly atmosphere of
the Brotherhood "Game Nite" Stag Meeting.

Joint Brotherhood/Sisterhood projects included the annual Chanukah Banquet and Dance, visitation at veterans' hospitals, and musical reviews, such as the highly acclaimed 1951 "Chizuk Amuno Gaieties." The two groups co-sponsored the first open-air carnival and bazaar in May, 1951 outside of the new School Center Annex. In later years, the outdoor carnival became part of the Congregation's Purim celebrations.

The "club" concept carried over into religious and educational programming as people with common interests banded together. The Choral Society rehearsed weekly and performed several times a month. The Usher Corps was honored at a special dinner held after the High Holy Days. In 1950, after only *"twenty-five worshippers marched in the procession with the majestic Lulavim and fragrant Esrogim,"* Goldman invited families to *"Join the Lulav Club"* for Sukkot in 1951. The rabbi introduced induction ceremonies for first graders beginning Hebrew school and new students of the Sunday school. Held during Simchat Torah services, the ceremony included Rabbi Goldman presenting small gifts to the children. Class field trips and projects helped create a cohesive group of students at each grade level. School principal Hymen Saye commented in the 1955 Sisterhood Donor Book, that the buzz of activities around the synagogue created *"the symphony which is Chizuk Amuno."*

Rabbi Goldman strove to create a sense of family fellowship among the members of the Congregation. Israel and Mildred Goldman graciously opened their home to many auxiliaries of the Congregation and visiting guest lecturers. On December 31, 1951 they hosted a tea for returning college students. The rabbi made a point of collecting the addresses of each college student so that he could correspond with them during the school year. Anxious to make a personal connection with as many families as possible, the rabbi often asked to be notified about events affecting congregants. As America entered the Korean Conflict, the following note from Rabbi Goldman appears on page one of the March 9, 1951 Bulletin:

Dear Members and Friends:

We are living, once more, in trying times. Again we are faced with the difficult task of saying farewell to the sons of Chizuk Amuno entering the armed forces of our country. I would appreciate a call from you telling me when a member of your family is leaving, so that I may join you in bidding him farewell and best wishes. I would like to see our young people who go into uniform at the Sabbath Services preceding their departure, at which time I will have a little gift for them.

When the rabbi traveled abroad, he sent letters back to the Congregation relating his experiences. Reprinted in the Bulletin, the messages were the topic of conversation at the synagogue, just as if people had gotten a postcard from a member of their family. Young Anna and Tobie Goldman often accompanied their father on Shabbat afternoon walks, as he visited elderly and ill members of the Congregation living in the neighborhood. Politely accepting offers of cookies and sweets, the girls quickly endeared themselves among the synagogue community. However, the warmest relationship was the community's embrace of Mildred Goldman.

Often referred to as "my dear wife Mildred" by her husband, Mrs. Goldman was the first rebbetzin at Chizuk Amuno in thirty years. A native of Cleveland, Ohio, she devoted her early adult years to the field of Hebrew literature and Jewish culture. Mildred moved to New York and accepted a position as secretary to Dr. Louis Finkelstein, president of JTS. It was there that she met young Rabbi Goldman, the man she married in January, 1943. Within three months of arriving in Baltimore, Mildred Goldman had already taught adult Hebrew classes for the Women's Institute, and delivered her first keynote address to guests at the Sisterhood's annual donor luncheon. It was, however, Mrs. Goldman's literary review sessions that attracted the most praise. Announcement of an upcoming meeting in April, 1951 included words of praise for the rabbi's wife:

> *It's always nice to look forward to something, especially when we know it's going to be a book review by our own Mrs. Israel M. Goldman. We know from our past experiences, that were we to look the city, or yes, the country over we could not and would not find a more wholesome, refreshing, cultured and inspiring person to review the new book by Ruth Gruber, "Israel Without Tears." So, in our very midst, we have the person most sought after in the city.*

Mildred Goldman's reviews were promoted as *"enlightened interpretations"* and the Sisterhood termed her *"Our Gem."*

For Rabbi Goldman, synagogue attendance was a means for members to strengthen their sense of a Jewish community. Announcement of the Selichot service in 1950 invited families *"For a Grand Congregational Reunion,"* and described the evening as *"an opportunity to get together in good fellowship after many of us have not seen one another during the summer months."* Underlying Goldman's messages of social fellowship were his efforts to engage congregants in serious worship and study. Sermons with titles such as "The Contest Between Good and Evil" and "What is Man?" provided members with spiritual leadership and an increased understanding of the tenets of Judaism.

Sometimes the rabbi tried to cajole members to attend services, and sometimes he tried to scare them into attending. Touching on the fear of future assimilation, in a 1950 Bulletin article Goldman wrote:

> *The day of reckoning is not far off for parents who have estranged themselves and their children from the Synagogue! The tragic price of such estrangement from the Synagogue is not infrequently, estrangement from Juda-*

ism and sometimes God forbid, from one's own family. Mothers, don't rear a potential stranger in your midst – come with your children this Saturday morning at 10 o'clock. Fathers – if you are not employed Sabbath mornings, come with your children. Draw your family close to yourself and be at home in the Synagogue.

Shabbat attendance was not just an issue at Chizuk Amuno. Many Conservative congregations faced the same problem. Some pulpit rabbis postulated that as members moved to the suburbs, traditional restrictions against riding on Shabbat kept them from attending services. In his essay, "JTS and the Conservative Movement," Jack Wertheimer comments that congregational rabbis were frustrated with *"the failure of leading Talmud professors to find warrants in Jewish law to address new challenges."* The tension between academic scholars of the Seminary and their graduates was summarized at the 1950 Rabbinical Assembly (RA) Convention by the group's president, Rabbi David Aronson: *"The rabbis of the Assembly are spiritually married to their congregations. The Seminary, as an institution, is not."* Disputes continued as the RA, JTS, and the United Synagogue of America all struggled to refine their role in the growing Conservative movement.

After years of complaining to the Seminary, the Rabbinical Assembly's Law Committee issued a milestone decree in 1950, permitting limited driving on Shabbat. In their "Responsum on the Sabbath," the rabbis wrote:

Refraining from the use of a motor vehicle is an important aid in the maintenance of the Sabbath spirit of repose. Such restraint aids, moreover, in keeping the members of the family together on the Sabbath. However where a family resides beyond reasonable walking distance from the synagogue, the use of a motor vehicle for the purpose of synagogue attendance shall in no wise be construed as a violation of the Sabbath but, on the contrary, such attendance shall be deemed an expression of loyalty to our faith.

The Assembly identified the decrease in Shabbat observance as a symptom of the disintegration of Jewish religious life in America.

While attending the 1950 RA Conference, Israel Goldman heard Rabbi Ben Zion Bokser, of the Forest Hills Jewish Center in New York, speak on a creative program that the president of his congregation initiated to stir Shabbat attendance. Ironically, the president at Forest Hills was Fred Katzner, formerly of Chizuk Amuno Congregation, and brother of Board member J. Benjamin Katzner. The plan intrigued Goldman and he presented the idea to the Board in the fall of 1952. During the rabbi's Kol Nidre sermon, "All Our Vows," the Synagogue Attendance Pledge was introduced. Preaddressed cards were placed on members' seats describing three categories of membership based on Shabbat attendance. Gold Star members pledged to attend late Friday night or Shabbat morning services every week. Silver Star members pledged attendance at either of those services at least twice a month. Blue Star members made the commitment to attend once a month. After extolling the virtues of participating in communal worship, the rabbi asked those present to turn down a tab on the card indicating which attendance plan they would meet. On October 14, 1952, wallet-size membership cards – 542 blue stars, 215 silver stars, and 163 gold stars – were mailed to those who had responded to the pledge card.

The rabbi continued to bombard congregants with messages intended to promote participation in worship services. Adding to the variety of excuses why a member was not in synagogue, Goldman now faced competition from the advent of television:

Into the routine of your life, the Friday Evening Services will bring a new note to inspire, to stimulate and to uplift. Our Choir and Cantor will chant the stirring melodies of the synagogue. The congregation will join in community singing. There will be a warmth and a friendliness which can be found nowhere else in life. The words spoken from the pulpit will endeavor to bring you inspiration and instruction.

Don't let anyone or anything take away this wonderful experience from you. Neither comedians on television or friends who invite you to dinner or neighbors seeking to lure you towards cruder pleasures.

The conversion to mixed seating slowly led to other smaller strides in other rights for women. When applications for membership were reviewed at the September 5, 1950 Board meeting, the names of two women were listed. The minutes of that meeting describe the challenge that occurred when the Board was asked to vote:

They were all unanimously elected as members of Chizuk Amuno, with the exception of the women, whose legality toward membership was questioned since the Constitution provides that women can only become members upon the death of their husbands, in which case they would take over their husbands' membership. In discussing the matter, it was brought up that in the last two years since we opened the balcony for membership, women members were elected. This question was left in abeyance until a later meeting.

The issue was not mentioned again until 1953, when the Constitution Committee was instructed to *"look into the matter."*

As the baby-boom generation blossomed, stay-at-home women directed their leisure time to synagogue activities and communal worship. The Sisterhood's small fund-0raising drives had developed into major campaigns for Building Funds and on behalf the Seminary's Torah Fund, and the Associated Jewish Charities' Combined Campaign. The tradition of providing advanced religious education only for sons was questioned, as the women realized that they had not been adequately prepared for the worship service in which they now participated. The Board of Jewish Education supported this modern approach and advertised for parents to enroll their daughters in a Hebrew school. One ad in the January 23, 1948 issue of the Jewish Times asked:

IS YOUR DAUGHTER A STEP-CHILD?

Your daughter goes to public school just as boys do. You want her to get as good an education as a boy receives. If at all possible, you will see to it that she goes to college. She will have the right to vote and to be elected to office. As a mother she will have even more responsibility for raising the children than her husband. WHY, THEN, DO YOU TREAT HER AS A STEP-CHILD ONLY AS REGARDS HER JEWISH EDUCATION?

Rabbi Goldman personally joined the crusade for educating young women, presenting his own family as an example of modern Jewish parenting. In his September 7, 1951 article published in the Bulletin, the rabbi describes the *"thrill"* that he and his wife experienced when enrolling seven-year-old Anna in the congregational Hebrew school. Entitled "I Send My Daughter To Hebrew School," the column questioned why any parents would deny themselves the happiness of seeing their daughters *"possess the treasures of Judaism."*

One of the most important milestones for women was the approval of Bat Mitzvah ceremonies in 1952. Although Dr. Mordecai Kaplan had introduced the ritual service at his Reconstructionist congregation in the 1920's, few Conservative congregations had adopted the practice by 1950. Goldman's synagogue in Rhode Island had initiated Bat Mitzvah services in 1935, and he was anxious to establish the concept at Chizuk Amuno. On February 28, 1952 the Divine Service Committee unanimously approved the Shabbat morning *"Bas Mitzvah"* ceremony as follows:

At the conclusion of the prayer for the Government or the prayer preceding the New Moon, and before the chanting of the 145th Psalm (Ashrei), the Bas Mitzvah is to ascend the pulpit upon which the scroll of the Torah will be lying, closed and fully clothed...She will then recite a few lines both in Hebrew and in English from either the scriptures or the Prophets. After which she will turn around, facing the Ark and say a few words of personal prayer. The Rabbi will then give her the benedictional blessing and present her with a diploma and suitable gifts. She will then descend from the pulpit to her seat in the audience.

It was made quite clear that the young girls would not sit on the bimah, approach the Ark, or join in the Torah processional. They would speak the words of all blessings and biblical text – not sing them. The Board voted to accept the recommendation.

A group of ten girls attended Chizuk Amuno's first bat mitzvah class on October 23, 1952, taught by Miss Rosemarie Salinger, and supervised by Rabbi Goldman. Miss Ruth Blum, daughter of Dr. and Mrs. Louis Blum, had the honor of becoming the congregation's first bat mitzvah on January 31, 1953. Rabbi Goldman's sermon that day was appropriately titled, "Girls Are Children Too." Major revisions to the girls' service were adopted in late 1956, as the ceremony was shifted to the late Friday night services. Without the Torahs removed from the Ark, the young ladies were now permitted to chant a portion from the Prophets and have a more active role in the service.

As the young women of Chizuk Amuno were exposed to their first taste of participation in the prayer services, their mothers were still targeted to serve the traditional role of Jewish mother. In the fall of 1951, the Sisterhood launched the Judaism-In-The-Home Institute with curriculum provided by the National Women's League. The series of Wednesday morning lectures included "Learning How to Read Hebrew in 8 Easy Lessons," taught by Mildred Goldman. Members of the Sisterhood's Committee on Customs and Ceremonies conducted sessions explaining the meanings of various symbols and rituals of Jewish holidays. The Committee on Food presented samples of kosher recipes, and the Committee on Publications recommended Jewish literature and recorded music appropriate for children. The stated mission of the Institute was to:

...help the modern Jewess who desires a truly beautiful Jewish home life. It will provide her with the techniques, skills and materials which will imbue her and her children with a love and understanding of the Jewish way of life.

Rabbi Goldman supplemented the women's learning by using the Bulletin to review the traditional rituals associated with Shabbat and festivals.

In 1958, Brandeis scholar Dr. Marshall Sklare commented on how the bat mitzvah ceremony conveyed the illusion that women were being granted ritual equality. His remarks, reprinted in the 1981 essay, "Women in the Conservative Synagogue," stated:

Although the sexes do sit side-by-side during worship and the women take part in all the responses indicated in the liturgy, they are still excluded from certain worship activities...the ritual surrounding the handling and reading of the Torah scrolls is still generally reserved for males...Conservative women have generally been satisfied with their limited status – a great advance over the age-old segregation.

With the benefit of hindsight, Jack Wertheimer interpreted the significance of the bat mitzvah innovation much differently, writing in his 1987 essay, "The Conservative Synagogue":

The activities of Bat Mitzvah girls pioneered the way for adult women: First, by their participation in Torah and prayer-related rituals, Bat Mitzvah girls began the process of legitimizing the involvement of all females in such rites. Second, when they grew into adulthood, women who had at an earlier age participated more in synagogue services during their Bat Mitzvah ceremonies, re-

fused to accept their present exclusion from prayer and Torah rites; they thus formed an important body for change in the status of women in the synagogue.

Another generation would come of age before women at Chizuk Amuno would be granted full ritual equality.

Without any fanfare, the administrative management of Chizuk Amuno had matured along with its programming. As the first half of the twentieth century drew to a close, the title of Joseph Weinstein's position, previously known as "Executive Secretary," was renamed "Executive Director." The synagogue employed *"three full-time girls"* for clerical support in the office. The increase in professional staff prompted the Board to draft formal job descriptions for the rabbi, cantor, school principal, shammas, executive director, choral director, and youth director. With the exception of the rabbi and shammas, each employee was responsible for *"controlling the budgetary expenditures of his department."* All employees were instructed to work in a manner that would *"create the spirit of harmony and cooperation among all members of the staff."* They were asked to schedule vacations with the president and *"leave address where vacationing so contact can be made, if necessary."*

Additional employees were necessary to coordinate the multitude of activities revolving around the Chizuk Amuno family. As pressure mounted for more of a suburban presence, the staff would soon be coordinating suburban locations, both a school and auxiliary holiday services.

The format of the eighty-first Annual Meeting of the Congregation, Sunday afternoon, January 20, 1952, was quite unlike any previous meeting. Promoting a theme of "Toward New Horizons for Chizuk Amuno," the gathering featured a one-hour business meeting, guest speaker, social hour, and a menu of eight seminar options. In the session entitled, "A New Location for Chizuk Amuno – Where and When?," Bernard Manekin presented the Board's plans for relocation, citing *"a definite need for the establishment of a location in the suburban area for a branch school, recreational center and for an additional place of worship during High Holidays."* The Jewish migration toward the northwest was entering its final stage. Semi-detached brick cottages in Mt. Washington were selling for $12,800. Greenfeld's Kosher Meat Market had opened on Pimlico Road.

Articles in the June 13, 1952 issues of the Jewish Times and Bulletin announced that the Congregation would be holding holiday services in the Pikesville Armory on Reisterstown Road. Isaac Potts stated: *"These religious services will follow the philosophy and program of Conservative Judaism and will adhere to the practices and rituals of Chizuk Amuno."* Rabbi Jerome Labovitz of Philadelphia and Cantor George Pomerantz officiated at the services, which had nearly 400 people attending. Members paying $46 annual dues plus a minimum $10 pledge received two seats. As an enticement to join the Congregation, non-member seats were rented for $15 each. In September, 1952 Chizuk Amuno provided worship services for close to 2,500 people in four locations – the main sanctuary on Eutaw Street, the Macht Assembly Hall, the Pikesville Armory, and the School Center on Eutaw and Whitelock Streets. By 1954, total holiday attendance had climbed to 3,000.

Shortly after the announcement of plans for the suburban service, the Board completed negotiations to open a suburban branch of their Hebrew and Sunday schools. The University of Baltimore allowed Chizuk Amuno use of one of the buildings they had recently acquired from St. Paul's School located at 2207 Enslow Avenue, near Greenspring Avenue in the Mt. Washington area. The Suburban Sunday School, headed by Kate Miller Gordon, included students from kindergarten through age twelve. Hymen Saye supervised the Suburban Hebrew School, which provided instruction for children ages seven to eleven. First year enrollment exceeded one hundred students.

While the Board planned the suburban schools and holiday services, co-chairmen of the Planning and Location Committee, Bernard Manekin and Leonard Stulman, continued their search for land on which to build a new synagogue. On Sunday, June 15, 1952 the entire Board inspected two tracts of land on Stevenson Road – one seventy-one acres with an asking price of $3,000 per acre and the other forty-two acres at a fee of $4,500 per acre. At the Semi-Annual Congregational Meeting on June 30, 1952, members voted to give the Board authorization:

> ...to negotiate and purchase on the best possible terms such land as seems in its judgment best suited for the future needs of Chizuk Amuno and second, that this purchase be made at a price and on terms which seem in the judgment of the Board of Directors, proper and satisfactory.

Negotiation for the larger tract dragged on through the summer. With the dedicated legal assistance of Julius Novey, agreement was finally reached in early October, 1952, and a $5,000 deposit put down on the seventy-one acres on the west side of Stevenson Road, north of Old Court Road. In the October 17, 1952 Bulletin, Milton Fleischer announced the acquisition, adding that development of the property was from ten to twenty years away. The initial vision for the site included *"a series of buildings and court-yards...surrounded by beautiful gardens in keeping with the suburban landscape of woodland and meadow."* Interest from the Jewish community was strong, as the announcement of Chizuk Amuno's plans became public.

Although the sellers agreed to a $100,000 mortgage, the Board needed an additional $75,000 at time of settlement. Donald Levinson headed solicitation efforts resulting in gifts and loans from thirty-eight members sufficient to cover the requirement. The six men representing the Congregation at the signing of documents transferring ownership of the Stevenson Road property were photographed to preserve the historic moment. Rabbi Israel Goldman, Milton Fleischer, Isaac Potts, Joseph Weinstein, and Donald Levinson gathered in the law offices of Julius Novey on Erev Pesach, March 30, 1953. Planning for the fourth synagogue location of Chizuk Amuno Congregation could now begin.

Excitement surrounding the relocation plans was put aside in January, 1953, as Milton Fleischer decided to step down from the presidency of the synagogue after serving as an officer of the Congregation for fifty-five years – thirty-one of them as president. Chaired by Joseph Davidson, the Testimonial Committee planned a weekend of salutes to their retiring leader. The Jewish Times, published on January 16, 1953, pictured Fleischer on the cover and included an editorial in recognition of his devotion to Chizuk Amuno:

> *There are too few Milton Fleischers. Would that we had more creatures of such habit. If such were the case, Baltimore would have the strongest synagogues in America...in the world. For Chizuk Amuno has not reached its lofty position as one of the country's outstanding conservative congregations by luck, or by good fortune. Behind it, pushing it, planning for it, wrestling with the problems and the crises that faced it was a somewhat shy and retiring gentleman named Milton Fleischer.*

Late Friday Evening Services on January 16, 1953 included a choral anthem, "*Ve-Haya Be-Acharit Hayamim,*" composed by Cantor Abba Weisgal for the occasion and dedicated to his long-time friend. Dr. Simon Greenberg, executive director of the United Synagogue of America and vice-chancellor of JTS, delivered a keynote address and presented Fleischer with a certificate honoring him as the "Dean of Synagogue Presidents." Notable leaders of the Jewish community were invited to Shabbat services the next day as Goldman delivered a sermon entitled, "Milton Fleischer – The Synagogue Leader." Three hundred men attended the Brotherhood's testimonial dinner in the Macht Assembly Hall where Rabbi Israel Herbert Levinthal of the Brooklyn Jewish Center was the guest speaker.

Isaac Potts was installed as the eighth president of Chizuk Amuno on Sunday, January 18, 1953, after serving as vice-president for the previous six years. In his acceptance remarks, Potts reminisced about how, at age four, he had hurried *"into the side entrance of the old Lloyd Street Schule, to line up for a sip of the Kiddish wine."* After graduating with a Master's degree in chemistry from Johns Hopkins, Potts briefly taught in Pennsylvania before returning to open a business in Baltimore. Joining Chizuk Amuno in 1927, Potts quickly became involved with the Congregation, heading the School Board and serving on several committees. Highly qualified to assume his new position, Potts was a past president of the Baltimore Board of Jewish Education and the Baltimore Zionist District, and had served as treasurer of the Jewish Welfare Board.

Social programming continued to expand as members awaited building of the suburban campus. In 1952, Rabbi Goldman introduced the first Congregational Pesach Seder, held on the second night of the holiday in the Macht Assembly Hall. Over two hundred people attended the ceremony, which featured participation by many adults and children and included the appearance of Elijah the Prophet. A gala evening was presented on the eve of Purim in 1953 with six hundred people in attendance. Megillah reading was followed by a Purim Shpiel – *"South Persia,"* a parody of the musical "South Pacific." To complete the evening, the audience was entertained by a magic show and the Manny Schwartz Orchestra.

A "Festival of Synagogue Music," coordinated by Bernice Kolodny, was held on May 3, 1953 and featured renown New York cantor Arthur Wolfson as soloist. Dr. Hugo Weisgall conducted a choir of seventy-five voices and an orchestra of forty musicians in three works by French-Jewish composer Darius Milhaud. The concert attracted citywide attention as more than 1,200 listeners crowded into the sanctuary.

The Planning Committee launched a national search to locate an architect for the Stevenson Road complex. After interviewing a dozen prominent professionals, Leonard Stulman, chairman of the committee, announced that Daniel "Duke" Schwartzman of New York would be granted the contract. President of the Architectural League of New York, and a contributing editor of the book, "The American Synagogue for Today and Tomorrow," Schwartzman had traveled extensively through Europe while in a graduate program. No stranger to Chizuk Amuno, Schwartzman had been a student of the Religious School and became a bar mitzvah at the McCulloh Street synagogue. The architect had designed the reconstruction of the Eutaw Place vestry three years earlier.

Rabbi Goldman was keenly interested in the plans for the new buildings. As he traveled to different cities he often made notes in his personal workbook of interesting sculpture, landscaping, or interior designs. Even before a contract was executed with the architect, Goldman prepared notes outlining his vision. In preparation for a meeting with Schwartzman and Stulman, the rabbi recorded the following notes on February 17, 1954:

1. *The buildings to be arranged so as to give the effect of a campus and to have organic unity throughout.*

2. *The most imposing and the tallest building should be the Synagogue Building. It should face in an easterly direction...and should have a modern tower of pylon, at the top of which should be a large and magnificent Menorah which would be illuminated for special occasions. In this way the Synagogue will serve as a land-mark and focal point for the entire countryside.*

3. *The buildings should be so arranged as to make possible a series of gardens, court-yards, terraces, walks, and outdoor playground areas.*

4. *The main garden shall be designated as THE HEBREW CULTURE GARDEN. It might be laid out in the form of a Mogen David. It should incorporate a Bible Garden which would have in it Bible trees, plants and flowers imported from Israel if necessary.*

5. *We will have an expandable sanctuary...in its largest form accommodates 2000 worshippers. Classroom wings on each side of the sanctuary should add 1000 seats. The sanctuary should not look like an auditorium or a theatre. It must have*

majesty, mystery, reverence and simplicity. The front of the sanctuary should not be a stage. It should be an elevated area consisting of steps leading from the floor of the sanctuary and composed of several levels. Such an elevation at the front of the sanctuary expresses the democracy of Judaism by means of which each worshipper can have access to the Holy of Holies.

6. *The social hall should be separate from the Synagogue and not to be used as part of the expandable sanctuary. It should have a luxury appearance.*

7. *Use Israeli building materials wherever possible.*

The first architectural drawings presented to the public included most of Goldman's concept. Gracing the cover of the Jewish Times on September 10, 1954, the sketch showed the sweeping contour of the sanctuary roof and glass walls on either side of the Garden Lounge. A model of the proposed complex was unveiled on June 15, 1955, at a special dinner held at the Lord Baltimore Hotel. Reviewed in the next day's Baltimore Sun, the design was hailed as *"contemporary in style, though incorporating traditional Hebrew symbols."*

Rabbi Goldman had spent a great deal of time studying examples of modern American architecture, especially those found in public buildings and schools. He wanted Chizuk Amuno to reflect twentieth century culture, just as historic synagogues had mirrored the Romanesque and Byzantine eras. With the expansive space available, Goldman expressed his wish for equality in all parts of the building – the sanctuary, schoolrooms, and meeting areas:

The new Synagogue architecture has banished the old musty vestry, the dark basement classrooms, the stuffy, small kitchen. Many of the old synagogues of Europe were built like fortresses to protect our people from hostility and attack. Thank God here, in America, we can build in glass, for we build in freedom.

Covered walkways connecting segments of the campus were designed to create a sense of serenity. Access to natural daylight and gardens signified freedom to the rabbi.

To manage the financial burden, construction was scheduled to be carried out in five stages – the Social and Educational Center, Synagogue, Chapel and Library, Administrative Wing, and Educational Building. Using the motto *"Build Now for Generations to Come,"* Finance Committee Chairman Albert Esterson launched the two-million-dollar Building Campaign. Lay leaders had always been successful in soliciting donations when needed for a variety of past campaigns. Isaac Taylor headed the "Yeshivah and Tzedakiah Fund" annual appeal and J. Max Abramowitz chaired the Israel Bond Campaign. When additional prayerbooks or taleisim were needed, congregants rose to provide the money. The magnitude of the funds needed for the Stevenson Road development far exceeded any past project and justified calling for professional assistance.

With the unanimous consent of the Board, Esterson engaged Ketchum, Inc. of Pittsburgh to manage fund-raising efforts. Two consultants remained in Baltimore for twelve weeks and established campaign headquarters on the first floor of the Emersonian Apartments on Eutaw Place. Under their guidance, the Building Fund Campaign enlisted the aid of nearly two hundred men organized as an army of solicitors. Announcement of the Kick-Off Dinner to be held on January 4, 1956 proclaimed:

All Counselors eat with your Captains.
All Captains: Get your Teams together.
All Majors: Organize your Groups.
All Vice-Chairmen: Round up your Sections!

The men selected prospect pledge cards and received their "Campaign Kits for Action." The goal was to personally contact and solicit every member and organization affiliated with the Congregation. A series of weekly mailers aimed at stirring enthusiasm for the project answered questions about the new campus. The *"Campaign Corner"* column printed in the <u>Bulletin</u> highlighted a variety of fundraising facts – lists of volunteers, donors, and results.

One large gift was announced just before the second phase of the fundraising campaign concluded. During Sisterhood Shabbat on

March 10, 1956, President Sayde Sklar disclosed that along with their customary $500 donation to the Building Fund, the Sisterhood *"most enthusiastically pledged $50,000 to build and furnish our kitchen in the 'New and Greater Chizuk Amuno.' We know that it is not going to be too easy a task, but it will be a labor of love."* By March 18, 1956, pledges totaling $936,965 had been subscribed and the Steering Committee authorized the architect to prepare full blueprints and request bids for the first phase of construction.

The plans for the Social and Educational Center reflected what is currently the Krieger Auditorium area. The April 20, 1956 <u>Bulletin</u> described the building as having three levels:

> *The lower level will have in it a Foyer, a Sisterhood Hall, a Brotherhood Club Room, both of these with kitchen facilities, as well as cloak rooms, telephones, and storage space. The first floor will contain a Grand Lobby together with a Social Hall which will seat one thousand people. On this floor there will also be the kitchen and other service facilities. On the second floor there will be eight permanent Class Rooms, two Lounges, and three Offices. This building will also have an elevator in it and will be air-conditioned.*

Rabbi Goldman had hopes of including groundbreaking ceremonies during the celebration of Chizuk Amuno's eighty-fifth anniversary in the spring of 1956, but those plans would be delayed. One more issue still needed resolution. The State Roads Commission had informed the Board that eighteen acres of the Congregation's property was needed for the proposed Route 695 Beltway. Architectural drawings accounted for the loss of ground, but negotiations with the State as to the price which should be paid for the property had stalled. Final settlement with the Commission carried into 1960.

The construction firm of Baltimore Contractors, Inc. was awarded the contract to build the first unit of Chizuk Amuno's building project. On Thursday, September 13, 1956, a delegation of members joined Goldman, Weisgal, and Potts in Julius Novey's law office to witness the signing of the contract worth almost one million dollars. Potts spoke of the event in his Yom Kippur address to the Congregation: *"We have taken a progressive step forward...No fossilized folk are we, no dead and dried-up relic of a civilization and culture that has long passed its zenith."*

Invitations to the Ground Breaking Ceremonies on October 14, 1956, included directions – *"go one block east to Stevenson Road, then turn north one mile and on the left of the road is our new site."* The eight hundred students of Chizuk Amuno's schools were among the 1,500 people present to witness Isaac Potts use a silver shovel for the first ceremonial turn of earth. Other leaders of the Congregation, the rabbi, cantor, and one representative from each school class took turns scooping their shovel-full of dirt. Leonard Stulman drove the contractor's bulldozer a few yards and announced that construction had begun. At Goldman's suggestion, founder Jonas Friedenwald's great-granddaughter, Julia, was invited to participate in the ceremony. Although her father, grandfather, and great-grandfather had all served as presidents of Chizuk Amuno, she was the only member of the Friedenwald family still actively involved with the Congregation. Widowed at an early age, Julia Friedenwald Strauss married widower Isaac Potts in 1953.

On September 15, 1957, seven hundred people returned to the building site for the ceremonial "Laying of the Cornerstone Service." The presidents of the Brotherhood, Sisterhood, and Congregation participated in the service, which included selections by Hazzan Weisgal and remarks from Leonard Stulman and Albert Esterson. Rabbi Goldman spent considerable energy orchestrating the event to be both symbolic and meaningful. After months of correspondence with historic congregations around the world, Goldman collected an array of items that would help link the new Chizuk Amuno building with the ancient traditions of Judaism. Deposited into a metal box to be placed behind the cornerstone were prayerbooks and historical booklets from the five oldest synagogues in America. Sand from the

Mikve Israel Synagogue in Curaçao, West Indies was placed in the box as a gift from the oldest synagogue in the Western Hemisphere. Representing the present, membership lists from various Chizuk Amuno organizations were included as well as current issues of local newspapers and coins from Israel and the United States. Two stones were cemented onto the face of the cornerstone. One, a gift from the State of Israel, had been taken from Mount Zion in Jerusalem. The other stone had recently been excavated from the ruins of a fifth-century synagogue near Tiberias and sent to Goldman by the Director of the Department of Antiquities.

A message to future generations accompanied the items sealed in the metal box. Written on parchment paper by Israel Goldman, the letter summarized the history of the Congregation and reflected on current conditions in America:

> *We are building our Synagogue in what has become known as the Atomic Age. This is an anxious and fearful time in which we live. There is much unrest in the world. The nations of the East, dominated and enslaved by war-mongering Soviet Russia, are set against the free peoples of the West under the leadership of our own peace loving United States of America. This Atomic Age, unless dedicated to the acts of peace, can foreshadow the most dreadful potentials for the destruction of mankind.*

A major administrative change had occurred before the first shovel of dirt was lifted on Stevenson Road. After twenty-two years with Chizuk Amuno, Executive Director Joseph Weinstein submitted his resignation in October, 1955. During his employment, the annual budget had grown from $22,000 to over $113,000 and membership from 140 to 770. Weinstein was honored for his years of faithful service at an "Appreciation Breakfast" co-sponsored by the Brotherhood and Sisterhood. Harold Hammer, of Brooklyn, New York, was hired to fill the position of Administrative Director. One other familiar face was not present at the cornerstone ceremony on

Stevenson Road. In January, 1957 Chizuk Amuno's guiding spirit for over half a century, Milton Fleischer, passed away.

With the new suburban Social Center nearing completion, another gala tribute was held in the Eutaw Place synagogue. A three-day celebration was held March 27-29, 1958, honoring Hazzan Abba Weisgal on the fiftieth anniversary of his becoming a cantor. On Thursday night, nearly four hundred men and boys, trained for their bar mitzvah studies by Hazzan Weisgal, gathered in the Macht Assembly Hall wearing badges proudly proclaiming, "I Am One Of Adolph's Boys." An original skit by Weisgal's son, Fred, entitled "Have Tuning Fork Will Travel," roasted the popular cantor's career:

To the tune of "Get Me to the Church on Time"

I will audition in the morning
Brush off my Homburg, get my cane
Don't make me nervous
Before Mincha service
Get me on time to the train.

I'll take my Tsissis, it keeps me warm
I'll take my tallis – I hope they're not reform.

I will audition in the morning
Get me my schnapps I'll feel devine
I'll kiss the Messusah, I won't be a loser
Get me to the shul
Don't make for me a fool
Be sure and get me to that shul on time.

On Friday evening, invitations to "A Festival of Synagogue Music" drew hundreds to enjoy some of the original compositions written by Weisgal and performed by the Chizuk Amuno Choral Society. In 1950, with the financial support of devoted congregants, Abba Weisgal publish a book of his compositions entitled, <u>Shirei Hayyim Ve-Emunah, Songs of Life and Faith</u>. In his foreword to the volume, Weisgal cited his motivation to publish these scores:

Following the great catastrophe which overtook our
people in Europe, with its accompanying destruction of
the Jewish Synagogue and its music...I have gathered
together these leaves and am publishing them as a par-
tial replacement for all the Jewish spiritual values which
were lost and destroyed through brute force.

During the March 29, 1958 Shabbat service dedicated to
Weisgal, Rabbi Goldman devoted his sermon to recounting the
cantor's thirty-eight years of service to Chizuk Amuno. In recognition of that dedication, the Congregation presented Weisgal with a
trip to Europe and Israel.

Although formal dedication of the Social Center would not be
held until September 7, 1958, Chizuk Amuno's Institute of Jewish
Studies for Adults convened in the building on March 4, 1958.
Mildred Goldman reviewed <u>Remember Me to God</u> at the Sisterhood's
first meeting on Stevenson Road on April 7, 1958. Those women
needing transportation from the Eutaw Place area were offered a fifty-
cent, round-trip ride from the synagogue. The following evening,
the new Art Gallery on the second floor of the building's lobby opened
with an exhibit loaned from the Jewish Museum of New York. Dr.
Stephen Kayser, curator of the New York museum, presented a lecture entitled, "The Synagogue As a Work of Art."

The Social and Educational Center was a work of art. Architect Daniel Schwartzman wrote a detailed description of the building for the Congregation that appeared in the April 25, 1958 <u>Bulletin</u>.
The dominant feature of the exterior was the curved line of the roof
that peaked at twenty-eight feet in height with a full glass wall. That
wall would soon become the barrier between the lobby and the sanctuary. Panels of Italian Venetian glass mosaic in shades of blue
complemented Maryland fieldstone walls trimmed with cypress
wood. The entrance to the building was lined with magnolia trees,
soon joined by red maples, moraine honey locust, and sycamore trees.
The auditorium was designed with two levels, the sides and rear two

steps above the main floor separated by mahogany flower boxes. The architect noted that the room had been designed *"in accordance with the most advanced principles of acoustical engineering, with the sound distribution from the stage by means of low level ceiling diffusers and acoustical treatment of the ceiling, as well as the sound absorbing drapery at the back wall."* The mezzuzah at the main entrance, a gift from Mr. and Mrs. Hymen Saye, had been used on the doorway of the Palestine Pavilion at the 1940 World's Fair in New York City.

The new Social and Educational Center, referred to as the "Center Building," opened for the eight hundred students of the religious school on March 16, 1958. Enrollment was high enough to schedule two shifts of classes – one beginning at 9:00 a.m. and one at 11:00 a.m. A single section of fourth and fifth grade students met at the main synagogue for those families still living in the area. A bus was added to the *"transportation fleet,"* shuttling students to school in the afternoon. Beginning with the 1957 school year, the Congregation raised their educational standards by discontinuing the "Sundays Only" option. Following the recommendations of the United Synagogue's Commission on Jewish Education proposed at the organization's Biennial Convention, pupils in grades four, five, and six were now required to attend one weekday afternoon Hebrew class in addition to Sunday mornings. Hymen Saye continued to lead the school as principal – now serving his twenty-sixth year.

Early childhood education on Stevenson Road began in the fall of 1958 as the Pre-School Department was organized to establish nursery and kindergarten classes. Daily morning kindergarten was available at the Center for the annual fee of $245, plus transportation charges. At their convention, the United Synagogue of America also hailed the establishment of day schools formed under the aegis of affiliated congregations and called for a national network of Solomon Schechter Day Schools. It would be more than two decades until Chizuk Amuno launched its day school.

One week before Rosh Hashanah, formal ceremonies marked the dedication of the new building. The High Holy Day Services of

5723 (1958) were held in three locations – Eutaw Place, Stevenson Road, and the Pikesville Armory. The suburban service was for members only, but unaffiliated members of the community were welcome to purchase seats at the other locations. Children's services were conducted at each location, and for the first time, a Teen Service convened in the new Social Center. With hundreds of members worshipping downtown and an even greater number uptown, the attentions of the Congregation's primary rabbi and cantor needed to be split. Rabbi Goldman and Hazzan Weisgal officiated at the Eutaw Place sanctuary for Rosh Hashanah, while Rabbi Moshe Davis and cantorial candidate Joseph A. Levine were in Stevenson. Goldman and Davis exchanged pulpits for Kol Nidre and Yom Kippur. Cantor Levine continued working with the Congregation on a part-time basis over the following year.

At age seventy-five and in failing health, Isaac Potts stepped down from the presidency in March, 1959 after serving six years. The Brotherhood honored Potts at their Sunday morning meeting on April 5, 1959. Efram Potts, son of the retired leader, saluted his father for his profound influence:

> *Dad's example of refusing to permit his vocation to be the "be all and the end all" of each day, but his insistence on himself that he serve the community as well as his higher self, has certainly had an effect on the outlook of each of his children...To use his own words, he has shown me an "almost forgotten set of three R's – Right, Responsibility, Reverence."*

Joseph Davidson was installed as the ninth president of Chizuk Amuno at the Annual Meeting.

Rabbi Goldman's address at the dedication of the Center Building, "Promise and Fulfillment," set the stage for the next phase of the planned building project. Co-chairmen of the fund-raising effort, Albert Esterson and Solomon Rogers, organized the "Finish the Job" campaign. While fund-raising continued, the Ritual Committee, which included the rabbi and cantor, discussed the question of moving the main Shabbat service to Stevenson. After reviewing the matter for six months, the Committee provided their recommendations to the Board who unanimously accepted them.

The eighty-ninth Annual Congregational Meeting was held on February 21, 1960 in the Center Building. President Joseph Davidson announced the Board's plans for transferring the focus of Chizuk Amuno activities to the Stevenson campus. Beginning with Passover of 1960, the main services, including all bar and bat mitzvah ceremonies, were to be held in the Center Building, led by Rabbi Goldman with the assistance of Cantor Joseph Levine and the choir. A parallel service would continue on Eutaw Place under the guidance of Hazzan Weisgal assisted by the sexton, Hyman Bassan. The main High Holy Day services would remain in the downtown synagogue until the new sanctuary was constructed. Finally, Davidson announced the Ritual Committee's adjustment of the Shabbat service:

> *The Festival and Sabbath Services in the Center Building shall begin at 9:30 A.M. and conclude at 12:00 noon. This will create not only a shorter service, but also a more vital service without eliminating any parts of the traditional service. This service will be in strict accord with the traditions of Chizuk Amuno, at the same time taking account of the progressive trends in the outstanding Conservative Congregations in the country.*

In the words of Israel Goldman, *"Chizuk Amuno is now ONE congregation with two synagogues."* He viewed the new arrangement as a *"welcome opportunity and a vital challenge."* Rabbi Michael Hecht was engaged to officiate at festival and Shabbat services "in-town" from Pesach until Shavuot. Goldman was particularly proud to announce that Hecht, completing his studies at JTS, was the son of Chizuk Amuno members, and a graduate of the Congregation's religious school.

During the summer of 1960, the Board decided that the growth of the Congregation dictated the need for an assistant rabbi *"to give effective service to our growing adult membership and to our many young people."* Recently ordained, Rabbi Leonard S. Berkowitz was hired in September, 1960 to work with high school and college students. Rabbi Goldman frequently traveled, visiting congregations across America and Europe on behalf of the Rabbinical Assembly and the World Council of Synagogues. The addition of a permanent assistant rabbi assured that continuous spiritual leadership would be present throughout the year.

Rabbi Berkowitz served as advisor for the Chizuk Amuno branch of the United Synagogue Youth (USY). Organized in 1958, the chapter was open to teenagers between the ages of fourteen and seventeen. Among their social, religious, and cultural activities, the USY sponsored the first Purim Carnival at the Social Center in 1960. The Stevenson Road complex continued to host the multitude of youth programs that had begun on Eutaw Place. Afternoon and weekend clubs focused on drama, dance, journalism, and art. Within the next two years, however, many of these activities were no longer successful at Chizuk Amuno as the Jewish Community Center (JCC) opened its Park Heights Avenue building. With community-wide youth activities now in the hands of the JCC, Chizuk Amuno concentrated its efforts on developing the USY and Bar Mitzvah Brotherhood.

As soon as expanded banquet facilities became available at the Stevenson Road campus, Chizuk Amuno auxiliary organizations began using them for social events. The Sisterhood and Brotherhood jointly sponsored the formal "Inaugural Spring Cotillion" on Saturday evening, April 26, 1958, in the new Social Center. Later that year, nearly seven hundred people attended the annual Chanukah Dinner Dance and Rabbi Goldman's Tenth Anniversary Celebration held in the new building. The Couples Club, established in 1957, used the large room for songfests, cha cha lessons, and lectures. In January, 1959 members of the USY chapter and other youth auxiliaries joined together for the "Snowman Swing" winter dance in the *"main ballroom of the new Center Building."* The Congregation's

Chanukah Dinner Dance in 1959 transformed the main auditorium into a European café, complete with a replica of the Eiffel Tower:

> 'Twas the third light of Chanukah, and all thru the house
> Not a creature was stirring, for the man and his spouse
> Were dining and dancing in festive décor
> At the Stevenson Center, which was filled to the door.
> The menu was French, continental cuisine,
> The flowers and wines were fit for a queen.
> "Chanukah in Paris" was the theme de jour
> And the guests were guided on a Parisian tour.

Celebrating seventy-five years of service to the Congregation, the Sisterhood's Diamond Jubilee Donor, Show and Dance attracted hundreds to the building on November 12, 1960. Hazzan Weisgal's younger son, Fred Weisgal, wrote and directed the Sisterhood's spectacular musical production, "Have Congregation Will Travel." Sisterhood members engaged in a variety of activities at the Center, including Mother-Daughter luncheons, book reviews, musical lectures, and the annual Spring Fair. The October 7, 1959 Sisterhood meeting welcomed the Goldmans back from their trip to Europe and Israel. *"Mrs. Goldman's back and the Rabbi's with her,"* announced the notice. *"Don't miss hearing their first-hand stories and delightful experiences."*

Brotherhood Donor Dinners, initiated in 1940, were also hosted in the Social Center. Prominent guest speakers, such as Congressman James Roosevelt in 1960, drew large crowds, helping to raise funds in support of the Congregational school. The format of the annual donor was changed in 1961, as the Brotherhood attempted to attract an even larger audience. On Sunday evening, February 12, 1961, the Brotherhood's first "Festival of Stars Donor" was held at the Lyric Theatre headlining comedian Alan King. Over the next few years the event featured Liberace (1962), tenor Jan Peerce and comedian Jackie Mason (1963), Gordon MacRae (1964), Jane Morgan and Jack E. Leonard (1965), and Jimmy Durante (1966).

In late spring 1960, commitments to the Building Fund were sufficient for the Board to approve the commencement of the next phase of the building project. Bold, banner headlines in the Bulletin of July 8, 1960 proclaimed, *"MAZEL TOV! Ground Breaking for New Sanctuary in Fall 1960, Occupancy Expected for Fall 1961."* E. Eyring and Sons were engaged as general contractors for the half-million-dollar sanctuary project. Although groundbreaking ceremonies took place on November 13, 1960, the construction schedule soon fell behind. Severe winter weather and excessive rainfall in the spring resulted in seventy-three days of delay. The cornerstone, placed on September 24, 1961, contained parchment cards signed by nearly one thousand members and affiliates of the Congregation. Each card stated that the signatures signified *"an earnest expression of our love for our Congregation and of our devotion to the House of God."*

Interviews to find a full-time hazzan for Stevenson Road were held in the spring of 1961. On March 11, 1961 Cantor Abraham Salkov of Los Angeles officiated at Shabbat services. A native of Rochester, New York, Salkov had served more than fifteen years in the cantorate, and was an accomplished liturgical composer. A few weeks later, on April 27, 1961, the Baltimore Sun announced *"Chizuk Amuno Elects Cantor."* The Salkov family moved to Baltimore over the summer and the cantor began his tenure in the temporary sanctuary at the suburban Social Center on July 1, 1961.

With two rabbis, two cantors, and two locations, members needed a reminder to keep track of who was going to be where for the High Holy Days of 5722 (1961).

Rosh Hashanah – Eutaw Place: Rabbi Goldman and Hazzan Weisgal
Stevenson Road: Rabbi Berkowitz and Cantor Salkov

Yom Kippur – Eutaw Place: Rabbi Berkowitz and Hazzan Weisgal
Stevenson Road: Rabbi Goldman and Cantor Salkov

The <u>Bulletin</u> suggested that members *"keep this calendar for reference."* Immediately following Rosh Hashanah, a daily minyan was established at the Social Center. Men were asked to volunteer their attendance one day a month at either the 8:00 a.m. or 7:30 p.m. service. Stressing the mitzvah of communal prayer, the <u>Bulletin</u> of September 1, 1961 announced, *"Here is Your Chance to Become a Minyanaire."* The latest edition of Rabbi Morris Silverman's week-day prayerbook was introduced for use at services. Endorsed by both the Rabbinical Assembly and the United Synagogue, the Silverman weekday, Shabbat, and High Holy Day prayerbooks were used by the majority of Conservative congregations by the mid-1960s.

In the spring of 1959, the Chizuk Amuno Choral Society, under the direction of Hugo Weisgall, recorded an album of Jewish liturgical music. "Choral Masterworks of the Synagogue" was released for national distribution, and copies were available for $2.98 at the synagogue office. When Dr. Weisgall accepted a position out-of-state, William J. Milner was engaged as assistant conductor of the choir and choral society for the 1959-1960 season. Milner often conducted the choral society in concerts featuring Cantor Salkov and in celebrations during National Jewish Music Month. Assistant Cantor Joseph Levine resigned in fall 1961 to accept a position with Beth Tfiloh Congregation. Three years later, Milner joined him.

The New Sanctuary

After months of delays, Chizuk Amuno's second building at Stevenson Road was dedicated on April 1, 1962. Exactly ninety-one years after Chizuk Amuno's founding members gathered for their first Shabbat service, over one thousand people attended the first worship service in the new sanctuary. Reminiscent of the Lloyd Street dedication in 1876, the choir sang "Mah Tovu," followed by the entrance of the rabbis and cantors of the Congregation. Members of the Board formed a processional carrying the Torah scrolls that would now be enshrined in the Ark. Beatrice Levy, widow of past president William Levy, was given the honor of kindling the Ner Tamid. Seminary Vice-Chancellor Dr. Simon Greenberg delivered the dedication sermon. One month later, Chancellor Dr. Louis Finkelstein accepted Rabbi Goldman's invitation to address the Congregation at a special "Service of Dedication to Jewish Community Fellowship." Goldman had written to President John F. Kennedy for a message of greeting to the Congregation, but it was the President's Special Assistant who responded in a letter dated March 27, 1962:

> *While the ever-increasing demands upon the President's time prevent his personally sending a message, he does want me to extend his warm greetings to all who will be gathering for this important event. Through the years your congregation has added much to the strength and vitality of the community and the Nation and it is hoped with these additional facilities the sphere of your beneficent influence will ever widen.*

A state-of-the-art communication system was installed on the rabbi's stand that enabled him to call for an usher, or signal the cantor to slow down or speed up. When Dr. Theodore Schwartz addressed the Congregation from the bimah at the first Brotherhood Shabbat to be held in the new sanctuary, he remarked on the technology:

> *I wish you could all come up and inspect closely this space-type pulpit in which I am standing. There is an instrument panel with more buttons and controls than in Colonel Glenn's Friendship VII and my only fear is that inadvertently I might touch the wrong one, shoot through the escape hatch and disappear from sight.*

Public reviews of the new structure were glowing. The Sun featured a full-page article on the new synagogue on page three of their Sunday, April 1, 1962 issue, commenting that the sanctuary's *"contemporary architecture, and its spaciousness, give it a touch of the spectacular."* The exterior eastern wall of the Social Center lobby, measuring over four stories high, now served as the interior separation between the Center and the sanctuary. The lower portions of the ten glass panels on the wall were converted to four sets of mahogany doors. The main floor contained seating for 1,300 people, with an additional 500 seats placed in the balcony. The sides of the 300-foot long sanctuary each contained nine windows. Rabbi Goldman explained that the ten glass panels in the rear represented the Decalog (Ten Commandments), while the nine side windows symbolized the nine major and minor Jewish festivals. The exterior walls continued the appearance of the Social Center – Maryland fieldstone and blue Italian glass mosaic.

Sections of Israeli marble were centered on the interior of the sanctuary's east wall framing the Ark. Muralist Samuel Weiner, Jr. designed the tapestry which covered the doors of the Ark. Weighing over three hundred pounds, and measuring fifteen feet wide and twenty-four feet high, the tapestry had been handmade at the V'Soske shops in Puerto Rico. Rabbi Goldman had suggested that the theme of the piece be *"the origin, contents and effects of the Torah."* The artist described his interpretation of the motif in an interview with reporters:

> *The origin is represented by the mountain and the fire and smoke accompanying the revelation. The contents are represented by the tablets of the law. The effects are represented by the Tree of Life on the two sides, which also suggest the two columns of the Temple of Solomon.*

The three sculptures above the bimah were designed and constructed by Robert Cronbach of Long Island, New York. Hanging on the curved mahogany wall were two seven-foot-tall Menorahs – each made from hammered and welded bronze and brass, polished and lacquered. Cronbach explained that one piece, "The Olive Tree Menorah," symbolized Zachariah's dream in which two olive trees standing of either side of the menorah supply it with oil. The other 180-pound sculpture, "The Chanukah Menorah," incorporated the Lion of Judah. Suspended from the sanctuary ceiling, the Eternal Light was made from polished and lacquered bronze. The two-foot-wide sculpture symbolized *"the wings of the Cherubim surrounding and protecting the ever-burning flame."* Before the religious ornaments were placed in the synagogue, the sculptures and tapestry were loaned to the Baltimore Museum of Art for a month-long exhibit. Cronbach installed his twenty-four-foot-high "Burning Bush" on the exterior of the sanctuary over the course of the summer. Set against a background of beige-colored Venetian glass, the bronze sculpture had been hand-hammered, and oxidized in a green patina. Floodlights positioned on the ground highlighted the artwork nightly.

Eight museum cases were recessed into the lobby walls outside of the sanctuary to display the Congregation's collection of eighteenth-and nineteenth-century religious and ceremonial objects. Dr. Stephen Kayser, curator of New York's Jewish Museum, returned to Baltimore to assist at the dedication of Chizuk Amuno's museum on April 27, 1962, bringing items with him to fill the cases. Mr. and Mrs. Albert Hendler made the first gift to the museum – a Chanukah Lamp made about 1780 in Holland. Within the following year, Rabbi Goldman collected several archaeological antiquities from Israel to establish the synagogue's Biblical Museum. An interview with the rabbi, published in the November 4, 1963 Baltimore Sun, disclosed that the Israeli Ministry of Education and Culture, Department of Antiquities, had issued a special export license to Goldman. The rabbi explained why rare items, such as a primitive flint ax from the Stone Age and cooking pottery dated circa 970-840 BCE, were allowed to leave Israel and be exhibited:

> *Modern Israel is a relatively young country, but to prove they are a nation with an ancient civilization they are literally digging in the past to find evidences of their culture; hence their desire to keep these archaeological discoveries in their own country, allowing only those objects to leave which will be used abroad in furthering a knowledge of their culture.*

During Shavuot services on June 8, 1962, President Joseph Davidson proudly announced that the Krieger family had made a donation in the amount of $125,000 – the largest gift ever received by the Congregation. Brothers Abraham and Zanvyl Krieger had been active Chizuk Amuno members for decades, and assumed leadership positions in various civic and Jewish organizations. In appreciation of the generous contribution, the Board agreed to designate the assembly room of the Social Center as the "Krieger Auditorium."

The focus of Chizuk Amuno's ritual activities slowly shifted uptown to Stevenson Road. The February 9, 1962 Bulletin announced that Rev. Moses Amsterdam had assumed the job of sexton at the Center Building. After the new sanctuary was dedicated in April, 1962, Stevenson Road services were termed the "Main Service" and those at Eutaw Place labeled the "In-Town Service." Rabbi Goldman now officiated only on Shabbat and festivals at the uptown location. As Rabbi Berkowitz's two-year contract expired in the summer of 1962, Hazzan Weisgal regularly officiated at Shabbat services without the assistance of a rabbi. The Board publicly announced that the Eutaw Place synagogue would close after Shavuot in 1962, but members and non-members residing in the area successfully appealed to the Board to reverse their decision.

An article in the July 27, 1962 Jewish Times announced that Dr. Louis L. Kaplan, Dean of Baltimore Hebrew College, would officiate at High Holy Day services to be conducted at the Eutaw Place synagogue. A committee, headed by William Greenfeld, contacted people residing in the areas surrounding the in-town synagogue informing them of the Conservative services. The wording of subsequent advertisements implied that the downtown service was being scheduled as a courtesy to the old neighborhood: *"Chizuk Amuno Congregation is pleased to announce that as a service to the Baltimore Jewish Community there will be held Community High Holy Day Services at Eutaw Place and Chauncey Ave."* Hazzan Weisgal was accompanied by a choir directed by his son, Hugo. The new suburban sanctuary allowed Chizuk Amuno to admit a limited number of new members who would be assigned seats in the main service. Without an assistant rabbi on staff, only one adult service was held at Stevenson Road in 1962. A JTS rabbinical student led services for teenagers in the Krieger Auditorium, while Hymen Saye supervised the Children's Services in the downstairs Sisterhood and Brotherhood rooms.

Although the <u>Bulletin</u> continued to print the in-town synagogue's schedule of services, those announcements appeared in smaller type at the bottom of the page. In November, 1962 Efrem Potts began assisting Hazzan Weisgal with weekly Shabbat services. Twenty-seven new members requested holiday seats at the downtown location in 1963. The October 18, 1963 <u>Bulletin</u> printed the president's Yom Kippur message, in which he commented: *"I am very pleased to report to you that this year the number of worshippers at Eutaw Place has increased considerably and that we have 950 worshippers there now."* Throughout the next decade, the Eutaw Place facility functioned as a self-sufficient, satellite branch of Chizuk Amuno, with a governing Board and operating budget.

On March 24, 1963 J. Benjamin Katzner was installed as the tenth president of Chizuk Amuno Congregation. A former president of the Associated Jewish Charities, Katzner was keenly aware of the need to set priorities. His acceptance speech outlined the four goals of his term: balance the budget, complete the building project, increase membership, and involve all age groups in congregational activities. Within a few weeks, the Board announced a new membership plan structured to attract young families. For a fee of $100, plus a minimum "maintenance pledge" of $50, a family would be entitled to full privileges of membership, reduced tuition for children attending the religious school, and two seats for the auxiliary High Holy Day Services to be held in the Krieger Auditorium. No Building Fund pledge was required. Advertisements warned that only a limited number of memberships were available at this special price. Three months later, the <u>Bulletin</u> announced that forty-one new families had affiliated with Chizuk Amuno, *"a friendly, warm, cor-*

dial Congregation with a modern and progressive philosophy and program for American Jews." Results of the membership drive reflected an illusion of success. As new members enrolled, resignations of existing members counteracted any growth in the membership base. Financial difficulties motivated many of these resignations, but increased competition also caused many defections.

Young Jewish families in Baltimore continued settling in northwest suburban neighborhoods in the late 1950s and early 1960s. Beth El, a fellow Conservative congregation, had purchased the plot of land behind Chizuk Amuno, dedicated their new synagogue/school complex in the fall of 1960. A third Conservative congregation, Beth Israel, organized in 1956, dedicated their multi-purpose synagogue center in December, 1959. The educational wing of Beth Israel's Randallstown complex opened in September, 1962. Nationally, migration to suburban areas, coupled with increasing interest in the middle-of-the-road policies of the Conservative movement, had created an explosion of new congregations. In his essay, "The Conservative Synagogue," Jack Wertheimer noted:

> *United Synagogue membership, which stood at approximately 350 affiliated congregations at the end of the war, leaped to 800 congregations within two decades. The United Synagogue inducted 131 new congregations from 1955 to 1957, another 58 during the next two years, and 80 affiliates from 1959 to 1961.*

Wertheimer added the fact that between 1965 and 1971 no new Conservative congregations formed.

Chizuk Amuno's Stevenson Road complex had been designed to accommodate 1,200 families. However, the April 26, 1963 <u>Bulletin</u> mentioned that *"membership numbers 840 families."* In an effort to stimulate growth, ads were placed in the <u>Jewish Times</u> which proclaimed, *"Now is the Time to Join Chizuk Amuno," "Chizuk Amuno Offers Inspiring Religious Services," "Chizuk Amuno Offers Your Child a Fine Jewish Education,"* and *"Chizuk Amuno Interests Intelligent Adults."* Members were urged to contact the synagogue office with the names of any friends or neighbors who might be potential members.

In his 1963 Yom Kippur address, Katzner shared both good and bad news with members. He reported that 1,800 people worshipped in the main sanctuary during Rosh Hashanah and another 280 attended the auxiliary service in the Krieger Auditorium. Katzner also revealed that the Congregation was operating at a deficit. The heavy investment in real estate was now coupled with larger than expected operating expenses. Rumors circulated through the Congregation that the Board was planning to sell off some of the Stevenson Road land to generate much needed cash. In an open letter to members, printed in the June 14, 1963 Bulletin, Katzner explained that real estate developers interested in Chizuk Amuno's property had occasionally approached the Board. After the sale of acreage for Beltway development, the Board determined that the Congregation owned twenty-six acres of land *"for which the congregation had no present or future use."* Katzner appointed a Real Estate Committee to recommend a plan for the disposal of the excess land. Several congregants and neighbors of Chizuk Amuno opposed the concept of subdividing the property, and the issue was temporarily tabled for the next few years.

Social Action and Interfaith Programs

In 1954, the Commission on Social Action was established through a joint effort of the United Synagogue, the Rabbinical Assembly, and the National Women's League. Seven years later, Dr. Bernard Segal, Executive Director of the United Synagogue, defined the goal of the Commission as attempting to *"bring to our people a fuller understanding of the universal teachings of our tradition and help to translate these teachings in the affairs of the general community and the world."*

In the late 1950s, America's relationship with the Soviet Union became increasingly strained as the Cold War intensified. The explosion of the first hydrogen bomb by the Soviets in 1954, and the launch of the Sputnik satellite in October, 1957, intensified the

public's fear of nuclear attack. Many Chizuk Amuno auxiliary organizations included social action programs in their scheduled events.
In a speech to the Sisterhood on November 4, 1957, Hymen Saye
commented: *"There is a very close connection between the atomic
warheads on the scientific missiles and the anxiety which has seized
all of us who think about this problem."* On October 19, 1955 Dr. R.
Carson Dalzell of the Atomic Energy Commission delivered an address entitled, "Atoms for Peace" at the Brotherhood Breakfast Minyan. The Couples Club welcomed Johns Hopkins professor Dr. H.
Bentley Glass on January 12, 1958, for a discussion of "The Dangers
of Radioactive Fall-Out."

Before the keynote speaker at the January 5, 1958 Brotherhood Breakfast Minyan, Robert Katzoff presented a d'var Torah entitled, "Time for Torah: A Social Action Message." In his passionate
message, Katzoff noted that *"the world is pregnant with possibilities
for good or evil."* He stressed the urgency to *"grasp the Torah as a
tree of life to equip us for living with the physical changes that man's
intelligence has achieved."* Katzoff was appointed as the chairman
of the Brotherhood's first Social Action Committee in the fall of
1958. The Sisterhood formed their own Social Action Committee
soon after, and in March 1959, encouraged members to attend Civil
Defense classes citing: *"This training is essential! Join now and
learn how to protect yourself and your family."*

The United Synagogue of America debated the issue of nuclear
weapons testing at its November, 1959 convention and adopted a
"Resolution on Atomic and Hydrogen Weapons Testing." The resolution condemned the proliferation of nuclear bombs, hailed the
United Nations' stand on disarmament, and called on religious leaders:

> *...to use the full weight of their moral influence, by the
> printed word and by preachments, and by rallying the
> best human impulses of mankind, to help to establish an
> era of lasting permanent world peace, firmly to weld the
> might of society to the cause of atoms for peace only, lest
> we all perish.*

The full resolution was published in the May 5, 1961 <u>Bulletin</u> in anticipation of Chizuk Amuno's "Synagogue Social Action Sabbath." The program, jointly sponsored by the Sisterhood and Brotherhood Social Action Committees, took place the following Friday evening. Dr. William L. Neumann, professor of History at Goucher College, delivered a sermon entitled, "Can Man Abolish War?" and participated in an open forum after services.

As the Cuban Missile Crisis passed, Dr. Neumann returned to Chizuk Amuno in November, 1962 to address the Sisterhood and Brotherhood on the controversial issue of nuclear testing. Throughout the country, children of all ages were preparing for a possible nuclear attack by practicing "duck and cover" drills. At the Annual College Shabbat on December 28, 1962, student Jonathan Azrael remarked:

> *Today's college student, the first generation of the Atomic Age, is painfully aware of the fact that never before has man had the power to make free choices which will so profoundly affect the destiny of mankind. Never before has man's choice between good and evil meant so much to his future happiness and security and, indeed, his very survival.*

Rabbi Israel Goldman was personally involved in social action causes, especially the fight for civil rights. Appointed vice-chairman of the Baltimore Commission of Human Relations, Rabbi Goldman often commented on social issues from the pulpit and in his written remarks. On October 15, 1954 the <u>Bulletin</u> reprinted the Commission's statement on integration of Baltimore's public schools, which said: *"The example which is set by parents urging children to stay out of school can only serve in the end to encourage truancy and delinquency and to perpetuate prejudice."* After returning from a weeklong speaking tour to Savannah, Macon, and Columbus, Georgia, and Birmingham, Alabama in March, 1955 the rabbi addressed the Brotherhood Breakfast Minyan on the subject of "America the Beautiful – and the Not So Beautiful."

Eager to engage young people in the issue of civil rights, Rabbi Goldman arranged for the Morgan State College Choir to sing at the Young People's League (YPL) meeting on December 16, 1956. Following the program, Rabbi Goldman joined Professor Wickwire of Johns Hopkins University and Dr. Wilson of Morgan College to discuss "Can We Eradicate Prejudice?" Several months later, on November 17, 1957, the YPL monthly meeting featured a discussion on "block busting" with a panel comprised of representatives from the Baltimore Jewish Council, the Baltimore Urban League, and Bernard Manekin of the Baltimore Real Estate Board.

Many young people of the Congregation followed Goldman's lead and took an active interest in the civil rights movement. The Annual Homecoming Sabbath for college students, held on Friday evening, December 29, 1961, focused on "How Can We Make Religion Vital in Modern Life?" Emily Shiling spoke of her experience after being arrested for joining in protest at a segregated diner:

Religion does have something to do with civil rights, restaurants, public accommodation laws and jails; for modern man, unlike Cain, knows how to "slay" his brother without killing him and to sin, without bloodshed, in the name of the law. This is not the time to ask that religion provide us with a refuge from an evil world. We must rather hope that religion will continue to set before us questions and challenges and that we ourselves will have the strength to give courageous answers.

Barely two weeks later, the Baltimore Board of Rabbis adopted a resolution supporting efforts to secure equal access for all races in Maryland restaurants. Published in the February 9, 1962 <u>Bulletin</u>, the resolution declared that *"it is to be expected that Jews be in the vanguard of the effort to assert the rights of all citizens of America, regardless of race, color or creed."*

Rabbi Goldman's personal involvement in the civil rights movement became legendary on July 7, 1963, when he participated in a demonstration for integration of a private amusement park in Baltimore County. In his capacity as vice-chairman of the Maryland Commission on Interracial Problems and Relations, Goldman had spent hundreds of hours implementing desegregation efforts around the state. On Monday, July 8, 1963, the Baltimore Sun reported that about one hundred people had been arrested at Gwynn Oak Park, including three rabbis and several other members of the clergy. Rabbi Goldman, the article reported, was *"in the forefront of the first wave to brace the policemen"* and owners of the park. Ironically, due to the large number of arrests, the police set up temporary holding cells at the Pikesville Armory – site of Chizuk Amuno's Auxiliary High Holy Day Services years earlier. A photograph of the rabbi being fingerprinted by a police officer appeared not only in the local newspaper, but was also on the cover of the Summer 1963 United Synagogue Review. The editor applauded Goldman's efforts, as well as those of nineteen other rabbis who joined protests in Birmingham, Alabama, *"as witnesses for freedom."*

The United Synagogue publicly declared its support of the Civil Rights Movement, joining in the March on Washington in August, 1963, and honoring Dr. Martin Luther King at its November convention. Abraham Joshua Heschel, Seminary Professor of Jewish Ethics and Mysticism, was an outspoken advocate for Jewish ideals of universal justice and equality. Frequently a guest speaker at Chizuk Amuno Institutes in the past, Heschel was quoted in the Summer 1963 United Synagogue Review as saying, *"You cannot worship the God of Abraham and at the same time look at man as if he were a horse."*

Within the Congregation, support for Rabbi Goldman's actions was almost unanimous. In the first Bulletin printed after his arrest, September 6, 1963, the rabbi reported that he had received close to one hundred telephone calls and letters with words of encouragement and support. However, he did receive one anonymous, typewritten note condemning his actions and alluding to the fact that the writer represented *"a number of Chizuk Amuno members."* The rabbi expressed his disappointment at not being able to meet personally with those people critical of his involvement, and discuss the issues with them. JTS Chancellor Dr. Louis Finkelstein wrote to Goldman from Jerusalem after hearing of the arrest:

> *I want to congratulate you on your courage and determination to do what is right under these trying and terrible circumstances...We have to take hold of the problem of the Negro and get it straightened out as quickly as possible, or unspeakable harm will come to our country and to each of us.*

The rabbi concluded his <u>Bulletin</u> article by repeating one of his basic tenets of faith, *"that the Synagogue today must be a living witness to the ethical teachings of Judaism."*

Nearly 1,500 people, shocked by the news of President John F. Kennedy's assassination, filled the sanctuary for a memorial service on November 25, 1963. Goldman paid tribute to Kennedy, calling him a *"pillar of fire who led America and the world through the Wilderness of Modern Times."* Two weeks later, the Brotherhood and Sisterhood Social Action Committees met to discuss the Social Action Resolutions passed by the United Synagogue in November, 1963 that dealt with Church-State Relations, Civil Rights, and World Peace. Witnessing the enthusiasm of members and the national precedent set by the Rabbinical Assembly and the United Synagogue, the Chizuk Amuno Board established a Social Action Committee at the Congregational level. Announced in the January 17, 1964 <u>Bulletin</u>, the Board explained that the new sixteen-member committee would be comprised of five Brotherhood, Sisterhood, and Congregation members, and a chairman appointed by the president. Dr. Irvin Cushner was appointed chairman and Robert Katzoff, vice-chairman.

In May, 1964 a consortium of Baltimore rabbis, including Israel Goldman, publicly declared their support of the Civil Rights Act, and urged their constituents to vote against George Wallace in the May primary election. *"The Rabbinate rarely reacts as such, but we feel compelled to speak out against this rabid, racist governor...."* The annual Social Action Sabbath, held on May 22, 1964, followed the rabbi's lead and featured the chairman of the Baltimore County

Human Relations Commission, the executive secretary of the Maryland Commission of Interracial Relations, and members of Chizuk Amuno's Social Action Committee. The subject of the forum following services was, "Governor Wallace in Maryland – the Next Steps in Civil Rights."

In conjunction with their involvement in social action causes, the Congregation also participated in several activities intended to strengthen interfaith relations. Abraham Karp, in his essay, "The Synagogue in America," commented that post-war acceptance of Judaism as a prominent religious group in America brought:

> ...a whole network of interfaith activities: joint church-synagogue visitations; teams of minister-priest-rabbi that made joint platform appearances at civic functions and college campuses and offered prayers at state occasions – activities that accorded Judaism parity and the Jew equal status.

Rabbi Goldman had actively participated in interfaith events in Rhode Island, frequently exchanging pulpits with the leading clergy of the state. He had served on interfaith commissions with Archbishop Francis Keough, who had moved to Baltimore from Providence shortly before Goldman.

After joining Chizuk Amuno, Rabbi Goldman formed strong ties with colleagues of other faiths and continued his efforts to strengthen understanding and respect between religious factions. Christian clergymen were invited to speak at the annual Thanksgiving Service, Institute of Jewish Studies for Adults, Laymen's Institute, and Sisterhood luncheons. The rabbi addressed Methodist, Catholic, Protestant, Unitarian, and Episcopalian congregations, and often appeared as the keynote speaker at interfaith conferences on human relations. In 1958, the Brotherhood sponsored a five-week series of Breakfast Forums centered on the theme of "Religions and Peoples in America." The presidents of Westminister Theological Seminary, and Loyola, Dropsie, and Morgan State Colleges spoke on the Protestant, Catholic, Jew, and Negro in America. Rabbi Goldman concluded the series with his lecture, "The Jew in Christian America – Problems of Integration and Separation."

An historic event in Chizuk Amuno history occurred on Sunday evening, February 14, 1965, when Cardinal-designate of Baltimore, Lawrence Shehan spoke at a special Brotherhood Convocation in the Social Center auditorium. The evening included a concert of sacred music performed by the Chizuk Amuno Male Choir and the Cathedral Choir of Gentlemen and Boys. As reported the following day in The Sun, Shehan's remarks entitled, "The Ecumenical Council, the Jews and Judaism," included the comment: *"We are entering a new world of relationships between the Christians and particularly the Catholic Church and the Jewish people."* Goldman presented the speaker with a leather-bound translation of the Five Books of Moses, *"as a token of appreciation and as evidence of the common basis of the Hebrew-Christian tradition."*

Rabbi Donald D. Crain was hired as assistant rabbi in August, 1963 to fill the position left vacant at the departure of Rabbi Berkowitz in June, 1962. A graduate of JTS, Crain had experience on the pulpit, as well as many years of experience with Ramah and USY programs around the country. The August 2, 1963 Bulletin explained that the rabbi was hired to provide *"greater service to the growing number of young married couples, young adults, college and high school youth in the Congregation."* Shortly after arriving, Crain and his wife invited other young married couples to their home and organized the "Mr. and Mrs. Club," intended to create a closer bond between the young couples and the Congregation. In late August, Rabbi Crain directed the first annual Youth Kallah (conclave), held at Camp Wohelo, site of the annual Brotherhood Laymen's Institute. The four-day encampment was designed to provide the teenagers with *"the Jewish skills, knowledge and enthusiasm which are essentials for proper leadership."*

Sandra Crain shared her husband's interest in promoting Judaism among the young people of the Congregation. She served as advisor to the Chizuk Amuno Teen Sisterhood (C.A.T.S.), a group of girls thirteen and over. Interestingly, just as the November 15, 1963 Bulletin announced that the director of "Stewart's Charm School for Teens" would lecture the girls on the topic of *"inner charm and graciousness, and the art of dress and make-up,"* Betty Friedan's classic book, The Feminine Mystique, hit the bookstores. Suburban women, many of whom had a college education, were becoming disillusioned with life centering on the home. Although Sisterhood- and synagogue- sponsored adult education courses were intellectually stimulating, most learning opportunities for women focused on current book reviews, creating a Jewish home, and contemporary Jewish issues. While they did participate in Bible and Hebrew language classes, Sisterhood members were still excluded from most ritual activities and advancement within the lay leadership.

More than a decade would pass before the first public calls for women's ritual equality surfaced in the Conservative Movement, and until women were encouraged to assume leadership responsibilities. Chizuk Amuno women did hold top leadership roles in regional and national organizations, but only in women's groups. Members sat on the Boards of the National Council of Jewish Women, the National Women's League, and the Seaboard Branch of the League, which they had helped to establish. Women were able to conduct successful conventions and lucrative fund-raising events, but were excluded from utilizing their strong administrative and organizational skills in top positions on any congregational committee other than those dealing with children.

Each year, a mother and her daughter were selected to speak from the pulpit during the Annual Mother-Daughter Shabbat Service held on Mother's Day weekend. Remarks made by Anna Shoubin and her daughter, Shoshana Cardin, in 1963, printed in the May 24, 1963 Bulletin, illustrate emerging attitudes toward women's role in contemporary Judaism. Mrs. Shoubin shared her memories of spending all day on housework, cooking, and attending to the needs of her husband and children:

> *We also had our version of a car pool but without the car. We walked our children to school in the morning, picked them up for lunch, took them back to school and brought them home at 3:15, after which we walked them to Hebrew School, five times a week. This was our reducing exercise, not golf or bowling...We helped their religious training by keeping a true Shabbos atmosphere, lighting the candles, saying Kiddush, even singing Zmiros after the Sabbath meal.*

Shoshana Cardin referred to the role of women in past generations as being a *"virtual social imprisonment,"* but announced that *"twentieth century culture and thinking have emancipated and educated us."* She emphasized that the responsibilities of the modern Jewish woman had not changed, they had merely increased. Women were still expected to maintain an efficient household, raise responsible children, and serve *"as the inspiration and gentle force behind their husbands."* However, Cardin urged women to also direct their energies outside of the home:

> *With our newly found freedom comes greater responsibility to the civilization and the culture which has deemed us sufficiently mature to assume an active role in community life and charitable endeavors. The modern Jewess can and must become a participant, not a spectator in religious, civic and charitable projects.... If we are to insure a more stable and wholesome society, a safer and more progressive community, we must work for it... The complexities of our society, and the many problems which are manifest in our community require our atttentions and assistance.*

Shoshana Cardin went on to direct many local, national, and international communal and philanthropic organizations. She served as the first woman president of the Council of Jewish Federations.

Civil rights protests, international hostilities, and the sexual revolution marked the early 1960s. At the Annual College Student Shabbat Service in 1962, Joanne Goldman described the anxiety young people felt about the future and their loss of innocence:

During the recent Cuban crisis students all over the country formed picket lines. "Ban the bomb," – "Disarmament," and so forth. While the feelings of the world showed disharmony, those of the college students were in complete unison with people both inside and outside of his collegiate environment. Suddenly destruction for him was no more and no less of a threat than it was for his Catholic, Protestant and Negro neighbor. The insignificance of these religious and racial barriers became emphasized to the hilt.

While college students were coping with the prospect of an uncertain future, their parents and grandparents were worrying that the young adults might forget or reject the Judaism of their ancestors. Many young men and women of Chizuk Amuno had left their homes to attend colleges where, for the first times in their lives, they were in the religious minority.

Assimilation and intermarriage, unspeakable among the Eastern European immigrant generation and their first-generation American children, were now threatening to undermine the future of American Judaism. Rabbi Goldman offered a session entitled, "The Rising Tide of Intermarriage" at the Institute of Jewish Studies for Adults in October, 1964. The following month, an open forum led by guest Rabbi Albert Gordon examined *"the ever-growing problem"* of intermarriage. In November, 1965 members received a flyer questioning, "Is Jewish Youth in Danger of Being Lost in a Christian Majority?" Three experts on youth, including a rabbi, Catholic priest, and Episcopal chaplain, participated in a panel discussion *"on the ever-growing problem"* of assimilation.

Three students presented their views on "The Threat of the Majority Culture" during the College Student Shabbat of 1965. Beth Cullen elaborated on the problem of secularism:

On the college campus, beliefs are constantly being challenged. If, after eighteen years at home, the student does not feel his religion to be inextricably precious to him, he will surely tend to lose in college much of the feeling he did have. If he has vague notions about the fundamental teachings and worth of Judaism, he might reject Judaism as intellectually dishonest and even as fraudulent.

Cullen suggested that the answer to combating acculturation among Jewish youth was to have *"stimulating and dynamic Jewish leadership"* devote more energy toward the college-age community. In an effort to assist Chizuk Amuno college students deal with the turbulence of the world, Rabbi Crain distributed the College Cryer, a monthly publication containing news from the Congregation and articles of interest to *"intelligent, thinking young Jewish adults."* Occasionally, books on topics of Jewish interest, such as Justice and Mercy by Dr. Max Arzt, were also mailed to students on college campuses.

The Congregation promoted Camp Ramah as an alternative summer experience to secular camps, and encouraged Hebrew school students to apply. After describing the physical characteristics of the facilities, an article in the November 29, 1963 Bulletin explained that the summer program was conducted in Hebrew as the child experienced the *"riches of his heritage."* Included in the program were sessions on synagogue skills, attended by both boys and girls. Annual Ramah Shabbat Weekends, held in the winter, showcased the children's learning as they conducted special Mincha, Maariv, and Havdallah Services in the main sanctuary. Three years later, Chizuk Amuno sponsored their first Israel Pilgrimage, supervised by Rabbi Crain. In the summer of 1966, twenty-nine teenagers between the ages of fifteen and seventeen participated in the trip to Israel. The students spent seven weeks studying and touring the country, meeting with Israeli youth groups, and attending theatrical and musical events. The all-inclusive cost of the trip was $840.

In appreciation of Rabbi Goldman's, and Hazzan Weisgal's years of service to Chizuk Amuno portraits of the two men were commissioned. Artist Henry Cooper, the cantor of Har Sinai Congregation, used the Eutaw Place sanctuary as a background for his oil painting of Weisgal holding his tuning fork. As reported in The Sun of March 9, 1964, *"the hazzan's portrait has shown him as a man of great artistic integrity with the bearing of a venerable patriarch."* Goldman, depicted with the Stevenson Road sanctuary behind him, is shown holding his prayerbook. The newspaper reviewer commented:

> *Mr. Cooper, in painting the rabbi's portrait has caught his benign, mild expression, a contrast to his administrative drive and strength of the sort that betokens accomplishment. It is an expression showing a man who is happy in his calling and who would never wish to do anything else but what he has chosen as his career.*

Gifts of Mr. and Mrs. Bernard Polan and their family, the portraits were presented to the Congregation on March 15, 1964. Cantor Cooper joined Cantor Salkov in a musical tribute at the ceremony.

Two months later, Chizuk Amuno hosted the Philadelphia Cantors Ensemble as part of their "Triple Star Program" at the Annual Jewish Music Festival. Promoted in the Bulletin as the *"largest aggregate of Cantors ever to appear in one program in Baltimore,"* the group presented popular Jewish music and synagogue liturgical selections. Later in the program, the Chizuk Amuno Youth Chorus performed a musical/drama based on the Book of Daniel, with Cantor Salkov as narrator. Over the following decade, the cantor composed many liturgical compositions and appeared as a guest artist at various cantorial concerts throughout the country.

On July 20, 1964, The Sun announced the appointment of Saul E. Lilienstein as the new Director of Choral Music at Chizuk Amuno. Lilienstein had joined the choir as a baritone in 1958, after moving to Baltimore from New York. At the time of his promotion,

Lilienstein was a faculty member at Essex Community College, and director of the Jewish Community Center Choral Society, the Handel Choir, and the Harford Choral Society. In June, 1966 Lilienstein conducted members of the Baltimore Symphony Orchestra for a performance of Igor Stravinsky's "Abraham and Isaac." Presented in honor of the Sisterhood's eightieth anniversary, the ballad featured Cantor Salkov as soloist. The Chizuk Amuno Choral Society and Children's Choir shared the program, performing Honegger's "King David."

New Year's Eve fell on a Friday in 1965, prompting the Baltimore Board of Rabbis to issue a statement urging the Jewish community not to schedule any New Year's Eve parties on Shabbat. The rabbis applauded several local country clubs and Jewish organizations that cancelled celebrations in deference to the sacredness of the day. Rabbi Goldman's sermon at the late Friday Night Service on December 31, 1965, was entitled "What Will 1966 Bring – A Forecast." He could not have predicted the alarming events that soon followed.

In January, 1966 a four-foot swastika was painted on the façade of the synagogue. Two months later, during the early hours of March 5, 1966, a second episode of vandalism occurred. As worshippers arrived at Shabbat services, they were greeted with anti-Semitic slogans spray-painted directly under the bronze sculpture of the Burning Bush. A photograph, published in the newspaper on the following day, showed two men wearing talesim, standing on the lawn outside of the sanctuary staring at the words:

> *Perish Judah! Perish Integration!*
> *Communism is Jewish!*
> *Race Mixing is Filthy!*
> *Support American Nazi Party!*

The graffiti remained visible until after Shabbat, when work could begin to remove the paint. At eight o'clock that evening, members returned to the synagogue to hear the reading of the Megillah in celebration of Purim. There was no mention of the vandalism in the Bulletin, but reports of the defacement appeared in the New York Yiddish daily paper, The Forward. An Orthodox synagogue, Liberty Jewish Center, had also been defaced that morning – the seventh attack they had suffered in ten years.

The March, 1966 incident brought swift condemnation by the community. An editorial in The Sun compared the act to recent cross-burning episodes and labeled the actions *"blots on the community."* The Jewish Times called for severe felony laws for vandalism and announced a $1,000 reward offered by the Baltimore Jewish Council for information leading to the conviction of the perpetrators. Rabbi Goldman received letters of support from the Maryland Council of Churches, the local Methodist church, the editors of The Baltimore Catholic Review, and the Jewish War Veterans. One handwritten note from a woman in Phoenix, Maryland, simply stated: *"As a Christian I wish to tell you and your Congregation how appalled I am at the desecration of your temple. It leaves me ashamed and disturbed."*

Vandals defaced the front of the synagogue for the third time on July 18, 1966. This time, a huge swastika was accompanied by the words, *"Hitler Was Right."* Pikesville police announced that they would fully investigate the crime and order special patrols to prevent future destruction. The Sun quoted Rabbi Goldman as stating, *"anti-Semitism in this country is not just a Jewish or a Baltimore problem. It is an American problem."* Two years later, the rabbi was summoned to testify at the trial of the man accused of the March, 1966 attack. A brief article appearing in The Sun of August 30, 1968 reported that attorneys for the thirty-four-year-old man entered an insanity plea to charges relating to the destruction of property. The defendant was committed to Clifton T. Perkins State Hospital specializing in mental disorders.

The baby boom of the post-war decade flooded the religious school with children, causing overcrowded conditions. As the 1960

school year began, four mobile classrooms were positioned behind the school to handle the overflow. The rabbi referred to the high school students using the temporary rooms on Sunday mornings as the "Trailer Club." Station wagons used for shuttling students provided insufficient seating and were replaced by a professional bus service. Classrooms could only accommodate three groups of students for High Holy Day Children's Services in 1963, making it necessary for students age twelve to fifteen to conduct services under a tent erected on the south lawn of the synagogue property. Faculty members and parents, frustrated with the lack of facilities, complained to the School Board. In a letter dated April 16, 1964 the School Board warned the Board of Trustees that declining enrollments were *"due to parents' dissatisfaction with our facilities and their seeking schools with better physical plants and better conditions for their children."* While the Board expressed their hesitancy to obligate the Congregation in a building program, President Katzner personally began soliciting for major gifts, raising $295,000 in pledges by fall 1965. Heeding the School Board's warning, the Board re-activated efforts to raise funds for the third phase of the Stevenson complex. On October 3, 1966 Katzner gathered lay leaders of the Congregation together to organize teams for the million-dollar campaign. Abraham Krieger served as campaign chairman, overseeing nearly one hundred solicitors.

A second letter from the School Board, read at the trustees' monthly meeting on October 25, 1965, stressed the urgency of beginning the building program as soon as possible. The memo cited complaints that confirmation classes were being held in the hallway outside of the Rabbi's robing room, and four classes were meeting in windowless rooms never intended for use as classrooms. School Board President Sigi Strauss read the letter aloud:

> *We are faced with such a growing list of complaints about the intolerable physical conditions in the school that we fear for the future of our school. ....In the face of the opening of other Congregational Schools in this area (within a radius of 1-2 miles) we dread to speculate on the num-*

ber of parents who, having viewed our facilities, have gone on to other Congregations for their children's schooling. And gentlemen, you know that a good percentage of our new membership must be based on young parents with school-age children.

After raising pledges and collections totaling $973,000, the Building Committee granted the construction contract to the firm of E. Eyring & Sons Co. Several hundred people attended groundbreaking ceremonies on Sunday, March 12, 1967. A photograph of the entire Chizuk Amuno complex accompanied an article about the project that appeared on the first page of the Sunday Sun Real Estate section. Brochures were mailed to each member showing an artist's rendering of the proposed buildings. The first floor of the new School Building was designed to house the pre-school department, youth center, and administrative offices. Ten classrooms, a library, and teachers' room were planned for the second floor. A school auditorium, which would accommodate two hundred people and include a stage and full kitchen, was positioned on the east end of the building.

The Garden Lounge, named for the Biblical Garden visible through the glass walls of the hallway, connected thed school wing with the sanctuary and Krieger Auditorium. In the center of the Lounge was a 150-seat chapel, complete with two stained glass window and a tapestry by Samuel Wiener, Jr. The Biblical Garden, located in the courtyard outside of the chapel, contained plants and shrubs mentioned in the Bible. Accacia, almond, fig, broom, and cedar of Lebanon were planted initially, but few survived the decade. One of Rabbi Goldman's original concepts for the Stevenson Road complex – the reflecting pool with a menorah tower – was eliminated without explanation.

Severe winter weather caused construction delays. The February 2, 1968 Bulletin announced that most of the interior work had been completed, and the curbing of the circular driveway was nearly done. Additional construction expenses brought the final cost of the

School Building project to $1,175,000. A large portion of the funding came from a few major donors, including a matching gift from the families of Abraham and Zanvyl Krieger to pay an amount equal to ten percent of all other pledges received. The opportunity to dedicate a portion of the new building, in honor or memory of an individual, attracted nine other gifts of over $50,000 each.

Rather than a single dedication ceremony, Rabbi Goldman suggested that the Congregation celebrate *"a year of dedication and re-dedication."* Members received a booklet describing areas of the new buildings and acknowledging the generous donors who had funded the project. Under the general theme of "A Revolutionary Age," nine Friday evening services were designated as Dedication Services – four with guest speakers.

Personnel changes in the early 1960s resulted in the replacement of several long-standing employees of the Congregation. After Rev. Moses Amsterdam, sexton of the Stevenson Road complex, died on October 30, 1965, the Board hired Rev. Yehuda Dickstein for the position. The new sexton commuted from his home downtown during the week, and lived in overnight quarters located in the Krieger Wing for Shabbat, until a suitable home was built in the neighborhood. Sexton Hyman Bassan, who had served the Eutaw Place synagogue for thirty-two years, announced his intention to retire effective November 1, 1966, and settle permanently in Israel. In honor of Bassan's retirement, Rabbi Goldman made a rare Shabbat appearance at Eutaw Place, officiating at services on October 29, 1966. Irving Hertzberg was hired to replace the retiring sexton.

Executive Director Harold Hammer submitted his resignation on February 11, 1965, after serving Chizuk Amuno for over nine years. The Brotherhood paid tribute to Hammer at a farewell breakfast on March 21, 1965. Bernard Lehman was hired to replace Hammer, but resigned after only sixteen months on the job. A special meeting of the Board was convened on January 11, 1967 to discuss the unexpected vacancy of this key staff position. Melvyn Pugatch, chairman of the Personnel Committee, reported that the committee recommended Stanley I. Minch to be the next Executive Director. Inspired by the dedication to Chizuk Amuno that his father had shown decades earlier, Minch had been an active participant in congregational activities since his own membership had been approved. Having served on the Brotherhood Board for ten years, including a term as president, and on various committees through the years, the new Executive Director had significant insight into synagogue matters. Election of the affable and highly organized Stanley Minch was widely applauded. He would fulfill the role of chief operating officer for the next thirty years.

Chizuk Amuno endured the turbulence of the late 1960s along with the rest of the city, the country, and in fact, the entire world. The September 1, 1967 <u>Bulletin</u> listed the titles of Friday evening sermons for the coming month: "Race Riots in American Cities," "Red Hot China," "Israel Crisis – Six Days of War," and "Israel Crisis – The Seventh Day of Peace?" Jews around the world celebrated the restoration of the Old City of Jerusalem to the Jewish people, but recognized the instability of the region. The Israel Bond Committee stressed Israel's critical need for financial support during its period of economic reconstruction. Members of Chizuk Amuno responded enthusiastically to Judge Albert Sklar's bond appeal during the High Holy Days of 5728 (1967), pledging a record high $368,950.

Twenty-five years earlier, the horrors of World War II had motivated Jews to affiliate with congregations for the comfort and support of a religious community. In the 1960s, no such surge in membership occurred. Many second- and third-generation American Jews maintained their synagogue membership primarily for the education of their children. A review of the lists of resignation during this period reveals that families frequently resigned after their youngest child became bar mitzvah. In a memorandum to the Board dated May 22, 1967, Irving Melnick, chairman of the Membership Committee, outlined the committee's campaign for the coming year.

Melnick reported that 972 families were members of the Congregation, 134 with seats at Eutaw Place and 838 at Stevenson Road. He compared the current figures with earlier projections:

> *When we projected our new Building Program we projected our planning for a quarter of a century hence. In other words we started to plan in 1953 and we projected our planning to the year 1978. We estimated that we should build for a congregation with a membership roster of 1200-1300 families in the new Stevenson synagogue. Because we arrived at this number of families, we planned a seating capacity in our new Sanctuary of close to 1800 and a maximum seating capacity in the Krieger Auditorium of over 1000. It is obvious from the above that we certainly are an <u>under-populated congregation</u>.*

A goal of two hundred new members was set. The Board approved the Committee's recommendations to establish a new category of membership for those under thirty years old. Announced to the Congregation in the June 16, 1967 <u>Bulletin</u>, the plan offered young married couples full membership benefits and two seats in the Krieger Auditorium for the High Holy Days at a cost of $85. When the *"male member reaches age 30,"* the cost would revert to the current dues in effect. As an additional incentive, the Board authorized that couples married by the rabbis of the Congregation and under age thirty be granted a complimentary membership for the first year of their marriage. On October 29, 1967 seventy-nine new members were invited to the annual New Members Breakfast, which featured a discussion led by Rabbi Goldman and Dr. Daniel Thursz, dean of the University of Maryland School of Social Work, on "What the American Jew Expects from his Synagogue" and "What the Synagogue Expects from the American Jew."

Growing interest in social action issues precipitated the expansion of the Congregation's Social Action Committee to thirty members. Student protests, civil rights marches, the conflict in Vietnam, and the oppression of Soviet Jewry were all topics of discussion at adult learning sessions and youth activities. Author Elie Wiesel addressed a group of more than eight hundred in Krieger Auditorium on October 31, 1967. A review of the evening, printed in the November 17, 1967 <u>Bulletin,</u> noted: *"Mr. Wiesel held his audience spellbound as he interpreted the meaning of the recent victory of Israel over the Arab attackers and the silence of the three million Jews in Soviet Russia."* The following month, Chizuk Amuno congregants joined hundreds of others at a citywide mass meeting held at the JCC to express concern for Soviet Jewry.

In anticipation of Passover, 1968, the <u>Bulletin</u> explained, *"What You Should Know About Passover,"* detailing the traditional home rituals associated with the festival. The April 5, 1968 issue included a statement drafted by the American Jewish Conference on Soviet Jewry urging every family to reflect on the plight of fellow Jews under Soviet rule by reciting the following statement during their Seder:

> *This matzoh, which we set aside as a symbol of hope for the 3 million Jews of the Soviet Union, reminds us of the indestructible link that exists between us. As we observe this festival of freedom, we know that Soviet Jews are not free to learn of their Jewish past, to hand it down to their children. They cannot learn the languages of their fathers. They can only sit in silence and become invisible. We shall be their voice, and our voices shall be joined by thousands of men of conscience aroused by the wrongs suffered by Soviet Jews. Then shall they know that they have not been forgotten, and they that sit in darkness shall yet see a great light.*

Saturday, April 6, 1968 was designated as the annual Brotherhood Shabbat Service. Although David Whitman, president of the Brotherhood, still delivered the sermon announced the previous week entitled, *"The New Meaning of Brotherhood,"* his remarks were altered by the tragic events that had occurred less than forty-eight hours earlier in Memphis, Tennessee. The assassination of Rev. Martin

Luther King ignited racial rioting in major cities across America, including Baltimore. As National Guard units were responding to the violence on city streets, Whitman spoke on the role the Brotherhood plays in bridging the life of the synagogue with the life of the community:

> *As Americans, and as American Jews, we share the feelings of sorrow and grief brought to our Land by the senseless act of violence which has taken from us one of our great Leaders. But we will also share the sense of rededication to the ideals of equality and of brotherhood between men of different races and creeds...*

Whitman, himself the owner of a small business in the heart of the inner city, had always prided himself on the relationship that he had established with his customers.

The following Friday, while Chizuk Amuno families were preparing for the start of Passover at sundown, Rabbi Goldman stood on the pulpit of the Cathedral of the Incarnation to address the crowd gathered for the Good Friday Service. The text of his message, *"Rejoice With Trembling,"* was reprinted in the April 26, 1968 Bulletin. In it, the rabbi described what a miracle it was that *"a humble Rabbi of Israel"* would be privileged to speak in a cathedral on the saddest day in Christendom. He related the terror he had felt as a child in Poland, barricaded in his home on Good Friday as non-Jewish neighbors attended church services where they were *"inflamed anew with hatred towards the Jew."* Goldman stressed the kinship between Judaism and Christianity, and commented on the positive steps taken by the Vatican Council and Protestant Church Synods to reject historic religious hatred. In closing, the rabbi invoked Martin Luther King's murder as a rallying call to *"stand together and serve together in common causes."*

Against the backdrop of dramatic world events, the Congregation celebrated the twentieth anniversary of Israel Goldman's tenure in Baltimore, and honored retiring President J. Benjamin Katzner at the ninety-seventh Annual Meeting. Katzner, concluding twenty-

seven years of continuous service to Chizuk Amuno, received tributes at the May 19, 1968 black tie Dinner-Dance catered by a local
kosher caterer. Over the next few months, the nation watched while
U.S. Attorney General Robert F. Kennedy was assassinated and student riots in Chicago threatened to disrupt the Democratic National
Convention.

Anxious to involve themselves in contemporary issues, the
auxiliaries of the Congregation sponsored the first "All-Congrega-
tion Assembly" on Sunday evening September 15, 1968, featuring
Senator Joseph D. Tydings discussing the topic, *"Dare We Kill Gun
Control Laws?"* Many political leaders spoke at the synagogue over
the following years. Chizuk Amuno member Governor Marvin
Mandel shared the pulpit with Rabbi Goldman at a late Friday
Evening Service on February 7, 1969. Former Secretary of State
Ramsey Clark addressed the Brotherhood Donor on February 19,
1969 and Senator Charles McC. Mathias, Jr. spoke at a Brotherhood
Breakfast the following month.

The youth of Chizuk Amuno experienced the late 1960s much
differently than did their parents. Protests surrounding the civil rights
movement and military draft had expanded the concept of free expression, challenged traditions, and dispelled unquestioning respect
for government actions. Within a few short years controversial topics such as the sexual revolution, feminism, campus sit-ins, draft
evasion, drug abuse, and nihilism dominated conversation. Rabbi
Goldman reflected on the climate of American society in his <u>Bulle-
tin</u> column on September 20, 1968 – two days before Rosh Hashanah
5729:

> *We are caught in a series of bewildering and overwhelm-
> ing paradoxes. This is an age of brilliant achievement
> and unparalleled advances in every field of human en-
> deavor. It is also an age of darkness and despair in which
> famine and poverty stalk over large portions of human-*

ity. It is an age with visions of Utopia of people living in peace and security. It is also an age of moral deterioration, of crime and war and of spiritual emptiness.

At first glance, the schedule of synagogue activities planned for December, 1968 seemed typical of past years. The Sisterhood's donor luncheon featured a "Parade of Fashions" with fur coats. Hazzan Weisgal's eightieth birthday was marked with a concert and formal congregation party. However, closer examination reveals some complex issues facing the Congregation:

- December 1 – senior high school students hear guest speaker on the topic of *"What Does Black Power Mean to White Suburban Youth?"*
- December 8 – Rabbi Goldman responds to the "God is Dead" movement with lecture at a Brotherhood breakfast entitled *"God is a Living Question!"*
- December 22 – wives invited to attend Brotherhood breakfast with guest speaker discussing *"What is Happening to Morality – In Marriage?"*
- December 29 – Rabbi Crain moderates panel questioning college students *"...about the Sexual Revolution and the New Morality, about the 'Playboy' philosophy and its effect on our younger generations, about pornography and especially about the effects and interest in religion and religious experience."*

Rabbi Crain, recognizing the widening gap between college students and their religion, used the December 20, 1968 Bulletin to urge adults to attend a College Homecoming Service scheduled for the following Friday evening. Noting that these students represented the future leadership of the synagogue, Crain stressed the message: *"We want them to know that geographic distances will not be a detracting element in our continuing love for them and interest in their lives."* The young rabbi concluded his tenure at Chizuk Amuno when his contract expired in July, 1969. Four months later, Rabbi David Nelson assumed the office of assistant rabbi. Ordained by the Seminary in 1967, Nelson had spent two years serving a large congregation in Brazil before coming to Chizuk Amuno.

Discussions of morality and sexual attitudes continued as Rabbi Goldman reviewed contemporary literature at Brotherhood and Women's Institute meetings. Portnoy's Complaint, Couples, and Sexual Wilderness were among the books reviewed. The Mr. & Mrs. Club focused on the sexual revolution as they invited members to hear discussions on "The Double Standard in Marriage" and "Marriage and Sex." Just five weeks after Goldman's November 28, 1969 sermon entitled, "The Modern Over-Emphasis on Sex," the Bulletin announced that a discussion of Jacqueline Susann's novel, The Love Machine, would launch the 1970 Book Review Series.

In the late 1960s, American educators reacted to changing standards by introducing sex education courses into public school curricula. Hoping to provide a frame of morality around the topic, the Synagogue Council of America issued a position statement on the role that religion should play in the sexual education of children. Rabbi Goldman's column in the November 7, 1969 Bulletin published the Council's statement which said, in part:

> *Responsibility for sex education belongs primarily to the child's parents. A home permeated by justice and love is the seedbed of sound sexual development among all family members…. It is important that sex education not be reduced to the mere communication of information. Rather, this significant area of experience should be placed in a setting where rich human, personal and spiritual values can illuminate it and give it meaning.*

The issue of sex education remained controversial. In January, 1970 the Brotherhood invited an educator from the Baltimore County school system to address the topic, "Sex Education – What are They Teaching Our Kids These Days?"

Exploring the Concept of a Day School

The concept of a Conservative day school was first mentioned in the April 19, 1957 <u>Bulletin</u>, as the United Synagogue of America established a Department of Day School Education within its Commission on Jewish Education. Rabbi Josiah Derby, chairman of the Commission, was quoted as saying:

> *The child attending day school will have the opportunity to acquire an intensive education in Hebrew language, Bible, Talmud, medieval and modern literature. It is the day school which will furnish an important reservoir of intensively educated Jewish leaders, the teachers, rabbis and scholars of the future.*

A day school at Chizuk Amuno was still decades away; however, the School Board did participate in some non-traditional efforts to improve religious education. In the fall of 1965, the Congregation was selected to participate in the Melton Research Project, exploring new methods of instruction. The Confirmation Department was revitalized in 1965, adding field trips, guest speakers, and films to their programming. A new music education program supplemented the core curriculum of the schools.

The idea of a day school remained of interest to the Board. Herbert Goldman, chairman of the School Board, and Principal Hymen Saye represented Chizuk Amuno at the Conference on Jewish Day Schools in the Conservative Movement held in New York on December 26-27, 1965. In the following months, members of the School Board listened to authorities on education speak about the virtues of the Solomon Schechter Day School system and spent several years exploring the possibility of opening a school.

In late 1968, representatives of Beth El, Beth Tfiloh, and Chizuk Amuno met to discuss establishing an inter-congregational day school. Acknowledging that Beth Tfiloh already had a school serving grades kindergarten through eight, the rabbis of the three congregations recommended that one Hebrew Day School be formed through joint sponsorship. In a memorandum to the Boards of Trustees dated January 7, 1969, Rabbis Goldman, Jacob Agus, and Samuel Rosenblatt suggested that different grade levels of the proposed school could be located on each congregation's property, noting the close proximity of the synagogues. Although pre-school levels were not included in the inter-congregational school, a high school was projected.

J. Benjamin Katzner, the chairman of the Subcommittee on the Day School Resolutions, presented formal resolutions for a day school to the Board on November 24, 1969. As a protection against any unexpected financial burden, the Board approved the joint day school resolutions amended to limit each congregation's liability to a maximum of $8,500 for each of the first two years of operations. The proposal for a combined day school is not mentioned again for several years. Written minutes of the Congregation offer no further explanation as efforts to make the plan a reality continued "behind the scenes."

Following the success of the Youth Pilgrimage to Israel in 1966, the Sisterhood organized a two-week tour of the country in March, 1969. Led by Rabbi and Mrs. Goldman, sixty adults from the Congregation celebrated Purim in Tel Aviv. Festivities were dampened, however, by the death of Prime Minister Levi Eshkol and mounting terrorist activity. Tension in the Middle East intensified in 1969 as Egyptian President Nasser used military force while attempting to regain the Suez Canal, which had been captured by Israel two years earlier. In a letter to the Congregation reprinted in the March 21, 1969 <u>Bulletin</u>, Rabbi Goldman reported that Israeli citizens were maintaining routine activities and enduring daily acts of terrorism, but were *"very anxious about the policy of the Nixon Administration toward Israel.... The hope here is that America will not abandon Israel."* Historians later postulated that it was apprehension about U.S. support of Israel that muted American Jewry's public reaction to the country's involvement in the Vietnam conflict.

Although active in his support of civil rights, Rabbi Goldman was noticeably passive on the matter of Vietnam in 1968 and 1969. As a naturalized citizen, the rabbi fully appreciated the freedom that America offered and trusted the system of government that created foreign policy. Many leaders of the Conservative Movement were also reluctant to publicly question the government's actions overseas. In her essay, "Texture of Seminary Life during the Finkelstein Era," Baila R. Shargel, social and cultural historian, commented on the dilemma faced at the Seminary:

Several faculty members, vocally pro-civil rights, cautioned compliance with governmental policy lest Jewish opposition to the Vietnam War endanger America's pro-Israel stance. Their logic escaped the students, who generally embraced the antiwar position of their peers.

Students at the Seminary, as well as Chizuk Amuno's youth, attempted to reconcile the ethical teachings of Judaism with what they considered to be the immoral bombing of Vietnam.

Other than the Social Action Committee's position statement on Vietnam, mention of the hostilities was noticeably absent from the programming at Chizuk Amuno during the escalation of U.S. involvement in 1968 and 1969. In contrast to the Congregation's activities during World War II and the Korean Conflict, synagogue communications of the late 1960s never mention Brotherhood or Sisterhood involvement in support of members serving in the armed forces. There is no record of gifts sent to servicemen, Bulletins sent overseas, or visitations to injured veterans.

University of Maryland student Richard Forman, invited to speak from the pulpit on the seventh day of Passover, 1970, observed that synagogues across the country were *"empty of youths"* on Shabbat. He described the contemporary college student as follows:

Young people today are religious even to the point of superstition. Nothing sells in paperbacks so much as theology and religious writings. What are the hottest items on campus? Tarot cards, Yoga, Ouija boards, mind-expanding drugs, mysticism, astrology, the occult. Youth today are incredibly religious. They just don't buy organized religion.

Forman attributed anger against institutional Judaism as being a part of the larger protest that young people were voicing. Their complaints were *"against the bigness of the institution, against its inhumanity, against the tendency of institutions to exist for themselves in their own right, as power gone mad and turned against the very persons the institutions are intended to support and protect."*

The restlessness and dissatisfaction of Jewish students was national in its scope. A 1967 essay by JTS student Robert J. Saks, entitled "Jews, Judaism, and the New Left," noted that rebellious Jewish students condemned the multi-million dollar synagogues and hypocritical, overdressed Jews whose attendance at services was limited to three days a year. Saks identified the characteristics of the synagogue community that offended the liberal, altruistic, younger generation:

Our extravagant bar mitzvah parties, pre-selichot dances, and gaudy arks are turning thousands of our best youngsters away from Judaism. Our practice of occasionally giving awards to the unrighteous but rich, infrequently addressing ourselves to social issues (and when we do so, in lukewarm terms) and rarely, if ever, showing ourselves on picket lines has born the bitter fruit of a generation which at best ignores us, and at worst holds us in disdain.

The safe, suburban life that parents in the 1950s wanted to create for their children was no longer relevant in the age of political unrest. Bob Dylan and Abbie Hoffman served as their Jewish role models.

Saks's essay presented the advice of leading rabbinic experts on youth to combat the disillusionment of their younger members. Rabbi Isador Hoffman, past director of the Jewish student society at

Columbia University, explained that Judaism should not attempt to dissuade students from the humanitarian tradition of the religion, but should rather show them how the teachings of Judaism can help develop a person's ethical sensitivity. Hoffman stated: *"It gives one a sense of greater confidence and rootedness to know that one's people and history validates such a stance."* The role of the rabbinate, commented Hoffman, was to show youth why and how their concern for social causes was attributable to their Jewishness.

By late 1969, public opinion on the war had shifted and in November, protestors organized a massive Peace March on Washington. Rabbi Goldman's sermon on November 15, 1969, the weekend of the March, compared the divisiveness of the country to the week's Torah portion on Jacob and Esau: *"The hands of Esau are tragically prolonging the Vietnam War. They are trying to choke off all protest against this horrible war. They are determined to crush criticism and stifle dissent."* The rabbi warned that restrictions placed on freedom of speech and assembly could ultimately lead to Fascism in America.

Reacting to perceived contradictions between the standards of Judaism and the position of the synagogue, students challenged the validity of organized religion and questioned the wisdom of those in authority. Addressing the Congregation on the first day of Passover in April, 1970, Rabbi Goldman commented on the alienation of many young adults from Jewish values and traditions. He stressed the need to keep paths of communication open between parents and children as together they struggled to find answers to the questions of the day. Goldman proposed replacing the traditional Four Questions asked at the Seder table that year with the following:

Why get involved in society when we live under the constant threat of nuclear annihilation?
Why continue in the Vietnam War?
Why are we in such a mess?
Who am I and why shall I remain a Jew?

The theme of the June, 1970 Convention of the National Federation of Jewish Men's Clubs held at Grossinger's was "The Quest for Jewish Identity in the Midst of Changing Values." The men examined the relevance of synagogue worship, and discussed why they were losing the participation of Jewish youth. Chizuk Amuno's Youth Activities Board promoted a series of creative programs to attract students and help them define their own Jewish identity. High school students were invited to an "All-Night Shul-In" on Selihot beginning at midnight. The schedule included a movie, discussion with Rabbi Nelson, outdoor exercises, and a sunrise service in the Biblical Garden. Teenagers were encouraged to help decorate the synagogue's sukkah and given printed instructions on how to build their own sukkah at home. Rabbi Nelson also conducted a series of Home Learning sessions for young couples in his home.

Distrust of authority continued to swell as law enforcement officers were summoned to control student revolts on college campuses – Columbia, Brandeis, and Kent State Universities. The image of the synagogues, perceived as grand buildings ruled by aging rabbis and lay leaders, suffered, as those leading academic institutions and state governments resorted to violence as a means to flex their control. Many of the well-intentioned programs to attract college students back into synagogue were met with apprehension. Announcements in the weekly Bulletin reveal the frustration felt by lay leaders:

October 9, 1970:
We, the so-called Jewish Establishment, have an invitation for you. Bring along a friend – if you have one – and come to our Sukkah Brunch on October 18...Why should you forsake your campus for even one hour? The answer is: A chance to meet and talk with interesting people.... You can also tell your rabbis and cantors from Beth El and Chizuk Amuno how much you love them – plus the added attraction of free good food. Come even if your parents want you to!

December 18, 1970:

Get together with your friends to vent your hostilities against the establishment over lox and bagels. Come to the Brotherhood sponsored Breakfast on Sunday morning, December 27. First of all, it will provide "spiritual stimulation" (assuming you come to our service, which starts at 9:30);

Secondly, it will be a gastronomic treat (assuming you don't eat before you come); and

Thirdly, it will be intellectually challenging. You can hear Howard Lifshitz, one of the Jewish Theological Seminary students discuss "College Students and the New Left."

A hannukiah and candles were mailed to every college student in the Congregation along with a ritual guide.

Adult social activities continued – art exhibits, Jewish music festivals, dances – but the role of the synagogue as a social haven and cultural museum was slowly fading. No longer would the youth of the Congregation be satisfied with involvement in "junior" models of adult auxiliaries and record hops. A new sense of seriousness prevailed. Although adult education and traditional Jewish study had been prevalent at Chizuk Amuno for nearly one hundred years, the emphasis in the early 1970s was to explore classical Judaic texts as a means to understand and react to contemporary issues.

In the midst of social upheaval, the Board faced the threat of financial collapse. A review of bar mitzvah statistics in 1969 indicates that those born at the crest of the baby-boom era were now past the age of attending afternoon religious school but not yet self-sufficient adults. Total membership was not shrinking, but it was aging. Traditional sources of revenue – dues and donations – were not sufficient to support the cash needs of the expansive Stevenson Road complex. This cash crunch was felt not only at Chizuk Amuno, but also at many congregations that had expanded during the boom years of the post-war decade. The Seminary was hard-hit with the same problem and became increasingly dependent on the United Synagogue and Women's League for funding. Chizuk Amuno participated in the National Enrollment Plan, wherein each congregation affiliated with United Synagogue was assessed a per capita fee. The Sisterhood took a leadership role in support of the Seminary's Torah Scholarship Fund and efforts to finance the Mathilda Schechter Residence Hall.

In light of mounting fiscal problems, the Board returned to the question of selling excess land. Those members who had witnessed the problems caused by inadequate space at Eutaw Place were especially sensitive to the proposal and expressed their opinion at the Annual Meeting on May 25, 1969. In an effort to control rumors, President Herbert Goldman released a four-page letter to members on June 23, 1969, detailing the chronology of the Board's decision to sell thirty acres of the Congregation's land that was deemed excess six years earlier. The letter emphasized that the decision to sell land was not done in haste, but rather was, *"thought through over a long period of years and was the result of recommendations of capable, qualified and sincerely interested members of the Chizuk Amuno family."* The Board met privately with the dissenters and reviewed the objections of surrounding neighbors to rezoning the property for multi-family units. A vote taken at a special congregational meeting on August 18, 1969 indicated that the membership was divided on the issue, with over 150 families voting in opposition to the Board's plan to request rezoning. With a majority vote in favor, but clearly no mandate, the matter was referred back to the Planning and Real Estate Committee for further study.

The Budget Committee struggled to draft a balanced budget for the approaching fiscal year. On February 23, 1970 the Board considered eight suggestions to clear the forecasted deficit, including selling real estate and issuing non-interest-bearing debentures. Cognizant of the continuing opposition to the real estate option, the

Board agreed to develop a plan to issue up to $500,000 of debt. One month later, the Real Estate Committee recommended that the Congregation also make application for rezoning of the excess thirty acres. Within days, Herbert Goldman received a letter representing the "Chizuk Amuno Committee to Oppose Rezoning," restating the group's strong disapproval of rezoning. Meanwhile, sale of the Congregation's debentures was critically hampered by the Board's action to pursue the zoning petition. At a meeting held on September 4, 1970, the newly organized Executive Committee of the Board agreed to recommend to the Board of Trustees that the petition for rezoning be recalled in an effort to unify the Congregation. After *"much discussion"* at the September 14, 1970 Board meeting, the recommendation was unanimously approved, and the application for rezoning was withdrawn. With the conflict settled, the Debenture Committee proceeded with their campaign and reported sales of $206,000 of debentures at the December 28, 1970 Board meeting.

In order to retain members and encourage affiliation among younger families, the Membership Committee proposed a new category of dues. On August 24, 1970 the Board approved a reduction of standard dues for families between the ages of thirty and thirty-five. The following year, the Building Fund requirement for membership was reduced, and the length of time to pay was extended from five to ten years.

On the recommendation of the Cemetery Committee, the Board accepted a net $132,500 settlement resulting from the *"condemnation suit with the City of Baltimore relative to the acreage that the city took over for the Northern Parkway and Wabash Avenue Thruways."* The new roadways had split the Congregation's cemetery property, leaving fifty-seven acres north of Northern Parkway separated from the main grounds. Seven months later, after approving the release of this plot on May 24, 1971, the Board accepted a purchase price of $1.2 million for their land.

The 100th Anniversary

Rabbi Goldman and the Board of Chizuk Amuno viewed the hundredth anniversary of the Congregation's founding as an opportunity not only to look back, but also as an opportunity to plan for the future. On December 23, 1969, more than a year before the official anniversary, the 100th Anniversary Committee convened to brainstorm a list of issues that the Congregation should address in the coming years. As a result of that discussion, the Board agreed to the Committee's recommendation to conduct a survey. With input from various auxiliaries of the Congregation, Dr. Paul Ephross, a social welfare researcher, designed separate questionnaires for Chizuk Amuno adults and youth. In order to ascertain each group's opinion on the direction that the synagogue should take in the future, considerable energy was devoted to structuring the survey questions, which were to be completed anonymously. Besides items relating to demographic characteristics, questions included:

THE ADULT STUDY

- *Rank the three parts of Chizuk Amuno's program that have the most, and least, meaning to you and your family.*
- *Do you favor the establishment of a Hebrew Day School by Chizuk Amuno? If there were a Hebrew Day School, would you send one or more of your children to it if the tuition were about $700?*
- *Do you read Hebrew well enough to read prayers in Hebrew?*
- *Level of observance regarding kashrut – buy Kosher meat?, use separate dishes?, eat only Kosher food outside of the home?*
- *Rank the three most important things that are essential to being a good Jew.*

THE YOUTH STUDY

- *What my parents value most in life is..... What I value most in life is....*
- *If the synagogue were to move in the next ten or fifteen years,*

I would want it to be: larger, smaller, more elaborate, less elaborate?

- *Would you want to attend an all-day Jewish high school instead of the public or private school which you now attend?*

- *The most important way Chizuk Amuno should help the Jews of Israel is…*

Unfortunately, the Board minutes of December 27, 1971 report that, *"the response by the congregation was not sufficient for the data to be analyzed for a report but that there were sufficient returns for a report to be rendered on the college students."* Although only 135 responses (sixty-nine female and sixty-six male) were received from the 375 college-age members sent the survey, an interpretation of the results was printed in the December 15, 1972 Bulletin. The profile revealed that students were strongly liberal in their views on racial equality, abortion, and the legalization of marijuana. They valued the effect of Israel on American Jews and supported conventional ways to provide aid to the country. *"There is deep and broad evidence of a commitment to being Jewish and to the Jewish people. There is a serious questioning of the traditional forms of Jewish life."* The students' attitude toward Chizuk Amuno as a synagogue was summarized as *"it's nice to know it's there but don't expect me to invest much of myself."*

Rabbi Goldman highlighted the anniversary by publishing articles and presenting lectures about the history of Chizuk Amuno, its Brotherhood, Sisterhood, school, lay leadership, and spiritual leaders. Centennial year activities began with over 1,200 people attending the 47th Annual Union Thanksgiving Service honoring Dr. Louis Finkelstein. On Friday evening, February 12, 1971, Chizuk Amuno conducted a Centennial Interfaith Service. Lawrence Cardinal Shehan, Bishop David K. Leighton, and Rabbi Israel Goldman spoke on the spirit of unity and the advancements made in interfaith understanding. The United States Naval Academy Choir, comprised of 110 midshipmen, provided musical entertainment.

Marking the precise date that the first Congregational meeting was held in 1871, on April 2, 1971, Rabbi Goldman entitled his Friday evening sermon, "How Chizuk Amuno May Change in the Next One Hundred Years." Two days later, Professor Salo W. Baron, considered the foremost Jewish historian of the twentieth century, delivered the Founders Day Convocation address entitled, "American Jewry in the Next 100 Years."

Unlike celebrations of the Congregation's earlier milestone anniversaries, the 1971 occasion did not include a lavish banquet or dance. A formal *"Champagne Ball"* was considered during the planning phase, but the idea was dropped. In a decade of social unrest and worldwide political tension, a serious, reflective approach to marking Chizuk Amuno's 100th anniversary was deemed more appropriate.

The 101st Annual Meeting was held on Wednesday evening, June 9, 1971. Before installing new members of the Board of Trustees and the officers, Rabbi Goldman commented on the future:

The beginning of our second century will be a period of youthful and zestful activity which will be inspired by the past, but which will be geared to the future. We will be guided by the wishes and suggestions of our membership, young and old, and we will plan services, programs and activities which will be relevant to the needs of our times.

As the serious portion of the evening concluded, the cast of "The Building Bug" took their places backstage in the Krieger Auditorium. Written, directed, and produced by Chizuk Amuno's creative Executive Director, Stanley Minch, the satirical musical production traced the one-hundred-year history of the Congregation and paid homage to retiring President Herbert Goldman. One of the show's highlights was a song mocking the synagogue complex on Stevenson Road:

To the tune of Matchmaker, Matchmaker

Contractor, contractor build us a schule
A chapel that's cool, a big swimming pool
We want Beth Tfiloh and Beth El to drool
So build us a perfect schule.

Architect, architect draw us a plan
Survey some land, make it look grand
Send me the papers for Arlington acres
And find us some perfect land.

For Rabbi, make it look holy
For Hazzan, make acoustics that ring
We need a cool place in summer
For cream cheese and bagels and our praying.

Contractor, contractor build us an Ark
Some places to park, with lights when its dark
Contractor, contractor build us an Ark

And find us some land
Make it look grand
A big swimming pool
Even a school

Oh, build us a perfect schule!

When Herbert Goldman stepped down as President of Chizuk Amuno in June, 1971 he summarized the Congregation's philosophy regarding its lay leadership:

Our changing society has telescoped centuries of progress and development into a relatively short span of years. Changes are not restricted to machines but have taken place in society and man's relationships as well. Current generations are a thinking people who are not willing to accept the old ideas but develop new philosophies of life. So it is that religion must modernize and keep abreast of the needs of today.

The Congregation experienced a period of significant change during the next few years – in personnel, ritual practice, and educational programming. Chizuk Amuno was not alone. The principles of Conservative Judaism continued to be examined and adapted in response to an evolving American Jewish community. In 1971, Wolfe Kelman, vice-president of the Rabbinical Assembly, published an essay entitled, "The American Synagogue: Present and Prospects," which aptly fit Chizuk Amuno's status:

> *The generation of rabbis, leaders and teachers who grew to maturity in the 1950-1970 period will gradually replace the aging present leadership which has been blessed by longevity. Unlike most other contemporary human institutions, the Jewish Establishment is, with rare exception, still controlled by the same leaders, elected or appointed, who emerged during or immediately after the post-World War II period of dynamic expansion.*

Kelman commented that rising young leaders would bring with them a new perspective, having matured *"in a more self-confident era of Jewish history."* Many of Chizuk Amuno's future leaders were second- and third-generation descendants of earlier members of the Congregation. Their religious identity had been formed in the very synagogue that they would now lead.

Hymen Saye had been responsible for religious education at Chizuk Amuno for forty years. His retirement was announced in the May 14, 1971 Bulletin. The article detailed the Educational Director's long career, commenting that school enrollment had grown from sixty-five to nearly five hundred during his tenure. The following week, Dr. Philip Wendkos was announced to head the Congregational schools. Wendkos, described as *"a brilliant and progressive educator,"* possessed impressive academic credentials. His approach to Jewish education included the use of recordings, films, field trips, and implementation of the Melton Method of "Inquiry and Discovery" to teach Bible and prayer. Fifteen teenage graduates of the school were hired by Wendkos as instructional aides to assist classroom teachers and to further motivate students. Wendkos also encouraged student involvement by forming the first School Student Council. Intended to serve as a liaison between the students and the School Board, faculty, and administration, the Council helped to plan retreats and other activities.

A more informal system of learning took place six days each week, as a dedicated band of men attended morning services to assure that mourners and those recognizing the yahrzeit of a loved one were supported by a minyan. In earlier decades, coffee and buns were served to the minyanaires after the 7:45 a.m. service, but beginning in 1969, the worshippers were treated to sit-down breakfasts served on long tables set with tablecloths, napkins, and flatware. Those who did not need to rush to work lingered over warm bagels, eggs, and occasionally, mondel bread. Rev. Dickstein used the time to explain the week's Torah portion, discuss a section of Talmud, or answer questions on ritual practice. In 1971, Leonard Feinglass established the coveted "Golden Bagel Award." The plaque, shown in a photograph in the June 2, 1972 Bulletin, was engraved, *"in appreciation of outstanding devotion to the daily breakfast minyan."* Sexton Dickstein tutored several men on how to lead the prayer service, creating a cadre of laymen capable of conducting services, not only in the chapel, but also at homes observing shiva.

At the request of Rabbi Goldman, the Ritual Committee recommended several innovations to the High Holy Day services of 5732 (1971). Listed in the September 17, 1971 Bulletin, the changes included:

- Open seating for the evening services of Rosh Hashanah
- 9:00 a.m. starting time on Rosh Hashanah and Yom Kippur mornings, necessitating *"an abridgement of the Shacharith Service"*
- a booklet of contemporary prayers to supplement the traditional machzor

- twelve new pages in the <u>Wings of Memory</u> booklet replacing historical examples of Jewish martyrdom with pages citing modern day martyrdom taken from Holocaust literature

In addition to adult services in the Eutaw Place synagogue, Krieger Auditorium, and the main sanctuary, five separate children's services were scheduled for students ages three to thirteen.

Older students exhibited their own sense of ruach on the eve of Simchat Torah. In what was described in the October 29, 1971 <u>Bulletin</u> as an *"unprecedented way,"* the young people took over the service: *"Their singing and their dancing with the Torah on the Bimah and all around our large synagogue, simply brought gladness to the hearts of all who were present."* The youth program had expanded to provide social interaction among students of all ages. A series of Youth Directors organized activities for the many student clubs within the Congregation. These organizations included Leadership Training Fellowship (eleventh and twelfth graders), United Synagogue Youth (ninth to twelfth graders), Bar Mitzvah Brotherhood (boys ages thirteen to eighteen), Bat Mitzvah Sisterhood (girls ages thirteen to eighteen), Kadima (seventh and eighth graders), Olim (fifth and sixth graders), and Bonim (third and fourth graders). Events such as the annual *"Hanukkah Latke Luau,"* youth encampment at Camp Holiday, Sukkah Decorating party, and toy drive were designed to promote observance of Jewish holidays, the development of synagogue skills, prayer, social action, and synagogue service projects.

As early as 1970, Rabbi Goldman began discussing the details of his inevitable retirement. The Board considered questions pertaining to pension benefits and provisions for his wife. Heading Goldman's list of future plans was the wish to be granted a sabbatical to travel, study, and write. The rabbi's first book, <u>The Life and Times of Rabbi David Ibn Avi Zimra</u>, was published by JTS in the fall of 1970. He was anxious to begin on his next literary project, a volume detailing the evolution of Jewish adult learning. On June 28, 1971 the Board approved a six-month sabbatical leave for Rabbi

Goldman to begin on January 1, 1972. The rabbi arranged a schedule of guest clergy to occupy the pulpit during his absence.

News of the rabbi's sabbatical was announced in the December 17, 1971 Bulletin. Rabbi and Mildred Goldman began his period of "rest" with a two-month cruise to South Africa and South America. The rabbi had been invited by the cruise line to serve as both Jewish and interdenominational chaplain aboard the *S.S. Leonardo da Vinci*. In his letters to the Congregation, Rabbi Goldman reported that the leader of the Jewish community in Senegal invited him to conduct their Friday night service. Returning for a brief stay in Baltimore, the Goldmans recounted their impressions of the foreign Jewish communities they had visited at services on February 25, 1972. On March 8, 1972, Rabbi and Mildred Goldman left for Jerusalem. During their three-month stay, the couple enrolled in several courses at the Hebrew University, met with Israeli dignitaries, and enjoyed *"both renewal and replenishment of mind and spirit."* Although he described the sabbatical leave as *"a dream come true,"* Rabbi Goldman also expressed his homesickness in a letter addressed to *"Dear Friends,"* printed in the May 19, 1972 Bulletin:

> *Let me tell you at the very outset that I miss you. This is the first time in the 24 years of my Rabbinate with you that I have been away for such a long time. The routine of my life at Chizuk Amuno day in and day out, has been so full, so crowded and so meaningful, that it is something of a wrench and a dislocation in my life to be without it and to be away from it.*

As the Congregation welcomed Rabbi Goldman back to the pulpit in June 1972, they also bid farewell to Assistant Rabbi David Nelson. During the summer, twenty-seven-year-old Rabbi Charles Sherman arrived in Baltimore to fill the position of assistant to Rabbi Goldman.

In 1972, the Rabbinical Assembly published a new edition of the High Holy Day Mahzor, edited by Rabbi Jules Harlow. At Rabbi Goldman's recommendation, the Ritual Committee strongly endorsed the updated volume. The basic integrity and traditional structure of the service were maintained; however, the English translation of the text reflected modern thought and experiences, including the Holocaust and establishment of the State of Israel. Rabbi Goldman explained: *"Several of the revisions of the Hebrew text reflect current liturgical practice in the Conservative Movement. By adding extensive transliteration, congregational participation will be encouraged."* A committee successfully solicited donations for 826 prayerbooks in time for their use during the High Holy Days of 5733 (1972). Responding to a desperate appeal, Chizuk Amuno shipped five hundred copies of their old prayerbooks to Temple Israel in Wilkes-Barre, Pennsylvania. The September 15, 1972 <u>Bulletin</u> explained that the Conservative congregation had been completely destroyed by recent flooding.

Another Jewish community in crisis drew the attention of Chizuk Amuno members in the early 1970s as the plight of Soviet Jewry became known. In 1970, students sent New Year cards to more than sixty synagogues in the Soviet Union to remind the Jews of Russia that American Jewry had not forgotten them. A large contingent of members joined the Baltimore Committee of Soviet Jewry in a bus cavalcade to Washington, D.C. on June 15,1971, to demonstrate concern for Soviet Jews who had been harassed and restricted from leaving the Soviet Union. In the fall of 1972, a school literary contest was held to help children develop an empathy for, and awareness of, problems facing Jews in hostile countries. Students were asked to respond to the question, "What would I feel like if I were a Jew in an Arab Country?" Each class winner was given a year's membership in the American Association for Iraqi and Syrian Jewry.

Outrage over the murder of eleven Israeli athletes at the 1972 Munich Olympics prompted Hebrew school faculty to have their classes write condolence letters to the bereaved families. One note, written by a ten-year-old, was especially poignant:

> *I am very sorry that your son was 1 of the 11 young men that was murdered. It is a shame in today's world, man cannot leave a Jew alone and live in harmony. I know*

*the sorrow you must feel and if wishes and prayers could
undo the wrong I would pray very, very much that this
tragedy would never have happened.*

The Brotherhood Breakfast Forum held on October 22, 1972, featured the Israeli Ambassador to Burma speaking on "After Munich, Is Peace Possible in the Middle East?"

Unfortunately, that question was answered less than a year later when Egyptian and Syrian military forces attacked Israel on October 6, 1973 – Yom Kippur 5734. Chizuk Amuno members reacted with their hearts and with their wallets. Shortly after the annual appeal for Israel Bonds on Yom Kippur Day, an emergency meeting was called to encourage additional bond purchases. Bulletin articles emphasized: *"In this crisis your conscience commands you to make a compulsory loan to Israel through State of Israel Bonds."* Hebrew school children collected over $600 in cash donations. Flyers promoting the Sisterhood Fall Dance to be held on November 10, 1973 stated that proceeds would be sent to the Israel Emergency Fund. At their October Board meeting, the Brotherhood voted to contribute $1,000 – half of their existing bank account balance – to the Emergency Fund.

Following the cease-fire declared on October 25, 1973, Rabbi Goldman announced plans to travel to the Middle East in January. In addition to visiting Israel, the rabbi and his wife cruised the Mediterranean, exploring the Jewish communities in Barcelona, Casablanca, and Athens. The December 28, 1973 Bulletin disclosed that the rabbi would be *"met and briefed by representatives of the Joint Distribution Committee for the latest findings on Jewish conditions."* In a letter to the Congregation dated January 24, 1974, Rabbi Goldman reported on conditions in Jerusalem. After meeting with government officials at the Foreign Ministry, the Goldmans visited wounded soldiers at Hadassah Hospital and the rehabilitation center in Natanya. Faced with stalled tourist activity, the Israeli economic community desperately needed American Jews to visit. Responding to an urgent plea from El Al Airlines, Rabbi Sherman organized a ten-day Study Mission to Israel, departing February 23, 1974, less than one month after notice of the trip was announced.

Economic conditions in America also suffered as a result of the Middle East conflict. From October, 1973 until November, 1974 the oil-producing Arab countries maintained an embargo on oil exports to Western nations, causing gasoline shortages and inflated oil prices. Executive Director Stanley I. Minch outlined the steps that Chizuk Amuno was taking in response to the energy crisis in the December 14, 1973 Bulletin:

- *Promoting the use of carpools to and from the synagogue whenever possible.*
- *Encouraging parents to dress children in heavy sweaters during cold weather because the temperature will be set lower throughout the buildings*
- *Holding services in the Chapel whenever there is no bar or bat mitzvah scheduled for a Friday night or Shabbat morning*
- *Extinguishing all ornamental lighting*
- *Reducing electrical fixtures by fifty percent*
- *Using oil-burning boilers sparingly*

Even with these austerity measures, Chizuk Amuno expenses spiraled upward during America's inflationary times.

Two innovative programs in religious education began at Chizuk Amuno in 1973: the Parent Education Program (PEP) and the Hillel High School of Jewish Studies. Developed by the United Synagogue Commission on Jewish Education, PEP sought to effect a positive change in the Jewish lifestyle of the family through greater observance of and involvement in Jewish living. The November 9, 1973 Bulletin described how twenty families with children in the Alef Class had enrolled in the program. For two hours every Monday evening, participating parents received classroom instruction in Hebrew language, the *"Jewish experience,"* and the concepts of Torah. The School Board strongly felt that parental involvement in the learning process would enable parents *"to guide their own children better Judaically, and to serve as shining examples for their children starting out in Hebrew School."* A special PEP Family Sabbath Dinner, held on December 14, 1973, provided families the opportunity to experience Shabbat rituals explained by *"Abba and Ima,"* Rabbi and Mildred Goldman.

The establishment of the Hillel High School at Chizuk Amuno provided a structured educational experience for teenagers without placing unreasonable demands on their time. As explained in the September 28, 1973 <u>Bulletin</u>, students attended courses on either Sunday morning or Wednesday evening for two ten-week mini-semesters. *"Young, dynamic instructors"* endeavored to examine the Jewish experience in contemporary terms. The first class of over ninety students chose from among courses that included: *"Mama Loshon: From Pinsk to Pikesville," "Where is God? The Mind-Blowing Jewish Mystique," "My Son and Daughter...The Shul Maven,"* and *"Keyn Enhora: Jewish Magic and Superstition."* To help prepare teenagers for summer experiences in Israel, the program also offered a seminar in the Ulpan approach to the study of spoken Hebrew.

Although Rabbi Goldman was pleased with the Hillel High School program, he still advocated the concept of a day school. The Board had expressed interest in an inter-congregation day school in 1969, but basic ideological issues were raised during conversations with Beth El and Beth Tfiloh that could not be resolved. In late 1972, the Committee on Communal Schools of Baltimore's Board of Jewish Education requested a position paper regarding the establishment of a Communal Day Co-educational High School. Dr. Herbert Birnbaum, Executive Director of the Board of Jewish Education, and Carmi Schwartz, Director of Social Planning of the Associated Jewish Charities, released Draft #2 of that position paper on December 12, 1973. At the time, there were five day schools in Baltimore – four Orthodox single-sex schools and Beth Tfiloh, an Orthodox coed school. Combined enrollment totaled over one thou-

sand students. Beth Tfiloh was the only existing day school interested in considering co-educational classrooms.

Birnbaum and Schwartz questioned the rabbis of six congregations as to their perceived need for a communal day high school
and the ideological philosophy of such a school. All six rabbis agreed
that there was a need for a Hebrew Day High School; however, the
researchers noted *"significant differences among the six rabbis regarding the philosophy, ideology and general atmosphere guiding
this enterprise."* Page ten of the position paper reveals Rabbi
Goldman's stand on the matter:

> *While Rabbi Goldman would have personally opted for
> a school whose affiliation would be with the conserva-
> tive Solomon Schechter schools, in deference to the needs
> of this community he suggested that no ideological af-
> filiation be attempted in the formation of this school. It
> should also be noted that Rabbi Goldman's major em-
> phasis was on a viable strong feeder system for a coedu-
> cational high school. He felt that the number of students
> coming into such a school from the Hebrew school of the
> congregation would be minimal. He, therefore, felt
> strongly that the first priority of the community ought to
> be the development of a sound, viable coeducational
> Hebrew day elementary and junior high school program
> on a communal basis.... Inasmuch as a potential elemen-
> tary and junior high school feeder system was at present
> on the Beth Tfiloh grounds, he felt that Chizuk Amuno
> should house the high school in the eight and more class-
> rooms which are available on its grounds.*

The Board of Jewish Education position paper concluded that
it was *"eminently clear"* that basic differences in religious philosophy left *"little room for commonality of purpose and direction."*
Chizuk Amuno's involvement with a day school was tabled once
more.

Rabbi Goldman took great pride in the communal involvement of his congregants, frequently publishing news of their leadership appointments in the Bulletin. Continuing the example set by previous generations, Chizuk Amuno congregants served in top leadership positions in the Associated Jewish Charities, Baltimore Jewish Council, Sinai Hospital, Hadassah, Jewish Big Brothers, YMHA, Levindale, Board of Jewish Education, Hebrew Free Loan Association, and American Jewish Congress. Ties to the Seminary remained strong as members served on the JTS National Board of Directors.

In 1969, the rabbi expressed special pride in the election of Maryland's first Jewish governor, Marvin Mandel, a member of the Congregation. On April 25, 1973, Mandel received the Brotherhood's first Distinguished Leadership Award, presented at the sold-out Donor Dinner. U.S. Senator Hubert Humphrey delivered the keynote address. Governor Mandel returned to the annual Brotherhood Donor Dinner the following year, this time to present the auxiliary's Distinguished Leadership Award to Massachusetts Senator Edward M. Kennedy on May 8, 1974. A strong supporter of Israel, Kennedy reported on his latest trip to the Middle East and included a few sarcastic remarks about the current Watergate hearings.

The most prestigious choice for the leadership award was Dr. Henry Kissinger, Secretary of State. The May 9, 1976 dinner attracted the attention of local, national, and international press, all of whom crowded their cameras against the railing of the sanctuary balcony. More than 1,400 people passed through the Secret Service security checkpoints in the synagogue to get to their seats. President Gerald R. Ford sent a lengthy telegram to Chizuk Amuno congratulating the Brotherhood on their selection. Quoted in the May 21, 1976 Bulletin, the President stated:

You are honoring a great Secretary of State. His efforts to achieve a final peace in the Middle East and to maintain and strengthen them, the long standing and close relationship which our nation enjoys with Israel are among his many achievements.

An editorial appearing in the May 11, 1976 issue of <u>The Sun</u> congratulated Chizuk Amuno on showing *"courage and wisdom"* in selecting Kissinger for their award.

As the buildings on Stevenson Road aged, expenditures for repairs and maintenance mounted. Board minutes of August 26, 1974 noted *"the appearance of termites within the building."* The expense of parking lot, boiler, roof, and compressor repairs, coupled with inflationary wage and utility costs, forced the Board into announcing a dues increase effective January 1, 1975. Congregations across the nation faced financial problems, as did the United Synagogue of America, who indicated that their assessment of five dollars per congregation family would be doubled to ten dollars a year effective July, 1974. Stanley Minch attempted to justify the need for a dues increase in a <u>Bulletin</u> article, reminding members of the multitude of activities that filled the building seven days a week. He stressed that dues did not fully cover Chizuk Amuno's expenses and explained that the synagogue depended upon generous contributions to balance the deficit budget.

The Fair Share Committee, headed by Henry Shor, was established in August, 1974 to solicit additional voluntary offerings. Rather than impose a greater burden on all Congregation families by raising dues excessively, the Committee attempted to solicit funds from families with a greater ability to pay. The campaign was set to begin a year earlier, but emergency fund-raising efforts in support of Israel forced the Fair Share Committee to temporarily postpone their solicitations.

Budget cutbacks continued in 1975. The <u>Bulletin</u> was issued biweekly instead of weekly; no evening meetings or events were scheduled on Tuesday or Thursday evenings to save utility costs. Hanukah candles were no longer sent to families, and no refreshments were served after "Under the Stars" services. The Executive Director promised to conserve wherever possible and eliminate waste.

Sale of the Eutaw Place Synagogue

The dedication of loyal members kept the synagogue on Eutaw Place viable throughout the 1960s, but just as financial concerns plagued the Stevenson Road campus, the in-town location had difficulties of its own. Incidents of vandalism, break-ins, and harassment are noted in Board minutes as early as 1970. In 1973, the Board determined that $15,000 was required for building repairs. Led by Efram Potts and I. William Schimmel, members at Eutaw Place raised sufficient funds to cover the improvements.

Although Chizuk Amuno had received several unsolicited offers to buy the synagogue building over the years, the Board honored their commitment to retain the site as long as it was feasible. At the October 28, 1974 Board meeting, the Eutaw Place Committee presented a resolution that had already received the approval of Eutaw Place members and the Executive Board. The resolution stated that, as of December 31, 1974, *"the Eutaw Place Synagogue would no longer be operated as part of Chizuk Amuno Congregation."* Services were to be held under the auspices and leadership of a newly formed congregation, Beth Am, which would be given a twelve-month grace period before paying a $65,000 purchase price. Provisions detailing issues of administrative assistance, insurance coverage, and property ownership were also addressed.

In only six months, Beth Am had raised $29,000 toward the purchase price. Long-time member Isaac C. Rosenthal offered to contribute $21,000 if Chizuk Amuno's Board would accept a reduced price of $50,000 in cash. On July 1, 1975, the Board accepted the offer. As agreed, a committee headed by Rabbi Goldman reviewed which three Torah scrolls would remain at Eutaw Place. An article by Stanley Minch printed in the September 26, 1975 Bulletin announced that on September 5, Erev Rosh Hashanah, documents were signed that formally sold the Eutaw Place synagogue. After receiving a letter of "mazel tov" from Chizuk Amuno President Dr. Samuel Rochberg, Efram Potts responded with a note of thanks:

The very fact that Beth Am exists at all is something of a modern miracle, but that it should be fostered in so many constructive ways by Chizuk Amuno, I believe, must be very close to unique in the area of synagogue relations. In behalf of the entire Beth Am family, I want to express our appreciation to the officers, executives, rabbis, and board for their cooperation during the transition and to the entire congregation for their good will and good wishes.

Sadly, I.C. Rosenthal passed away on September 9, 1975, merely four days after the sale he had facilitated took place.

Women's Ritual Equality

The first hint of a challenge to the traditional role of women in synagogue rituals appeared in 1955. After returning from the Rabbinical Assembly Convention, where a decision was reached to permit women to be granted aliyot, Rabbi Goldman entitled his May 14, 1955 sermon, "Shall Women Be Called to the Torah?" Unfortunately, no excerpts from that address were reprinted in future issues of the Bulletin. Merely the introduction of the topic indicates Rabbi Goldman's openness to enter into a discussion about women's equality in ritual well before women themselves expressed any public interest in the topic. Throughout the 1960s, women were welcomed to the pulpit on Mother's Day and Sisterhood Shabbat to deliver messages to the Congregation. Even at these special services, aliyot, Torah reading, and other bimah honors were still reserved for men.

The most controversial matter relating to women's involvement in worship seemed to focus on their headwear. Under the headline, *"YOUR ATTENTION, PLEASE,"* the January 20, 1961 Bulletin reminded women: *"It is the custom at Chizuk Amuno that all women wear hats when they come to the Synagogue for religious services."* As an issue of synagogue decorum, the matter was later brought before the Ritual Committee for discussion. At a meeting of that committee on October 15, 1964, the Sisterhood's representative was asked to have her auxiliary *"make available a chapel cap to women entering the Sanctuary without a suitable head covering."* Enforcement of this tradition proved uncomfortable for ushers. Six months later, the Ritual Committee minutes note that *"a great deal of tact is needed when offering the lace chapel caps."* The Committee agreed that two women ushers should be present at services to handle the head-covering dilemma diplomatically.

Settlement of this emotional issue was brought to Rabbi Goldman. In his February 6, 1970 <u>Bulletin</u> column, the rabbi placed the hat controversy in the context of increasing informality at religious services, commenting that he had noticed men attending daily chapel services *"in sweaters or sport shirts without ties."* Citing that there was no Jewish law that states that women must wear hats at services, Rabbi Goldman added:

> *When women wear an appropriate head covering at religious services a different mood prevails among the worshippers and there is a feeling that there is a striving for something higher, for excellence, for dignity and for decorum. This kind of attitude should not be enforced by rigid sanctions of any kind. It belongs only in the heart and in the mind of the worshipper who understands the importance of maintaining the sanctity and the dignity of the synagogue service.*

The question of girls participating in Shabbat services was first raised by members attending the Eutaw Place service. With no Friday evening service, there was no opportunity for holding a bat mitzvah ceremony at the downtown synagogue. At a meeting on December 22, 1964, the Ritual Committee resolved that the ceremony for young girls could consist of reading the Haftorah, following the Torah reading. The minutes note: *"Maftir Aliyah may be given to the girl's father...there would be no calling to the Torah of a woman."* Emphasizing that their decision was merely a concession to accommodate the lack of a Friday evening service, the Committee recorded the statement: *"The Ritual Committee reaffirms its stand that at no time shall a Bas Mitzvah be permitted at Stevenson on a Saturday morning."* The 1964 meeting also addressed the question of female Hebrew School students reading Torah at Junior Congregation services. To determine if this practice was conducted at *"a service or a religious experience, the matter was tabled in order to actually witness what is taking place."*

The 1964 Civil Rights Act, which banned discrimination in employment opportunities based on race, also banned gender discrimination. In the late 1960s, many young women who had actively joined campaigns for civil rights formed consciousness-raising groups to explore the inequality of sexism. The growth of the emerging feminist movement forced a reexamination of gender roles in many facets of daily life. Within the next few years, the question of a woman's role in Jewish ritual practice filtered into the synagogue. On March 1, 1971 the Sisterhoods of Chizuk Amuno and Beth El joined together to hear a luncheon speaker address the theme, "Women's Lib and the Jewish Tradition."

In a memorandum dated June 1, 1971, Rabbi Goldman forwarded a list of six recommendations to the Ritual Committee for consideration. Two of those suggestions pertained to the advancement of women's status in the synagogue – allowing women to sit on the bimah during Friday evening services, and calling women to the Torah on Simchat Torah morning. Both proposals were approved by the Committee on July 7, 1971, and subsequently passed by the Board of Trustees. Announcement of the Simchat Torah honor appeared in the October 8, 1971 Bulletin:

> *...all women who will be present...will be called upon in a group, to stand around the Torah, thus extending to the women of the congregation the same privileges for honoring the Torah as are extended to the groups of men, groups of young people and groups of children.*

Rather than have the women chant the traditional aliyah blessing, Rabbi Goldman distributed copies of a special prayer he had written for the occasion. The English verse expressed the women's gladness in the privilege of rejoicing with the Torah and of transmitting it to their children.

"Ezrat Nashim," a group comprised of the female activists of the North American Jewish Students' Network, pushed the issue of women's ritual equality to the forefront of the national Conservative agenda. The women had fully embraced Conservative Judaism through United Synagogue programs such as Camp Ramah and USY, then had been exposed to feminist activities on college campuses. As explained by an original member of the group, Judith Hauptman, in her essay, "The Ethical Challenge of Feminist Change," the young women *"discovered that a tradition that prided itself on its ingrained ethical stance did not apply the same high-minded principles to relations between the sexes."* Hauptman, who would go on to become a Professor of Talmud at the Seminary, recalled how frustrating it was to be enamored with Jewish observance, but restricted by *"entrenched male bias."*

The March, 1972 Convention of the Rabbinical Assembly was interrupted as Ezrat Nashim presented their manifesto charging that, *"to educate women and deny them the opportunity to act from this knowledge is an affront to their intelligence, talents and integrity."* Demands included counting women in the minyan, ordination of women as rabbis and cantors, eliminating barriers to women's equality in Jewish marital law, and full membership and ritual rights for women in the synagogue. In August, 1973 the RA's Commission on Jewish Laws and Standards voted to permit women to be counted in the minyan. One year later, the Commission approved proposals that extended women equal rights in all areas of Jewish ritual, including functioning as a witness. The United Synagogue of America endorsed the Assembly's resolutions at their biennial convention in November, 1973, stating that member congregations should *"take such action as will insure equal opportunity for its women congregants to assume positions of leadership, authority and responsibility in all phases of congregational activity."* The United Synagogue statement also included support for women's inclusion in ritual participation and the admission of women to the Rabbinical School of JTS.

At Chizuk Amuno, Rabbi Nelson offered the opportunity for a *"pulpit dialogue"* focusing on *"Women's Equality in the Synagogue"* on Friday evening, April 7, 1972, while Rabbi Goldman was on sabbatical leave. The Sisterhood, however, continued to highlight fundraising activities, and efforts to reinforce the traditional role of women in the Jewish home. Beverly Cohen, president of the Sisterhood, reported on the November, 1972 Women's League Convention in her message to the Congregation during the February 17, 1973 Sisterhood Shabbat service. She detailed five *"explosive"* resolutions that were brought before the national women's group for discussion and vote. The first two – the right of women to be elected to a congregational Board of Trustees, and the right of Jewish women to institute proceedings to secure a Jewish divorce – passed by overwhelming majority. On the other three resolutions – the right of women to be called for aliyot, to read from the Torah, and to be counted in the minyan – Cohen revealed that she and First Vice-President Vilma Sussman had both voted with the minority, in opposition. Justification for her position included the following comments printed in the March 9, 1973 <u>Bulletin</u>:

> *In most mitzvot in the synagogue women cannot be participants, however, there are many mitzvot in the home which men cannot perform. So, let the men keep theirs and the women theirs. I am perfectly happy to continue the status quo.*

> *If women were not so intent in doing everything which a man has been doing for lo these many years we might all be better off.*

> *Our participation at Chizuk Amuno is in no way conflicting with the traditions and religious obligations of our men, I prefer to keep it that way.*

On October 25, 1973 the Ritual Committee, which included Rabbis Goldman and Sherman, discussed the recent ruling by the Law Commission of the Rabbinical Assembly relative to counting women in the minyan. Minutes of that meeting record the decision to *"table any further consideration and to keep a constant alert for any reaction on the part of the women of the congregation."*

More than two years passed before a call for ritual equality surfaced in the Congregation. In early 1976, the Executive Committee of the Board of Trustees requested that the Ritual Committee conduct an informal survey of what changes, if any, the membership would suggest be instituted in the Congregation's worship services. In a report dated June 7, 1976, Ritual Committee Chairman Paul Wartzman summarized the suggestions, which included: *"grant aliyot to women... permit Bat Mitzvah to chant the current week haftorah...more involvement of women in services...and count women in minyan."* Further discussion on the recommendations was delayed until after the High Holy Days.

Rabbi Goldman's Retirement

As was his style, Israel Goldman drafted his official letter of retirement with humility and pride. Addressed to the President of the Congregation, the January 7, 1975 letter began:

The time has come for me officially to inform the dear people of my beloved Congregation that, upon my own initiative, and, at my own request, the Officers and Board of Trustees have agreed to allow me to retire as the active Rabbi of the Chizuk Amuno Congregation as of July 31, 1976.

The rabbi outlined the major highlights of his tenure, expressing appreciation for *"the warm response of the general membership and the leadership of many capable and dedicated men and women."* In closing, Rabbi Goldman commented that his relationship with the people of Chizuk Amuno had been more than that of rabbi and Congregation: *"We have been co-workers in a great cause. We have been together on occasions of joy and sorrow. We have laughed together. We have cried together. We have been to each other as dear and devoted friends."*

The final eighteen months of Rabbi Goldman's rabbinate were filled with activity. In April, 1975 he traveled to the Middle East and conferred with the chief rabbis of six Mediterranean communities. Shortly after returning, Rabbi Goldman taught a course at the annual Institute of Jewish Studies for Adults and attended the Brotherhood's annual Laymen's Institute at Camp Wohelo, both programs that he had established twenty-seven years earlier. His second book, Life-Long Learning Among Jews – Adult Education in Judaism From Biblical Times to The Twentieth Century, was published in 1975. Critically acclaimed, the volume traced the evolution of adult learning through nearly four thousand years of Jewish history. Tributes were paid to Rabbi and Mildred Goldman at a congregational dinner, Brotherhood breakfast, and Sisterhood luncheon. A testimonial service, held on Sunday evening, June 6, 1976, featured an address by Dr. Gerson D. Cohen, Chancellor of the Jewish Theological Seminary.

Three weeks before the start of the High Holy Days welcoming the year 5736 (1975), Rabbi Goldman was rushed to Johns Hopkins Hospital for emergency vascular surgery. While he recuperated, Rabbi Eliot Marrus, who had joined Chizuk Amuno in August, 1974, ably covered all of the senior rabbi's responsibilities. Executive Vice-President of the Rabbinical Assembly Rabbi Wolfe Kelman immediately offered his assistance to the Congregation, and officiated at holiday services in place of Rabbi Goldman.

THE CORSON & MARRUS TERMS 1976-1980

We are blessed with a large growing group of strong lay leaders who have accepted their synagogue as a major part of their lives. The laity makes decisions and sets policy. Our professional people, including the clergy, carry out policy. The final and only authority is vested in you, the members of Chizuk Amuno, first, with the committees, their chairman, and ultimately the Board of Trustees. This structure has always augured well, especially because of the total involvement of a large segment of our membership.... I am constantly amazed at the time spent on congregational affairs at definite expense to their personal lives and businesses.

Henry O. Shor
President of the Congregation
Passover, 1977

In early 1975, Chizuk Amuno began searching for their fifth senior rabbi. The twenty-five-member Search Committee, appointed by the president of the Congregation, Dr. Samuel Rochberg, consisted of the present officers, past presidents of the Congregation, presidents of the auxiliaries, chairmen of standing committees, and representatives from the Congregation. <u>Bulletin</u> articles assured the membership that the selection process would not be *"haphazard, hasty or accomplished by coincidence."* As they had three times before, Chizuk Amuno first turned to the Seminary for assistance. Members of the Search Committee met with the Rabbinical Assembly Placement Commission in New York to discuss the qualities the Congregation was seeking in their future rabbi.

Although the Placement Commission submitted more than a dozen names to the Search Committee for consideration, Board minutes of November 24, 1975 indicate that Dr. Rochberg was not pleased with the caliber of the candidates. Several of the rabbis were selected to visit Chizuk Amuno during the winter months, for a weekend of interviews and a chance to deliver a sermon on Shabbat morning; others visited on weekdays. With less than four months until the scheduled annual Congregational Meeting, the Search Committee still did not have a strong applicant. In January, 1976 Treasurer Leonard Jed suggested that the committee contact a rabbi in Philadelphia whom a relative had mentioned. On March 23, 1976, Search Committee members gathered to meet a candidate who was promised to be *"the last rabbi that we will be interviewing"* – Rabbi Maurice S. Corson. The forty-two-year-old rabbi was invited to deliver a sermon at Shabbat services on April 3, 1976. Three weeks later, based on the recommendation of the Search Committee, the Board approved Rabbi Corson.

The 106th Annual Meeting of Chizuk Amuno Congregation was held on May 26, 1976. Following the installation of Henry Shor as President of the Congregation, Israel Goldman was unanimously approved to be elevated to the position of Rabbi Emeritus. Rabbi Maurice Corson was then elected as Rabbi of the Congregation for a period of three years beginning August 1, 1976. Following his ordination from the Seminary, Rabbi Corson had served several pulpits across the country. Prior to accepting the position at Chizuk Amuno, the rabbi worked with the Jewish Community Relations Council of Philadelphia. In a break with tradition, Corson's November 28, 1976 installation ceremony did not feature the Chancellor of JTS. Instead, Rabbi Sidney Greenberg of Philadelphia's Temple Sinai delivered the installation address. The evening ushered in a period that would be scarred by a turbulent dispute within the membership, and marked by a historic revision in the ritual practices of the synagogue.

Ritual Equality Adopted

A milestone occurred in 1976, as Toba Rochberg became the first woman elected to serve as an officer of Chizuk Amuno. With her election, the Ritual Committee determined that *"there would be no exception to the policy of assigning officers a seat on the Bimah during the High Holidays, nor any exception in terms of the officers' participation in any procession."*

Leadership of the Ritual Committee was handed to Dr. Barry Lever in the fall of 1976. Actively involved in Chizuk Amuno for more than twenty years, Lever had served on the Youth, School, and Brotherhood Boards, as well as terms as secretary and treasurer. Although the Congregation adhered to the United Synagogue standard of respecting the rabbi as authority on religious matters, the Ritual Committee was charged with reviewing membership requests affecting the rituals and practices of the Congregation. Decisions of the committee were considered recommendations to the Board, not proclamations of policy. Picking up where his predecessor had left off, Lever approached the matter of women's ritual equality very seriously. The November 19, 1976 Bulletin described Lever's approach in his own words:

> *The rituals and practices of a large and historic congregation such as ours cannot be precipitously changed. Education of the congregation with factual knowledge about Jewish traditions, customs, and practices is the essential ingredient for achieving a harmonious consensus in areas of ritual practice. Together we will rethink and renew our traditions and through this process we will hopefully breathe new life and meaning into our congregational efforts at communal prayer and practice.*

Aware of the wide spectrum of opinions on the issue, Lever enlarged the membership of the committee to include representatives of the Sisterhood, Brotherhood, Youth, and School Boards.

The question of "Women's Role in Synagogue Ritual" was placed on the Ritual Committee agenda for their January 27, 1977 meeting. Although Rabbi Corson suggested deferring any serious study of the question until the following fall, the committee was anxious to deal with the issue in a timely manner. More than three years had passed since the Rabbinical Assembly had approved women being called to the Torah and counted in the minyan. Dr. Lever, with the guidance of Rabbi Goldman, searched for authoritative articles and essays related to the Rabbinic and Talmudic status of women in Jewish law. Minutes of Ritual Committee meetings indicate that committee members received several article reprints to study in advance of meetings. The Congregation was kept abreast of the committee's progress and encouraged to participate in the decision-making process. In the March 25, 1977 Bulletin, Lever reported:

> *During the coming months all source material sent to the committee will be placed on reserve in the library for anyone in the congregation to study. In the late spring the auxiliaries and major standing committees of the congregation will also have the opportunity of sharing their views with the Ritual Committee.... I strongly urge you to share your views and feelings with committee members or myself and avail yourself of any of the materials that will be placed in the library.*

Members serving on the Boards of the major committees and auxiliaries of the Congregation were invited to a learning session with Rabbi Seymour Siegel on May 11, 1977. The laity continued to explore background material on this controversial issue. Rabbi Siegel, chairman of the Committee on Jewish Law and Standards of the Rabbinical Assembly, reviewed the evolution of women's ritual participation in the synagogue from biblical times to the events leading to the RA's rulings. After his opening presentation, Rabbi Siegel responded to comments and questions from the audience. Women expressed their frustration at having to experience Judaism through the acts of their husbands and the humiliation of not being recognized as a member of the worship community. One unnamed gentleman commented on the potential "shock" of seeing a woman wearing a tallit and the effect that it might have on the Congregation.

After months of study and discussion, the Ritual Committee voted on the following resolution at its June 14, 1977 meeting:

RESOLVED THAT the Chizuk Amuno Congregation ex-
tend to women equality in synagogue ritual so that they
may henceforth enjoy the same rights, privileges, hon-
ors, and obligations that theretofore have applied solely
to men.

The resolution passed with the final vote recorded – eleven for, one against. A few weeks later, on June 27, 1977, Dr. Barry Lever introduced the same motion at the Board of Trustees meeting, where it was overwhelmingly approved – twenty-five for, two against, and two abstentions. The Board requested that a full membership meeting be held to cast votes on the same resolution.

Shoshana Cardin served as parliamentarian at the special congregational meeting convened on September 25, 1977. She explained that speakers would be bound by a three-minute time limit, and that this resolution would be the only item on the evening's agenda. Following discussion, *"a call for the question was made."* Two representatives, one male and one female, were appointed to count the paper ballots. Henry Shor announced that the results – 151 in favor, 34 opposed – exceeded the two-thirds needed to amend the mode of service. Rabbi Goldman, who had advocated this modification for years, was called on to deliver the closing prayer.

Implementation of the change in synagogue ritual was announced in the December 16, 1977 Bulletin. Effective on that date:

- *women were included as part of the minyan at all services held under the auspices of Chizuk Amuno*
- *women were granted the non-speaking aliyot of opening or closing the Ark and dressing the Torah*
- *b'not mitzvah were encouraged to accept an aliyah on the Shabbat following their bat mitzvah*

To assure that the first adult women to actively participate in a Chizuk Amuno worship service were adequately prepared, the milestone occasion was scheduled for the annual Sisterhood Shabbat, February 11, 1978. For the first time in the 107-year history of the Congregation, women were accorded all aliyot, as well as all nonreading honors of the service. Sisterhood President Bette Miller delivered the sermon and Shirley Evans chanted the entire Musaf service. Three young women read Torah portions, and Mildred Goldman was granted the privilege of chanting the Haftorah. Rabbi Goldman was hospitalized at the time. Executive Director Stanley Minch, knowing how important it would be for the rabbi to share this historic event, arranged for the telephone company to transmit the entire service into Rabbi Goldman's hospital room.

Eight months later, on Simchat Torah 5739 (1978), in addition to conferring two men with the traditional honors of Hatan Torah and Hatan Bereshit, a third honor, "Kallah Mafteret," was introduced. In recognition of her devotion to Jewish religious life and Chizuk Amuno, Cille Strauss was awarded the honor of chanting the haftorah. Several women expressed the desire to intensify their own personal connection to Torah by embarking on a structured two-year program of study. On May 12, 1979, Mother's Day Shabbat, the Congregation celebrated the group bat mitzvah of eighteen adult women.

One year after women were accorded equality in synagogue ritual, Sisterhood President Eileen Sacks spoke about the effects of the change in her sermon on February 10, 1979:

> *I think that you will agree with me that whatever trepidation and concerns people felt at that time were never realized. No one resigned from the congregation because of this change in ritual practice and no one stayed away from the synagogue in protest.... There is a growing awareness within the congregation of the strength and virtue of our women...Chizuk Amuno is blessed with suddenly discovering an additional 100 percent increase in the pool of personnel from which it can select its leaders and workers.*

The appointment of Louis I. Sternfield as the new Educational Director was announced in the August 6, 1976 <u>Bulletin</u>. With over twenty years of experience in the field of Jewish education, Sternfield was considered one of the leading educators in the Conservative Movement. After assessing the current status of the religious school, Sternfield conducted biweekly faculty meetings and required teachers to submit weekly lesson plans. In one of his monthly "Educationally Speaking" columns published in the Bulletin, Sternfield noted that many students performed well in all areas of the curriculum, with the exception of Hebrew language. Beginning with the 1977 school year, a two-track system was designed separating students above the second-grade level who were assessed to be "non-linguistic" based on their prior performance. These students continued their study of prayer and other traditional segments of the curriculum, but did not continue to receive instruction in Hebrew.

A project to overcome adult deficiencies in Hebrew was announced in the September 15, 1978 Bulletin as Chizuk Amuno launched *"a massive campaign to teach hundreds of our members how to read Hebrew."* The Hebrew Literacy Campaign, chaired by Dr. Jerome Buxbaum, was part of a nationwide program under the auspices of the National Federation of Jewish Men's Clubs. More than 250 men and women committed two hours per week, for twelve weeks, to complete the course taught by thirty-seven lay members of the Congregation. Hebrew language instruction emphasized Sephardic pronunciation, rather than Ashkenazic. Several years earlier, the religious school had adopted the Sephardic pronunciation. With the support of the Ritual Committee, on January 18, 1979 the Board approved *"the adoption of Sephardic as the official congregational pronunciation for synagogue ritual services."* Congregants were assured that they would quickly feel comfortable with the change.

Death of Rabbi Goldman

Rabbi Israel M. Goldman died on Friday, February 9, 1979, as Chizuk Amuno Congregation began a weekend marking the concluding service of the Hebrew Literacy Campaign, and the celebration of the first group bat mitzvah. His dedication to the field of adult Jewish learning had encouraged many such projects, and the lives of hundreds of members had greatly benefited from the rabbi's inspired vision and leadership.

A thoughtful and structured individual, Rabbi Goldman drafted a final message to his loved ones, and instructions for his own funeral and burial. The handwritten document began: *"The Bible teaches us that 'No man knowth the day of his end.'"* and continued:

> *My heart is filled with gratitude and with thankfulness. I think of the words of the Psalmist: "Bless the Lord, O my soul, and forget not all His benefits." (Psalm 103:2). Indeed, I have been greatly blessed by God and can never forget all His gracious benefits to me. I thank God for the gift of a fairly long, and I trust, a useful life. I thank God that He has guided my footsteps into the Rabbinate which has, as the Book of Chronicles declares, enabled me for more than half a century "to serve the Lord Our God and His people Israel." (II Chronicles 35:3)*

Rabbi Goldman wanted his *"Farewell Service"* to follow the same procedures used thirty years earlier for his *"distinguished predecessor, Rabbi Adolph Coblenz"*:

> *I want to make it clear that the arrangements here suggested are in <u>NO WAY intended to pay any honor to me</u>...My one and only intention is to have a Service that will reflect the standards and traditions of our dear Chizuk Amuno. The Service therefore should elicit dignity, decorum, inspiration, and uplift so that those present will feel that their <u>souls were satisfied</u>.*

As Israel Goldman had specifically requested, Rabbis Samuel Rosenblatt and Jacob Agus spoke at his funeral service, which was held on Sunday, February 11, 1979 in the sanctuary that Rabbi Goldman had helped to design. Dr. Simon Greenberg, a classmate of Rabbi Goldman, conveyed the sympathies of the Jewish Theological Seminary. Editorials, printed in the local newspapers, lauded the rabbi's contributions to the furtherance of interfaith and interracial understanding. The Congregation and Goldman family received hundreds of letters and telegrams of condolence from rabbinic colleagues, past congregants scattered around the world, and from several strangers who had been touched by Rabbi Goldman's words. Rabbi Stanley Rabinowitz, senior rabbi of the Adas Israel Congregation of Washington, D.C., delivered the memorial address at the Shloshim Memorial Service, on March 11, 1979:

> *One should conclude that Rabbi Goldman's greatest legacy was his insistence that a synagogue should not only be a place where people come to pray, to get married, to celebrate, to see their friends, it should be a place where people come to study and the Mishna was most appropriate as a tribute to his career and life.*

Rabbi Israel M. Goldman was laid to rest in the Congregation's Arlington Cemetery, next to Rabbi Coblenz.

On February 14, 1979 the Board unanimously approved the recommendations of the Ritual Committee relative to the observance of Rabbi Goldman's death:

- *The rabbi's chair on the bimah was draped in black and left vacant for a year.*
- *The Congregation was asked to rise and recite the Kaddish in Rabbi Goldman's memory during the thirty-day mourning period.*
- *On Mondays, Thursdays, and Saturdays, the sexton or cantor chanted El Molay Rachamin for a period of eleven months.*
- *The Congregation observed restrictions regarding music and entertainment during the thirty day mourning period, which included canceling the Purim Carnival.*
- *The history of Chizuk Amuno, which Rabbi Goldman was in the process of writing, was to be completed and published in his memory.*

The role of a rabbi in contemporary America was explored in an article by Murray Polner published in the February 24, 1978 Jewish Times. Entitled, "What's it Like to be a Rabbi?" the article described the multiple demands placed on a rabbi by his congregants. American Jews, Polner commented, wanted a rabbi who was comfortable with both Torah texts and his pastoral obligations.

On January 18, 1979 the Board of Trustees voted not to renew Rabbi Corson's employment contract. Only one dissenting vote was cast. Although the By-Laws of Chizuk Amuno's Constitution, Article 6, clearly stated that the rabbi's *"tenure of office and compensation shall be determined by the Board of Trustees,"* a group of members challenged the authority of the Board to make such a decision. Confident that they were acting in conformity with the procedures established by the founders, the officers confined their discussion of Corson's contract to the Board of Trustees. In remarks made to the minority opposition in March, 1979, President Henry Shor stated that this confidential approach was adopted *"in order to protect the privacy of Rabbi Corson, to shield him from any public disclosure, and to prevent a general airing of this most delicate subject by the congregation at large."* The dispute was resolved on March 15, 1979. Rabbi Corson resigned effective March 31, 1979.

In his "Year in Review" column printed in the June 22, 1979 Bulletin, Stanley Minch noted achievements in adult education programs, the Sisterhood play, and the twenty-two inches of snow during the United Synagogue Regional Convention in Baltimore. The article ended on a more serious note:

> *We would be less than candid if we did not acknowledge that this has been a most trying and difficult year for everyone. If there is anything positive to be gained from a situation in which people take different sides on an issue, it is the feeling that they are motivated by love and concern for their congregation, and that their actions are based upon what they think is in its best interest. As the year comes to a close that which has occurred should remain with the year that ended, so that all of us can*

*look forward to a new synagogue year full of hope and
promise.*

The Marrus Period – 1979-1980

Sigi Strauss began his term as president on April 1, 1979 –
exactly 108 years after his great-great-grandfather, Jonas Friedenwald,
had founded the Congregation. Strauss immediately reassured the
membership that until a new rabbi was engaged, arrangements had
been made to insure that a guest rabbi would officiate at Shabbat and
festival services, and would be available for life cycle events and
counseling. Hazzan Salkov officiated at funerals and visited members confined to the hospital.

The Search Committee, chaired by I. Leon Glassgold, contacted the Rabbinical Assembly Placement Commission in January,
1979, with hopes that a new rabbi could be elected within six months.
The committee carefully defined procedures that were to be followed
in the interview process. Although members were encouraged to
meet candidates when they were invited to officiate at Shabbat services, relatively few attended. On July 9, 1979 the Search Committee reported that no decision would be reached before the High Holy
Days. Rather than rush the interview process, they suggested that an
interim rabbi be engaged on a full-time basis until a permanent rabbi
could be hired.

On August 13, 1979 the Board agreed to hire Rabbi Eliot P.
Marrus for the ten-month period September 1, 1979 to June 30, 1980.
Ordained by JTS in 1972, Marrus had served as Chizuk Amuno's
associate rabbi from 1974 to 1976. He was concluding a three-year
term as rabbi at a De Witt, New York congregation when he received
the Board's offer. In order to avoid any misunderstanding, Rabbi
Marrus's contract clearly stated that he accepted employment with
the knowledge that he was not being considered as a candidate for
the permanent position. Familiar with the professional staff and many
of the members, Marrus quickly provided continuity in rabbinic leadership that had been missing since Corson's departure. Rabbi Wolfe

Kelman, executive vice-president of the Rabbinical Assembly, co-officiated with Rabbi Marrus during the High Holy Days of 5740 (1979).

In his quiet but professional manner, Rabbi Marrus fulfilled the rabbinic responsibilities of Chizuk Amuno. He provided much needed stability to the Congregation as they prepared to welcome their seventh rabbi to the pulpit.

THE ZAIMAN ERA 1980-

Rabbi Joel Zaiman – A younger man with his future in front of him...He is a leader who will have an impact upon the community, who will be aggressive and yet at the same time is schooled in the responsibility of pastoral obligations and the need to minister to a large congregation.

Memo from the Search Committee
July 25, 1979

Twice during the summer of 1979, Joel H. Zaiman, rabbi at Providence, Rhode Island's Temple Emanu-El, traveled to Baltimore for private meetings with representatives of the Search Committee. Several months later, he was invited to be a guest of the Congregation for Shabbat Noach, October 26-27, 1979, and to deliver sermons at both the Friday evening and Saturday morning services. Following Havdalah, the rabbi and his wife, Ann, met with the Executive Board and other lay leaders. In an attempt to form a clearer profile of their leading candidate, seven members of the Search Committee traveled to Providence and interviewed leaders of the local Jewish community and Rabbi Zaiman's congregation. A summary of those interviews, dated November 19, 1979, described the rabbi:

Hardworking, conscientious, honest, great integrity, intelligent, good character, sensitive but not overtly so, warm personality that may not be evident on first contact, superior intellect, sincere, open, fine reputation, flexible in his approach but rigid in belief and principles, high activity level, intolerant of mediocrity, committed to the rabbinate and vocation, great potential for growth...

Over the course of twelve months, the Search Committee had screened dozens of applicants, interviewed ten, invited six for weekend visits, and spent hundreds of hours researching, discussing, and evaluating the candidates. On November 29, 1979, the following motion was overwhelmingly passed:

> *The Board of Trustees approve the selection of Rabbi Joel Zaiman, of Providence, Rhode Island, for the position of Rabbi of Chizuk Amuno Congregation for a term of 37 months, beginning July 1, 1980, and recommend that the Congregation, at a specially convened meeting, on Wednesday, December 12th, issue Rabbi Zaiman a call to become Rabbi of this Congregation.*

Rabbi Zaiman was elected to be the seventh rabbi of the Congregation by a unanimous vote at the December 12, 1980 meeting. He spoke of the past and the future in his acceptance address:

> *A significant aspect of that past, yours and mine, is the fact that Rabbi Israel Goldman served but two congregations during his illustrious rabbinic career, Temple Emanu-El, Providence, and Chizuk Amuno, Baltimore.... The notion that I would serve the only two congregations which Rabbi Goldman served, the one which he helped to build, the other which he helped to rebuild, seemed so remote that I could not resist at least taking a look. As fate would have it, Mildred and her family visited Providence twice during the past year. Mildred used both occasions to encourage the Zaimans to come to Baltimore. Save for those ties, I seriously doubt I would be standing before you this evening...*
>
> *I come, not primarily because your past was great, but because our future can be ever greater.... I am looking forward, with great eagerness, to challenging you and to being challenged by you. I am looking forward to leading and to being led. I am looking forward to learning and living and working with you.*

Joel H. Zaiman's grandfather, Rabbi Hirsh Zaiman, emigrated from Kherson Guberniya, near the Black Sea, in 1915. Upon arrival, he served Congregation B'nai Zion in Chattanooga, Tennessee, while his older brother, Rabbi Mattus Tsaimon, officiated at a synagogue in Syracuse, New York. Hirsh Zaiman relocated to Syracuse in 1918 following his brother's death. By 1925, Hirsh's wife and three sons had joined him in America. Nathan, the middle son, received his rabbinic ordination and assumed a pulpit in Annapolis, Maryland. Solomon, the youngest son, enrolled in a Chicago, Illinois yeshiva and eventually served a Traditional congregation in Chicago. Joel Hirsh Zaiman, the only son of Rabbi Solomon and Ruth Zaiman, was born in 1938.

At age nineteen, Joel Zaiman graduated from DePaul University with a degree in economics. Although he briefly considered a career in criminal law, the young man discovered that he was not comfortable with the prospect of occasionally defending a guilty client. Imbued with an intrinsic love of learning, of Torah, and of the Jewish people, Zaiman chose to pursue a career in the rabbinate. He attended Union Theological Seminary and Hebrew University in Jerusalem before receiving his ordination from JTS in 1962. Upon graduation, Rabbi Zaiman accepted the position of Assistant Rabbi at Temple Emanu-El in Providence, Rhode Island – the same congregation Rabbi Israel Goldman had served from 1926 to 1948. Rabbi Zaiman was placed in charge of the congregation's youth programs and, in 1964, was promoted to Associate Rabbi. As Temple Emanu-El elevated their senior rabbi to Rabbi Emeritus in 1973, there was never a question that Rabbi Zaiman would assume full rabbinic responsibility for the congregation. By 1973, Joel Zaiman had become widely respected for both his pulpit ability and his scholarly achievements. A guest lecturer at Brown University's Department of Religion, Rabbi Zaiman had authored several articles which appeared in national journals and assumed leadership positions in local communal organizations. At the time of his election, he was serving as national chairman of the United Synagogue Commission on Jewish Education after being the first chairman of the Commission's Parent Education Committee.

Rabbi Zaiman began preparing for his transition to Chizuk Amuno soon after his 1979 election. He visited Baltimore with his family in late December, then returned on January 23, 1980, to address the Brotherhood's Donor Kick-Off Dinner. The 110th Annual Meeting of the Congregation on April 20, 1980 featured remarks by Rabbi Zaiman based on the phrase, "We Are What We Do," expressing his opinion that the true function of the synagogue is to influence the quality of a person's life. On each visit, the rabbi drafted notes of his impressions, and detailed summaries of his conversations. In a letter dated December 27, 1979, he described his expectations:

> *The list of things to be decided grows. And, frankly, anything which can be decided this year will be a plus. And if, in order to accomplish that, I should spend more time in Baltimore – or longer stretches of time – I will certainly try to do so. Given the fact that the effects of many agenda items will not be felt for at least two years, I would hate to have those two years be three years. When I was young, or younger, it was suggested that I was impatient because of my youth. Now its either because I am older, or because, by nature, I am impatient.*

Joel Zaiman's time schedule was delayed. Within weeks of the rabbi's election, his youngest son, Rafi, was diagnosed with a terminal illness, which led to his death on June 15, 1980. The July 25, 1980 Bulletin announced that the rabbi would be, *"available to the Congregation officially on August 1."*

In an effort to acquaint Chizuk Amuno members with the new rabbi, a series of informal parlor meetings was hosted in private homes. Using an alphabetical roster of membership, the first seventy-five families were invited to meet Rabbi Zaiman after the High Holy Days. Acquiescing to Rabbi Zaiman's wishes, the Board planned a simple installation ceremony for November 16, 1980 that included an address by Rabbi Gerson D. Cohen, Chancellor of the Jewish Theological Seminary. However, Ann Zaiman's father passed away in early November and the installation ceremony was cancelled.

Within his first few months at Chizuk Amuno, Rabbi Zaiman made personal appearances before most segments of the Congregation. He joined nursery school students for Shabbat and Hanukkah celebrations, and held once-a-month Shabbat afternoon learning sessions for USY members in his home or study. The rabbi met with the Young Couples Club, spoke at the Brotherhood's Breakfast Forum, and addressed the Sisterhood Women's Series, speaking on "Jewish Art – What is it?" Classroom teaching was also scheduled into the rabbi's busy agenda. He instructed the Adult Bat Mitzvah class in *"how to study Torah,"* and offered two courses in Chizuk Amuno's Spring, 1981 Adult Academy. The new rabbi's popularity was evident, as Stanley Minch reported in the June 12, 1981 <u>Bulletin</u>: *"members nearly fought in the aisles in order to be the highest bidder for dinner at the Zaimans,"* an item auctioned off at the Sisterhood's fund-raising event.

Anticipating the election of a new rabbi in 1980, the Ritual Committee discussed the question of conducting bat mitzvah ceremonies on Shabbat morning rather than at late Friday evening services. Although there was general agreement to institute such a change, the motion was tabled until the new rabbi could be consulted. In late August, 1980, the rabbi concurred with the Ritual Committee, and prepared a three-page memo in support of according girls equality with boys in scheduling their b'not mitzvah during the morning service. Citing that boys and girls were receiving identical training in the Hebrew School, Rabbi Zaiman argued that girls must be *"afforded similar and equally meaningful opportunities."* Assignment of bar/bat mitzvah dates occurred over a year in advance therefore, the change was scheduled to go into effect in September, 1982.

The Board, anxious to determine the popularity of an early Friday evening service, experimented with a change in format for eight weeks beginning in December, 1980. Services were conducted in the chapel without the participation of the choir. For the first four weeks, the Friday evening service began at 8:15 p.m. and included a dialogue with the rabbi. Traditional Kabbalat Shabbat services during the second four weeks began at 6:00 p.m., giving families the opportunity to worship prior to Shabbat dinner. Although some congregants expressed disappointment, attendance proved what the Ritual Committee had expected – few members attended the late service when there was no bat mitzvah or special program scheduled. In early 1983, as b'not mitzvah transitioned to Shabbat morning, the Board voted to discontinue the late Friday evening service.

The nursery school program, renamed the Early Childhood Education Department in the 1970s, expanded to offer full day classes, and an afternoon kindergarten to supplement the Baltimore County program. As additional classes were established, space was at a premium. In 1980, Sandee Lever, the department's director, requested that classes be relocated to the rooms beneath the Krieger Auditorium, originally used by the Sisterhood and Brotherhood. New curriculum centered on basic learning skills and Jewish values and traditions. Parent involvement in classroom activities and creative extracurricular activities added to the success of the program.

Formation of a Day School

Discussions continued with the other two Conservative congregations in Baltimore concerning the formation of a community day school. In order to assess interest among members of the respective congregations, a questionnaire was distributed in December, 1979 asking the question: *"Would you seriously consider sending your child(ren) to a Solomon Schechter Day School if one were to be established in Baltimore?"* Upon his arrival, Rabbi Zaiman encouraged the Board to proceed, even though the other congregations determined that there was insufficient interest among their membership. He requested a meeting with the Board's Executive Committee in January, 1981 to present his concept of a Hebrew Day School at Chizuk Amuno.

Following debates on whether the Board should purchase their first "mini computer" and the pros and cons of acquiring a new photocopier, Rabbi Zaiman made his presentation. The eight lay leaders of the Executive Committee recognized the seriousness of the proposal and its potential impact on the entire Chizuk Amuno community. Rather than deliberate the question of committing resources toward a day school at the Board level only, the rabbi was asked to make a full presentation two weeks later at a special meeting, convening not only the Board of Trustees, but also the Brotherhood, Sisterhood, Youth and School Boards.

On Thursday, January 29, 1981, Rabbi Joel Zaiman and Executive Director Stanley Minch introduced and analyzed the feasibility of implementing a day school at the meeting of lay leaders gathered to represent all facets of the congregational community. An outline of the rabbi's presentation clearly defined his thoughts on why the Congregation should move forward:

A. *Chizuk Amuno wishes to make a serious statement regarding its concern for a quality Conservative Jewish Education. Chizuk Amuno has the opportunity to play a leadership role in providing a day school education to traditional non-Orthodox Jews.*

B. *Chizuk Amuno welcomes the opportunity of attracting to its membership and welcoming at its services serious young Jews and their families.*

C. *Chizuk Amuno recognizes its responsibility to aid in the development of Jewish leadership. Through the establishment of a Solomon Schechter Day School it will at once be train-*

> *ing a future generation of knowledgeable and committed Conservative Jews – parents and children.*

After much discussion, the Board of Trustees convened in private session to consider the following motion:

> *To direct the professional staff to establish a Solomon Schechter Elementary Hebrew Day School, with implementation of a Kindergarten and/or a First Grade by September 1, 1981, if feasible, but no later than September 1, 1982.*
>
> *The Day School is to be structured as a wholly owned, but separate entity of the Chizuk Amuno congregation, with its own Charter and Board.*
>
> *The congregation, through its Capital Fund, will provide a sum not to exceed $25,000 as initial capital. Further funding must be provided through tuition, voluntary contributions, and endowment funding.*

The motion was approved with one negative vote cast. Board minutes note that the opposing vote *"was not against the concept of the Hebrew Day School, but only to the name."* In an article announcing the historic decision, Rabbi Zaiman reflected on the evening: *"Everyone involved sensed the importance of the decision being made, the challenge it presented and the opportunities it promised."*

In April, 1981 the Board voted to amend the middle paragraph of the motion recasting the day school from an independent entity to a standing committee of the Congregation subject to the authority and control of the Board of Trustees. Past President Henry Shor assumed chairmanship of the Day School Committee and began soliciting pledges for a two-million-dollar Day School Endowment Fund. Initially, no Building Fund would be needed – day school classes would be held in the rooms used by the afternoon Hebrew school.

Consistent with the mission of other Solomon Schechter Day Schools, Chizuk Amuno's program was committed to educational excellence and intellectual integrity in both Jewish learning and general studies. Applications would be accepted for enrollment in kindergarten and first grade for the 1981-1982 school year. Each year thereafter, an additional grade level would be added until the school served students through grade six. Announcement of the plans was made in a letter to members dated February 23, 1981. The letter's last paragraph reflected Rabbi Zaiman's vision for the Congregation: *"Now is the time to train a future generation of knowledgeable and committed Conservative Jews – parents and children."*

In the Solomon Schechter Day School Manual, author Pesach Schindler postulated as to why the idea of a Conservative day school was acceptable by1970:

> *The pluralism of American society is now taken for granted. The old "melting pot theories," by and large, have evaporated. There is a consensus that America would be that much poorer were ethnic and religious groups to merge in a common nondescript background.*

Immigrants arriving in America around the turn of the century knew how to be Jewish, but struggled with how to become American. First-generation American Jews suffered through anti-Semitic challenges to their patriotism and taunts at their ethnicity. The next generation, parents in the 1950s and 1960s, were comfortable with their equality in a democratic nation, and considered it un-American not to send their children to public schools. As the third generation of American-born Jews matured and became parents in the 1970s and 1980s, they sensed that Jews could be proud of their ethnic heritage within the American culture. For the first time in decades, non-Orthodox Jewish parents were willing to reinstate rituals and traditions publicly that had been considered outdated by earlier generations. Parents viewed day school not as an escape from a substandard public school system, but rather as a commitment to a more intensive Jewish education for their children, conducive to a strong Jewish identity.

Educational Director Sternfield searched for day school faculty who would be effective models of the Conservative perspective.

On September 8, 1981, Faye Pollack and Marjorie Hoffman welcomed their first classes of eight kindergarten and eight first grade students. Months earlier, Rabbi Zaiman had been questioned as to whether there would be sufficient interest in day school education to justify the project. He responded: *"There is no way of determining the answer to this question with certainty. Indications are that once the viability and the quality of such a school is established, it will not lack the requisite number of students."* The rabbi's prediction proved accurate. Forty-two students enrolled for the school's second year, eighty-one for the third year, and 113 students in kindergarten through fourth grade for the 1984-1985 school year.

Restructuring Educational Programs

With the successful opening of the day school accomplished, Rabbi Zaiman shifted his attention to the reorganization of youth programs at Chizuk Amuno. A brief memo from the rabbi invited the Executive Committees of the School and Youth Boards and the officers of the Congregation to join him for breakfast on February 21, 1982:

At this time I will present a proposal for a new system of delivering informal Jewish Education. It will involve a change in structure and responsibilities for laymen and professionals alike. I know that we share the perception that despite the vigorous efforts we have made these past few years to provide the best informal program to our youngsters, we are not at all satisfied with the results. I will share with you my views as to why success has eluded us and a proposal concerning how we should proceed.

Rabbi Zaiman attributed the lack of success to parent apathy, over-programming, the nature of the Jewish community, and the composition of Chizuk Amuno's membership.

Minutes from the Executive Committee meeting on March 15, 1982, summarized Rabbi Zaiman's recommendations. The Youth and School Boards would be combined into one Education Committee.

The director of the religious school would be responsible for both formal and informal programming of the Hebrew school. Youth groups representing students in grades two through eight would be disbanded, and related activities would become part of the formal program of the Hebrew school curriculum. The Bar Mitzvah Brotherhood would also be discontinued, although Sunday morning davening by both girls and boys would be scheduled as part of the Vav Class curriculum. Following general discussion on the proposals, the Executive Committee members voted unanimously to approve the rabbi's recommendations.

Principal Louis Sternfield informed the Board of his plans to retire after the 1982-1983 school year. Rabbi Zaiman recommended that the Board hire either an Educational Director or an Assistant Rabbi during the summer of 1982. The following year, the remaining position would be filled. Unfortunately, the rabbi was unable to recruit suitable candidates for either position and on October 11, 1982, requested approval to hire both an Educational Director and Assistant Rabbi.

Rabbi Zaiman was anxious to assemble a team of dedicated professionals who would share in his vision – a vision centered on developing a community of committed Jews. The pathway to that goal would be education, first of children, then adults. Cognizant that a quality educational program depended on quality educators, Rabbi Zaiman requested that the Board allocate sufficient funds for personnel costs to meet this critical need. The rabbi personally interviewed candidates, and finally recommended men of integrity with solid foundations in Conservative Judaism. In March, 1983 the Board unanimously agreed to engage Rabbi James S. Rosen as Assistant Rabbi, and Rabbi Paul D. Schneider as Superintendent of Schools.

Ordained at JTS a year earlier, Rabbi Jim Rosen held a Master's degree in social work and had experience in geriatric and hospital counseling. His wife, Nancy, quickly acclimated to the Congregation and offered her teaching skills leading classes in Torah reading and Israeli dancing. Rabbi Rosen's compassion and ethical sensitivity, coupled with the strength of his religious convictions, quickly endeared him to the Congregation. His association with Chizuk Amuno would last nine years.

Rabbi Paul D. Schneider received his ordination at JTS in 1974, and his Doctorate in education from the Teachers College of Columbia University in 1980. Originally from Detroit, Michigan, Dr. Schneider had been raised in a traditional Jewish home which included his Yiddish-speaking grandmother. Prior to moving to Baltimore with his wife, Marilyn, and three young sons, the rabbi served for seven years as Educational Director of a large congregation in Los Angeles, California. Dr. Schneider brought administrative expertise to Chizuk Amuno's day school, as well as a thorough understanding of educational theory. Although not originally hired to fulfill pulpit or pastoral responsibilities, Dr. Schneider's personal warmth and professional skill enabled him to assume rabbinic functions when called upon. His ability to weave tales of biblical heroes and modern-day sages delighted schoolchildren, who became intrigued by his passion for Jewish education.

To assist Dr. Schneider with his responsibilities, the Board approved the hiring of Jeffrey Lasday as administrator for the religious school. Lasday held a Master's degree from the Harvard Graduate School of Education, and had experience developing curriculum and teaching materials.

With the assistance of Rabbis Rosen and Schneider, Rabbi Zaiman began to shape his vision of integrating synagogue activities and study. Rather than maintain distinctly separate communities of learners – pre-school, religious school, day school, and Adult Academy – faculty and staff responsible for one segment crossed over to join in the programming of other segments. This "team approach" utilized the depth of knowledge and dedication of professionals to motivate, instruct, mentor, and support Chizuk Amuno's families as they broadened their understanding of Judaism.

One such integration of staff occurred on February 25, 1984, as the Early Childhood Education Department, now known as the

Early Childhood Education Center (ECEC), sponsored a "Havdalah Happening." Attracting nearly 350 parents and children, the service, led by Rabbi Rosen, was followed by a storytelling session with Dr. Schneider. Later that year, Rabbi Zaiman conducted a Parent Education Program for religious school families where he discussed aspects of Jewish parenting, and issues of Jewish self-image, identity formation, and special life circumstances. A few weeks later, Rabbi Zaiman addressed the day school's PTA Study Group on the topic "Conservative Judaism in Thought and Action."

Enrollment in the Solomon Schechter Day School (SSDS) grew as the school developed a reputation for excellence. Dr. Schneider informed the Board that by March, 1984, qualified applications for the following year's kindergarten class had exceeded available openings and additional students would be turned away for lack of space. The Headmaster credited the strength of the school to its outstanding faculty. Expansion had allowed Dr. Schneider to hire top-quality faculty for both the secular and Judaic departments. In a letter to school parents dated March 1, 1984 he commented:

> *There is a unity of purpose among the faculty at Solomon Schechter which transcends departmental lines. In order to achieve curriculum integration, Judaic and General Studies teachers meet together regularly to coordinate and support each others' work. I am delighted to work with such talented, creative and caring individuals.*

Dr. Schneider believed that exposing students to curriculum in an integrated manner would expand their thinking process, thus providing them with a deeper understanding of and appreciation for the material.

Historically, afternoon religious schools had difficulty recruiting top educators because of the limited schedule of working hours. The day school attracted excellent Judaic teachers who taught half day for the day school, then remained at Chizuk Amuno teaching religious school students, thus creating full-time positions. At the February 23, 1984 meeting of the Sub-Committee on Educational Resources, Chairman Dr. Barry Lever explained that SSDS had strengthened the Congregation's afternoon religious school *"by providing better teaching quality and other educational resource support."*

The day school enhanced the educational image of Chizuk Amuno's other segments as well. Dr. Schneider supported Sandee Lever's philosophy that faculty members should continue their Jewish studies, and encouraged pre-school teachers to enroll in continuing education courses. The ECEC curriculum continued to evolve as more parent-child programming, such as the Sunday morning "Bagels and Blocks," and Shabbat Torah for Tots, was introduced.

Working with the youth groups within the Congregation, Rabbi Rosen established a program for post bar/bat mitzvah students that paired learning with social experiences. Open to eighth and ninth graders, the Chavurah program began in 1985, and featured study with the rabbis, exploration of personal and Jewish identity, the opportunity to socialize with friends, and extracurricular activities.

Commitment to adult education increased as a new generation of parents was inspired by their children's excitement for learning. Chizuk Amuno still participated in the community-wide Adult Institute established by Rabbi Goldman in 1948, but in December, 1984 the <u>Bulletin</u> announced *"the inauguration of a most ambitious and exciting concept in Adult Jewish Education."* Sessions, conducted on various mornings and evenings, covered a host of interests including textual study of Bible, Rabbinics, Jewish Mysticism and Philosophy. Rabbis Zaiman, Rosen, and Schneider also taught such varied courses as:

- *The Jewish Dietary Laws*
- *Appreciating Jewish Humor*
- *Medical Ethics: Jewish Perspectives*
- *Conservative Judaism*
- *Parents and the Jewish Adolescent*

Cantor Salkov offered instruction on "Chanting the Weekday Service," and Stanley Minch held a five-part seminar on "Leadership Training."

Hazzanim

On November 15, 1981, Hazzan Abba Weisgal died after a long illness. Although the final years of his active cantorate were spent serving the Beth Am Congregation in the Eutaw Place synagogue, Weisgal was buried at Chizuk Amuno's Arlington Cemetery, in the area reserved for clergy of the Congregation. Final tribute was paid on December 18, 1981, as the Friday evening service was conducted using the traditional Eastern European melodies that Weisgal had sung at Chizuk Amuno for over fifty years.

Hazzan Abraham Salkov was honored by the Brotherhood on May 21, 1986, for his twenty-five years of service to the Congregation. The event also marked Salkov's retirement. It was during Hazzan Salkov's tenure that a mixed-voice choir was first introduced at Chizuk Amuno's Shabbat morning service. On August 25, 1980 the Board voted to institute the ritual change, which had motivated Jonas Friedenwald to establish Chizuk Amuno 109 years earlier.

In 1986, Iranian-born Farid Dardashti accepted the Congregation's invitation to become the Hazzan of Chizuk Amuno. Descended from a long line of distinguished singers, Hazzan Dardashti studied at the Mannes Conservatory of Music and graduated from the Cantors Institute at the Seminary. He had served congregations in several states before coming to Baltimore from a synagogue in California's San Fernando Valley. The Dardashti family included his talented wife and three daughters, who often performed in concert with the hazzan.

Procedures to prepare students for their b'nai mitzvah were restructured by Hazzan Dardashti. After meeting with the Hazzan to practice diction and learn trope (cantillation), most youngsters were matched with an older student tutor. Eliminating the use of tape recordings to aid memorization, tutors met with their students weekly over a period of several months. This enabled the bar/bat mitzvah students to acquire the skill needed to chant not only their parashah and haftorah, but also enabled them to chant any Torah portion or haftorah. The close learning relationship between the tutor and student often created a mentoring bond that lasted well past the child's bar/bat mitzvah day.

Building Expansion

Constantly aware that physical space in the Chizuk Amuno complex was being stretched to its limit, an ad-hoc Space Utilization Committee was formed in 1982, to forecast the needs of not only the Solomon Schechter Day School, but also those of the afternoon Religious School and Early Childhood Education Center. As enrollment increased, so, too, did the necessity of allocating limited space and sharing scare resources. The Committee concluded that the Congregation would once again need to expand the campus.

In a break with tradition, the Congregation's appeal for Israel Bonds was presented on the first day of Rosh Hashanah 5746 (1985), rather than during Kol Nidre. President Mende Lerner used the solemn spirit of the Yom Kippur evening service to deliver a message stressing the urgency and importance of the Congregation's new Building and Endowment Campaign. He reaffirmed the Board's commitment to Jewish education for all segments of the Chizuk Amuno family. Allocation of the five-million-dollar fund was projected as:

- *New building construction - $3,000,000*
- *Renovation of existing facilities - $500,000*
- *Endowment Fund - $1,500,000*

More than two hundred pledge cards were collected that evening with an aggregate contribution of approximately $400,000.

By the summer of 1986, collections and pledges had reached eighty percent of the campaign goal. On March 2, 1987, President I. Leon Glassgold signed a contract with NSC Construction, Inc. to build over forty thousand square feet of additional space. Two months later, more than 750 people were seated in the courtyard to participate in the cornerstone-laying service for the new educational campus. As had been the case more than a century earlier, although more than seventy percent of the membership participated in the campaign, the majority of the funds had been gifts of a handful of prominent members. Certificates of appreciation were presented to: Mrs. Jean Berman, Mr. and Mrs. Zanvyl Krieger, Mr. and Mrs. Harold Goldsmith, Mr. and Mrs. Leonard Stulman, and Mr. and Mrs. Lowell Glazer. Rabbi Zaiman thanked the generous donors, and announced the naming of the Jean and Allan Berman School Building, the Krieger Gymnasium, the Goldsmith Early Childhood Education Center (GECEC), the Stulman Auditorium, and the Glazer Media Center. The rabbi spoke of the Talmudic expression, "As my forefathers planted for me, so I plant for my children," and added, *"Even as we have been the beneficiaries of those who proceeded us, it is our obligation to be of benefit to those who will follow us."*

When completed in 1988, the new building housed administrative offices for the schools, a health suite, computer laboratory, two-story library, and specially designed rooms for science, music and art. A one-story wing in the rear of the complex contained twelve new classrooms for the pre-school. Older classrooms above the administrative wing and the Krieger Auditorium were renovated, replacing electrical fixtures and carpeting, and upgrading air-conditioning systems.

Religious School

Jeffrey Lasday notified the Board that he would resign in June, 1985 to pursue other interests in Jewish education. Ethel Fischer assumed the job of Religious School Administrator, working under the supervision of Dr. Schneider. An experienced teacher, Fischer had previously served as program director for the High School Division of Baltimore Hebrew College. She served as Administrator for three years.

In the Spring of 1988, Rabbi Zaiman recommended Rabbi

Stuart Seltzer for the position of Director of the Religious School. Recently ordained at JTS, Rabbi Seltzer had spent two years studying at the Hebrew University of Jerusalem and had extensive classroom and camp experience. His responsibilities would include not only the afternoon religious school program, but also Junior Congregation, Shabbat and holiday programming, and teaching several classes in the Solomon Schechter Middle School.

For decades, many children considered afternoon supplemental religious school "a necessary evil." In a March, 1992 article, Rabbi Seltzer stated his opposing view: *"It is possible to create an afternoon school program of Jewish education that is effective, dynamic, and innovative, and which deepens not only the children's experience of Judaism, but that of the whole family, the congregation, and the community."* The rabbi recognized that six hours of classroom instruction each week was insufficient to provide a full Judaic education, and, therefore, guided the faculty in designing innovative courses that would concentrate on fewer subjects in greater depth. Each grade offered a program of instruction that was different, thus combating the complaint, *"Oh, we learned this last year."* With the assistance of highly motivated teachers, Rabbi Seltzer led the charge to escape the confines of the classroom. Students could often be found on the auditorium stage, in the synagogue's kitchen, on a scavenger hunt throughout the complex, or outside hiking through the woods.

Central to the objectives of the religious school was an emphasis on family learning. In a 1993 letter to parents, Rabbi Seltzer remarked:

> *I wish I could write you all a personal note because if there is anything I want our religious school to be, it's personal – a place where you don't just drop your kids off at the curb, but where you come in and participate and learn with your children. I consider religious school education to be family education.*

It was not sufficient for teachers to be viewed as Jewish role models; the school endeavored to bring the knowledge and excitement of Jewish experiences directly into the home. Rabbi Seltzer's unbounded enthusiasm stimulated increasing numbers of parents to explore their own response to ritual and tradition. The Family Mentor Program, established in 1993, provided two professional educators who were available to meet with families, discuss their goals and needs, and help them make lifestyle changes so that they might *"discover the joy in the practice of significant mitzvot and study."*

Family-centered learning was also stressed in the day school. Frequently, day school students were assigned homework projects that involved cooperative research with their parents. While studying contemporary Jewish history, seventh-grade families researched their own ancestral roots. The three-month project culminated in a Family History Museum where students displayed the results of their research. A <u>Jewish Times</u> article on Jewish education, published in November, 1992, commented: *"Chizuk Amuno is the acknowledged leader in the field of Jewish family education in Baltimore."*

Sharing facilities with the day school greatly enhanced Chizuk Amuno's religious school program. Computer, art, and music rooms were utilized by both schools, as was the extensive library and media center. When afternoon students arrived in the building, they walked into a welcoming educational environment steeped in Jewish culture. Classrooms displayed student projects and assignments, faculty chatted to each other in Hebrew, and hallways were filled with day-school friends ending their day of learning. Through fourth grade, students were encouraged to attend Shabbat Junior Congregation services, which included an aerobic reenactment of Moses splitting the Red Sea during "high tide – low tide." Students in grades five through eight davened together on Shabbat at "Middle School Minyans," and enjoyed bi-monthly luncheons and birthday celebrations sponsored by the PTA Council. Several times a year, religious school and day school students joined together for informal learning activities, concerts, holiday celebrations, and Shabbat sleepovers at the synagogue.

Through the late 1980s, the Solomon Schechter Day School continued to flourish. The Board approved extending the school through grade eight and by 1989, enrollment had grown to 260 students. In appreciation of Zanvyl Krieger's continuing guidance and financial support, Chizuk Amuno's Solomon Schechter Day School was renamed "Krieger Schechter Day School" (KSDS) at a modest ceremony on September 9, 1992. The following year, Chizuk Amuno's Religious School was renamed the "Ben and Esther Rosenbloom Religious School." The generous support of the Rosenbloom family enabled the Congregation to construct a second floor addition above the pre-school wing providing additional classrooms, a technology lab, and administrative offices.

With the hiring of Rabbi Seltzer, Chizuk Amuno now boasted four Conservative rabbis on the professional staff – two primarily responsible for handling the pastoral needs of the large Congregation, and two supervising the education of the Congregation's children. On May 27, 1992 the Congregation bid an emotional farewell to Rabbi Jim Rosen and his family after a nine-year association. Chizuk Amuno's new Associate Rabbi, Richard Camras of Los Angeles, California, arrived a few months later.

At first glance, Rabbi Camras's resume appeared typical – JTS ordination in 1992, a year studying in Israel, rabbinic internship, hospital chaplaincy – but one item was anything but typical: *"Backpacked through Asia living with indigenous population learning their culture and spiritual beliefs, 1985-1986."* Several years later, Rabbi Zaiman recounted his first impressions upon meeting the young Seminary student:

> *The first words out of his mouth that I remember were: "I already have a job. I don't need your job." Boy, I*

*thought to myself, am I going to have fun describing this
guy to Ann, knowing full well that I could hardly do him
justice. Irrepressible. Irreverent. A Rabbi? When I
asked the young chap what he saw himself doing ten years
from now, he enthusiastically replied: "A friend of mine
and I want to open a restaurant and a shul on a mountain in Colorado." He was serious. I thought to myself:
What a great place to start on such a career path – Chizuk
Amuno Congregation!*

Despite Rabbi Zaiman's initial impression, Richard Camras
was unanimously endorsed by the rabbi's trusted sources at the Semi-
nary, and was invited to Baltimore for an interview. Much to Rabbi
Zaiman's surprise, the Committee liked the young rabbi. In late 1992,
Rabbi Richard Camras began his seven-year tenure with Chizuk
Amuno where *"his enthusiasm, his boldness, his graciousness, his
love for Judaism and the Jewish people,"* were described by Rabbi
Zaiman as *"contagious."*

In addition to his pulpit, pastoral, and teaching responsibilities, Rabbi Camras assumed oversight of the high school and college
outreach programs. The rabbi and his wife, Carolyn, graciously hosted
Shabbat afternoon "Lunch and Learn" sessions in their home, establishing a warm relationship with the young adults of the Congregation.   In order to strengthen the USY program, Rabbi Camras
introduced a variety of social programming ranging from coffee
houses to field trips.

Although religious school students had the option of extending their Jewish education in Chizuk Amuno's Chavurah program,
there was no suitable supplemental program for KSDS graduates. In
1994, Rabbis Camras and Seltzer developed the Netivon (path of
wisdom) program. Designed to provide high school students with
an opportunity to build on the skills and knowledge they acquired in
the day school, the program welcomed seventeen day school graduates to the first year's class. Study sessions, meeting six hours each
week, were led by the rabbis of the Congregation and lay congregants.

Adult Learning

The success of Chizuk Amuno's day and religious schools not only shaped the minds and characters of children, but also propelled the synagogue community into a new phase of adult education. Parents and grandparents were inspired to resume their own path of Jewish study after witnessing the accomplishments of their school-age children. Several KSDS secular studies teachers, similarly inspired by their students, enrolled in the two-year Adult Bat Mitzvah program. However, adult learning at Chizuk Amuno was not focused exclusively on the school population.

Rabbi Zaiman's vision of fostering a congregation of educated, committed laymen was based on attracting adult learners from across the spectrum of the synagogue community. His objective mirrored the ideological platform, Emet Ve-Emunah: Statement of Principles of Conservative Judaism, released in 1988 by a joint commission of rabbis and academicians from the Seminary. The last section of the document defined "the ideal Conservative Jew" as one whose life is shaped by Jewish values and practices, who considers Jewish learning a lifetime pursuit, and who is constantly striving toward greater observance and knowledge. Using the Statement as a teaching tool, the Congregation embarked on a year-long study program. Several noted scholars, including many contributors to the landmark document, participated in a Speakers Series through the winter of 1988-1989. As a follow-up to these lectures, over one hundred people met in small study groups to explore the ideology of Conservative Judaism.

In a meeting with Board officers on June 10, 1991, Rabbi Zaiman suggested forming an Adult Education Committee comprised of representatives from Chizuk Amuno's separate communities – Brotherhood, Sisterhood, Religious School, Day School, Early Childhood, and the Congregation at-large. The Committee would oversee programs sponsored by the individual groups and, in addition, plan *"two to four major congregational Adult Education Programs involving everyone."* The new committee, chaired by Linda Blumenthal, distributed their first catalogue of courses, entitled "In

Search of Knowledge," in December, 1991. Some sessions were targeted to specific groups of parents, such as Rabbi Rosen's "A Jewish Philosophy of Discipline," and "Saying Good-Bye the Jewish Way: Explaining Death to Your Child," taught by Rabbi Zaiman. Other courses, such as "If Rashi Wrote the English Translation of Torah," and "Jewish Theology: A Do-It-Yourself Guide," were intended to be of interest to all members.

Even with a variety of adult programming offered, some members felt that an unfair percentage of resources was being expended for the benefit of families with schoolchildren. Rabbi Zaiman turned that complaint into a rallying call as he addressed the Congregation on Yom Kippur 5754 (1993):

> *We have, plain and simple, one of the finest Jewish school systems in the entire nation. We educate over 1,200 kids. We don't have room in any one of our four schools for more children and we turn away children – qualified children, in each of our schools. But what about you? We do so little for you… As a congregation we are doing for our children and we can be, and should be, very proud of ourselves. It's about time we started doing for ourselves, with one another.*

Six months later, the Congregation celebrated Jewish learning with an Adult Beit Midrash. One hundred participants spent three consecutive weeks studying a single biblical verse in a traditional Jewish manner. Groups of ten, each led by a facilitator, reviewed traditional sources to discover how to bring the verse into a modern context.

As the new year 5755 (1994) began, the Board announced the establishment of the Stulman Adult Academy in recognition of Leonard Stulman's generous support of Chizuk Amuno for more than fifty years, and his interest in education. All future adult education and scholar-in-residence weekends were held under the auspices of the Stulman Adult Academy, renamed The Stulman Center for Adult Learning in 1996.

Dedication to adult educational programming precipitated the decision to engage a Director for Chizuk Amuno's Stulman Center of Adult Learning. In Fall, 1996, Judy Meltzer, former Dean of Undergraduate Studies and Continuing Education at Baltimore Hebrew University, was hired to assume that responsibility.

The day school and restructured religious school built a base for future congregational membership. The dynamic environment of the schools exposed adults to a vibrant Jewish community learning together, and sparked new interest in synagogue affiliation. Hundreds of new members had joined Chizuk Amuno in the 1970s and 1980s, but similar numbers of resignations had caused membership levels to remain relatively constant. A 1979 national study found that the majority of the country's Conservative synagogue members were aged forty-six to sixty. Very few members were in the twenty-six to forty-five age group. In his essay, "The Conservative Synagogue," Jack Wertheimer summarized the study's conclusion:

> *Although American Jewry, in general, is aging, the membership of Conservative synagogues is aging even more rapidly. Put differently, Conservative synagogues were simply not retaining the allegiance of their younger people. Instead, they were populated mainly by Jews who had come of age during the great postwar expansion....*

Chizuk Amuno's population had aged along with the national trend. In September, 1981 members organized a new social group, Club Hatikvah, for those over the age of fifty. Monthly meetings featured a light supper and an entertaining program.

As the day school continued to expand, requests for membership in the Congregation rose and resignations slowed. Total membership jumped from a reported 1,199 families on November 27, 1989, to nearly 1,375 in 1994. Many parents expressed the desire to worship together with their children on the High Holy Days. The availability of seats in the main sanctuary and Krieger Auditorium was nearing capacity, and the dues charged for those locations were prohibitive for many young families. In 1988, with the completion of the educational wing addition and the availability of another rabbi on-site (Dr. Schneider), the Board agreed to establish a new category of membership. Families not presently affiliated with Chizuk Amuno were invited to become members at a reduced rate and be seated in the Stulman Auditorium for High Holy Day Services. Dr. Schneider welcomed lay involvement in the service, encouraging both children and adults to participate. Over the following few years, his family-oriented style and thought-provoking sermons attracted a growing assemblage.

Over the years, the Ritual Committee frequently discussed requests for changes to the Shabbat service. Some members wanted a shorter service, some more English, and some asked for more lay participation. On October 24, 1992 Chizuk Amuno adopted the triennial cycle of reading Torah according to the Rabbinical Assembly's schedule, slightly shortening the service. A corps of talented high school students was regularly called on to read Torah in the main sanctuary, and more congregants received official approval to lead Shaharit, but the formality of the Shabbat service remained. As more and more members availed themselves of Chizuk Amuno's educational offerings, the base of Jewishly educated laymen, proficient in their understanding of the worship service, widened.

With the strong support of newly-elected President Florene Goldner and Rabbi Camras, the Ritual Committee approved plans to offer an alternate Shabbat morning service. A rabbi of the Congregation would be present, but the egalitarian service would feature laymen, both adults and children, leading the Hebrew and English portions of the service and delivering the d'var Torah. As a supplement to the new service, the Adult Education Committee presented a five-week program entitled "Iyyun Tefilah," probing the meaning of prayer. On January 12, 1995 the first Alternative Shabbat Minyan worshipped in the Esterson Auditorium. The service attracted a loyal following, and, within the year, was meeting twice monthly.

The 125th Anniversary

As Chizuk Amuno approached its 125th anniversary, synagogue buildings were bustling at all hours of the day and night. During the 1950s and 1960s, meeting rooms were utilized for social and club functions. By the 1990s, Synagogue Administrator Dorothy Rainess spent hours each month scheduling classrooms, meeting rooms, and auditoriums for learning activities. In October, 1994 Ronald N. Millen assumed the administrative post of Executive Director for School Management in anticipation of succeeding Stanley Minch as Executive Director.

Cognizant that the cost to provide quality programming and facilities for the multifaceted Congregation far exceeded the amount that could be assessed through membership dues, the Board launched an ambitious development plan in 1995. Under the leadership of Lee M. Hendler, the 125th Anniversary Campaign set a goal of $7.1 million – $6 million in endowment funds for programming, and another $1.1 million for necessary capital improvements. Fundraising methods were redefined as lay leaders considered the membership's wide spectrum of financial wherewithal. In late summer 1996, a fully staffed Development Office was established within the synagogue.

To commemorate the Congregation's milestone anniversary, a "Celebration of Study" was designed. Congregants received a booklet containing twenty-seven units of study based on three themes – Torah, Avodah, and Gemilut Hasadim. Each unit contained Hebrew and English text, questions based on the text, and questions that went beyond the text. Throughout the year, the units were discussed in small study sessions, in the synagogue schools, and at faculty, Board, and committee meetings.

Education had always played a prominent role at Chizuk Amuno. In the September 6, 1996 Bulletin, Rabbi Zaiman explained why educating oneself "Jewishly" would remain one of the central objectives in the Congregation's future:

In Jewish tradition, education is not an end unto itself. Education in Judaism is a triad – a Jew studies Torah so that his or her actions are grounded in ethical behavior which leads by example to teaching others how to lead a moral life. Thus, education is not passive, it is action-oriented and practical. This is how education transforms – by projecting a vision of what a meaningful life is about, education enables us to aspire to a higher standard in our own lives.

The anniversary of Chizuk Amuno's founding was viewed as an opportunity to reexamine the goals of the Congregation, and draft a concise Mission Statement. The Mission Committee, chaired by Lee M. Hendler, solicited input from members, and guidance from the rabbis. The resulting statement centered on three foundational pillars – life-long learning, observance, and acts of loving kindness.

CHIZUK AMUNO CONGREGATION MISSION STATEMENT

Chizuk Amuno has a long history of proud service to Baltimore's Jewish community. As a traditional, Conservative, egalitarian congregation, founding member of the United Synagogue for Conservative Judaism and strong supporter of the Jewish Theological Seminary, it is dedicated to perpetuating and affirming Judaism by strengthening the faith and nurturing the religious development of its members. In pursuit of this mission, Chizuk Amuno, guided by its rabbinic and educational staff, and lay leaders, ascribes to the rabbinic teaching: "The world is sustained through Torah, worship and acts of loving kindness." Pirkei Avot 1:2

Chizuk Amuno Congregation had evolved into a community of self-assured Jews, built on the principles of Conservative Judaism, and imbued with a commitment to their synagogue and Jewish learning. In his Yom Kippur sermon delivered on Shabbat morning, September 25, 1993, Rabbi Joel Zaiman offered his wish for the future of the Congregation:

> *Maybe some day soon when a person says, "I'm a member of Chizuk Amuno Congregation," it will mean much more than "this is where I pay my dues."*
>
> *What am I looking for? A sacred place, a place where Jews can gather together to do things that make their lives better, more vibrant, more meaningful, fully alive. A sacred place where we see beyond the face, beyond appearances, beyond circumstances. A sacred place where we see the possibilities...the redemptive possibilities. A sacred place where we can laugh and cry together, where we can learn, confirm and rejoice in our Judaism, our Covenant with God. A sacred place where what we can't pull off alone, we can manage together, encouraging one another to be the kind of people we should be; giving one another the courage to do that. A sacred place where expectations are just, where expectations are high, where expectations – the expectations of Torah – are met. A sacred place where we can be morally strong, spiritually sound, a place where together we can reach for Shlemut, wholeness. A sacred place where we can say to one another Chazak V'nitchazek, be strong, because we are committed to strengthening one another."*

Left to right: Rabbi Israel M. Goldman
before his relocation to Baltimore;
Installation Service program, 1948.

Chizuk Amuno Congregation
Installation Service
of
Rabbi Israel M. Goldman D. H. L.
Sunday Evening, November fourteenth
nineteen hundred and forty-eight

PROCESSIONAL
(Congregation will please rise and remain standing until after the Invocation)
"Se-u She-arim"—"Lift up your heads, O ye gates".....Psalm 24 - Sulzer
THE CHOIR

INVOCATION.................................RABBI BENJAMIN AXELMAN,
Perach Tikvah Congregation

"HINEH MAH TOV".................................CANTOR AND CHOIR
"Behold how good and pleasant it is for brethren
to dwell together in unity"—Psalm 123 - Sulzer

WORDS OF WELCOME.................MR. ISAAC POTTS, Chairman
Rededication Week Committee

GREETINGS IN BEHALF OF THE BALTIMORE RABBINATE
RABBI SAMUEL ROSENBLATT, Beth Tfiloh Congregation

SCRIPTURE READING (Numbers 27:15-23)......RABBI URI MILLER,
Beth Jacob Congregation

CHARGE TO THE CONGREGATION...RABBI ADOLPH COBLENZ,
Rabbi Emeritus, Chizuk Amuno Congregation

CANTORIAL SOLO.............................CANTOR ADOLPH J. WEISGAL
Selections from Isaiah, Chapter 41, and Mishna Uktzin
(Composed by Cantor Weisgal for this occasion and
dedicated to Rabbi Goldman)

GREETINGS IN BEHALF OF THE CONGREGATION
MR. MILTON FLEISCHER, President Chizuk Amuno Congregation

INSTALLATION ADDRESS AND CHARGE TO THE RABBI
DR. LOUIS FINKELSTEIN, President
Jewish Theological Seminary of America

RESPONSE.................................RABBI ISRAEL M. GOLDMAN

CLOSING HYMN..............CANTOR, CHOIR AND CONGREGATION
Adon Olam—Traditional

BENEDICTION...THE RABBI

RECESSIONAL—Hallelujah - Psalm 150.....................THE CHOIR
(The Congregation will please remain standing in their places
until after those on the platform shall have reached the lobby.)

(Piano Accompaniment by Dr. Hugo D. Weisgall)

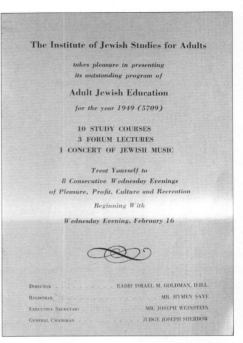

A JEWISH PEOPLE'S

UNIVERSITY

for

MEN, WOMEN AND YOUNG PEOPLE

❦

at the

CHIZUK AMUNO CONGREGATION

BALTIMORE, MARYLAND

1949-5709

The Institute of Jewish Studies for Adults

takes pleasure in presenting
its outstanding program of

Adult Jewish Education

for the year 1949 (5709)

10 STUDY COURSES
3 FORUM LECTURES
1 CONCERT OF JEWISH MUSIC

Treat Yourself to
8 Consecutive Wednesday Evenings
of Pleasure, Profit, Culture and Recreation

Beginning With

Wednesday Evening, February 16

DIRECTOR	RABBI ISRAEL M. GOLDMAN, D.H.L.
REGISTRAR	MR. HYMEN SAYE
EXECUTIVE SECRETARY	MR. JOSEPH WEINSTEIN
GENERAL CHAIRMAN	JUDGE JOSEPH SHERBOW

Clockwise from top left: Adult education program, 1949; Adult education program, 1949; Synagogue attendance pledge card, 1952; Facing page top: Adult education registration form, 1955; Bottom: Children's Passover seder, Eutaw Place, 1954.

GOLD STAR MEMBER
Fold Along Dotted Line

SILVER STAR MEMBER
Fold Along Dotted Line

BLUE STAR MEMBER
Fold Along Dotted Line

Synagogue
Attendance Pledge
by

The Sabbath is the pillar of our faith

Worship heals the spirit of man

GOLD STAR MEMBER

I pledge regular attendance at the late Friday night* or Saturday morning services

every week

SILVER STAR MEMBER

I pledge regular attendance at the late Friday night or Saturday morning services at least

twice a month

BLUE STAR MEMBER

I pledge regular attendance at the late Friday night or Saturday morning services at least

once a month

(The late Friday night services are conducted for 14 Friday nights from October 31 to January 30)

CHIZUK AMUNO CONGREGATION

No._____ No._____

For *quick and easy registration, fill out this form and mail with check to*

INSTITUTE OF JEWISH STUDIES FOR ADULTS
CHIZUK AMUNO CONGREGATION, EUTAW PLACE AND CHAUNCEY AVE., BALTIMORE 17, MD.

ENROLLMENT BLANK
Date_____1955

I wish to enroll as a member of the Institute for the current year of 1955 and shall attend: *(Please check)*

STUDY COURSES: 8 P. M.

☐ 1. Beginners' Hebrew   ☐ 5. Jewish Ceremonial Objects and Their Use Today
☐ 2. Elementary Hebrew   ☐ 6. A Guide To Conduct—The "Ethics" of Maimonides
☐ 3. Yiddish for Beginners   ☐ 7. Books and Plays In Review
☐ 4. The Prayer Book In Our Lives   ☐ 8. A Film Forum—The Faith We Live By

☐ FORUM LECTURES at 9 P. M. on
"CHARTING THE 4th CENTURY OF AMERICAN JEWRY"

Name   Mr. and Mrs.
         Mr. or Mrs.
         Miss   _____Fee $_____   check ☐   cash ☐

Address_____   Zone ____ Phone No._____

Enrollment Fees: Single $3.00—Husband and Wife $5.00—Young People $2.00
Admission Card will be issued upon completion of enrollment.

For the Institute
Date _____
No. _____
Enrollment fee paid $ _____
Name _____
No. _____
check ☐ cash ☐

"SURE...My Mother and Father are going! Everybody's going! It's the best and biggest SPRING CARNIVAL and BAZAAR Chizuk Amuno has ever had! They're giving away FREE PRIZES like a TV Set...and a 'million' other things to win and see! We'll see you there ... both nites ... don't forget!"

"Yes ... 2 BIG NITES ... OUTDOORS"

Tuesday ---➤ ... MAY 22nd

Wednesday ---➤ ... MAY 23rd

ON THE GROUNDS OF THE SCHOOL CENTER
EUTAW PLACE AND WHITELOCK STS.

SPONSORED BY THE CHIZUK AMUNO SISTERHOOD AND BROTHERHOOD

Facing page top: Sisterhood luncheon, Eutaw Place, 1945; Bottom: Cast of Purim spiel, 1957. This page top to bottom: *Bulletin* announcement of Spring Carnival, 1951; Religious school students, Eutaw Place, 1946.

Top: Brochure for first suburban High Holy Days service, 1952; Pikesville Armory prepared for holiday services, 1958; Facing page top to bottom: Eutaw Place sukkah, 1953; USY Board, 1957.

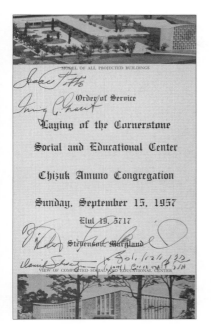

Facing page top to bottom: 85th Anniversary Banquet at Lord Baltimore Hotel, 1956; Groundbreaking for Stevenson Road complex, 1956; This page clockwise from top left: Autographed program from cornerstone ceremony, 1957; Ticket for Couples Club dance, 1958; Groundbreaking for Stevenson Road complex, 1956.

CHIZUK AMUNO COUPLES CLUB

Annual Cabaret Dance

Saturday, November 1, 1958

SOCIAL AND EDUCATIONAL CENTER
STEVENSON ROAD

Set-ups Provided   Breakfast at Midnight

DANCING FROM NINE TILL ONE
FIVE-AND-A-HALF DOLLARS PER COUPLE

N⁰   0146

Clockwise from top left: Stevenson Road campus, 1963; Sample of cards inserted in cornerstone, 1961; Cornerstone ceremony, Stevenson Road, 1957.

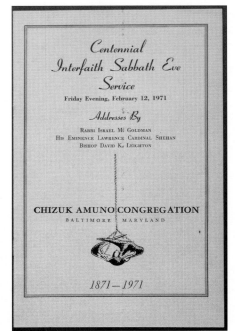

Clockwise from top: Bar Mitzvah Brotherhood,
1958; Program from Interfaith Service, 1971;
Announcement of concert, 1968.

APPROVED

CHIZUK AMUNO CONGREGATION

Sunday, September 25, 1977

OFFICIAL BALLOT

RESOLVED THAT

The Chizuk Amuno Congregation extend to
women equality in synagogue ritual so
that they may henceforth enjoy the same
rights, privileges, honors and obligations
that heretofore have applied solely to men.

☒ YES (For Women Equality in Synagogue
Ritual)

☐ NO (Against Women Equality in Synagogue
Ritual)

*The Chizuk Amuno
Sisterhood*
*Invites You, Your Family
and Friends
to a
Milestone in the Life
of our Congregation*

Sisterhood Shabbat

Saturday, February 11, 1978
*Kiddush Luncheon
Following Services*

Services at 9:15 a.m.

*SERMONETTE:
BETTE MILLER*

*HAFTORAH:
MILDRED GOLDMAN*

*MUSAF:
SHIRLEY EVANS*

*Ladies of the Sisterhood will participate
in the Service and
receive Aliyot*

*Kiddush Luncheon Chairperson:
Shirley Sloe*

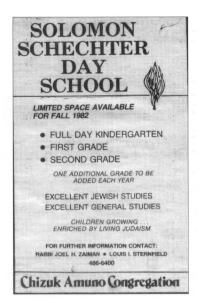

Facing page clockwise from top left: Friday evening "Service Under the Stars, 1975; Invitation to Sisterhood Shabbat, 1978; Ballot for vote on women's ritual equality, 1977; Clockwise from top left: Adult education program, 1981; Advertisement for day school, 1981; Rabbi Joel H. Zaiman, 1981

School and Youth Program
1987-1988

Chizuk Amuno Congregation
Baltimore, Maryland

GENERAL INFORMATION

YOUTH GROUPS

EARLY CHILDHOOD EDUCATION CENTER

RELIGIOUS SCHOOL, HAVURAH

SOLOMON SCHECHTER DAY SCHOOL

Facing page clockwise from top left: Hazzanim Abraham Salkov and Farid Dardashti, 1987; Rabbis Richard Camras and Joel H. Zaiman, 1996; Stevenson Road synagogue sanctuary, 1980s. Clockwise from top left: Day school kindergarten class, 1981; Youth program brochure, 1987; Educational campus cornerstone ceremony, 1987.

The Chizuk Amuno Annual Appeal

וֶהְיֵה בְּרָכָה...וְנִבְרְכוּ בָךְ כֹּל מִשְׁפְּחֹת הָאֲדָמָה   BE THOU A BLESSING

We are counting on you to help Chizuk Amuno maintain its tradition of excellence in religious, educational, and communal programming. Your contribution will enable us to support a range of programmatic initiatives intended to benefit *every member* of the Chizuk Amuno community.

FOR OUR SCHOOLS AND OUR CONGREGATION

BE THOU A BLESSING   BE THOU A BLESSING   BE THOU A BLESSING   BE THOU A BLESSING   BE THOU A BLESSING   BE THOU A BLESSING   BE THOU A BLESSING   BE THOU A BLESSING   BE THOU A BLESSING

And Now The Future Begins...

Top: Annual Appeal pledge card, 1996; Bottom: Aerial view of Stevenson Road complex, 1990s.

CHRONOLOGY

YEAR	EVENT
1871	Twenty-three men gather to establish Chizuk Amuno Congregation
1876	Dedication of synagogue on Lloyd Street at Lombard Street, Rev. Dr. Henry W. Schneeberger hired as lecturer and to establish religious school
1886	Ladies Auxiliary formed
1886	Rev. Schneeberger and Aaron Friedenwald invited to be among the twelve men gathered in New York to establish the Jewish Theological Seminary
1890	Hertz Oppenheimer legacy establishes first endowment gift
1895	Congregation moves to new synagogue built at McCulloh and Mosher Streets
1908	Formation of Ritual Committee
1910	Change from German machzor to English edition
1912	Rabbi Eugene Kohn elected second rabbi of the Congregation
1913	William Levy represents Chizuk Amuno at meeting establishing United Synagogue of America
1918	Chizuk Amuno Ladies Auxiliary founding member of Women's League of Conservative Judaism
1918	Hazzan Herman Glass assumes spiritual leadership following resignation of Rabbi Kohn
1920	Rabbi Adolph Coblenz elected as third rabbi of the Congregation
1921	Hazzan Adolph (Abba) Weisgal hired
1922	Congregation moves to Eutaw Place and Chauncey Avenue synagogue
1922	Junior Congregation established
1924	Young People's League established
1925	Chizuk Amuno Brotherhood formed

1930	First Confirmation Class graduates
1944	Sisterhood allowed representative seat on Board of Trustees
1946	Arlington Cemetery dedicated
1947	Membership votes to institute mixed seating
1948	Rabbi Israel M. Goldman elected rabbi of the Congregation
1952	Ritual Committee approves bat mitzvah service
1952	Auxilliary High Holy Day Service held at Pikesville Armory
1956	Ground broken at Stevenson Road for first phase of new synagogue complex
1960	First assistant rabbi hired
1961	Hazzan Abraham Salkov hired
1962	Sanctuary dedicated
1974	Board accepts plan by Beth Am Congregation to purchase Eutaw Place synagogue
1976	Rabbi Maurice S. Corson elected rabbi
1977	Members approve resolution granting women full ritual equality
1979	Rabbi Eliot Marrus elected interim rabbi
1980	Rabbi Joel H. Zaiman elected rabbi of the Congregation
1981	Solomon Schechter Day School established
1986	Hazzan Farid Dardashti hired
1988	Dedication of Educational Campus buildings, third High Holy Day service formed
1994	Mission statement approved
1995	Alternative Minyan conducts first Shabbat service
1996	125th anniversary of Chizuk Amuno Congregation

APPENDIX A
Rabbis of the Congregation

1876–1912	Rev. Dr. Henry W. Schneeberger	
1912–1918	Rabbi Eugene Kohn	
1920–1948	Rabbi Adolph Coblenz	
1948–1976	Rabbi Israel M. Goldman	
1960–1962	Rabbi Leonard S. Berkowitz	(A)
1963–1969	Rabbi Donald D. Crain	(A)
1969–1972	Rabbi David A. Nelson	(A)
1972–1974	Rabbi Charles S. Sherman	(A)
1974–1976	Rabbi Eliot P. Marrus	(A)
1976–1979	Rabbi Maurice S. Corson	
1979–1980	Rabbi Eliot P. Marrus	
1980–	Rabbi Joel H. Zaiman	
1983–1992	Rabbi James S. Rosen	(A)
1992–1999	Rabbi Richard P. Camras	(A)
1999–	Rabbi Robert L. Tobin	(A)
1999–	Rabbi Deborah Wechsler	(A)
1983–	Dr. Paul D. Schneider	(Ed)
1988–	Rabbi Stuart Seltzer	(Ed)

A – Associate   Ed – Educator

APPENDIX B
Hazzanim of the Congregation

1871–1877	Rev. Lehman Heilner
1877–1878	Rev. L.M. Lilienthal
1878–1921	Hazzan Herman Glass
1921–1975	Hazzan Abba Yosef Weisgal
1961–1986	Hazzan Abraham Salkov
1986–1997	Hazzan Farid Dardashti
1997–	Hazzan Emanuel C. Perlman

APPENDIX C
Secretaries/Executive Directors of the Congregation

1871–1890	Henry S. Hartogensis
1890–1898	Alfred Scholle
1898–1910	Milton Fleischer
1910–1933	Benno W. Hummel
1933–1955	Joseph Weinstein
1955–1965	Harold W. Hammer
1965–1966	Bernard Lehman
1967–1996	Stanley I. Minch
1997–	Ronald N. Millen

APPENDIX D
Presidents of the Congregation

1871–1879	Judah Rosewald
1879–1892	Jonas Friedenwald
1892–1902	Dr. Aaron Friedenwald
1902–1911	Michael S. Levy
1911–1921	Dr. Harry Friedenwald
1921–1922	William Levy
1922–1953	Milton Fleischer
1953–1959	Isaac Potts
1959–1963	Joseph Davidson
1963–1968	J. Benjamin Katzner
1968–1971	Herbert Goldman
1971–1974	Edward B. Sandler
1974–1976	Dr. Samuel Rochberg
1976–1979	Henry O. Shor
1979–1982	Sigi R. Strauss
1982–1984	Irwin M. Sussman
1984–1986	Mende Lerner
1986–1988	I. Leon Glassgold
1988–1990	Fred Hittman
1990–1992	Dr. Jerome Buxbaum
1992–1994	Lowell R. Glazer
1994–1996	Florene Goldner
1996–1998	Alan N. Kanter
1998–2000	Lee M. Hendler

APPENDIX E
Sisterhood Presidents

1886–1900	Rosa W. Rosenfeld
1900–1906	Betsy Levy
1906–1912	Bertha Friedenwald
1912–1920	Birdie S. Friedenwald
1920–1922	Beatrice Levy
1922–1932	Hannah Silverman
1932–1934	Leah Potts
1934–1935	Bertha Hecht
1935–1938	Nellie Baker
1938–1941	Flora S. Rosenbloom
1941–1943	Helen Greenfeld
1943–1945	Florence A. Rogers
1945–1948	Bernice Kolodny
1948–1951	Sylvia Katzner
1951–1954	Toba K. Rochberg
1954–1956	Sayde J. Sklar
1956–1958	Sylvia R. Scherr
1958–1960	Lillian W. Forman
1960–1962	Jane K. Cohen
1962–1964	Patsy K. Gilbert
1964–1966	Isobel Kemper
1966–1968	Lottie K. Jandorf
1968–1970	Cille Strauss
1970–1972	Alberta C. Hyman
1972–1974	Beverly K. Cohen

1974–1976	Vilma B. Sussman
1976–1978	Bette Y. Miller
1978–1979	Eileen D. Sacks
1979–1981	Jackie Glassgold
1981–1983	Sharon Rose
1983–1985	Harriet Udell
1985–1987	Barbara E. Leibowitz
1987–1989	Ferne Abramowitz
1989–1991	Edna Crystal
1991–1993	Shirley Shor
1993–1995	Linda Diamond, Selma Frank, Ronnie Kleiman
1995–1997	Gerry Berman, Sharon Edlow
1997–1999	Susan Sklar
1999–	Lynne Lichtig

APPENDIX F
Brotherhood Presidents

1925–1927	Charles Abramson
1927–1929	Leslie W. Moses
1929–1931	I. William Schimmel
1931–1933	Fred E. Katzner
1933–1935	Alvin Neuberger
1935–1937	Joseph Kolodny
1937–1939	J. Benjamin Katzner
1939–1943	William Greenfeld
1943–1945	Joseph Davidson
1945–1946	Frank Fisher
1946–1948	Irvin F. Blumenfeld
1948–1950	Leon Lebow
1950–1952	Dr. Elmer N. Hoffman
1952–1954	Stanley Scherr
1954–1956	Nathan H. Karu
1956–1958	James I. Waranch
1958–1960	Herbert Goldman
1960–1962	Dr. Theodore A. Schwartz
1962–1964	Ralph Steinbach
1964–1966	Stanley I. Minch
1966–1968	David Whitman
1968–1970	Norman Apatoff
1970–1972	Henry O. Shor
1972–1974	Gilbert S. Levine
1974–1976	Leonard J. Attman

1976–1978	Frank Sacks
1978–1980	Calvin I. Hamburger
1980–1982	David J. Schwaber
1982–1984	Dr. Ronald Goldner
1984–1986	Donald Kerbel
1986–1988	Gerald Zentz
1988–1990	Bruce Raskin
1990–1993	Dr. Jeffrey Platt
1993–1995	Dr. David Roffman
1995–1997	Theodore S. Levy
1997–1999	Howard Brill
1999–	Robert H. Wolf

BIBLIOGRAPHY

Adler, Cyrus. I Have Considered the Days. Philadelphia: The
    Jewish Publication Society of America, 1941.

Adler, Morris, Jacob Agus, and Theodore Friedman. "Responsum
    on the Sabbath." Proceedings of the Rabbinical Assembly
    of America Volume XIV (1950): 112-137.

Aronson, David. "President's Message." Proceedings of the
    Rabbinical Assembly of America Volume XIV (1950): 91-
    105.

Blum, Isidor. The Jews of Baltimore: An Historical Summary of Their
    Progress and Status as Citizens of Baltimore from Early Days to
    the Year Nineteen Hundred and Ten. Baltimore: Historical
    Review Publishing Company, 1910.

Bokser, Ben Zion. "Forest Hills Plan." Proceedings of the Rabbinical
    Assembly of America Volume XIV (1950): 189-192.

Cahn, Louis F. The History of Oheb Shalom 1853-1953. Baltimore:
    Oheb Shalom Congregation, 1953.

_____. Man's Concern for Man:The First Fifty Years of the Associated
    Jewish Charities & Welfare Fund of Baltimore. Baltimore:
    Associated Jewish Charities and Welfare Fund, 1970.

Fein, Isaac M. The Making of an American Jewish Community: The
    History of Baltimore Jewry from 1773-1920. Philadelphia: The
    Jewish Publication Society of America, 1971.

Feingold, Henry L. The Politics of Rescue: The Roosevelt
    Administration and the Holocaust, 1938-1945. New York:
    Holocaust Library, 1970.

Fishman, Bess, and Eric Levi. The Chronicle of Beth Tfiloh
    Congregation 1921-1981. Baltimore: Beth Tfiloh Congregation,
    1981.

Friedenwald, Harry. Life, Letters, and Addresses of Aaron Friedenwald, M.D. Baltimore: The Lord Baltimore Press, 1906.

Goldman, Israel M. Lifelong Learning Among Jews: Adult Education in Judaism from Biblical Times to the Twentieth Century. New York: KTAV Publishing House, Inc., 1975.

_____. "Henry W. Schneeberger: His Role in American Judaism." American Jewish Historical Quarterly Volume LVII Number 2 (December 1967): 152-190.

Greenberg, Rose. The Chronicle of Baltimore Hebrew Congregation 1830-1975. Baltimore: Baltimore Hebrew Congregation, 1976.

Hauptman, Judith. "Conservative Judaism: The Ethical Challenge of Feminist Change." The Americanization of the Jews. Ed. Robert M. Seltzer and Norman J. Cohen. New York: New York University Press, 1995. 296-310.

Hyman, Paula E. "Ezrat Nashim and the Emergence of a New Jewish Feminism." The Americanization of the Jews. Ed. Robert M. Seltzer and Norman J. Cohen. New York: New York University Press, 1995. 284-295.

Joselit, Jenna Weissman. "The Special Sphere of the Middle-Class American Jewish Woman: The Synagogue Sisterhood, 1890-1940." The American Synagogue: A Sanctuary Transformed. Ed. Jack Wertheimer. Cambridge: Press Syndicate of the University of Cambridge, 1987. 206-230.

Kahn Jr., Philip. Uncommon Threads: Threads that Wove the Fabric of Baltimore Jewish Life. Baltimore: PECAN Publications, 1996.

Karp, Abraham J. A History of The United Synagogue of America 1913-1963. New York: United Synagogue of America, 1964.

_____. "The Origins of Conservative Judaism." Conservative Judaism Volume XIX Number 4 (Summer 1965): 33-48.

_____. "The Synagogue in America - A Historical Typology." The American Synagogue: A Sanctuary Transformed. Ed. Jack Wertheimer. Cambridge: Press Syndicate of the University of Cambridge, 1987. 1-36.

Kass, Alvin, ed. Proceedings of The United Synagogue of America 1973 Biennial Convention. New York: United Synagogue of America, 1974.

Kaufman, David. "Jewish Education as a Civilization: A History of the Teachers Institute." Tradition Renewed: A History of the Jewish Theological Seminary, Volume I: The Making of an Institution of Jewish Higher Learning. Ed. Jack Wertheimer. New York: The Jewish Theological Seminary of America, 1997. 565-630.

_____. Shul With A Pool: The Synagogue Center in American Jewish History. Hanover: University Press of New England, 1999.

Kelman, Wolfe. "The American Synagogue: Present and Prospects." Conservative Judaism Volume XXVI Number 1 (Fall 1971): 3-24.

Levin, Alexandra Lee. Vision: A Biography of Harry Friedenwald. Philadelphia: The Jewish Publication Society of America, 1964.

_____. The Szolds of Lombard Street. Philadelphia: The Jewish Publication Society of America, 1960.

_____. Dare to Be Different: A Biography of Louis H. Levin of Baltimore, A Pioneer in Jewish Social Service. New York: Bloch Publishing Company, 1972.

Levin, Neil W. "Music at JTS." Tradition Renewed: A History of the Jewish Theological Seminary, Volume I: The Making of an Institution of Jewish Higher Learning. Ed. Jack Wertheimer. New York: The Jewish Theological Seminary of America, 1997. 717-792.

Levine, Joseph A. Emunat Abba. Doctoral Dissertation. 1981.

Marcus, Jacob R., ed. The American Jewish Woman: A Documentary History. New York: KTAV Publishing House, Inc., 1981.

Perlman, William J., ed. The Jews in America. Baltimore: Leading Jews of America Publishing Co., 1918.

Pruce, Earl. Synagogues, Temples and Congregations of Maryland 1830-1990. Baltimore: The Jewish Historical Society of Maryland, Inc., 1993.

Rozenblit, Marsha L. "Choosing a Synagogue: The Social Composition of Two German Congregations in Nineteenth-Century Baltimore." The American Synagogue: A Sanctuary Transformed. Ed. Jack Wertheimer. Cambridge: Press Syndicate of the University of Cambridge, 1987. 327-362.

Rubinstein, Louis Baruch. "Temple Emanu-El of Providence: The First Half Century." Temple Emanu-El: The First Fifty Years 1924-1975. Ed. David Hurvitz. Providence: Temple Emanu-El, 1975. 24-94.

Saks, Robert J. "Jews, Judaism, and the New Left." Conservative Judaism Volume XXI Number 4 (Summer 1967): 39-51.

Sarna, Jonathan D. "The Evolution of the American Synagogue." The Americanization of the Jews. Ed. Robert M. Seltzer and Norman J. Cohen. New York: New York University Press, 1995. 215-229.

_____. "The Debate over Mixed Seating in the American Synagogue." The American Synagogue: A Sanctuary Transformed. Ed. Jack Wertheimer. Cambridge: Press Syndicate of the University of Cambridge, 1987. 363-394.

Schindler, Pesach. Solomon Schechter Day School Manual. New York: United Synagogue of America, 1970.

Scult, Mel. "Schechter's Seminary." Tradition Renewed: A History of the Jewish Theological Seminary, Volume I: The Making of an Institution of Jewish Higher Learning. Ed. Jack Wertheimer. New York: The Jewish Theological Seminary of America, 1997. 43-102.

Shargel, Baila R. "The Texture of Seminary Life During the Finkelstein Era." Tradition Renewed: A History of the Jewish Theological Seminary, Volume I: The Making of an Institution of Jewish Higher Learning. Ed. Jack Wertheimer. New York: The Jewish Theological Seminary of America, 1997. 515-564.

Sklare, Marshall. "Women in the Conservative Synagogue." The American Jewish Woman: A Documentary History. Ed. Jacob R. Marcus. New York: KTAV Publishing House, Inc., 1981.

_____. America's Jews. New York: Random House, Inc., 1971.

Stanislawski, Michael. "The Pale of Settlement: The Czars' Edicts and Their Impact on Our Ancestors." 19th Annual Conference on Jewish Genealogy, New York City. 9 August 1999.

Wertheimer, Jack. "JTS and the Conservative Movement." Tradition Renewed: A History of the Jewish Theological Seminary, Volume II: Beyond the Academy. Ed. Jack Wertheimer. New York: The Jewish Theological Seminary of America, 1997. 403-442.

_____. "The Conservative Synagogue." The American Synagogue: A Sanctuary Transformed. Ed. Jack Wertheimer. Cambridge: Press Syndicate of the University of Cambridge, 1987. 111-152.

Zaiman, Joel H. "Jewish Parent Education." Conservative Judaism Volume XXVI Number 4 (Summer 1972): 67-71.

_____. "On Educating Our Children: Introduction." Conservative Judaism Volume XXXI Number 2 (Winter 1977): 80-81.

Other Sources

Minutes of the Congregation are held in the synagogue's archives with the exception of the volume representing 1913-1923, which has not survived. Various archival memoranda, pamphlets, audio tapes, correspondence, manuscripts, sermon notes, personal papers, and other materials consulted are also housed at Chizuk Amuno.

Acknowledgement of newspapers, periodicals, and other print sources has been cited within the text noting specific publication dates whenever identifiable. These sources include:

American Israelite (Cincinnati)
Baltimore American
Baltimore American and Commercial Advertiser
Baltimore City Directories
Baltimore Sun
Chizuk Amuno Bulletin
Chizuk Amuno Chronicle
Jewish Comment (Baltimore)
Jewish Times (Baltimore)

Photographic Credits

"Synagogue at McCulloh and Mosher Streets, 1910" by Joseph C. Christhilf, originally published in <u>The Jews of Baltimore: An Historical Summary of Their Progress and Status as Citizens of Baltimore from Early Days to the Year Nineteen Hundred and Ten</u>

"Groundbreaking for Stevenson Road complex, 1956" by Nat Lipsitz

"Cornerstone ceremony, Stevenson Road, 1957" by Nat Lipsitz

"Rabbi Joel H. Zaiman, 1981" by Susie Fitzhugh

Digital reproduction of existing images and photographs of archival materials by Steve Abrams

Every effort was made to provide credit for the photographs contained in this book. Unfortunately, notation of original photographers was not maintained in the archival files of the Congregation.

About the Author

Jan Bernhardt Schein is a third-generation Baltimorean. A certified accountant, Jan maintains a financial consulting practice specializing in not-for-profit organizations. While attempting to document her own family history, Jan developed a passion for Jewish genealogical research. Jan's fascination led her to develop classroom curricula aimed at linking students of all ages to the rich stories of their ancestors.

In search of genealogical items, Jan explored the vast archival material of Chizuk Amuno. Her discoveries prompted the writing of *On Three Pillars*. As members of the Congregation since 1994, Jan, her husband, Jay, and daughters Hallie, Johanna, and Chelsea, are actively involved in the synagogue community.